MAR 3 1

MEDIEVAL
OUTLAWS

For Judy, Molly, Fraser and Darby – members of my merry band

MEDIEVAL OUTLAWS

Ten Tales in Modern English

EDITED BY

Thomas H. Ohlgren

Sutton Publishing

First published in the United Kingdom in 1998 by
Sutton Publishing Limited · Phoenix Mill
Thrupp · Stroud · Gloucestershire · GL5 2BU

British Library Cataloguing in Publication Data
A catalogue record for this book is available from the British Library

ISBN 0 7509 1862 4

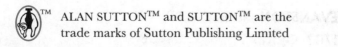

TM ALAN SUTTON™ and SUTTON™ are the
trade marks of Sutton Publishing Limited

Typeset in 10/12pt Baskerville.
Typesetting and origination by
Sutton Publishing Limited.
Printed in Great Britain by
WBC Limited, Bridgend.

CONTENTS

LIST OF PLATES

LIST OF CONTRIBUTORS

Thomas Hahn, Professor of English, University of Rochester

Shaun F.D. Hughes, Associate Professor of English, Purdue University

Timothy S. Jones, Assistant Professor of English, Augustana College

Thomas E. Kelly, Associate Professor of French Emeritus, Purdue University

Stephen Knight, Professor of English, University of Wales, Cardiff

Thomas H. Ohlgren, Professor of English and Medieval Studies, Purdue University

Carter Revard, Professor of English Emeritus, Washington University, St Louis

Walter Scheps, Associate Professor of English, SUNY, Stony Brook

Michael Swanton, Professor of English, Exeter University

PREFACE

My interest in medieval outlaws grew out of my undergraduate teaching at Purdue University, where I have offered a class on Robin Hood since 1992. While surveying the literary and historical accounts of the Prince of Thieves, my students inevitably asked me: 'Is Robin Hood *the original* English outlaw?' Turning to Maurice Keen's *The Outlaws of Medieval Legend*, J.C. Holt's *Robin Hood*, and Dobson and Taylor's *Rymes of Robyn Hood*, we discovered that Robin Hood was but one outlaw who left his mark on Western European literary culture. We found some answers, but, alas, no readily available texts to read for ourselves. While some translations did exist, such as Joseph Stephenson's 1875 English version of the Anglo-Norman *Fouke fitz Waryn* or W.D. Sweeting's 1895 rendering of *De Gestis Herwardi Saxonis*, they were either long out of date or inaccessible for teaching purposes. Another major work, the French *Li Romans de Witasse le Moine*, existed only in scholarly editions and a modern French translation. Thus began the five-year-long project to create fresh translations of the early outlaw narratives that lay behind the Robin Hood legend. My principal collaborator, Thomas E. Kelly, undertook the arduous task of translating the Anglo-Norman *Fouke fitz Waryn* and the Continental French *Eustache the Monk*. Along the way, we discovered that Michael Swanton at Exeter University had translated *Hereward the Wake* (*Gesta Herwardi*) in his 1984 book *Three Lives of the Last Englishmen*, and he graciously allowed us to publish a much-revised version in this collection. As time went on, we discovered seven additional stories, bringing the total to ten tales.

Each of the ten selections is accompanied by its own introduction, notes and select bibliography. The notes identify the major dramatis personae, place-names and relevant historical and cultural backgrounds. A thorough index has also been created to facilitate the location of the chief characters, places, episodes and themes.

This volume is not intended for academic specialists, who would no doubt insist on reading the texts in their original languages. Instead, it is intended for those who want to walk by themselves in the footsteps of Hereward, Fouke, Eustache, Robin Hood and William Wallace, among others.

Thomas H. Ohlgren,
Purdue University

ACKNOWLEDGEMENTS

As compiler and editor of this volume I have incurred many debts not only to the other contributors but to various institutions and people who furnished helpful information, materials and support. For help in locating photographs I want to thank Thomas Bilson, Courtauld Institute of Art; Mrs G.C. Cannell, Corpus Christi College, Cambridge; Kevin Carpenter, University of Oldenburg; Susanna Kerr, Scottish National Portrait Gallery; Stephen Knight, University of Wales, Cardiff; and Janice McFarlane, National Library of Scotland. For help in creating original maps, I thank Esther Scheps and Michael Swanton. For timely responses about particular issues: Glyn S. Burgess, University of Liverpool; Brian J. Levy, University of Hull; and Robert E. Lewis, Middle English Dictionary.

Since this anthology is the direct outgrowth of *Robin Hood and Other Outlaw Tales*, published in 1997 by Medieval Institute Publications at Western Michigan University, I want to thank Russell A. Peck, general editor of the Middle English Text Series, for his support and encouragement. In addition, I want to thank the Board of the Medieval Institute for permission to publish Thomas E. Kelly's translation of an excerpt from *Fouke fitz Waryn*, which in this volume is now complete.

At Purdue University I want to thank Margaret Moan Rowe, Dean of the School of Liberal Arts, and Thomas Adler, Head of the Department of English, for support of various kinds, including a sabbatical leave in fall 1997. For reading, discussing and writing about medieval outlaws, my students deserve my sincere thanks.

In academia it is often the 'custom of the castle' for scholars to work in isolation and, like porters at the gate, to guard fiercely their domains from unwelcome guests. By contrast, my experience as editor of this volume belied the stereotype – one could not find a more generous and affable group of contributors! Our frequent exchanges of information, advice and encouragement was greatly facilitated by the Internet.

Finally, I would like to express my gratitude to those friends and colleagues who offered help and support at every stage of this project: Ann Astell for listening, James Cruise for vetting my prose and Shaun Hughes for loaning me many books. At Sutton Publishing I would like to thank Roger Thorp, who solicited the project, Jane Crompton, who greatly helped me in the early stages, and Alison Flowers, who saw the manuscript through the production process.

FREQUENTLY CITED REFERENCES

Child, Francis J. (ed.). *The English and Scottish Popular Ballads*, vol. 3, 5 vols, New York, The Folklore Press, 1957

Dobson, R.B. and Taylor, J. (eds). *Rymes of Robyn Hood: An Introduction to the English Outlaw*, rev. (=3rd) edn, Stroud, Sutton, 1997

Holt, J.C. *Robin Hood: Revised and Enlarged Edition*, Thames and Hudson, 1989

Keen, Maurice. *The Outlaws of Medieval Legend*, revised edn, Routledge & Kegan Paul, 1987

Knight, Stephen. *Robin Hood: A Complete Study of the English Outlaw*, Oxford and Cambridge, MA, Blackwell, 1994

Knight, Stephen and Ohlgren, Thomas (eds). *Robin Hood and Other Outlaw Tales*, Middle English Texts Series, Kalamazoo, Michigan, Medieval Institute Publications, 1997

GENERAL INTRODUCTION

When most people hear the words 'medieval outlaw' they think immediately of Robin Hood. What they may not realize is that the basic ingredients of the Robin Hood story – an essentially good nobleman or commoner falsely accused, outlawed without due process, dispossessed of his titles and land, forced into exile in forest or fen, and only later pardoned – are rooted in stories composed hundreds of years earlier. The Anglo-Saxon Earl Godwin and Hereward the Wake, the French Eustache the Monk and the Anglo-Norman Fouke fitz Waryn are among the many ancestors of Robin Hood, but their stories are little known.

As this anthology of ten outlaw tales makes clear, outlaws and outlawry figured prominently in medieval literature, but these works have not received the attention they deserve. Of the research that has been done, Maurice Keen's *The Outlaws of Medieval Legend* (1961) is a pioneering study of the origins and development of the outlaw legend from the twelfth-century *Gesta Herwardi* to the fifteenth-century poems of Robin Hood and William Wallace.[1] Keen's main contribution was the identification of a coherent group of outlaw legends, which he called the 'Matter of the Greenwood' in order to differentiate them from the other three types of medieval romance: the 'Matter of Britain' (King Arthur), the 'Matter of France' (Charlemagne), and the 'Matter of Greece and Rome' (the Troy story). In the 'Matter of the Greenwood' the forest is no longer that transitional zone through which Arthurian knights ride from adventure to adventure, stopping briefly to encounter a hermit, damsel or mysterious challenger, but it takes centre stage:

> within its bounds their whole drama was enacted. If they ventured outside it, it would only be some brief expedition to avenge wrong done, and to return to it, when right had been restored and whatever sheriff or abbot was the villain of the piece had been brought low. (p. 2)

In applying the 'Matter of the Greenwood' to the outlaw tales, Keen developed three interrelated themes. First, despite their different origins, spirits and backgrounds, the tales display similarities in theme and incident too close to be accounted for by coincidence. They are, in Keen's words, 'the same stories, merely associated by different authors with the name of a different hero' (p. 65). Second, the tales grew by a process of accretion involving the addition, fusion or inclusion of story elements. Because versions of the stories were transmitted orally in English, it is not necessary to prove that the authors knew about or had access to the surviving manuscript texts in Latin, Old French and Anglo-Norman. Despite the fact that the unique text of the *Gesta Herwardi* is in Latin, other forms of evidence indicate that versions in English, now lost, once existed. Keen has observed that at the time of its compilation the *Book of Ely* records that peasants were aware of Hereward's deeds in the songs they sang (p. 13). Even the author of the *Gesta Herwardi* mentions that he translated into Latin a short account in English by Leofric of Bourne. And, after describing how Hereward killed a large bear in Northumberland, he adds that 'women and girls sang about him in their dances, to the great annoyance of his enemies'. The exploits of the pirate outlaw Eustache the Monk, especially his capture at sea and execution at the Battle of Sandwich in 1217, were widely known and recounted in the chronicles of John of Canterbury and Walter of Guisborough (Keen, p. 61). As for Fouke fitz Waryn, who led a rebellion against King John in the Welsh March, we know that an English version existed because John Leland, the sixteenth-century Tudor antiquary, printed excerpts from it (Keen, p. 41). Third, Keen detected a change in the social world of the early romances (*Hereward the Wake, Eustache the Monk* and *Fouke fitz Waryn*) and the later fifteenth-century Robin Hood ballads, with the *Tale of Gamelyn* providing the transition in the mid-fourteenth century. In the early stories 'historical rebels are trapped out as heroes of romance', while in *Gamelyn* and the ballads 'we have left the world of knights, in the romantic sense, for a world of landlords and peasants, the world in which Robin Hood himself moved' (Keen, p. 79). Like *Gamelyn*, the Robin Hood ballads were intended for a popular, i.e. peasant, audience expressing their discontent against a corrupt social order, the discontent manifesting itself in a series of violent uprisings, most notably the Peasants' Revolt of 1381 (Keen, pp. 160–1).

While Keen's claim of a peasant audience for the Robin Hood ballads was challenged by scholars such as J.C. Holt, causing Keen to change his original position, his book still provides us with a highly readable and informative survey of the medieval outlaw legends.[2] Directly inspired by *The Outlaws of Medieval Legend*, this volume assembles for the first time Modern English translations of many of the literary texts discussed by Keen. We have also added three works not covered by him: the Earl Godwin episode from the eleventh-century *Life of King Edward*, the early fourteenth-century protest poem *The Outlaw's Song of Trailbaston* and the fifteenth-century Icelandic outlaw tale, *Áns saga bogsveigis*. Although the tales differ in historical time (eleventh to the fifteenth century), in language (Latin, Old French, Anglo-Norman, Icelandic, late Middle English and Middle Scots), and in geographical setting (England, Wales, Scotland, France, Flanders and Spain), they exhibit similarities in character types, storylines and mind-sets too close to be accounted for by coincidence or common tradition. While external evidence for direct descent is lacking, readers of these tales will readily recognize the repetition of the core ingredients of the outlaw narrative.

To familiarize the reader with the varied worlds of the medieval outlaw, we have included brief summaries of each of the ten tales. The summaries not only give essential background information about the date, authorship and plot of each tale but point out the major similarities and differences. Following this section is a discussion of the critical issues that readers might wish to consider when reading the tales themselves.

1. THE OUTLAWRY OF EARL GODWIN FROM THE *VITA ÆDWARDI REGIS*

The translation consists of the third and fourth prose sections and the third, fourth and fifth poetic sections of the *Vita Ædwardi Regis qui apud Westmonasterurm Requiescit*, the anonymous life of Edward the Confessor, probably composed at the time of the Norman Conquest for Queen Edith, daughter of Godwin, Earl of Wessex. The excerpts describe Godwin's conflict with Edward's French advisor, Robert of Jumièges, leading up to the confrontation of 1051, Godwin's banishment and the earl's return and reconciliation the following spring. This narrative is the earliest extended account of outlawry in English literature. It introduces a number of themes to the outlaw tradition: the conflict between a Saxon nobleman and corrupt Norman royal officials, false accusations by a powerful cleric, outlawry and banishment of the hero, the hero's return with an armed force, popular support of the people and reconciliation with the king.

2. *THE DEEDS OF HEREWARD*

Written in Latin in the mid-twelfth century, the *Gesta Herwardi* celebrates the heroic revolt of Hereward, son of an Anglo-Saxon 'of very noble descent', against the Norman 'bastard', William the Conqueror, who successfully invaded England in 1066. Initially exiled to Flanders by his father and King Edward the Confessor for provoking strife, he returned to England after the Conquest to avenge the death of his brother, to reclaim his father's estates at Bourne and to lead a rebellion against King William at Ely. Unlike the *Vita Ædwardi Regis*, the *Gesta* develops fully the outlaw narrative and establishes the character-types, plot elements and themes seen in subsequent stories. He lives in the forests and fens of East Anglia; he forms a band of 'fugitives, the condemned and disinherited'; he is supported by the people who celebrate his exploits in song; he wields a deadly sword and bow; he uses disguises and trickery to reconnoitre, harass and confuse the enemy; he is captured and imprisoned but is rescued by his faithful companions; and, in the end, he receives the king's pardon and reclaims his lands and possessions.

3. *EUSTACHE THE MONK*

Another historical outlaw is Eustache the Monk (*c.* 1170–1217), son of Bauduin Busquet, a peer of the Boulonnais in northern France. Surviving in a single manuscript written between 1223 and 1284, the 2,307-verse romance in Old French recounts the adventures of the French knight, monk, sorcerer, outlaw, mercenary and mariner, who is unjustly outlawed by Renaud de Dammartin, the Count of Boulogne. After travels in Spain, where it is said that he studied necromancy in Toledo, Eustache becomes a monk at the Benedictine Abbey of Saint Samer near Boulogne. When his father is murdered by Hainfrois de Heresinghen, Eustache abruptly leaves his religious vocation in order to seek justice against his father's killer. After a series of events in which Eustache's champion loses a judicial duel, and Eustache himself, now the count's seneschal, disobeys a direct order, he is accused of financial irregularities by his enemy Hainfrois. Summoned to give an account of himself, Eustache, suspecting treachery, refuses to appear and instead flees to the forests of the Boulonnais where he begins his career as an outlaw. Because he is vastly outnumbered by the count's knights and men-at-arms, Eustache is forced to rely upon stealth, deception and daring tricks to elude capture and to wreak his revenge. Donning seventeen different disguises, Eustache terrorizes the count by burning his mills, stealing his horses and mutilating and killing his men. Several of these exploits closely resemble episodes in later outlaw tales – the capture and release of the Count of Boulogne paralleling Robin Hood's capture of the Sheriff of Nottingham in the *Gest of Robyn Hode* and the game of 'truth or consequences' in which those who tell the truth are allowed to keep their money, while those who lie are robbed. Eustache is eventually captured by the count, only to be rescued by William de Fiennes. Escaping to England, he offers his services to King John, who supplies him with thirty ships to rove the Channel Islands and the coast of France. Because the Count of Boulogne became the ally of King John against King Philip Augustus, Eustache again switches sides and joins the cause of Prince Louis who has plans to invade England. As the commander of the French fleet, Eustache is captured and beheaded at the Battle of Sandwich in 1217.

4. *THE OUTLAW'S SONG OF TRAILBASTON*

The untitled Anglo-Norman poem survives in a manuscript dated to about 1341. It was composed early in the fourteenth century at the end of Edward I's reign (1272–1307) when he established the commissions of trailbaston to deal with crime and public disorder. The word 'trailbaston' means literally 'one who trails or carries a club or cudgel'; that is, a brigand or outlaw (OED). Edward I appointed special judges in 1305 partly to investigate and to suppress increases in crimes of violence due to the lawlessness of returning soldiery from the foreign wars, factional conflicts and the corruption of judicial officials; also, however, to use the new fines to help pay for his wars. The first-person speaker of the *Song of Trailbaston*, boasting to have served the king in the wars in Scotland, Flanders and Gascony, protests that he has been unfairly indicted for robbery, homicide and other crimes, and instead of appearing when summoned he has fled to the forest of Belregard where he is living as an outlaw. Threatening to seek revenge against the corrupt judge and jury, he invites other criminals to join him in the forest where there is no treachery or 'twisting of laws'. Composed under a laurel tree, the ryme will be thrown on the highway where passersby can find it.

5. *FOUKE FITZ WARYN*

Surviving in a single manuscript dating from about 1330, *Fouke fitz Waryn* is written in Anglo-Norman prose, though scholars believe that it is based on a lost thirteenth-century poem on the same subject. Another version in Middle English alliterative verse is also lost save for some excerpts in a sixteenth-century synopsis by John Leland. Like *Eustache the Monk*, *Fouke fitz Waryn* is also set in the time of King John, and the outlaw narrative is but a part of the larger tapestry of complex dynastic and political relations stretching back to the Norman Conquest. The first third of the romance traces the history of the Welsh March from the time when William the Conqueror tried to pacify the Welsh borders by settling there three prominent Norman families – the Fitz Aleyns, Waryn de Metz and the Peverels – to the time of King Henry I when the Fitz Waryn's ancestral home, Whittington, is given to Roger de Powys. This loss of property sets the stage for the last two-thirds of the romance in which Fouke fitz Waryn III tries to regain his inheritance through vengeance against his family's enemies. The outlaw narrative consists of the now familiar elements: when King John refuses to return his lands and titles, Fouke renounces his homage and leaves the court; after killing fourteen of the king's knights, he is outlawed and flees to Brittany, only later returning to England, where he hides in the forests, assembles a gang of followers, dons various disguises and plays a deadly game of cat-and-mouse with the king's agents. After a four-year career (1200–3) of outlawry and rebellion, Fouke eventually wins back his lands and titles. In addition to the outlaw narrative and the largely factual history of the Welsh March, there is a third layer of fairy romance involving battles with giants, serpents and dragons.

6. *THE TALE OF GAMELYN*

The Tale of Gamelyn tells how the youngest of three brothers is deprived by his greedy oldest brother of the inheritance that his dying father wanted to leave to his baby son. When Gamelyn comes to maturity he realizes how he has been wronged and begins to exert himself, deploying both his great physical strength and the loyalty of his father's steward, Adam. In spite of various successes, however, including winning a wrestling tournament and beating up a group of monks and abbots, Gamelyn and Adam are outlawed through his brother's manipulation of the legal system. They are welcomed by the mysterious 'king of the outlaws', who is soon pardoned and leaves the outlaw band under Gamelyn's control. Gamelyn's second brother, Sir Ote, has gone surety for him at court, and the evil oldest brother plans to destroy them both. But with his faithful band of outlaws Gamelyn bursts into the court, seizes the judge's place and proceeds to hang the judge, brother and the whole jury – after which he is pardoned by the king and spends the rest of his life in honour as a warden of the royal forest. *The Tale of Gamelyn* has survived only because it found its way into one of the versions of the *Canterbury Tales*. As a result, it was then recopied many times, and also circulated in print. Many think Chaucer planned to use the story as a basis for an unwritten tale, perhaps for the Yeoman or even as the Cook's second tale after his first was interrupted for indecency. There is also the intriguing question about whether the 'king of the outlaws' is a reference to Robin Hood – there are some phrases used when Gamelyn stands and scans the forest which seem deliberately reminiscent of the opening of early ballads about the famous outlaw.

7. *THE SAGA OF ÁN BOW-BENDER*

In its surviving form *Áns saga* is a fifteenth-century example of a genre called the *Fornaldar sögur Norðurlanda* (Histories of the Early Period of the Northern Lands), and has become associated with a group of sagas including *Ketils saga hœngs* and *Örvar-Odds saga* set in the northern Norwegian district of Hrafnista. But there exists an earlier Latin version of the story from the twelfth century in book 6, chapter 4 of Saxo Grammaticus's *Gesta Danorum*, which suggests that the stories surrounding Án are of some antiquity. Much of *Áns saga* deals with his running conflict with King Ingjaldur of Naumdælafylki. The king uses the excuse that Án, in helping him to achieve victory in a dynastic struggle, has killed his two half-brothers. As a result, King Ingjaldur declares Án an outlaw 'throughout all Norway'. Suspicious of the king, Án makes his escape to the forest. After defeating another forest outlaw, Án takes up with a wealthy widow and they are soon married and run four large farmsteads in the forest. All the local people take Án as their leader and, in these surroundings, he enjoys popular support. Grímur, Án's nephew, comes to the forest and becomes his most trusted companion. Various of the king's retainers, either on their own or with the encouragement of the king, try to capture Án, but they are either humiliated and returned to the king or executed on the spot when their treachery becomes apparent. On one occasion Án calls an assembly of his followers in the forest to pass judgement on the king's emissary suggesting some kind of outlaw community. There are numerous comparisons that might be made between *Áns saga* and the stories of Hereward (feats of strength at an early age, Án's wife Jórunn and Hereward's wife Turfrida) and Gamelyn (feats of strength at an early age, the relationship of Án and his brother Þórir compared to that of Gamelyn and his brother). And, like Robin Hood and William Cloudesley of *Adam Bell*, Án is a master shot with bow and arrow. Among Án's other exploits are his prowess at wrestling, first in his match against Björn in the king's court and then against Garan the forest outlaw. In a final battle with King Ingjaldur, Án is left for dead and his farms destroyed. But he does survive and return to take possession of his forest properties after which time he and the king keep their distance. Án's son Þórir will eventually kill Ingjaldur and marry the king's sister, Ása. Four generations later, one of Án's descendants will be an important original settler in the north of Iceland.

8. *A GEST OF ROBYN HODE*

The best-known medieval outlaw is of course Robin Hood, but, as the *Gest* depicts him, he bears little resemblance to his modern images in film, television and fiction. The medieval Robin Hood is a yeoman, not the gentrified Earl of Huntington or Loxley; his base of operations is Barnsdale in the West Riding of Yorkshire, not Sherwood Forest in Nottinghamshire; his gang, consisting of Little John, Will Scarlok and Much the Miller's son, operates without Friar Tuck and Maid Marian. And the gang itself, driven by revenge and self-defence, commit real crimes, ranging from deer poaching, highway robbery and extortion to homicide. Our sympathies, however, are totally on the side of the 'good outlaws' as they punish the avaricious abbot of St Mary's, York and the treacherous and corrupt Sheriff of Nottingham. The narrative, which is arranged in eight parts or fitts, consists of five main episodes: Robin's rescue of the impoverished knight, Sir Richard at the Lee, by lending him £400 to save his property; Robin's punishment of the abbot by stealing £800 from his courier; Little John's revenge against the sheriff by stealing his money, silver and his cook; Robin's meeting, reconciliation and service with King Edward; and Robin's untimely death at the hands of his evil kinswoman, the Prioress of Kirkley Abbey. The *Gest* is not only the longest surviving poem on Robin Hood but also one of the earliest. Although the 1,824-verse poem arranged in 456 4-line stanzas survives in printed texts of the early sixteenth century, the poem was composed several generations earlier in the fifteenth century, either in the reign of Henry V (1413–22) or Henry VI (1422–61). The historical time depicted however is about a hundred years earlier in the reign of Edward III (1327–77). To further complicate matters, the surviving printed text is thought to be a compilation of earlier works along with material of the poet's own devising. Among these sources must be counted *The Deeds of Hereward*, *Eustache the Monk* and *Fouke fitz Waryn*.

9. *ADAM BELL, CLIM OF THE CLOUGH AND WILLIAM OF CLOUDESLEY*

Adam Bell and his associates in crime, Clim of the Clough and William of Cloudesley, were legendary outlaws whose recorded exploits extend back almost to the time of the earliest Robin Hood texts. Poetical accounts were circulated as early as the 1530s, and ballads and chapbooks celebrating these outlaws were published regularly through to the end of the seventeenth century. The surviving story falls into three parts: William decides to leave the forest in order to visit with his wife and children in Carlisle. There he is betrayed by an old woman of his own household; after a desperate and bloody fight, he is captured and sentenced to death. In the second part, Adam and Clim rescue William from the gallows and, in the course of their spectacular escape, kill several hundred officials and citizens of Carlisle. Safe in the forest once again, William convinces his companions to seek pardon directly from the king. In the final part, the monarch wishes at first to seize the outlaws, but his queen intervenes and obtains pardon for them, before the king learns the full extent of their recent crimes. William offers to redeem himself and his fellows though a daring escapade, namely shooting an apple from the head of his young son. The skill and mettle of the outlaws convinces the king that they will better serve as his allies than enemies, and the ballad ends with the outlaws happily taking up respectable positions at court. In its narrative style, its level of violence and its use of stock episodes, *Adam Bell* distinctly recalls a number of the Robin Hood ballads, as well as other outlaw tales such as William Tell.

10. FROM *THE ACTS AND DEEDS OF SIR WILLIAM WALLACE*

Sir William Wallace is perhaps better known as a general or *dux bellorum* as well as a Scottish patriot and national hero. But his first appearance on the public stage – from the English point of view at least – is as an outlaw, which he remained until his capture and execution in 1305. The primary source of information about Wallace's life is a poet variously known as 'Hary', or 'Blind Harry', or 'Henry the Minstrel', whose *Acts and Deeds of Sir William Wallace* (1482?) chronicles Wallace's struggle against the English. Much of Hary's poem deals with Wallace as a military figure who, by his strength of character and the sheer magnetism of his personality, draws to him thousands of freelances who form the core of his army. The translated passages, comprising approximately 1,900 lines or more than 15 per cent of the poem, however, ignore Hary's extensive accounts of pitched battles against the English and focus instead on the more personal causes and consequence of Wallace's outlawry. The episodes described in these passages often bear a striking resemblance to incidents and motifs found in the other outlaw tales in this volume: e.g., Wallace's supporters, his skill with bow and sword, his killing of young Selby, his encounter with the potter, his disguise as a woman, his debate over the fish, his betrayal by his mistress, the murder of his beloved, among others. There is little doubt that Hary fleshed out the historical facts concerning Wallace with material from literary sources, both written and oral.

MODELS OF OUTLAW IDEOLOGY

To put the ten tales into a broader critical perspective, we offer the following models of outlaw ideology: the 'Social Bandit', the 'Good Outlaw', and the 'Trickster'. While these concepts share certain common features, we will treat them separately.

The 'Social Bandit'

A useful model for studying the outlaw tale is provided by Eric Hobsbawm's classic study, *Bandits*.[3] Taking a broad cross-cultural and diachronic approach, Hobsbawm seeks to explain 'why social banditry is so remarkably uniform a phenomenon throughout the ages and continents' (p. 11). The model that he constructs excludes 'simple criminals' and focuses instead on 'peasant outlaws whom the lord and state regard as criminals, but who remain within peasant society, and are considered by their people as heroes, as champions, avengers, fighters for justice, perhaps even leaders of liberation, and in any case as men to be admired, helped and supported' (p. 13). He demonstrates that social banditry is universally found in agrarian societies, where peasants and landless laborers are ruled, oppressed and exploited by lords, towns, governments and lawyers. Often the outlaw's career is precipitated not by a criminal offence of his own making but by an act of injustice by others, and his main goal is to right the wrongs done to him and his family or people. Sometimes the justice is rough, involving vengeance and retribution. The outlaw is not only 'invisible' due to the frequent use of disguise and trickery but invulnerable because of his almost mythical prowess with weapons. He is not usually the enemy of the king, who frequently pardons him, but of the local gentry, clergy or sheriff. If he survives, he returns to his people as an honourable citizen, but if he is killed, it is through treachery, and sometimes a woman is implicated in his capture. Hobsbawn localizes banditry in remote and inaccessible regions such as forests, fens, mountains, waterways and particularly near highways and trade routes where 'pre-industrial travel is naturally both slow and cumbrous' (p. 16). While banditry can occur at any moment in history, Hobsbawn identifies those disruptive times that cause tension and crisis, such as war, famine, plague and political chaos. Wars in particular left behind bands of marauders and desperados, making weak or divided civil authorities powerless to control them (p. 18). Banditry, however, seldom results in major transformations of society. Instead, it seeks to right wrongs, avenge injustices and restore the traditional order of things. Some outbreaks, however, may presage genuine revolutionary movements caused by 'the disruption of an entire society, the rise of new classes and social structures, the resistence of entire communities or peoples against the destruction of its way of life and the social breakdown that makes the approaching end of a relatively long cycle of history, heralding the fall of one dynasty and the rise of another' (pp. 18–19).

While Hobsbawm's model of the social bandit offers many important insights, it also requires some tailoring to fit the tales in this collection. The most important qualification concerns the social class of the outlaws. None of the ten outlaw tales in this collection concern peasant heroes. Godwin was Earl of Wessex; Hereward was an Anglo-Saxon 'of very noble descent'; Eustache's father was senior baron of the Boulonnais; Fouke fitz Waryn descended from Anglo-Norman lords of the Welsh March; Gamelyn's father was a landed English knight; William Wallace was a Scottish commoner, but certainly not a peasant; and Robin Hood and Adam Bell were yeomen. Furthermore, a distinction should be made between those outlaws who desire genuine revolutionary change (Hereward, William Wallace and, to a certain extent, Fouke fitz Waryn) and those outlaws who want to right the wrongs done to them, their families and their friends. The private wrongs in these instances often involve the loss of property, titles and inheritance (Eustache the Monk, Fouke fitz Waryn and Gamelyn).

The 'Good Outlaw'

Another outlaw model is Ingrid Benecke's the 'Good Outlaw'.[4] While sharing some of the same features as Hobsbawm's social bandit, this model draws upon four English medieval literary works: *Hereward the Wake*, *Fouke fitz Waryn*, *Gamelyn* and *A Gest of Robyn Hode*. All of the heroes in these stories pose the paradoxical problem of being outlaws, having committed real crimes, but they are admired and supported by the people. Their outlawry does not bring shame upon them, but instead proves them to be superior to their opponents, both in martial prowess and, most importantly, in moral integrity. As Benecke observes, the moral superiority of the outlaw heroes is highlighted in a number of ways:

> either by relating that God honoured them more than others, even working a miracle for them (Hereward, Fouke, Robin Hood), or by describing how the outlaws' victory over their outnumbering enemies was part of a mission they were destined to fulfill (part of a curse – Gamelyn, or of a prophecy – Fouke), or else by presenting the heroes in such a light that they rightly appear as the judges of their enemies' crimes (Gamelyn and Robin Hood). (p. 157)

In addition to demonstrating the moral superiority of the English outlaw heroes, some of the tales, according to Benecke (p. 160), defend the knights' *legal* rights to reclaim feudal titles, lands and privileges lost as a result of arbitrary, unjust actions either by the monarch (Hereward, Eustache, Fouke, William Wallace) or the kings' representatives (Gamelyn, Robin Hood, Adam Bell). They have a legal right to rebel against a royal tyrant as guaranteed by the provisions contained in *Magna Carta*. Articles 39 and 52 are especially relevant.

> Article 39: 'No free man shall be arrested or imprisoned or disseised or outlawed or exiled or in any way victimised, neither will we attack him or send anyone to attack him, except by the lawful judgment of his peers or by the law of the land'.
> Article 52: 'If anyone has been disseised of or kept out of his lands, castles, franchises or his right by us without the legal judgment of his peers, we will immediately restore them to him: and if a dispute arises over this, then let it be decided by the judgment of the twenty-five barons who are mentioned below in the clause for securing the peace'. [5]

The concept of the 'good outlaw' is not only paradoxical but morally ambiguous, particularly when the outlaw's violence goes beyond what is necessary to preserve one's life or to right a wrong. Some of the tales contain at least one troubling incident: Eustache the Monk forcing the young boy to hang himself; Fouke fitz Waryn ordering the impostor knight to behead his accomplices; and William Wallace sparing 'no one who was of English blood'.

Natural Law

Implicit in Benecke's treatment of moral and legal superiority is the opposition between natural law and statutory or positive law. According to medieval political theory, man's law ought to follow the law of nature, which in turn reflected the eternal law of God. By using reason man was able to deduce a body of principles or ethical norms from God's law that were universal, unchangeable and morally obligatory.[6] These universal principles – human existence is meaningful, humans possess equal dignity and rights, humans are naturally social and have a moral duty to contribute to society – were a rational ethical ideal forming the foundation for existing legal systems and the standard by which they were judged. Governments exist as the means of fulfilling the social and political nature of man and achieving the common good.

Conformity to the order in nature results in harmony, virtue and happiness, but violation of natural law results in disorder, evil and unhappiness (Sigemund, p. 7). As long as the legal authority is legitimately obtained, man is obligated to obey his superiors or temporal rulers. But, if a civil law violates natural law, man is not obligated to obey it. The justification of civil disobedience is contained in St Thomas Aquinas's *Summa Theologia*:

Man is bound to obey secular Rulers to the extent that the order of justice requires. For this reason if such rulers have no just title to power, but have usurped it, or if they command things to be done which are unjust, their subjects are not obliged to obey them. [7]

Although Aquinas elsewhere condemned tyrannicide because it may result in some worse kind of oppression, he recognized that 'the government of a tyrant cannot be of long duration' because 'those who are kept down by fear will rise against their rulers . . . '.[8]

The influence of these ideas on the practical politics of the fourteenth and fifteenth centuries was tremendous, 'as is apparent from sources like petitions to parliament, contemporary poems and songs of complaint, and popular manifestoes at times of rebellion such as the Peasants' Revolt of 1381 and Jack Cade's rising in Kent in 1450'.[9]

The 'Trickster'

The third model of the outlaw to be considered here is the 'Trickster', which as defined by Paul Radin is one of the world's oldest expressions of counter-culture:

Trickster is at one and the same time creator and destroyer, giver and negator, he who dupes others and who is always duped himself. He wills nothing consciously. At all times he is constrained to behave as he does from impulses over which he has no control. He knows neither good nor evil yet he is responsible for both. He possesses no values, moral or social, is at the mercy of his passions and appetites, yet through his actions all values come into being.[10]

While Radin's examples are drawn from Winnebago Indian mythology, it is clear that the concept of the 'Trickster', like the 'Good Outlaw', is cross-cultural, and examples can be located in many different cultures throughout history. For example, Carl G. Jung, in the afterword to Radin's book, brings us back to the Middle Ages when he notices the same 'contradictoriness' and 'reversal of the hierarchic order' in the medieval jester, the ancestor of the modern-day circus clown. The jester, the clown and the fool all belong to the world of carnival with its spectacles, celebrations and rituals, such as the Feast of Fools, Feast of Asses and the Boy Bishop in the Church itself or the play-games and mock events in agricultural fairs and other civil and social celebrations (Radin, pp. 196–8). The fullest account of this 'carnivalesque' spirit of the late Middle Ages and early Renaissance is Mikhail Bakhtin's *Rabelais and His World*, in which 'a boundless world of humorous forms and manifestations opposed the official and serious tone of medieval ecclesiastical and feudal culture'.[11] These festive celebrations not only offered 'temporary liberation from the prevailing truth', but also 'marked the suspension of all hierarchical rank, privileges, norms, and prohibitions' (Bakhtin, p. 10). The traditional order was in fact frequently reversed, producing what has been called the 'topsy-turvy' world in which low is high and high is low, bottom is top and top is bottom (Bakhtin, p. 11).

Reversal of position in the moral and social hierarchy also epitomizes the outlaw tale, in which the lowly 'wolf's head' paradoxically is shown to be superior to the very authorities who should uphold the law. A striking example of reversal occurs in the *The Tale of Gamelyn* when Gamelyn violently ejects the corrupt judge from his bench, breaking his jaw and arm, and assumes his position. He then sentences the judge and the twelve bribed members of the jury to death, and they along with the sheriff and Gamelyn's evil brother are all hanged. As Keen observes, 'the only champions of justice are those who are, officially, criminals' (Keen, p. 92).

To right the wrongs done to him and others, the outlaw must first resort to subterfuge or disguise. The tales display four different types of disguise, and they are often used in combination: alteration of physical appearance; voice or language spoken; clothing; and gender. To confuse the enemy, several of the outlaws actually alter their physical appearance. When Hereward is in exile in Cornwall, he rescues a Cornish princess from being forcibly married to a king's son and returns her unharmed to her betrothed in Ireland. To infiltrate the wedding party in Cornwall he changes his physical appearance by 'using a lotion which changed his blond hair to black and his youthful beard to a ruddy colour'. John de Rampaigne, Fouke fitz Waryn's chief lieutenant, takes the more drastic step of swallowing a herb that causes his face to puff up and discolour so that even 'his own companions scarcely knew him'. Dressed in poor clothes and carrying juggling equipment, he then goes to Whittington to spy on Fouke's enemy, Moris fitz Roger. John later disguises himself as an Ethopian minstrel by staining his hair and body jet black. To make their disguises more believable, several of the outlaws even alter their voices: when John of Rampaigne pretends to be a Greek merchant he deliberately speaks 'bad Latin' in King John's court. Similarly, after defeating the pirate Red Reiver on the high sea, William Wallace speaks to him in the 'Latin tongue'. The chief means of altering one's appearance is of course by changing costume or clothing. In *Eustache the Monk* alone, seventeen different disguises, often in conjunction with a trick, are used to deceive the enemy. Interestingly, a number of these disguises are also used in other tales, suggesting either a well-known common tradition or direct influence. In four of the tales, for instance, the outlaw disguises himself as a monk or priest (Hereward, Eustache, Fouke and Wallace). Three tales use the potter disguise (Hereward, Eustache and Wallace, as well as Robin Hood in the ballad and play, *Robin Hood and the Potter*). Finally, in several of the tales, the hero changes gender to fool the enemy. Hereward gains entrance into his ancestral home at Bourne by wearing a 'maidservant's cloak' under which he hides his mail-coat and helmet.

William Wallace twice disguises himself as a woman, once as a spinner after he killed the constable's son in Dundee and, again, when he dons his lover's gown and coverchiefs to escape from a trap laid by the English. The most outrageous example of all, however, unfolds when Eustache disguises himself as a prostitute and 'seduces' one of the count's men!

The tales also abound in what we can call 'strategic tricks' involving stealth and deception designed to achieve various ends: to reconnoitre or gain information; to gain entry; to confuse the enemy; to entrap the enemy; to effect a rescue; to effect an escape; and to harass or rob the enemy. In order to seek peace with the count, Eustache, disguised as a monk, audaciously sits down next to him and offers to intercede on his *own* behalf; upon being identified by a man-at-arms, Eustache escapes with one of the count's favorite horses. In *Adam Bell*, in order to gain entry into the town of Carlisle, Adam and Clim trick the porter at the locked city gate by pretending to be messengers from the king. Knowing that the porter cannot read, they show him a false letter and the king's seal. After the gullible porter lets them in, they rescue William of Cloudsley from the gallows. The trick of reversing the horses's shoes to confuse the pursuers is used by three outlaws – Hereward, Eustache and Fouke – 'so it could not be discovered from their tracks where they were or where they were going' (*Hereward*, chapt 26). Eustache so confuses the count that he follows the horse-tracks back to the smith who reversed the shoes! The trick of using bait to lure the enemy into a vulnerable position occurs in two tales. Disguised as a charcoal burner, Fouke encounters King John and three knights. When the king asks him if he has seen a stag or doe pass by, Fouke replies that he has just seen a long-antlered stag and offers to lead the king deeper into the forest to find it. Upon arriving at the thicket, Fouke and his men rush out and capture the king. The sheriff in the *Gest* is captured in a similar manner when Little John, disguised as Reynold Greenleaf, promises him a 'right fair hart' and 140 other sharp-antlered deer; the master-hart turns out to be Robin Hood himself who is accompanied by 140 men armed with sharp arrows – a perfect case of the 'hunter hunted'.

THE APPEAL OF THE OUTLAW TALE

A variety of explanations can be offered to account for the appeal of the outlaw tale. One psychological theory suggests that the tales provide a safety valve for the channelling and release of aggressive impulses in the reader. We imaginatively identify with the outlaw, letting him perform the antisocial behaviour in our place and in the process we feel relief as if we performed the acts ourselves. To gain our admiration, however, the outlaw must possess the redeeming qualities of loyalty, courage and cleverness; he must also be the victim of a corrupt legal or political system; and he must not engage in indiscriminate murder and mayhem but right the wrongs done to him, his family and friends, and his country. Another explanation sees the outlaw as a cultural hero who challenges the rigidity of a closed political or economic system. By breaking taboos and violating societal norms, the outlaw not only reveals the 'bad' statutory laws but reaffirms those values, such as the natural laws of self-preservation, freedom, equality and justice, that have been subverted. Yet another explanation, and perhaps the most important one, is that the outlaw tales are just good stories with sturdy and honest heroes, vile villains, adventurous chases, daring deeds, bold disguises and tricks, and lots of narrative suspense.

1

THE OUTLAWRY OF EARL GODWIN FROM THE *VITA ÆDWARDI REGIS*

Timothy S. Jones

INTRODUCTION

The earliest life of Edward the Confessor, the *Vita Ædwardi Regis*, survives in a single manuscript, British Library Harley MS 526, which was assembled in the seventeenth century by the antiquarian Sir Simonds d'Ewes from several smaller pieces.[1] The portion of the manuscript containing the *Vita Ædwardi* (fols 37r–58r) appears to have been copied in about 1100, perhaps at Christ Church, Canterbury. However, the *Vita* was probably initially composed between 1065 and 1067 by a priest or clerk in the household of Queen Edith.[2] Unfortunately the manuscript appears to lack a quire between folios 40 and 41, leaving us without the end of Verse I and the whole of Prose II.

The *Vita* is a difficult text to categorize. It falls into two parts, the first written in prosimetric form and the second entirely in prose, but the prose is rhymed, following the fashion popular in western Europe in the eleventh century. One cannot, however, easily call the *Vita* a work of hagiography. While the latter half of the text describes the religious life of Edward the Confessor, including miracles which occurred during his life and after his death, the former half is almost entirely concerned with the secular actions of Earl Godwin and his sons. Prominent among these episodes is an account of the crisis of 1051 and 1052, when Godwin and his sons were outlawed from England after a stand-off which nearly resulted in civil war.

Earl Godwin was a man of obscure origins who made his way through the convoluted politics of early eleventh-century England to become the most powerful man in the kingdom. He was awarded the earldom of Wessex by King Cnut in 1017, and at the time of the Norman Conquest his sons controlled all of southern and western England. Harold, his eldest surviving son, was able to declare himself king upon the death of Edward the Confessor. Such a prominent rise to power may seem to be an unlikely source for an outlaw legend, but the competing interests for the control of England at the time have left us with complex and partisan depictions of an enigmatic character. Opinions, such as those concerning any outlaw, are split along lines of social and political interest.

The Norman historians of the twelfth century despised Godwin as the father of Harold, the oath-breaker.[3] Meanwhile the *Anglo-Saxon Chronicle* and the Icelandic *Knýtlinga saga* present a more sympathetic and even heroic figure, and later works, such as Walter Map's *De Nugis Curialium*, reflect the complexities of the competing traditions. Depending on whom we read, Godwin may be a clever politician, a scheming parvenu, a treacherous murderer, a wily trickster, an inspirational leader or a loyal vassal.

Outlawry was an expedient judicial procedure for a legal system lacking a centralized police force and facilities for imprisonment. Legal practices of the early Germanic tribes indicate that anyone caught in a crime was a de facto outlaw and might be pursued and killed with impunity.[4] The same appears to have held true for murderers in England as late as the tenth century. But gradually the sentence became reserved for a suspect who failed to appear before the local judicial council at the fourth summons.[5] As an outlaw he lost all his rights of property, contract and inheritance. No one was allowed to assist him and all were called upon to hunt him down.[6] Anyone who came upon an outlaw in the Anglo-Saxon period could kill him without receiving any legal reprisal. An outlaw's only hope was to abjure the realm, but he had no hope of returning unless he received a royal pardon. Bede's *Ecclesiastical History* and the *Anglo-Saxon Chronicle* both give a number of examples of the practice of outlawry used as a judicial process and as a political tool. King Cnut, for instance, outlawed several notable men during his reign, apparently because he perceived them to be threats to his own power.[7] This was a practice that the powerful would continue to employ throughout the Middle Ages.

Godwin does not fit conveniently into Maurice Keen's division of the English medieval outlaw legends into earlier tales of chivalric adventurers and later stories of forest outlaws. Neither the *Vita Ædwardi* nor any of the other texts about Godwin contains a fight with a monster, the illusions of a magician, the rescue of a princess or other romance conventions. Nor does Godwin ever lead a band of men in the Greenwood in a guerrilla war against injustice. However, like other outlaws, Godwin resides on a border, in this case a historical one between Anglo-Saxon and Anglo-Norman England. Moreover, the materials on Earl Godwin iterate several themes common to later medieval English outlaw stories, including anti-Norman sentiment, respect for kings, religious devotion, trickster behaviour and anti-clericalism.

The *Vita* is quite forthright in its placement of blame for Godwin's troubles on the Norman Robert of Jumièges. In doing so it reflects a conflict from Edward's reign. Edward had been raised in exile in Normandy after the line of his father, Æthelred, had been displaced from the throne of England by the Danish viking Cnut. As a result, he had many Norman friends whom he rewarded with lands and powerful positions in England. This favouritism aroused jealousy and anxiety among the English and the *Vita* author makes a point of placing these tensions at the centre of the 1051 conflict. In contrast, the Worcester (D) and Peterborough (E) versions of the *Anglo-Saxon Chronicle* put the blame on a skirmish instigated by Eustace of Boulogne at Dover.[8]

By placing the blame for the events of 1051 on Robert rather than either Godwin or Edward, the *Vita* adopts a typical strategy of the medieval English outlaw narrative. Edward himself is not unjust or tyrannical, but merely led astray for a time by corrupt advisors. Nor does Godwin challenge the authority of the king. In fact, by applying the Biblical model of David and Saul to Godwin and Edward, the author of the *Vita* reinforces the divine right of the king, for Godwin like David will not take it upon himself to injure God's anointed ruler. When he has the king outnumbered at Southwark, Godwin's followers urge him to attack, but the horrified earl responds: 'May God be in my heart today as a testament to its faithfulness; indeed, I would rather die than have done, or do, or while living permit to be done, anything indecent or evil against my lord the king'. The passage implicitly echoes the protest of David in I Samuel 24:6, 'God forbid that I should do anything to my lord the anointed one of God' and I Samuel 26:9, 'and David said to Abisai, "Do not kill him, for who may extend his hand against the anointed of God and be innocent?"' Furthermore, in his actions Godwin follows the procedure for correcting an errant superior outlined by Gregory the Great. Commenting on the response of David to the opportunity to kill Saul, Gregory writes:

> For what can be mentioned more merciful than David, what more humble, who received from the reprobate king insults for his victories, who by his strength rescued the nation of the Israelites from the hand of their enemies, and yet fled away himself lest he should die, as one of no strength?[9]

Such humility was the key, according to Gregory, to correcting the errors of a superior: 'Now, what is symbolized by Saul but bad rulers, and what by David, but good subjects?'[10] Rulers are to be admonished so that they do not become proud in their position, so that they act justly and so that they exercise their power moderately. Proper admonition, however, is a problem – Gregory warns that subjects observing the faults of their leaders should beware of pride and disrespect in themselves, and 'their private judgment should be such that constrained by the fear of God they still do not refuse to bear the yoke of reverence in subjection to them'.[11] So, despite the opportunity to kill his adversary, 'David shrank from smiting him, because subjects with a dutiful conscience keep themselves completely free from the plague of disparagement, and do not attack with the sword of the tongue the way of life of superiors, even when they find fault with their imperfections'.[12] And so Godwin bears neither the sword of his hand nor the sword of his tongue against Edward, but rather allows his humility and loyalty to speak for him. In this regard he anticipates both the fidelity and the gentle criticism that Robin Hood embodies by doing the work of the king's appointed officials.

Respect for God's ordained king is only one dimension of Godwin's religious devotion in the *Vita*. Unlike the clever, self-possessed character in other accounts of his life, Godwin here constantly interprets the events of his life in the light of divine providence and measures his actions according to divine law.[13] His devotion stands in notable contrast to Robert's repeated disrespect for the laws of Church and kingdom. Godwin, for instance, appears self-sacrificing when he offers to 'satisfy the king according to his will, either within the law or beyond it', whereas Robert appears tyrannical and lawless when he convinces Edward to demand the impossible, to return 'his brother alive with all his men'. Likewise, the author is quick to criticize Robert for having Edith sent away 'against the law of Christian religion', while Edward's complicity in the action is assuaged by the 'honest reason' he provides.

Though Godwin does not play the trickster in this selection from the *Vita*, such behaviour is common enough in other accounts of the earl's character that it deserves mention. Map's *De Nugis Curialium*, *Knýtlinga saga* and the *Vita Haroldi* all include tales of Godwin's use of deception to get what he wants. The most famous is a play on language that has its echoes in *Fouke fitz Waryn* and various tales of Robin Hood. Walter Map reports that the earl once approached the Archbishop of Canterbury and stated, 'You give me Bosham'. When the startled Archbishop asked, 'I give you Bosham?' Godwin took the town, claiming the Archbishop had said, 'I give you Bosham'. Elsewhere the earl cleverly gains a position in Æthelred's court, marries Cnut's sister and confiscates the property of a convent. Such behaviour conflicts with the earnest and holy character that the author of the *Vita* describes, but this dimension of Godwin's reputation clearly has affinities with many other outlaw stories.

TRANSLATION FROM THE *VITA ÆDWARDI REGIS*

Prose III

The order of this story demands an explanation of events that happened earlier, so that what follows does not blunder away from the truth. When the aforementioned King Edward of holy memory returned home from France, quite a few not ignoble men of that land accompanied him, and the king kept them with him and enriched them with many honours and, since he ruled the entire kingdom, he made them his own privy counsellors and controllers of affairs of the royal palace.[1] Among these came an abbot named Robert, who had led the monastery at Jumièges across the sea, and he, so they say, was very powerful and always standing by the king in private. Through his advice many things both good and bad were done in the kingdom with mixed results, as it often happens in the world.

When the bishop of London passed away, Robert succeeded to that bishopric by royal favour.[2] Assuming such advanced authority, he immersed himself more than necessary in arranging royal councils and acts, to such an extent that it proves the saying, 'good habits are corrupted by evil companions'; for the king listened to his advice due to its proximity rather than to more useful counsel.[3] Hence, as it usually happens, Edward offended many of the kingdom's nobles through the fault of another, and on account of such circumstances his kingdom gradually began to be disturbed. For when the possessors of dignified seats died, some men desired the vacant seats for their own, and other men alienated them to foreigners. Then while the royal court was upset by this storm, Eadsig Archbishop of Canterbury died.[4] However, a certain monk named Ælric had grown up in that same church of Christ, educated from youth in monastic discipline and from the lineage of the aforementioned Earl Godwin. He was a man clearly industrious in secular affairs and endowed with wisdom in things of the world, but not less beloved in that same congregation. The brothers of the entire church and the monks of his monastery implored him to become archbishop and chose him according to the desire of the community and by petition as dictated by rule. They sent to Godwin, who by royal favour ruled in that part of the kingdom, reminding him of his own kinship, and asking that on account of love of family he approach the king and, inasmuch as Ælric was raised in the same church and elected according to canon law, to designate him their pontiff. The famous earl faithfully put his own power into the undertaking and, approaching the king, made known the petition and election of the ecclesiastical community. But because, as we have said, the holy king gave more ear to the opposing party in those days, the earl's petition was rejected. Indeed, Robert of London, leaving his seat, moved to the Canterbury church to be rewarded with the archbishopric by the king, while all the brothers of the church protested this injury with great outcry.[5]

Finally, possessing his own desire and having attained a dignity of highest honour, the archbishop began to irritate and oppose the earl with all his power and effort. And because he stood with the king in the principle place of private council on account of reverence for his superior rank, he often attacked Godwin with counsel, and troubled him with injuries when he was vulnerable. However, the fact that certain lands of the earl bordered lands which belonged to Christ Church came near to expediting the movements of the hostile party into a just cause for the bishop. There were also frequent controversies between them because Robert said that Godwin had invaded the lands of his archbishopric and injured him by holding them for his own uses.[6] However, the industrious earl bore the heedless fury of the bishop peacefully, both for the king's honour and the innate custom of his family, for they do nothing quickly or lightly, but by most perceptive counsel they wait and watch the head-long rush to see the matter either dissipate or die on its own. Nevertheless, the injuries to the earl deeply disturbed some of his men, and they would have punished the bishop very often with abuse had Godwin not stopped them by prohibiting it.

And although Robert had proven evidence of this, nevertheless he did not desist, but adding madness to madness, with all his effort he turned the king's mind against Godwin and persuaded Edward to believe that Godwin planned to attack the king by guile, just as he had once attacked his brother, which was not mentioned before because the matter did not arise. This same King Edward had a full brother named Alfred. When their stepfather Cnut died, through the effort of the Danes, who at that time had power and following in the kingdom, Harold, a certain of Cnut's sons, born illegitimately, as they say, 'of his blood', a man of insolent bearing and not of good character, succeeded to the kingdom.[7] Alfred unadvisedly entered Britain with a few armed Frenchmen and, acting rashly about attaining the paternal kingdom, he was wrongfully captured and, it is said, tortured to death at the command of the aforementioned king. [See plate 1.] Indeed, they say his companions were deceitfully disarmed and some murdered and the remainder given in servitude to the victors.[8] And so, as we have said, Archbishop Robert put it in the king's ear that this crime of his brother's death and the loss of all his men had been done on the advice of the same glorious earl, because at that time, as before, he was the bailiff of the royal council, and Robert persuaded Edward as much as he was able that Godwin intended to ruin King Edward himself, his own kinsman, in the same manner. So, through continual persuasion, Robert made the king to believe more of this than was certain.

Therefore, the king being disturbed by such things more than was just, all the nobles and earls for all of Britain convened at the royal palace at Gloucester, where, hearing this complaint from the king, the innocent earl endured the accusation of the crime.[9] When he found this out through certain faithful companions, he sought the king's peace via messengers, offering without effect to purge himself by law from the criminal charge. For up to this point the king had so set his mind upon believing in this crime that he could not hear any word of the offered purgation. At the convention were Siward, Earl of Northumbria, called 'Digra' in the Danish tongue, that is 'strong'; Earl Leofric, a most eminent man and very devoted to God; Ælfgar, son of the same Earl Leofric. When they had all struggled together in vain to legally transfer the foul accusation to an ordeal, the royal court moved from that place to London.[10] Likewise Earl Godwin, innocent and trusting in his own conscience, and entirely guiltless of such a crime, approached from a different direction with his men and set up alongside the same city's River Thames at his own manor. Sending messengers from there, he again asked that nothing be brought against the prejudgment of his innocence by the king, and he showed himself by all means prepared to satisfy the king according to his will, either within the law or beyond it. By the efforts of Stigand, then Bishop of Winton but later also Archbishop of Kent, who served as an intermediary, the day of judgement was put off while the king made use of his council.[11] Meanwhile, Archbishop Robert hostilely pressed the earl by obstructing him, and through his action this indissoluble judgement was at last passed against the earl by the king: namely, that he could hope for the king's peace when he gave back to him his brother alive with all his men and restored entirely all that had been taken from them living or dead. Bishop Stigand, weeping abundantly, was the sorrowful bearer of this message. And when the earl saw his cause made impossible through the action of his adversaries, he pushed away the table which stood before him, and mounting a horse made his way quickly to Bosham on the sea. There, compelled into exile on readied ships he begged God faithfully and with tears to direct his life and his way in the sea and in that exile, for he was faithful to his lord Edward the king, and he stood innocent of all these things which provided the occasion for such great animosity. After he had expressed completely the quality of his innocence, with general tears, with wife and children and his property at hand, a favourable wind blowing, he came to where Count Baldwin V, an ancient friend of the English people, ruled.[12] Yet the archbishop did not desist, being truly driven by his madness; many soldiers from the king's palace rode all night so that they might kill the aforementioned earl if they could catch him within the borders of the kingdom.[13] But because the goodness of God frustrated this, the great madness of the bishop grew. And, so that no part of Godwin's family might adhere to the royal side to work for the welfare of the kingdom, he directed all counsel so that even the queen, daughter of the same earl, was separated from the king against the law of Christian religion. Nor did the king oppose this plan, although he allowed it to be moderated, offering this honest reason for the separation, that at Wilton monastery, where she had been raised, she would await the calming of the turbulence in the kingdom. Thus with royal honour and an imperial retinue, yet mourning, she was led into the enclosure of Wilton monastery, where for nearly a year with prayers and tears she awaited the day of salvation. This sadness penetrated more deeply and injured more the heart of the crowd of courtiers than the departure of the earl. No wonder, for she was in all the royal councils, and as we might say, a moderator and principle of all honesty, and preferring most strongly what benefited the king to all powers and riches.

Verse III

Sing, sister Muse, on this sad song,
About that man of God, whom we called
A clear fountain in paradise, known for a faithful heart,
But fouled by the filth of Scylla's poison;
And although he never before bore the guilt of one accused,
Tell why the weight of crime stuck to him.
Hardship comes to many who do not deserve blame,

Who are acclaimed with greater distinction once fear is defeated;
And the more anyone is pronounced devout,
The more he is marked to bear great pressures.
Have you not read of Susanna, full of life,
Led to the stones by her virtue, having repulsed with pure mind
The evil they sought?[14] Don't you recall that
Hebrew boy, relying on the munificence of heaven,
Who feared to sin, yet bore the penalty of sin?[15]
Our Lord himself, born of a true virgin,
Came to us without sin and nevertheless received
Many punishments of the world during his life.
The present is full of this, as was the former age;
There are a thousand examples that this is often the case.

Prose IV

The exiled earl Godwin was received with great honour by Count Baldwin V both on account of their ancient alliance and in exchange for the many favours of the earl. This occurred during the marriage of Godwin's own son, Earl Tostig, when he received as his wife Judith, niece of that most renowned King Edward and sister of Count Baldwin V. Thus it came about not a little undeservedly that after the chalice of exultation Godwin was made to drink the cup of sorrow. In turn, his sons Harold and Leofwine had crossed over to Ireland so that, by gathering military forces, they might avenge their father's injury. This commotion befell the English kingdom around the calends of October, and the earl wintered with Count Baldwin V in Flanders and the sons with King Dermot in Ireland.

Since, as we have said before, all the English honoured Godwin as a father, the heart of the people was terrified by the news of his sudden departure. They held his absence or flight to be their own ruin, the destruction of the English people, indeed, the downfall of the whole land. He thought himself fortunate who was able to follow Godwin into exile. Some went after him and others sent messengers that they were prepared, if he should wish to return, to receive him with military aid into the land, to fight for him, and, if necessary, they were just as willing to die for him. And this was proclaimed not secretly or in private but openly and publically, and not limited to a few but by nearly all the natives of the land. And when sought by the whole kingdom with good will and desire, this man, notable for faith and virtue and upset by such a scandal, sent again to seek peace and mercy from the king his lord, that he might be allowed by his grace to come into his presence and legally clear himself. The king of the Franks also sought this through his own messenger on account of his love and respect, and the Marquis of Flanders, with whom Godwin was wintering, urged the same.

And yet those men supplied this satisfaction in vain; for the malice of perverse men blocked the ears of the pious king.

When the active earl saw himself wrongly overthrown and denied access to a trial by law through the efforts of iniquitous men, he recalled his old virtue and all of the labours of his youth, and in the middle of the next summer prepared a fleet of many ships in the River Yser and put to sea.[16] With a favourable wind blowing directly from the east, he slipped into a port on the shore of Britain. All the southern and eastern English who were able came to the ship; they all came to him, I say, just as sons to their long-awaited father. At that same time, aroused by the report, the two previously mentioned sons came to him from Ireland with great fleets, and they devastated with sword, fire and the seizure of spoils everything from those westernmost limits of the Britons or English up to where the earl waited. With great joy the father and brothers caught sight of each other in turn, and mutually admired their own completed labours and perils. The sea was covered with ships; the heavens reflected the closely packed weapons. So finally, the warriors having strengthened their resolve through mutual encouragement, they crossed what is called the Kentish sea, and with a long line of ships entered the course of the River Thames.

When the king heard of this violent and unauthorized entry into his kingdom, although he did not put faith in the messengers, he came to London with all the military force he could, and because he was fierce in spirit and most vigorous and quick to act, he tried to prohibit them from entering the city by what means he held. But the whole city went out to meet the earl and to aid and protect him, and all those people acclaimed his coming joyfully in a single voice.[17] And because resources from every side provided him with superior strength, many urged that he force his way in upon the king himself. Faithful and devoted to God, the earl was horrified by these words and advice. 'May God be in my heart today', he said, 'as a testament to its faithfulness; indeed, I would rather die than have done, or do, or while living permit to be done, anything indecent or evil against my lord the king'. And having discouraged them all from this impulse, when he came into the presence of the king, he immediately threw down his weapons and prostrated himself at his feet, pleading humbly that in the name of Christ, the symbol of whose kingdom was upon the crown on Edward's head, the king would allow him to purge himself from the standing charge and, being cleared, grant the peace of his grace. And the king was compelled both by mercy and the satisfaction of the earl, who appeared to him quite superior in arms if he wished to make use of them, and also, indeed, because he had been abandoned, most notably by the flight of the archbishop and many of his men who were clearly the instigators of this turbulent disturbance and feared the face of the earl. Edward was also overcome by the prayers of the supplicants, and so, returning Godwin's weapons, he entered the palace with the earl, and there gradually his troubled mind was calmed. On the advice of his council of the wise, he offered a kiss to the earl, forgave all offences, and also granted his renewed favour to him and all his sons. Appropriately, after a short time a magnificent and suitable royal escort was sent to Wilton monastery, and just as after the dense clouds of rain or tempest have fled, the clear sky and pleasant splendour of the sun returns, so also the disturbance in the kingdom having abated, the queen, the daughter of the earl, was brought back to the king's marriage bed. Thus, after such great evil had been settled without bloodshed through the wisdom of the earl, the famous event was celebrated joyfully both at court and throughout the entire land.

Verse IV

You too, Muse, compose measured songs of springing lines
Joyfully with me for such a reconciliation of events.
So David was strong; so he thought to spare the king.
When for a time the evil spirit from God troubled the king,
The playing of the harp relieved it,
Because the graceful player followed the complex work
And playing the harp chased away the abominable vexation.[18]
The royal son-in-law conquered powerfully in battle,
Distributing foreskins as a marriage dowry;[19]
By which palms of victory he was beloved in the court of the king
And stands first, second only to the king.
But as honour grew, envy grew also,
And because of his own probity many traps were spread
Which the old warrior evades,
More prepared to seek flight or, when necessary, fight.
Therefore fearing fraud he hides, but envy often entwines
The fugitive. Yet God protects dutifully
And binds the king in David's hand. But he,
Devoted to such favour, decided to spare the anointed one.
With thousands of armed men waiting in a suspected place
Saul sought David, whom a hollowed rock concealed.
This Saul entered for a movement of the bowels,
The king alone, ignorant of he whom he desired to kill.
'Behold the day', said David's men, 'when it is given to you
To take vengeance upon the furious enemy.
Do not hesitate to kill, pull out the sword.
If you will not take the opportunity, let us.' But he said,
'God does not want our hand to destroy the anointed one of God.
Stand back, I order you, desist quickly from this deed.
We will not capture this one, for the high judge appraises us
And I will prove to be more devoted than his anointed one.

Let him fall into death on his own or to hostile weapons,
And the right hand of thunder preserve our innocence,
When he said this, he secretly cut off the edge of Saul's robe.
Then David, safely behind Saul's back, called out after him
And announced that he had found the power of death.[20]
Another time he made his way through the vast camp.
The king deep in heavy sleep, David's sole companion, Abishai,
Enjoying possession of the life of the king, prepared to strike;
But again David interrupted and taught the virtue of loyalty,
Lest under him should perish he whom the oil of anointment had
     consecrated.[21]
Behold, David, strong of arm but embracing peace,
Abhorred the scandal of killing a king.

THE DEEDS OF HEREWARD

Michael Swanton

INTRODUCTION

Hereward 'the Wake'[1] is one of the best-known English outlaw-heroes, and one of the very few for whom we have historical evidence.[2] The reason he is such a familiar figure is because he was taken up and reinvented by one of the most popular of nineteenth-century novelists, Charles Kingsley, whose *Hereward the Wake: Last of the English*, romantically illustrated, was influential not only at the level of popular culture, but to an unusual degree on professional historians.[3] Kingsley drew on a medieval Latin *Gesta Herewardi* which had in turn drawn on an Anglo-Saxon story-book. The significance and longevity of the story are due to the importance of the social setting from which it emerged, which was nothing less than a national trauma.

Historical Background

The Norman Conquest of England in 1066 had immediate and far-reaching consequences on every aspect of national life – political, social and religious. The situation was not dissimilar to that which we might imagine had the planned German invasion of the Second World War taken place. The English towns and countryside were patrolled by groups of armed men, giving orders and demanding reparations in a strange and barbarous tongue which few people understood. Their appearance, insignia and equipment were wholly alien; even their brutally cropped heads contrasted with the longish hair-styles favoured by fashionable Englishmen of the time. Forced labour was compelled to assist with the erection of new fortifications everywhere, and troops enforced wholesale eviction as foreign landlords arrived to oust their predecessors. Responsibility for the death of any of these foreigners would be visited on the district in which it occurred. In the ranks of the Church, Englishmen were steadily replaced, and schools were now directed by masters with different priorities.

While no section of society remained unaffected, it was felt most of all by the English land-owning classes. Some resisted. A troublesome element, referred to by the Normans as *silvatici*, took to the swamps and forests of the hinterland.[4] Some actively collaborated; the vast majority had little option but to acquiesce, albeit with bad grace. The Conqueror's policies were by no means racist. Together with Bretons and Flemings he was prepared to take into his service any Englishmen on whose loyalty he could depend. Many are known to have served in his armies. Nevertheless, all who had fought by William's side would expect to be rewarded with lands confiscated from those English families who had taken an active part in resisting the Conquest. Particularly great estates were bestowed on close friends of the king like the de Warennes. The Norman occupation came as a catastrophe from which the English landed gentry never fully recovered. Some of the dispossessed left to seek their fortune elsewhere, finding refuge abroad in Scotland, Flanders or farther afield. For the remainder it was by no means impossible to come to terms with the Conqueror. Only those who disputed his suzerainty were at risk. Those who had not personally borne arms against William might, at a price, be confirmed in possession of their estates. But, however smooth a transition of government was intended, the situation on the ground was more complicated.

The day-to-day realities of life under an alien army of occupation would give plentiful occasion for resentment. As reasons for revolt multiplied, hostility flared into open rebellion in a number of places. In the north and east of the country, an area of former Scandinavian settlement ('Danelaw'), persistent rumours of a large-scale Danish invasion would give the disaffected population continuing, if ill-founded, cause for hope. In 1070 a Danish raiding-party went briefly to Ely and were promptly joined by local discontents including a dispossessed Lincolnshire squire called Hereward. The Saxon abbot of Ely (Thurstan) had long been a thorn in Norman flesh, but because of the difficult terrain (Ely was defended by impassable swamps) had hitherto been ignored by the Conqueror. But when the Isle became a refuge for so many dissidents, and their harassment increasingly troublesome (holding to ransom the new Norman abbot of Peterborough and even slaying one of the de Warenne brothers), King William was obliged to subdue the town. Ely was not taken without considerable difficulty. The surrounding fenland was ideal guerrilla country and impossible for the Norman cavalry. But William bottled up the defenders, placing a naval blockade on the seaward side and then constructing a lengthy causeway to allow his land forces to advance through the swamps. Eventually the defenders surrendered to the king who 'dealt with them just as he wanted'.[5] Hereward escaped with some of his followers and is heard of no more in any official record. Later, like some other resistance leaders, he may have been reconciled with the Conqueror.[6]

Manuscript

The sole surviving copy of the Latin *Gesta Herewardi* is found added to the end of a thirteenth-century collection of legal documents belonging to Robert de

Swaffham, pittancer and cellarer of Peterborough Abbey (Peterborough Cathedral Manuscript I, fols 320–39; lodged in Cambridge University Library Manuscripts Department).

Author and Sources

The author of the *Gesta* explains the origins of his work in a Prefatory Letter. Seeking information for a 'Life of Hereward', he had begun by trying to read a decaying manuscript containing a collection of Anglo-Saxon stories allegedly compiled by Hereward's 'well-remembered' chaplain Leofric who had assembled all the doings of giants and warriors he could find 'in ancient stories as well as true reports'. On the basis of this, perhaps half read, half invented, the author constructed a plainly fictional account of Hereward's youthful exile (chapts 2–12). Frustrated at finding no more adequate source, the author laid his work aside, but later completed the book by adjoining a somewhat episodic account of Hereward's part in the defence of Ely, based on interviews with the hero's former companions in the anti-Norman campaign. If it is true that he drew on first-hand rather than second-hand accounts, he was probably working in the first quarter of the twelfth century, at a time when Hereward himself was dead, but a number of elderly veterans of the Ely campaign were still alive and capable of remembering their old companion, even if 'with advantages'. Some time in the mid-twelfth century an unnamed monk of Ely Abbey composed an eclectic history of his institution, in the course of which he says he drew on a *Gesta Herewardi* recently made by a respected and 'most learned' fellow monk called Richard.[7] There are some verbal parallels with our text, and it is reasonable to suppose that this Richard was the author of the extant *Gesta* or an earlier version of them. By that time Richard was dead ('of blessed memory'). His identity is uncertain, but he was clearly familiar with the locality and of sufficient status to be able to call on assistants.

Structure and Themes

Guerrilla exploits readily capture the popular imagination and a wide variety of stories had begun to attach themselves to our hero. The author says that women and girls sang about Hereward in their dances, and ballads celebrating, and no doubt exaggerating, his deeds apparently continued to circulate throughout medieval times.[8] It is unlikely that the content of these tales was ever strictly true, or 'historical' in any modern sense. Probably, as with those early story makers who told of Beowulf's deeds, the man's actual exploits will have been compared with those of other heroes – first by way of example, elaboration and variation, and eventually confusion.[9] After all, it was expected that every hero should slay giants, rescue maidens and so forth.

Because the Hereward figure has been available to historians as well as to those interested in fiction, it is of fundamental importance (more so perhaps than in any other story anthologized here) to recognize the nature of the interface between history and legend. The authority of any story is subject to primordial iconotropy – always open to 'creative distortion'. The fact that narrative in general is liable to penetration and accretion is half acknowledged by the author when speaking of his source material (Prefatory Letter). Those we traditionally term 'historians', who seek to restore something authentic but lost, will dismiss all of the first chapters and be properly sceptical about much of the remainder. Those others who recognize that fictive truth may inhere elsewhere than in trivial actuality, will be less concerned with telling true from false than with the value of narrative as a mode of making some sense of the world – providing the consolations of social or moral expectation. These are the stories we feel compelled to iterate or invent – the necessary national and personal myths by which we live. Of course in early medieval times history could still properly be regarded as merely one branch of narrative literature, and not yet a separate science. In the case of the *Gesta Herewardi* the story drew extensively on an album compiled by a man with a taste for ancient fables and then supplemented this with the oral recollections of old soldiers. In consequence it is now virtually impossible to unravel the various strands of differing status, although we might assume the author's account of Hereward's youthful exploits (chapts 2–12) to be largely fictional.

Like the material sources of the *Gesta* (see above), its structure and themes are bifurcate. The latter part seems to be a straightforward story of valiant resistance to oppression and ultimate reconciliation to royal authority, such as we find in almost all the tales anthologized here. No doubt the germ of the historical Hereward, give or take romantic exaggeration, lies at the heart of this part of the story. It is a powerful national and heroic statement: Danish presence at Ely is not mentioned; the defence of the Isle of Ely is represented as a wholly English affair – much as Hollywood would have us believe it was Errol Flynn and the Americans who won back Burma from the Japanese.[10] By the same token, Hereward the squire is portrayed as leader, despite the actual presence of significant figures like Earl Morcar and Siward. Indeed, the addition of several others who could not possibly have been there (Earls Edwin and Tostig were in fact already dead) merely serves to enhance Hereward's role in this respect.

Although our hero is shown taking part in tournaments earlier when in exile, the defender of Ely is no aristocrat. In general the story is presented in terms that were likely to appeal to a rustic rather than a courtly audience. Like their attitudes, their weapons (spear and shield, bow and arrow) are those of the yeomanry. Hereward has imported a fine Flemish mare (rather like a European sports car in twentieth-century America), but this is unlikely to have impressed genteel society. If he asks to be knighted, it will be in the traditional English, not the French, fashion (chapt. 15). He is not so much chivalrous as fair-minded – he will prevent too many attacking a lone enemy. It simply isn't right for a man to be outnumbered – though he himself is quite prepared to take on all comers! His adventures resisting the oppressor of course are dangerous and risk death, but also involve trickery and subterfuge; and he is a master of disguise.

The 'greenwood' ideal of the outlaw life appears to be already understood: good company and an abundance of food. In what seems a virtually pre-Lapsarian refuge, a just society is at one with Nature, despite all odds. The emphatic rightness of it all is made clear in the almost poetic description given to the king by a Norman eyewitness: 'the monks risk endangering themselves rather than be reduced to servitude . . . gathering to themselves outlaws, the condemned, disinherited, and orphaned . . . Although besieged by four kings and their subjects, the ploughman doesn't take his hand from the plough nor does the right hand of the reaper hesitate in reaping . . .' (chapt. 21).

The native Church, which was very distinctive at this time, formed a natural focus of cultural identity, as in present-day Poland or Ireland. An abbot was not yet stereotypically wicked, but depicted as good or bad depending on whether he was English or not. Thus it is comic that the foreign abbot intended for Ely is dumped at sea in a sack, prefiguring knock-about mockery of the abbot in later outlaw stories. Nevertheless, there is probably a good deal of historical interplay with the romance in this respect. The Norman Abbot Turold of Peterborough was *in fact* a tyrannical individual – and Ely *was* eventually betrayed by a dispirited English abbot. In practice, both Norman invader and English defender looted (or in Hereward's case 'liberated') church treasure.[11] Here the monks themselves bear arms against the oppressor (chapts. 21–2). At this time bishops and abbots were recruited mainly from the middle ranks of the nobility, surrounded by military bodyguards. Many had warlike proclivities. The Saxon abbot of Peterborough died as a result of wounds received at Hastings; and it was his successor, the embattled Brand, who helped foster Hereward's ambition. The 'law' outside which Hereward stands is illegitimate inasmuch as his is the bluff native code of behaviour with which we sympathize. Our hero is not the criminal 'wolf's-head', rather the protestant freedom-fighter. Like many later folk-hero outlaws, he represents underdog decency, and therefore what ought to be. The relationship the story has to its audience is one of shared, me-too, cultural identity. And the king himself, when he appears, is seen to be a fair-minded man. The fact that he recognizes Hereward's virtues will permit dramatic and moral *rapprochement* between hero and regal authority, whereas the king's minions will stoop to anything, even witchcraft, to gain their ends.

But the end was inevitable. Resistance to the Normans was ineffectual because it was piecemeal and local. The struggle of a doomed social order against a conquering invader could be made the occasion for romantic action, often violent, occasionally comic, sometimes both. But in practice uprisings were invariably suppressed with ferocity. The land was laid waste in the fashion of the time, leaving a legacy of bitterness which would last for generations to come. English fiction, as ever, was captivated by the glories of defeat rather than victory, quite content to dwell on the sentiment of righteous heroism in the face of overwhelming odds, Arnhem rather than Alamein. In order not to be unbearable, it could be presented in mythic terms. It was perhaps too early to clothe Hereward with the romance trappings of the later stereotypic 'greenwood' outlaw: merry men and feasts of venison. But not perhaps too early to see in Hereward the figure Charles Kingsley could identify as simply 'the last Englishman'.

In our imagination great heroes have great beginnings. One can readily understand why there attaches to Hereward's early life a whole array of stories. The young Hereward certainly shows signs of a difficult adolescence: truculent (which contemporaries might consider proper self awareness) and with a clear lack of regard for property rights. Great generosity was a heroic virtue, but with one's own, rather than one's father's goods – not recommended in what was already a feudal society! Proving rather more than a nuisance at home, he is sent into exile. It was conventional that a young man in such circumstances should visit the courts of foreign princes, and there prove himself in deeds of valour and prowess. [See plate 2.]

Hereward's absence from England at the time of the Conquest is convenient both dramatically and politically.[12] In practice, like many a neighbour, he might have been compromised. But at a local level it is unthinkable for the fictional hero to have been present during the humiliating seizure of his inheritance, since the enemy is demonstrably dismissible; moreover he could not otherwise fulfil his dramatic function as returning avenger with probity, redressing wrongs done to his people (though only locally and in microcosm). Thus the earlier part of the story is taken up with a farrago of adventures of the kind familiar from contemporary saga and romance: story rather than history, *geste* rather than *gesta*. Several of the formulae are found in Scandinavian sources,[13] as we might expect from its place of composition – an area of former Scandinavian settlement and continuing Danish sympathies. Our hero follows the traditional route of the fictional exile through the peripheral regions of Britain: combating a monstrous bear in the far north, rescuing a princess from an unwelcome suitor in Cornwall, slaying a great king in Ireland and suffering shipwreck in Orkney before eventually passing on to Flanders, the common resort of English refugees at this time. In the course of all this, the personality of the future guerrilla-fighter is anticipated: courageous, quick-witted, adept at disguise and ever-watchful, sleeping not in but to one side of his bed for fear of night-time attacks. In Flanders he performs deeds not unlike the 'exiled' Harold Godwinson – leading armies on behalf of a Continental ruler, after which he returns to England where the historical element of the tale is joined.

Separation of the *Gesta* into its two elements, however clumsy, would have been an authorial necessity to square with the known facts of such recent events. Falling so clearly into two halves, so different in style and intent, it would be easy to dismiss the surviving *Gesta* as merely bungled archival notes. But it might not be going too far to recognize an embryonic 'outlaw genre' emerging from the known forms of romance-saga tradition and awkwardly feeling its way towards the later popular tradition represented by Gamelyn and Robin Hood. Of necessity seeking to align recent reality with romance, it telescopes known events to allow the hero to take part or alters their sequence for dramatic effect. The result is not in any sense a 'finished' piece of writing.

In addition to structural faults, there are narrative inadequacies in detail: names of people and places are apparently arbitrarily introduced, which certainly carried clear connotations for a contemporary, and local, audience, but which require explanation for readers from another location or another time (see notes to the translation, *passim*). But here is clearly the material of another genre: that of 'dynastic romance'; there were soon noble families keen to trace their descent from the one-time brigand turned national hero. As the author himself admitted in his Prefatory Letter, the whole thing needed working over by another hand. Nevertheless, the story of Hereward would prove a potentially powerful theme.

Translator's Note

Translation cannot reproduce, or even adequately reflect, the style of the original without departing from its substance to an unacceptable degree. In this case we should remember that the surviving Latin text itself purports to be in part merely a translation from an Anglo-Saxon original, understanding which was not without difficulties. I have tried to present as close a translation as the language will allow without being awkwardly over-literal and with minimum intrusion of the academic voice. In particular I have thought it important not silently to 'improve' the original in places where I felt it to be clumsy, repetitive or obscure.

TRANSLATION OF *THE DEEDS OF HEREWARD*

Here begins the preface of a certain work concerning the exploits of Hereward the renowned knight.

Prefatory Letter [1]

When some among us wanted to know about the deeds of the great Englishman Hereward and his famous men, and to hear with our ears his generous acts and exploits, your brethren eked out our sparse information by enquiring whether anyone had left anything in writing about such a man in the place where he used to live. For when I informed you that I had heard somewhere that a short account had been written about him in English, you were immediately kind enough to have it sought out; and soon it was translated into Latin, with the addition of things we happened to hear from our own people with whom he was familiar, living a distinguished life as a great warrior. So, wanting to satisfy your wishes, I took care to enquire in many places, yet found nothing complete – only a few loose pages, partly rotten with damp and decayed and partly damaged by tearing. However, having taken up the pen, I have with difficulty extracted from it a few details as to his origin, his parents and reputation – that is to say the early achievements of the most famous outlaw Hereward, written down in English by the deacon Leofric, his priest at Bourne.[2] For it was the endeavour of this well-remembered priest to assemble all the doings of giants and warriors he could find in ancient stories as well as true reports for the edification of his audience; and for their remembrance to commit them to writing in English. And although I'm not sufficiently expert at this, or rather, unable to decipher what is obliterated in the unfamiliar writing, nevertheless I gather that on his return to the place of his own ancestral home, he found his brother killed – and so on. I leave this raw material, written in a rough style, to your care and to the efforts of some trained person, to be arranged and set out in a less ornate and complex manner. For I have been able to decipher nothing further than this, always hoping for more but still finding nothing in full. For a long time my assistants were deluded by a vain hope, stimulated by those who said that there was a large book about his exploits in such and such a place. But although they sent to the place they found nothing of what was promised. So giving up the search altogether, I abandoned the work I had begun. It could not have remained secret from you for long; but unexpectedly, you were kind enough to direct that at least the opening should not be denied you. Whereupon I took care, although not confident of any great ability, that your eyes might see the complete work. I took up the pen once more to unfold to you a little book in the style of a history, dealing with things I heard from our own people and from some of those who were familiar with him from the beginning and who were associated with him in many exploits. I have frequently seen some of these men – tall in stature, well built and exceptionally courageous. And you yourself, I hear, have also seen two of these men – that is to say his knights Brother Siward of St Edmunds[3] and Leofric Black, men of distinguished appearance, although having lost the beauty of their limbs due to the trickery of enemies, being deprived of certain members through envy.[4] And from these and others whom I have seen and tested in many matters, if on no other grounds, there is sufficient for you to understand how valorous their lord was, and how much greater his deeds were than those reported of him. For truly to know who Hereward was and to hear about his magnanimity and his exploits, is conducive to magnanimous acts and generosity, especially in those wishing to undertake the warrior's life. So I urge you to pay attention, especially you who are concerned to hear of the exploits of brave men; listen carefully to this account of so great a man who, trusting in himself rather than rampart or garrison, alone with his men waged war against kings and kingdoms, and fought against princes and tyrants, some of whom he conquered. Concerning these matters, beginning with his parents, everything has been arranged in due order, so that what is clearly set down here may be easily remembered.

1

Of what parents Hereward was born, and how from his boyhood he increased in the splendour of his deeds, and why he was driven forth by his father and country; whence he was surnamed 'The Outlaw'.

Many very mighty men are recorded from among the English people, and the outlaw Hereward is reckoned the most distinguished of all – a notable warrior among the most notable. Of very noble descent from both parents, his father was Leofric of Bourne, nephew of Earl Ralph the Staller; and his mother was Eadgyth, the great-great-niece of Duke Oslac.[5] As a boy he was remarkable for his figure and handsome in his features, very fine with his long blond hair, open face and large grey eyes – the right one slightly different from the left. However, he was formidable in appearance and rather stout because of the great sturdiness of his limbs; but despite his moderate stature he was very agile and there was great strength in all his limbs. From his childhood he exhibited such grace and vigour of body; and from practice when a youth the quality of his courage proved him a perfect man. He was excellently endowed in every way with the grace of courage and strength of spirit. And so far as generosity is concerned, he was particularly liberal with his own and his father's possessions, giving relief to all in need.[6] Although tough in work and rough in play, readily provoking fights among those of his own age and often stirring up strife among his elders in town and village, he had no equal in acts of daring and bravery, not even among his elders. So when young, and as he grew older, he advanced in boldness day by day, and while still a youth excelled in manly deeds. In the meantime he spared nobody whom he thought to be in any way a rival in courage or in fighting. In consequence he often caused strife among the populace and commotion among the common people. As a result of this he made his parents hostile towards him; for because of his deeds of courage and boldness they found themselves quarrelling with their friends and neighbours every day, and almost daily having to protect their son with drawn swords and weapons when he returned from sport or from fighting, from the local inhabitants who acted like enemies and tyrants because of him. Unable to stand this, eventually his father drove him out of his sight. He didn't keep quiet even then; but when his father went visiting his estates, Hereward and his gang often got there first, distributing his father's goods among his own friends and supporters. And on some of his father's properties he even appointed stewards and servants of his own to see to provisions for his men. And so his father ensured that he was banished from his homeland by King Edward,[7] disclosing everything that he had perpetrated against his parents and against the inhabitants of the locality. And this being done, he at once acquired the name of 'Outlaw',[8] being driven away from his father and his native land when he was eighteen years old.

2

How Hereward slew a giant bear, from which he earned a position among the knights where he was staying.

When Gisebert de Ghent[9] heard of this, that is his banishment, he sent for him. Hereward was in fact the godson of that wealthy man. So he set out with a single servant, Martin Lightfoot, and went beyond Northumberland,[10] forsaking his own district and his father's inheritance. He was not there for many days before a commendable thing happened. For at Easter, Whitsun and Christmas[11] that wealthy man had the custom of testing the strength and spirit of those young men who were hoping for the belt and arms of knighthood by letting wild beasts out from cages. At the beginning of his visit, that is to say at Christmas, Hereward being among their company asked to be allowed to take on one of the beasts – in point of fact a very large bear which was there. This was the offspring of a famous Norwegian bear which had the head and feet of a man and human intelligence, which understood the speech of men and was cunning in battle. Its father, so the stories and legends told, was said to have raped a girl in the woods and through her to have engendered Beorn, King of Norway.[12] Hereward couldn't get permission because, although the lord perceived the bravery of the young man, he feared for his youthfulness. The next day, however, the animal broke its chains and burst out of the bars of the cage, tearing to pieces and killing every living thing it could reach. When the lord heard about this, he immediately ordered the knights to get ready to attack it with spears, pointing out that it wasn't possible to take it alive. Meanwhile, alerted by the screams of the scared people, Hereward encountered the blood-stained beast as it was proceeding to the lord's chamber where his wife and daughters and the women had fled in fright. Straightway it wanted to rush at him. But he anticipated it, driving his sword through its head as far as the shoulder blades. Leaving the blade there, he lifted up the animal in his arms and held it out to those who followed, at which sight they were much amazed. From his lord and lady in fact he earned no little thanks, but from the knights and pages of the household deep hatred and envy. As a result of this deed he gained the status and rank of a knight, although at the time he put off being made a knight, saying that he ought to make a better trial of his courage and spirit. And so the people of the region extolled him with praises, and the women and girls sang about him in their dances,[13] to the great annoyance of his enemies. And because he daily increased in both bodily grace and maturity, and in strength and courage, leaving none to equal him in the chase and in hunting, nor in the sports of either the common people or of gentlemen, they looked for an opportune time and place to kill him. And one day when their lord happened to be absent hunting in the woods, the knights of the household tried to do away with him by means of a javelin hurled by one who was particularly familiar with him and whom three days earlier he had saved from death when captured by enemies. However, having learned of this plot from a servant just in time, Hereward transfixed with a spear his attacker in the act of throwing the javelin. Having disclosed this to his lady, and wanting to avoid such plots, he went away. But weeping, she repeatedly begged that he would at least wait for the lord to return or, if not, for the death of their sick son, declaring that if he would not leave he should become their adopted son and heir. But she couldn't persuade him.

3

How he overcame a certain tyrant, and took his famous sword.

From there Hereward went to join a certain prince of Cornwall called Alef. There he found a very wicked and arrogant man, Rough Scab by name, who had long hoped to win the prince's beautiful daughter through his remarkable courage.[14] Because of his relationship to them, this man was reckoned the strongest warrior among the two nations of the Scots and Picts, as if there was none to compare with him anywhere. Wherever he was staying crowds would flock to him, as if to some great spectacle, and to listen to his exploits. And he would freely, though untruthfully, din these into the ears of his audience, boasting that no man, nor any two or three, was his equal. He often did this before the royal family and the prince himself. On one occasion he was greatly disparaging the English nation for lacking the virtue of strength and being useless in battle, declaring that once he had killed three out of a number of men with a single stroke. Indignant at this, Hereward scornfully replied to him in front of them all: 'Since those men you say you killed were conceived in your own mind, begotten of your heart and not of a mother, it's appropriate that they should be slain by one blow of your mouth!' At this his future wife, the daughter of the aforesaid prince, dissolved in a fit of laughter. This greatly offended the bully, who immediately threatened Hereward: 'If it wasn't for the presence of the lord, you would now lie slain by my own hands, so help me!' To which Hereward replied: 'See that so tough a knight as you proclaim yourself to be doesn't employ trickery against a young man. Given that, if you want to set aside trickery and come looking for him of whom you speak, you'll always find me ready. So your triumph, if it comes, will be the more glorious.' Not forgetting what he had said, he happened to meet Hereward while he was unarmed, in a neighbouring woodland belonging to the aforesaid lord. 'Well,' said the bully at once, 'now is the longed-for time to take vengeance on an enemy', and so on. 'Today the gift of your scalp shall dissolve her either in laughter or in sorrow, she who earlier delighted in the obstinacy of your words, who praised your long hair, your features and the insolence of your reply.' To which Hereward rejoined: 'There's no glory in a famous man so well supplied with weapons and strength putting down an unarmed man. However, if I'm to fall, of your goodness if you have any, allow me the space of an hour to give my things to the priest to bequeath to the poor, and I'll return straight away.' And upon Hereward's taking an oath to this effect, he agreed, accepting his promise to disclose the matter to nobody. Departing therefore, Hereward armed himself – for it was for that reason that he had entered into discussion with him. Rapidly returning therefore, Hereward pierced the bully's thighs with a javelin at the first sign of onset; and struggling together, they struck blows at one another for some time. Well, continually advancing and attacking, the young man avoided the blows, and ducking and weaving, often inflicted blows that were unexpected and covert. When the detestable man saw the youth's spirit, he attempted to grapple with him hand to hand, for he was stronger and very much greater in stature. But Hereward continually evaded him until, as he was in the act of bending over and less careful of his rear, Hereward thrust his sword under the mailcoat into the groin. At which, wet with blood and feeling his death imminent, he said: 'Aaaaah! Look how I, so very tough, trusting in my own strength, through carelessness lie overthrown by a cunning lad! Ah, if only I had the blade which just now I handed to my future wife, which I got fighting with some tyrant, and with which I overcame such great men; if the goddess Fortune were kind to me I could at least avenge myself with one blow, half-dead as I am!' At this, hearing the noise of weapons, the pages of the household ran to the spot and meanwhile told of the affair to their lord, who sent armed men there to separate them, fearing the youth's death. Arriving, they found themselves preceded by a death they hadn't anticipated. Whereupon, because the abominable man was already spoken of as the prince's son-in-law, Hereward was apprehended and led before the prince. Immediately then the whole of that troublesome nation wanted to rise up against Hereward, declaring that their toughest man had been killed by treachery. But the prince himself curbed their anger and, in order that the youth might be saved, kept him in custody as though intending to decide what should be done about him. But his daughter, greatly delighted at what had happened because she very much dreaded that terrifying man with misshapen limbs, ministered to Hereward while in custody with the greatest solicitude. And finally, having presented him with gifts and the aforementioned sword which had been given her, contrived for him to leave in secret, begging him not to forget her. And, not without significant tokens, she sent him to the son of the King of Ireland,[15] telling in a letter how he had killed her enemy.

4

Of the war which took place in Ireland, and how Hereward with seven comrades slew the leader of the opposing army in the midst of his men.

When these things were known therefore, Hereward was honourably received by the son of the King of Ireland and by the king himself.[16] And they had him stay with them for several days, although he was unwilling to because, having carried out his errand, he wished to return to his father's household and his widowed mother. For he had come across two most distinguished men, Siward the Blond and Siward the Red, sons of his own uncle, who told him that his father was dead and that his mother was by herself on the estate now made over to him. He hadn't been staying there very long when it was announced that a war against the Duke of Munster was imminent.[17] And so on a given day all the king's adherents in the area begged and entreated Hereward and his men to take part in the battle and help them, since they had heard many instances of his bravery; and even now in the short time he had been with them they themselves had found out many things worth relating of him. Submitting to their entreaties therefore, Hereward was very active with his seniors in arranging and preparing everything for war, up to the very day of battle. He drew up the lines and led them. Meanwhile, if the outcome of the battle should prove doubtful or if their forces were giving way at all, seven of his comrades were assigned the task of attacking the leader of the opposing army in the midst of his men. Which they did. In the midst of the enemy battalions, killing to right and to left, they came right up to the leader's tent and found him lying at the entrance together with two of his chief men. Hereward rapidly told him the reason for their coming: he must immediately surrender and offer allegiance to his lord; otherwise he must realize that they would attack him. But knowing that his men were acting bravely, he refused. Shouting for help as he was surrounded by enemies, and defending himself with his own hand, he protected himself for a while after the two chief men were killed. Then while the others guarded the entrance to the tent, Hereward himself attacked and killed him. Then receiving a signal from the leader's sword and trumpet, they hastily returned through the cohorts which closely surrounded them. One of them, namely the king's nephew, was laid low, and they were almost overwhelmed in their retreat, having so far lost two comrades and with both of Hereward's nephews seriously wounded. Eventually reaching their allies, they sounded the leader's trumpet to advance, whereupon the enemy fled in great terror. As a result of this, Hereward's name was greatly praised throughout all the kingdom; and his fame increased daily among the neighbouring peoples round about. Hearing this, many tough men and the sons of leading families flocked to him to be instructed in arms and noble arts. Now having together with the king's son gathered together a band of soldiers, he subdued his enemies in the neighbourhood and then went on to subdue the entire area round about that was opposed to the king, all in the space of one year. None of his predecessor's courage approached halfway to his.

5

How Hereward in disguise was sent by his lord to a wedding, where he achieved a praiseworthy action in killing the bridegroom and carrying off the bride and conveying her to his lord.

While they were in a remote part of the country, leading their band into Cornwall, a messenger from the aforementioned Cornish princess hastened towards them with a letter which said: 'Ah, ah, how is it that you have forgotten your girl for so long! I would never have thought it of you that you would deceive a girl! Look, in front of your very eyes I'm being handed over to an Irish princeling, and his son is taking me against my will when I want to marry you! Would that I might come to know in this business the energy you display in the cause of others! But otherwise, if I can't escape, I shall always keep true in my heart to the promise I once made the famous lad, the son of the Irish king. But should you be tempted to abandon your honour like a barbarian, and not claim a girl for the husband she wants, then I beg you to remember what's happened between us.' Upon receiving this, the king's son directly sent messengers to the girl's father with two leaders and some forty men fully equipped in military dress, charging him to remember their former agreement, that his daughter was promised to him as a wife. Otherwise he must understand that he would make an attack on both him and the man who took his daughter, and get her from wherever she was married. Hereward, however, having disguised himself using a lotion which changed his blond hair to black and his youthful beard to a ruddy colour, undertook the same journey secretly by another road, with three companions. When at last he got there, he found the messengers of the king's son in custody and the intended son-in-law of the Cornish prince ready to journey the following day to his own people together with his bride. Therefore, Hereward went directly in so as to survey the nuptials, pretending that he was a foreigner from some way away travelling in those parts in service of a certain nobleman from the west. And although a stranger, he was received into the wedding party and welcomed by those feasting. So together with his men he took a seat at the far end of the table, choosing the lowest place for himself. The king's daughter observed this – and his distinguished figure – closely, but was puzzled by his colouring. Then, remembering the praiseworthy man Hereward whom she had recently freed from prison and sent to the son of the Irish king, she wept a little. And then, recollecting what he was like, she sent him a dish on a tray, saying: 'Since the man sitting apart at the far end of the table is a stranger and his status is unknown, let him accept this offering and its contents, that he may not disparage the bridegroom or young bride in a foreign country or denounce them at another wedding.' When the servant came up to him with the dish Hereward, realizing what was intended, stretched out his hands and took the plate, clenching the fingers of both his hands until blood flowed from under the nails. At this they cursed him roundly, shouting out that he was a fiendish and monstrous man and ought not to take part in the feast. To which he answered, referring to what he had on his mind: 'I will neither join in the pleasure of the feast nor share in the joy of this wedding until I can attend to you as you now serve me.' On being told of this, the girl kept on asking herself more and more who he could be; and she revealed the matter to her nurse in case she could find out more directly whether it was Hereward or a brother of his. When the nurse saw him she instantly declared that it was Hereward himself, with the colour of his hair altered. Nevertheless, she advised her to make sure.

After dinner, as the custom of the region is, the bride royally adorned went with the girls to offer drink to her father and mother's guests and attendants. As she left her father's house at the end of the day, someone went in front with a harp, and a cup was given to each person who played – which is a particular and characteristic kind of entertainment in those parts. Well, one of the girls offered Hereward a goblet full of wine while the man with the harp was standing by. [See plate 3.] But he refused to take it from the woman's hand because he and the Irish king's son had just taken a vow to accept nothing until they had received something they had long wanted from the hand of the prince's daughter. The guests immediately condemned him for this severe slight to the cup bearer, and the jester described the affair disapprovingly to his mistress while she was still offering the cup to the guests. When she drew near she offered Hereward a drink, standing opposite him. At a glance from her eyes she immediately recognized him, realizing from the likeness of the limbs that it was Hereward himself. And so, directing that he should be excused this time since he was unfamiliar with their customs, she promptly conveyed a ring from her hand into a fold of his clothing. But the jester, strolling about everywhere, wouldn't keep quiet, and as often as he passed by declared that a man who at a feast would slight the cup bearer with her cup simply wasn't fit to pluck the harp. Eventually stirred to anger by his conduct, Hereward gave him an answer which the fool stupidly spread about – that given the chance, he could perform that duty better than him. Indignantly, as if he alone were skilled in the art, the fool pushed the harp into Hereward's arms. Taking it, he touched the strings most adroitly, and for a while produced sounds and strains to the admiration of all, while the other was quite shamefaced at the business, and kept trying to snatch the harp from his hands. But in fact the guests reckoned him well worthy of a reward, and said that he should be allowed to keep the harp for the time being. Since they persisted in plying him with drink he acquiesced (perhaps so they shouldn't realize who he was), singing to the harp in a variety of ways. And he sang in different styles, now by himself, now in a trio with his friends in the manner of the Fenland people.[18] Whereupon everyone was greatly delighted; and by way of reward he obtained from the bride a fine cloak, and from the bridegroom whatever he cared to ask, except for his wife and his land. So he asked that the messengers from the Irish king's son should be released and set free without delay. However, while they were arranging to lead them out of custody, one of the sybarites on behalf of all, being jealous of the player, interrupted the lord, saying: 'This man is to be numbered together with those wicked messengers, and has come here to spy out your household, or rather to make fun of you, leading off your enemies through this paltry joke. Or because their force is so weak, this trickster, not only skilled in mockery but artful, hopes to get some of them back.' This suggestion seemed reasonable in his eyes, whereupon he told them to watch the vile fellow carefully. If he were apprehended at once there would be a disturbance at the party, but the following day Hereward was going to the display together with the messengers of the Irish king's son, while he himself returned to his own home with his bride. And he added that all these men ought to be deprived of their right eyes and sent packing thus. In fact, having directly learned of these things through the king's daughter, Hereward determined on flight. Then because of the seizure of his men, he called his companions and strove to get there first. They lay hidden in a nearby woodland close to some water which surrounds part of that kingdom and forms an inlet, and waited for the arrival and crossing of the advance party. And when nearly all of them had crossed over, and the aforesaid messengers were fettered so that they might be deprived of their eyes on the far side of the river, Hereward and his men sprang from their hiding place and, hurling javelins, surprised the tyrant and the others following. One by one releasing those who were found, they soon formed a not inconsiderable force. Finally, mounting the tyrant's horse and leading away his bride, Hereward and his companions hurried off to meet the Irish prince and his army which he had led round to help them. At length, after the space of three days, when all the horses were exhausted except for the tyrant's mount on which the girl was being led, and many of his companions were half-dead with heat, hunger and the flight, they arrived at the prince's camp in silence in the middle of the night. And heartily congratulating them, he was joined to the maid in marriage.

6

How he endured shipwreck on his return from Ireland, and in Flanders, being a second time overwhelmed by a storm, he there changed his name.

Now greatly kindled with the desire to visit his relations and parents, Hereward finally obtained from the king two ships fully fitted out with arms and naval equipment, although for a long time the aged king demurred, hoping that he would remain in the country, take an estate and marry one of his nieces or the daughter of any rich man in the land he liked. But Hereward would not agree to this before visiting his native land. Having embarked, however, he was driven by tempestuous winds on to the Isle of Orkney where one of the ships was lost on the coast.[19] And being carried by a hurricane from there to Flanders,[20] he suffered shipwreck for a second time, near to St Bertin.[21] But when they saw the ship's equipment and the splendidly armed men, the count of that land, known by the name of Manasar the Old,[22] and the noblemen of the country, sent to the place and had them brought before them, regarding them as the advance party of some army, or possibly spies in the land. Well, he was questioned as to his family and country, his name and the reason for his coming there. Hereward replied that he came from the race of the English, and might be going to serve as a soldier in a number of places and countries, or preferably trade or pursue any profession that luck might grant him, and that his name was Harold [23] and that he had been driven to those parts from Ireland by a storm, and had there suffered shipwreck. He had given orders that none of his men should mention the name Hereward, or disclose his status or rank. At length, dubious as to who he was or whence he came, the aforesaid count ordered him and his men to be honourably detained for a while.

7

Of his first fighting in Flanders, by which, and by his daily deeds of valour, he was eventually recognized, when much enquiry was made as to who such a man could be, or whence he could come.

At that time the Count of Flanders[24] was at war with a certain neighbouring Count of Guines;[25] and every day in this campaign his men engaged in single combat in front of the castles and manors. Hereward earnestly begged that he might be allowed to go out with them at least one day. At length it was agreed. And being well trained in the vigorous use of weapons and in the comradeship of battle, he behaved with enterprise that very day; for there was a soldier overwhelmed by another a long way away from the company, whom single-handed Hereward protected, freed and brought back, killing four attackers, to the admiration of everyone because they assumed that both had been taken prisoner. As a result of this he was greatly celebrated in the count's palace and distinguished among the toughest men, going in and out with them from that time on, accomplishing new deeds of bravery on the field of battle every day. However, the prince of the land being greatly intrigued as to who, what or from where, such a man might be, enquired for information about him from foreigners and merchants, if by chance his name or reputation were known in some distant part. And it was not long before the much-desired information was revealed by his enquiries. For someone said that three years earlier he had seen such a man in Ireland, similar to him in character and appearance; and that he had heard many stories told about him in which he was called by name. Being detected thus, he was summoned. The aforesaid count, together with his only son, questioned him as to the reason for his secrecy about his name and country, rank and family, assuring him with an oath that he would treat him as a very dear son. At length he admitted that what the count had heard about him was true, telling his name and country and how, driven out by his father, he had first gone to Cornwall, then Ireland, and about the reason for his coming to that place.

8

How Hereward overcame a famous soldier, and led him safe and sound to his companions.

There was sometimes present among the enemy party a nephew of the Count of Guines called Hoibrict, a knight magnificent in courage and knowledge of warfare, and who by reason of his bravery was reckoned in the army to be like a lion among the herd. One day, when he was alone, Hereward came across Hoibrict by himself; and in a spirit of bravery, without recognizing one another, they clashed together strongly, their lances breaking at the first shock. Upon this they immediately struck at each other with swords, and Hereward delivered a stunning blow under the ear. And while many rushed to Hoibrict's assistance, he evaded their hands, took him up in his arms and brought him to his friends, although meanwhile Hoibrict roused himself and struggled to break free from his hands. The Count of Guines was very much surprised at this, and very alarmed and saddened by the overthrow of so renowned a soldier as his nephew. The following day, still afflicted with grief, he offered due allegiance and service to his prince, and at the same time sent gifts and hostages. For he had heard of Hereward's laudable fame, of what he had done in Cornwall and Ireland; and now he had witnessed his bravery for himself.

9

Hereward was beloved by a certain girl, for whose sake he went forth to combat, and there with his men proved victorious.

At that time there lived in Saint-Omer[26] a noble and beautiful girl by the name of Turfrida, greatly devoted to the liberal arts and particularly skilled at handicrafts. Having heard of Hereward's many achievements, she fell madly in love with him. For love of him, she displayed her manifold talents, and in this way secured the young man's affections. But another man in the neighbourhood was in love with her – a famous soldier and the nephew of a very powerful man in St Valery.[27] And he was so desperately in love that he threatened to do Hereward's person some mischief – death even. And when Hereward was going to the tournaments which were held at Bruges and Poitiers[28] together with his lord's recruits, taking them to their first military trials, he unexpectedly came upon his adversary in company with his men, marching in the middle of the troop and sporting a favour from a girl's chaplet for his sweetheart's sake, as though he had been successful in combat. Catching sight of him, Hereward immediately charged and overthrew him at the first shock, seizing his horse and his favour. This he sent to the aforesaid girl together with other favours of his own, for he had overcome three others by himself, and had assisted his fellow soldiers in overcoming several others – accompanied by him and under his constant supervision. [See plate 4.]

And so, being especially honoured by his men thanks to this triumph, he confessed to his companions in front of them all that he was burning with love for the aforesaid maid, but did not know how he could get near her, in view of the snares of his many enemies. So he made his way to her with a small number of companions, directing that no one should be told of his absence. But neither his departure to this meeting nor the reason for his coming was concealed from his rival; wherefore he arranged ambushes in many places with robbers and villains to rush him. And on one day he killed twenty-five out of forty-odd attackers, while seventeen others hid, before resuming his interrupted journey. Although pressed by very many attacks on the road, he eventually arrived and announced that he was a messenger from Hereward, none other than his nephew called Siward the Blond, bringing her gifts and a message of love from his lord. Being so grateful, she immediately kissed him. And looking earnestly at the expression in his eyes, she finally recognized him by his handsome face, fair head of hair and the vigour of his body. At once she burst out with these words: 'Look, I'm holding in my arms the most distinguished of all men, gazing with my eyes at the most renowned soldier. Now at last I can be together with the man I most longed for. My vows and prayers are answered.' In fact he denied the suggestion and said that she was mistaken. But having closely questioned him as to certain marks on the body – scars indicating slight wounds – she insisted that, on the contrary, he was her beloved Hereward. At this he was beaten and admitted the truth. While they spoke about this privately, she took him and led him inside the house, showing him all her father's wealth of gold, silver and other materials and many things of her mother – and also a mailcoat of great lightness and very fine workmanship, and much brighter and purer than any iron or steel, and a helmet of similar beauty and strength. Speaking of these she added: 'There have been many rich and powerful men that have asked about these, making lots of enquiries as to their whereabouts and promising people rewards for their production, wanting to get them for themselves by trickery, threats, force, bribes or any stratagem whatever. But up to now I have kept their heirlooms – always the most treasured among my great-grandfather's, grandfather's and father's things – so that I could present them to my bridegroom. Now I favour you above all men for your bravery and courageous spirit; and it would give me great pleasure if my love should tell me he is glad of the gift. For I will myself guarantee that they are unsurpassed by anything of steel or metal.' Not a little pleased, Hereward thanked her for them. And thus they exchanged pledges of faith, and then he finally rejoined his fellow soldiers who were waiting for him.

But that same night in the guest quarters he unexpectedly encountered an enemy in one of the followers of the aforesaid knight, who in the dead of night went to attack Hereward with an axe while he was sleeping. But by chance he seems to have woken and, turning over in bed, the blow struck deep into the pillow. Everyone woke up and, seizing him, cut off his right hand when they found out from where and from whom he had come. From that time onwards it was an accepted custom that when Hereward was in a strange place he would rest to one side of his own bed, or else on the couch of one of his men as a precaution against enemy stratagems. The next night, however, he and his companions arrived at his lord's. And the lord heartily congratulated them, for he heard from them of Hereward's activities and achievements at the tournaments, for which he directly loaded them with rewards and honours. Hereward would accept nothing however, until he should claim and receive the aforesaid girl together with her estates.

10

Wherefore Hereward with a certain leader was sent into Zeeland with an army, and how he overcame the army in front.

Now, the Count of Flanders had sent officers into Zeeland[29] to secure taxes which had been long withheld, and to make a valuation of the territory. And about this time it was reported back to the place that, as an insult to him, these messengers had been deprived of the right eye and had had the left foot cut off. It seemed opportune to the prince and his advisers to send Hereward into that province together with an army under the prince's own general, in order to exact appropriate retribution and otherwise punish the enemy severely. And although it was difficult, Hereward at once gladly took the matter in hand. With good weather and a favourable wind, they went there in company with the fleet. But it was not long before they met with a host of the enemy who, wishing to drive them from their country, threatened either to overwhelm them with cruel javelins or to take them prisoner and reduce them to slavery. At this they were greatly exasperated, and very many were frightened, wanting to retreat. But Hereward easily strengthened the hearts of those who were afraid, declaring that from their own experience of battle they could be void of fear, even though they now met with such a great and disorderly host and rash audacity, because this was the confidence of rashness and the arrogance of annihilation. As a result of this their spirit was greatly kindled, and together they faced the attack of the opposing army more readily, with four out of the forty ships and the whole army backing them up, so that if some fell others might advance to take their place. Then as the others attacked, Hereward asked for the central place in the vanguard, so that the young men and youths might test their mettle, and being exasperated might be provoked to join battle, and that thus being as yet untried they might gain experience in battle before going on to greater deeds. Hereward directed them against the opposing army, who perceived the fact with delight, trusting in their own strength. They set one man in the middle, against whom Hereward immediately advanced; and when he was overthrown thus, they sent more, one after the other, for whom it was just the same – the occasion of death. Although armed, they did not know how to defend themselves, nor how to protect their awkward bodies with their weapons. But instead, declaring that they had been rendered incapable and thinking him a wizard, they attempted to rush him all together. He suddenly fell back towards his companions, so that his attackers were strung out behind him; and thus he got them within reach unawares, and in this way eventually overcame them all.

11

Of the second war with Zeeland, and how that nation advanced to the fight, and with what arms, and how Hereward arranged his army against them.

The rebellious people and the whole troublesome nation therefore instantly ordered everyone in the land from coast to coast to assemble and lay waste their borders, harrying and ravaging. They were to lay waste the face of the land thoroughly and hastily, within a fortnight, lest being insufficiently secure, they should be driven out, or even within that time become subject to foreigners like the English people were to the French – and it was no false report they had heard. And having assembled all together in one place against them, they ordered that the Flemish army was to be cut off. Those who had come there were to have their lives spared, but were to lose everything else except for a few ships and their tackle; and in addition the army's general, Robert,[30] and the soldiers' leader, Hereward, and the officers of the companies were to be handed over by them to be put to death on behalf of all. At the same time they had brought together wagons and carts with which to carry off all their weapons and goods. Seeing this, at a sign from Hereward the army set fire to the envoys' chariots and carts in front of them, and would have instructed the envoys themselves to have been thrown into the flames, were it not that the rights of intermediaries would seem thus to be broken, and the privilege of an envoy violated. Hereward therefore persuaded the army and its leaders that these envoys should be detained for a while, either by force or flattery, sending them back with gifts which might have the effect of delaying them, while in the meantime the rest of them could get ready for the battle, preparing their formations and appointing to each formation a leader and officer. In the event all this proved successful inasmuch as that impudent and inexperienced people, seeing some of the messengers returning loaded down with gifts and greatly coveting such things, made their way to them in great numbers, each wanting to secure the better things before the others. But as they ran in front of the army to look, three hundred picked soldiers under Hereward's leadership intercepted them and made no small killing among them, pursuing the others right up to their comrades' camp; at which all were completely struck with amazement, realizing how they had been taken by surprise. Consequently with great anger and supreme indignation, they advanced ready to do battle, swearing according to their custom not to let a single man escape alive. They were clothed and protected with this armour: coats of felt dipped in pitch, resin and incense, or with leather tunics reinforced with the bark of trees; their hands held spears, nailed and bound for thrusting and slashing, and three or four square-pointed javelins for throwing. Between every pair thus armed, was always set one with a sword or an axe, and also holding a shield in front of all three. Their host was certainly very large, numerous but disorderly. Now, seeing them go down into a hollow, the general of the Flemish army and the military leader Hereward positioned their troops on a slope against them. And when the others attacked them, they gradually all retreated, wishing to draw them all away from their camp. And then when they were separated some way from their defences, the Flemings stopped running away, turned and stood to fight.[31] Meanwhile, Hereward with a thousand knights and six hundred armed men killed those who were guarding the camp, setting fire to their tents, and so led his battalion to the rear of the Zeelanders, whom he found almost totally unarmed; and being quite unable to resist, they were routed. When those who were in the front line became aware of this unexpected event, and saw their men, inexperienced and untrained in war, fleeing in all directions, they finally fled themselves and found a defensible position in a secluded spot. But there the Zeelanders continued to be killed with javelins and missiles until nightfall. At last, with darkness covering everything, the moon shining very little that night, and before the rising of the morning star, the armies parted. Hereward with six hundred men whom he had left the day before to guard the ships, returned to the Zeelanders' camp at dead of night without anyone noticing, and there with javelins killed many and wounded a great many more, including some officers. This was an unprecedented affair and quite beyond anything they had ever experienced in warfare. And when full daylight returned and the armies were again drawn up in line on both sides ready to join battle, the Zeelanders hastily sent envoys praying and begging them to have mercy. A truce was arranged and they promised to make full reparations and to serve their lords like slaves so they might find favour with them, and to hand over to their authority all those who had laid hands on their messengers, or who had consented to it, or who had offended in word or deed, from the least to the greatest. And the Flemings gladly received the hostages they were sent, arranging to give them an answer within the week.

12

Where Hereward got a mare of very great speed, and a colt of conspicuous beauty, and what he experienced on the road.

Meanwhile it was reported to Hereward that there was a remarkable breed-herd of particularly swift horses[32] on a certain island of the country, so he went there with a few fellow soldiers and some people who were well acquainted with the difficulties of the road. There he bought a mare of very great speed with a colt of conspicuous beauty. The mother he named Swallow, and her colt Lightfoot. As he was returning from the place, however, he fell among a band of robbers in a certain secluded spot among the valleys, hills and woods. For two days he withstood their ambush vigorously, though by the third day he was quite weak from hunger and thrown into confusion by the violence of the brigands. But by the sixth day, making great speed, they rejoined their army which the next day was to make a response to the leaders of that land concerning the truce which they had requested. Indeed, on Hereward more than all the rest depended the favourable nature of the reply and the entire conclusion of the arrangements.

And so on the appointed day the Zeelanders came with their chief men and with fine gifts, offering their allegiance and earnestly praying and begging for a renewal of the ancient treaties and services, rather than merely a confirmation of them as they were in their fathers' time, and to do service under the most secure agreement from now on in perpetuity. The Flemings received them and, greatly enriched with gifts from the chief men of the country and with the valuation of the land and its taxation doubled, they left and returned to their own country delighted with the prize of courage and victory. But they found there neither their lord who had sent them nor his son, but a successor to the kingdom. Affected with the deepest grief and sadness, they bewailed the death of their most beloved lord. But eventually consoled after their grief, they asked the country's leaders and officers if, in return for their great effort they might be granted any reward by their lord, since they had brought back the subjection of the land to which they had been sent, which would now offer hostages and gifts and pay double taxation as a result of their efforts. They ought to be remunerated for their efforts in any case, they said. Eventually they realized that they were going to be given no compensation. Then at Hereward's suggestion the soldiers shared out among themselves everything they had brought from Zeeland – an act which afterwards caused ill feeling between Hereward and his lord's son.

13

How he returned to his country and to his father's house, where he found that his brother had been slain the day before, and of the grand vengeance he took the same night.

After Hereward had spent a few days in idleness there [in Flanders], thinking this disgraceful he left and immediately set out for England. He wished to visit his father's house and his homeland, now subject to the rule of foreigners and almost ruined by the exactions of many men, wanting to help any friends or neighbours who perhaps might still be alive in the place. He returned from foreign parts with his personal attendant Martin Lightfoot as his sole companion, leaving his two nephews, Siward the Blond and Siward the Red, together with the wife he had just taken. He arrived back at his father's manor called Bourne one evening time, and was entertained on the outskirts of the village by a certain soldier of his father's called Osred. There he found the head of the household and his neighbours very gloomy, all full of grief and in great fear, having been given over to the subjection of foreigners. And what was worse for them, they were bewailing the fact that they were subject to those who the previous day had slain the innocent younger son of their lord. Immediately therefore Hereward, who appeared as if a stranger, asked who their lord now was, who was responsible for the death of their former lord's son, and the reason for it. And they answered him: 'Although it is a help and a comfort in sadness to share one's grief, we shouldn't involve you in our misfortune, for we see that you're a great man with whom we ought to be joyful for the sake of hospitality. Nevertheless, because you appear to be in every way a great and famous man, we might look to you for some remedy for our sorrow, so we will readily explain the business to you. There was among us a certain younger son of our lord whom his father, when dying, commended to his people, together with his mother; and he was to be his heir if his brother, called Hereward, shouldn't return – a man most vigorous and conspicuous in all courage, whom while still a lad his father had driven away from his presence by way of punishment. And now, three days ago, certain men seized his inheritance with the consent of the king and took it for themselves, destroying our light, the son and heir of our lord, while he was protecting his widowed mother from them as they were demanding from her his father's riches and treasures – and because he slew two of those who had dishonourably abused her. By way of revenge because he had killed two Frenchmen, they cut off his head and set it up over the gate of the house – where it still is. Alas, wretched men that we are, we have no power of vengeance! Would that his brother Hereward, a very great man so we've often heard, were here now; for then truly before the moon set and the sun sent forth its rays of light, every one of them would be lying dead like our lord's son!' Hearing this, Hereward lamented greatly, sighing inwardly. At length, being drowsy after their conversation, they all retired to rest. After lying on his bed for a while, Hereward heard some way away the voices of people singing, the sound of harp and viol and the merriment of those applauding. Summoning a lad, Hereward enquired what the sound was that echoed in his ears. He immediately declared it to be the merriment of those joining in the party given on the occasion of their entering into the inheritance of his lord's son, who had been killed by them the previous day.

After a little while Hereward called his servant and, taking a mailcoat and helmet from beneath a black cloth – a maidservant's cloak – put on his tunic and took a sword. And thus, with his servant protected by light armour, he approached the party-goers who were now overcome with drunkenness, intending to pledge them for his brother's death with a draught of bitterness and wine of sorrow. When he came near, he found his brother's head over the gate. Taking it, he kissed it and concealed it, wrapped in a cloth. This done, he advanced through the entrance of the building to search out the guests. He saw them all by the fireside overcome with drunkenness, the soldiers reclining in the women's laps. Among them was a jester playing a lute, abusing the English race and performing antics in the middle of the hall meant in imitation of English dancing, who eventually demanded in payment from their lord something which had belonged to the parents of the remarkable lad killed the previous day. At this one of the girls at the banquet, unable to tolerate these words, replied: 'There still survives a distinguished soldier by the name of Hereward, brother to the lad killed yesterday and well known in our country (that is to say, in Flanders); and if he were here, none of these would be left alive when the sun spread abroad its rays of light!' Indignant at these words, the lord of the household answered thus: 'Well, I happen to know the man, and a great scoundrel he is, for he stole the gifts which were sent to the prince of our country from Zeeland and distributed them unfairly after the prince had appointed him leader of the soldiers. Now he would have suffered death on the gallows, if he hadn't ensured his safety by running away, not daring to stay in any land this side of the Alps!' On hearing this, the jester continued repeatedly to abuse him as he sang to the lute. Eventually unable to tolerate this any longer, Hereward leapt out and struck him through with a single blow of his sword, and then turned to attack the guests. Some were incapable of rising because they were drunk, and others unable to go to their help because they were unarmed. So he laid low fourteen of them together with their lord, with the aid of the single attendant whom he set at the entrance of the hall so that whoever escaped the hands of one might fall to the other. And that same night he set their heads over the gate where his brother's head had been, giving thanks to the Bestower of all grace that his brother's blood was now avenged.

14

For what reason some fled from him in alarm; and whence he chose for himself men of war.

In the morning, however, the neighbours and those living round about were filled with astonishment at what was done. And almost all the Frenchmen in the district were frightened, abandoning the lands assigned to them and fleeing, lest the same thing should happen to them at the hands of such a man should they have him for a neighbour. But having heard about him, the inhabitants of the country and his kinsfolk flocked to him, congratulating him on his return to his native land and to his father's inheritance, and advising him to guard it carefully in the meantime, dreading the anger of the king when he came to learn of the affair. In fact not unmindful of such matters, he lodged there forty-nine[33] of the bravest men from his father's estate and among his kinsfolk, equipped and defended with all necessary military accoutrements. Meanwhile he wanted to carry on for a few days taking vengeance on those of his enemies in the neighbourhood who still remained on their manors.

15

For what reason he wished to be made knight in the English manner, and where he was made knight.

When Hereward realized that he was the leader and lord of such men, and day by day saw his force growing larger with fugitives, the condemned and disinherited, he remembered that he had never been girt with the belt and sword of knighthood according to the tradition of his race. And so with two of the most eminent of his men, one named Winter and the other Gænoch, he went to the Abbot of Peterborough called Brand,[34] a man of very noble birth, in order that he might gird him with the sword and belt of knighthood in the English tradition, lest after becoming the chief and leader of so many men, the inhabitants of the country should disparage him for not being knighted. He received the accolade of knighthood from the abbot on the Feast of the Nativity of the Apostles Peter and Paul.[35] And in his honour a monk of Ely named Wulfwine, who was both a faithful brother and prior and also a friend of Hereward's father, made his comrades knights. Hereward wanted himself and his men to be knighted in this way because he heard that it had been ruled by the French that if anyone were knighted by a monk, cleric or any ordained minister, it ought not to be reckoned the equal of true knighthood, but invalid and anachronistic.[36] Opposing this regulation therefore, Hereward wished almost all those serving him and under his rule to be knighted by monks. So, if anyone wanted to serve under him he had to receive the sword in the manner the knight's tradition demands, from a monk at least, if from no one else. Often he would point out: 'I know from common experience that if anyone should receive the knightly sword from a servant of God, a knight of the kingdom of heaven, such a man will pursue valour most excellently in every kind of military service.' And hence arose the custom among those at Ely that if anyone there wished to be made a knight, he ought always to offer his naked sword upon the altar at High Mass and the same day receive it back again after the gospel reading from the monk who was singing Mass, the sword being placed on his bare neck with a blessing; and by making over the sword to the recruit in that way, he was made a full knight. This was the custom of abbots in those times. Later Hereward was to go to the Isle of Ely[37] and, together with its inhabitants, defend it against King William[38] who by that time had subjected almost the entire country to himself.

16

How he was sought out by a certain man who wanted to kill him, and how Hereward slew him.

Having returned to his own people, Hereward learned that a certain Frederick, who was the brother of the old Earl William de Warenne,[39] had been making frequent enquiries for him in many places, in order that he might either take him personally into the king's presence and hand him over to punishment for what was mentioned a little earlier; or alternatively cut off his head and set it up for a sign at a crossroads on the public highway, in the same way as he had exhibited over the gate of his house the heads of those who had stolen his inheritance and slain his brother; and further, that he might drive into exile or mutilate all those who continued to support Hereward or rendered him any assistance. But Hereward and his men immediately set about preempting him, intending to treat him in the same way if by chance they should meet with him. For Hereward had learned that Frederick was in Norfolk together with a military force, so that as soon as anything was heard of Hereward, Frederick might make his way there protected by a troop of soldiers. But what Frederick intended should happen to Hereward happened to himself instead. One evening time while he was plotting the death of Hereward, the outlaw himself arrived and slew him.

17

Why Hereward departed again into Flanders, where he soon performed some noteworthy deeds.

To allow the situation to cool down after this, Hereward went into Flanders to see the wife he had recently taken, promising those whom he left in England that he would return within the year. And there at Saint-Omer he came to his wife and the two nephews whom he had left with her. He had not been there a fortnight before he was invited by Baldwin,[40] a certain highly celebrated knight of that province, to join a campaign he had undertaken against the Viscount de Pynkenni.[41] The lord of Brabant[42] with his nobles was also to be present at this encounter. And on this expedition Hereward and his two aforementioned nephews Siward the Blond and Siward the Red, together with the aforesaid noble knight Baldwin who led them there, acted in such a way that even the opposing party did not withhold their commendation but greatly praised them, picking out Hereward especially as an object of admiration. Once when his boldness had carried him too far among the enemy, they killed his horse beneath him, and thus being alone and on foot they surrounded him on all sides. Not that this did them any good, for it proved the speedy destruction of his attackers, since he slew seven of those who rushed to seize him. At length when he was surrounded by a wall of enemies on all sides, several of the leaders of the opposing party, perceiving his spirit and courage, helped him by calling off his attackers. They said it was shameful for so many to be attacking a single man the whole day long, and scarcely finish the business in the end. 'And even if he were to be eventually overcome, what sort of victory would that be for us, for one man to be overcome by so many? There would certainly be a slur on our reputation. And even though he may fall in the end, he deserves to be esteemed above everyone else.' While Hereward was duly recovering a little from these attackers, unharmed by any weapon, a mounted comrade showed great enterprise, coming to his aid and snatching him up so that he was reunited with his men. Then from horseback he told everybody what had happened to him and recounted with what generosity the enemy had acted despite the fact that he had killed seven of their men who had unadvisedly attacked him. This event resulted in such goodwill on both sides that, out of respect for such a knight, all those who were formerly at odds were reconciled; and they honoured him with gifts.

18

How on his return to England his men gathered themselves together to him, on his giving the signal which he had arranged at his departure.

But as he had promised his men, Hereward, now eminent in all military matters, returned to England together with his two nephews and his loving wife Turfrida who was already superior to the usual feminine weaknesses and regularly proved capable in every exigency which befell her celebrated husband. There also came with him a certain chaplain of his, Hugo the Breton[43] by name, who although a priest, was no less trained in arms than endued with virtue, and Wivhard his brother, a splendid knight of soldierly courage. He obviously also brought with him those in his service. Some of these Hereward immediately sent to explore his own area and his father's house, so as to make careful enquiries as to what had been decided about him by the king's majesty, and with the utmost caution to find out from friends in his father's territory where those men whom he had left in England now were. When they eventually got there, they found his inheritance entirely undisturbed, no one having dared to enter it. Some of his men they found in hiding, thus ensuring their safety. And these, instantly delighted at his return, hastened to join him, namely: a certain Winter, a distinguished knight who was short in stature but particularly robust and strong; and Wenoth and Ælfric Grugan, notable in all courage and bravery, for they were as powerful in action as they were big and tall. In addition to these were three of Hereward's nephews: Godwine Gille, who was called Godwine because not dissimilar to Godwine the son of Guthlac who is so celebrated in stories of olden days;[44] and Duti and Outi, two twin brothers similar in character and appearance and both praiseworthy soldiers. The remainder of his band of followers, however, was scattered over the entire kingdom. At his departure he had arranged a signal for them – to set in flames three villages on Brunneswold[45] near to Bourne; and so he set fire to them and retired into the forest until his men were gathered around him.

And when they were all assembled, they were all the most eminent men, not one among them being counted of knightly rank without first having achieved some notable deeds. These are their names (with those mentioned above making up the number): Wulfric the Black, who got his name because he had once daubed his face with charcoal and gone unrecognized into a garrison, laying low ten of them with a single spear. And his friend was a certain Wulfric Rahere, or 'The Heron', so-called because he once happened to be at Wroxham Bridge[46] where four brothers were brought who, although innocent, were to be executed; and terrifying the hangmen who had called him 'heron' in mockery, he manfully caused the innocent men to be released, and killed some of their enemies. Others too were numbered among the more distinguished of Hereward's knights: Godric of Corby, a nephew of the Earl of Warwick;[47] and Tostig of Daveness, kinsman of the same earl and whose name he received at baptism; and Acca Hardy, the son of a gentleman from the outskirts of Lincoln who was personally responsible for one of the towers of the city;[48] and Leofwine Mowe, that is 'The Sickle', who got his name because, chancing to be alone in a meadow cutting grass, he had been set upon by a score of local peasants with iron pitchforks and spears in their hands, whereupon quite alone with only his sickle he wounded many and killed some, charging among them like a reaper, and finally putting them all to flight.

In company with these was also a certain Tunbeorht, a great-nephew of Earl Edwin,[49] and Leofwine Prat, that is 'the Dodger', who was called this because although often captured by enemies he had astutely escaped, frequently killing his guards. And in addition to these must be numbered others also very experienced in warfare: Leofric the deacon, the bailiff of Drayton, Thurcytel Utlamhe – that is to say, 'the Outlaw', Hereward's cook Hogor, Hereward's kinsmen Winter and Leofred, two distinguished men, and Regenweald steward of Ramsey. These were leaders; so also: Wulfric the Black and Wulfric the Blond, Ælfric Grugan, Yiardus, Godwine Gille, Outi – and the other Outi I mentioned before – and those two splendid men, Siward and the other Siward the Red, who were Hereward's nephews. Then with these there were other most eminent knights: Godric of Corby, the Norman priest Hugo and his brother Wivhard, Leofric the Deacon, Tostig of Rothwell, Leofwine Prat, Thurcytel and the bailiff of Drayton. All of these were among the most distinguished and splendid knights in the whole kingdom; and there were not a few others, whom it would take too long to name and describe separately.

19

*How the men in the Isle of Ely sent for Hereward; and how on the road he discovered an
ambush by the Earl de Warenne.*

Now when those who lived in the Isle of Ely, then beginning to hold out against
King William who had gained England in battle, heard of the return of such a
man as Hereward, they directly sent to him and negotiated through messengers
for him to join them with all his men, to take part together with them in the
defence of the homeland and their fathers' liberties, assuring him that such a
knight as he was would have the foremost position among them. This message
was delivered especially in the name and on behalf of Thurstan,[50] abbot of the
church at Ely, and his monks, who had lordship of the Isle, and by whom it was
put in a state of defence against the king, in particular because William intended
to set a certain foreign monk over them – one of those monks for whom he had
already sent from the French nation, to set as deans and priors in all the churches
of the English. [See plate 5.]

However, having prior knowledge of this, a certain well-known knight and
seaman, Brunman by name, being familiar with the coast, intercepted them at
sea, ducked them in the ocean in a large sack that he had tied to the prow of his
ship, and sent them back, thus freeing the English monasteries from foreign
domination for the time being. Hereward was delighted to receive this envoy and
finally directed his men to make preparations for the journey, boarding ship at
Bardney.[51] Hearing of this, the Earl de Warenne, whose brother Hereward
himself had recently slain, prepared many ambushes along his way in secret
hiding places near the routes out from the Isle through the swamp, cautiously
placing a guard round the waters on the land side and hoping to capture him
without serious loss to his own men. In the event, however, this was not hidden
from Hereward, certain of the guards having stumbled across some stragglers
from his force and assailed them with missiles. Coming to their aid and capturing
their attackers, he ascertained from these that the ambush was laid by the Earl de
Warenne, who was himself coming to Earith the following day. Whereupon,
hastening with his ships, Hereward assembled his men there. Concealing his
troops near the river bank, Hereward himself with three knights and four archers
well equipped with arms drew close to the edge of the river opposite to where the
earl and his men had just arrived. Upon seeing them, one of the earl's men
approached and said this to them: 'Are you from the company of that great
scoundrel Hereward who has ruined so much by trickery and has drawn so many
to help him in his nefarious deeds? Would that the villain could be betrayed to
our lord the earl. Anyone who agreed to do so would be well worth payment and
honours. For this hostile band, although not dangerous, may eventually force us
to live in this detestable swamp, and to chase them unarmed through muddy

marsh, swirling water and sharp reeds. Every one of them is destined to an early death, for the king has already surrounded the whole island on all sides with his army, and has closed off the area so that he may destroy its inhabitants.' At these words, one of them retorted: 'You good-for-nothing! How much longer are you going to incite us to betray our lord and desert our leader? Run off back; shift your feet, before you go down under fierce javelins. And tell your lord that the man he's asking for is here on this side of the water.' Learning this, the earl immediately approached and, catching sight of Hereward, urged all his men to swim across the water with him to avenge the blood and death of his brother. But they insisted that it wasn't possible, saying that Hereward had come there just to trap them in that very way. Whereupon, snarling, he railed against those lying across the water: 'Oh, would that your master, that limb of Satan, were in my grasp now; he should truly taste punishment and death!' Understanding these words, Hereward declared: 'But if by good luck we two happened to be by ourselves anywhere, you wouldn't be so keen to have me in your feeble grasp nor be glad that we met!' And leaning forward a little, Hereward stretched his bow and shot an arrow with force against the earl's breast. Although it rebounded from the protecting mailcoat, the earl was rendered almost lifeless by the blow. Whereupon his men, very anxious on their lord's account because he had fallen from his horse at the blow, quickly carried him away in their arms. Meanwhile Hereward went away and that very day withdrew his men into the Isle of Ely, where he was now received with the greatest respect by the abbot and monks of the place. And he was honoured by the important men in the Isle, that is to say by the former Earl of Leicester, Edwin, and his brother Morcar Earl of Warwick, and by another earl called Tostig,[52] all of whom had fled to join those in the Isle having suffered many wrongs at the hands of the aforesaid king and being harassed by many demands. Not a few of the country's distinguished men had fled and were led to the place for the same reason.

20

How the king attempted to take the Isle, where he nearly lost his entire army; while no man, except one brave knight, entered it.

Consequently, when the king heard about this he was moved to enormous anger and, goaded by deep indignation, furiously applied himself to taking the Isle by storm. In fact he moved his whole army to Aldreth where the surrounding water and swamp was narrower, the breadth there extending only four furlongs.[53] Having brought there tools and fitments of timber and stone, and heaps of all kinds of things, they built a causeway through the swamp, although it was narrow and quite useless to them. Moreover, close to the big river near this place, that is to say Aldreth, they assembled in the water large tree trunks joined together with beams, and underneath tied whole sheepskins, flayed and reversed and fully inflated so that the weight of those going over it might be better borne. When this was finished such a multitude rushed onto it all at once, greedy for the gold and silver and suchlike, not a little of which was thought to be hidden in the Isle, that those who went hurrying in front were drowned together with the road itself they had made. Those who were in the middle of the company were swallowed up in the watery and deep swamp as well. A few of those who were following at the rear got away with difficulty, flinging down their weapons, wallowing in the water and making their way through the mud. Thus in this way, with hardly anybody pursuing them, great numbers perished in the swamp and waters. And to this day many of them are dragged out of the depths of those waters in rotting armour. I've sometimes seen this myself. And out of this entire company I've talked of, not one got into the Isle, except by chance a single eminent knight called Deda who went on in front of everybody. But in any case, nobody from the Isle was caught in the trap. For some of them had made a heap of turves on the bank of the aforesaid river in front of the bulwarks and ramparts, laying ambushes to both right and left. The king, observing all these things from a distance, evidently saw where his men in front were swallowed up in the swamp and water; wherefore, groaning with deep, heartfelt sorrow, he left together with those of his men who still survived – very few compared with the number of those who were drowned – setting aside all hope of making any further attack on the Isle. Nevertheless, he set a guard there and positioned soldiers round about lest the islanders should have free passage to lay waste the district.

21

Of a soldier who went into the Isle, and resolved to be the first to give information to the king about the Isle and its inhabitants.

Now the cunning soldier whom I mentioned a little while ago as having got into the Isle, was captured and led before the chief men and dignitaries in the Isle of Ely. When he was asked his name and the reason for his coming, they found out from him that he went by the name Deda; and the reason was this. The king, in the presence of his men, had made a bargain that whoever was first to make his way into the Isle and inflict injury there, might ask him for any property in the Isle, and the king promised he should have it for sure. When they heard this, the islanders praised his boldness and courage and had him stay with them for a few days so that he might get to know their valour from personal experience, and realize what a secure position they held, being provided with the protection of a strongly fortified location and strengthened in no small way by companies of distinguished soldiers. For, as he often declared in their presence, he had heard many times that they were less proficient in war and less skilled in military affairs than other races. But before he left he recognized that they were quite excellent in all matters, and proficient in the art of warfare. And so he was given

permission to leave on these terms: that he should report about them nothing
other than what he had seen and heard – and this he had to affirm with an oath.
Enriched with a gift, he eventually got to the court of the king. On his arrival
everyone together there heartily congratulated him, and indeed the king himself
was delighted, for he was the most renowned among the more distinguished of
the king's knights. When questioned before the whole court, Deda explained how
by some lucky chance he had entered the Isle unharmed. As related above, great
numbers perished while going along the road which they had made. He said that
out of all of them he alone had been brought alive into the Isle by Hereward, the
leader of the soldiers in the island. He affirmed that through Hereward he had
been given an honourable place amongst the more distinguished of the troop of
soldiers. Then at Hereward's enquiry he had told them of the reason for his
coming – explaining to him the king's promise that the first man to enter the Isle
and inflict injury there should be rewarded with a very great honour. On the
king's closely questioning Deda still further, he went through the ranks of
the chief men in the Isle and their names, and recounted the splendid nature
of their activities in defence of the Isle, and how well strengthened they were by
troops of distinguished soldiers, and in no small measure protected by groups of
the toughest men. Those he ascribed to the first rank were: the three earls
mentioned earlier, namely Edwin, Morcar and Tostig, and the two noblemen
Ordgar and Thurcytel 'the Lad'.[54]

And in talking about them he extolled the outlaw Hereward and his men more
highly than themselves and above all the knights he had seen among the French,
or in the German Empire or at Byzantium, for valour and courage in all matters;
and although some might be equal to Hereward, none, he said, could surpass
him. At this the Earl de Warenne, whose brother Hereward had recently killed as
I explained above, moved to anger and goaded by deep indignation declared:
'Well, it's quite evident from what you say that you're not a little deceived, in that
you would induce our lord king to show kindness, by extolling his enemies with
false praise and arguments of this sort. Besides, are you going to set up that great
scoundrel Hereward for courage and bravery? Now leave off burdening his
respected majesty the king with such frivolous talk!' To whom the aforesaid
soldier replied, saying that he had not been seduced by a bribe or gift, nor was he
persuaded by any consideration; he had only to tell the truth about them without
fear or favour, and having taken an oath to this effect he had been allowed to
leave. And in replying, he asked how he could keep silent about such things when
they demanded to know what he had seen with his own eyes and had himself
experienced, without either offending the lord king or violating his oath by falsely
reporting other than the truth. So the king directed that he should tell them but
be considered without offence in this, declaring that he had long known him to
be a truthful soldier, and reckoned that he was not exaggerating in this now.
Once more, therefore, the aforesaid soldier was closely questioned, not only by

the king but by many others, asking if the enemy were in need of provisions or any other necessities, or if there were any further experienced men than those he had previously related, so as to find him out in any contradiction in his account, or rather that they might learn something to assist them in the siege. To this he made just one reply: 'Well, if you are still anxious to hear their cause, it is, as I understand it, as follows: it is because his respected majesty the king had given instructions that monks from overseas should be appointed deans and priors in all the churches of the English – and for whom your eminence had just recently sent, that is to say those whom a certain distinguished English knight called Brunman intercepted at sea because of this, ducking them in the ocean in a big sack and sending them back, thus freeing his kindred from foreign domination for the time being. For this cause, fearing subjection to foreigners, the monks of that place risked endangering themselves rather than be reduced to servitude, and gathering to themselves outlaws, the condemned, the disinherited, those who had lost their parents, and suchlike, they put their place and the island in something of a state of defence. There's no pressure on account of the numbers of the army over there, and they aren't oppressed by the enemy. For although besieged by four kings and their subjects, the ploughman doesn't take his hand from the plough, nor does the right hand of the reaper hesitate in reaping; the hunter doesn't neglect his hunting spears, nor does the fowler stop lying in wait for birds by the banks of rivers and in woods, so those in the Isle are well and plentifully supplied with almost all living things. At the time when the waterfowl are moulting and changing their appearance, I've commonly seen trappers there bringing in lots of small birds: very often a hundred, sometimes two hundred or more, and occasionally not far off a thousand from one stretch of water. Similarly from the woods that are in the Isle there is at one time of the year a good supply of heron, quite apart from the abundance of wild and domesticated animals. And certainly the waters which surround the Isle abound with all kinds of fish.[55] What more need I say! Indeed, every day during the time I spent there we made ourselves sick with the sumptuous English-style feasts in the monks' refectory – soldier and monk always going to dinner and supper together, at the high table the abbot with the three earls mentioned earlier, seated side by side with the two most distinguished men, Hereward and Thurcytel 'the Lad'. Above each and every knight and monk there hung against the wall a shield and lance; and down the middle of the hall from top to bottom on the bench were placed mailcoats, helmets and other arms, for the monks as well as the soldiers never scorned to take their turn and go out on a military patrol. Indeed, in what I noticed there, this one thing above all others struck me as remarkable, that almost all the monks of that place are so well versed in warfare – a thing I've certainly never heard of before, nor have I come across such anywhere else. Certainly I don't know that they are in need of anything as regards defence, let alone in spirit, when they have a fruitful island, so productive of every kind of grain and growing things, and so well fortified by waters and swamp, much stronger than any castle surrounded by walls. Nevertheless, I hope that my lord king will not cease attacking them, and then he will find that I haven't deviated from the truth, and will realize that in the end it would be better to make peace with them than be continually attacking them and getting absolutely nowhere.'

22

What they did when they were disheartened about the Isle, and how the king was disposed to make peace with them, had some of his own men not dissuaded him.

Well, just then while he was relating this, one of those soldiers the king had sent to effect the blockade at Reach dyke came in,[56] and as soon as the story was finished, expostulated: 'Why don't you believe it? Does it seem so unlikely? Only yesterday I saw several men coming out of the Isle – not many – only seven, but dressed for battle and girt with proper war-equipment, all but two of whom were manifestly monks, and like the others well versed in warfare. And exercising the rights of the military, they set fire to the village of Burwell and did damage everywhere – and not only these men but often others as well, rushing in all directions. Some of our men, ten in number who were engaged in the blockade, dashed in front of us all without consideration for themselves, thinking to capture them because they were fewer in number than us. Anyway, they finally intercepted them opposite the aforesaid dyke, within mutual lance-throwing distance. And after a long struggle all our men finally succumbed except for one distinguished soldier called Richard, who took his surname from his uncle Sheriff Osbeorht.[57] One of the outlaws called Wennoth, leaving the main body, had stuck closely to Richard in order to take him. While these two continued to struggle, those who had come out from the Isle stood by for a long time and could see neither of them prevailing. And observing us approaching from a distance with a force of soldiers, the leader of their soldiers, Hereward, had them separated and allowed no one to offer violence against Richard, saying that it was shameful for two or three to fight against one man, and would in no way allow such a thing to be done by his men; and this we learnt from the mouth of Richard himself. However, we finally pursued them right up to their ships, killing one of their boatmen with a javelin and capturing another who told us their ranks and described who they were, adding their names: the leader of the soldiers, Hereward, Wennoth, young Thurstan who was afterwards named prior,[58] Brother Siward of St Edmunds, Leofric and Acca Hardy, so named because he was hardy in enduring pain. Although monks, these were certainly most highly distinguished in all military matters and had frequently undertaken deeds of valour with Hereward and were well tried in their experience of battle.'

However, the king made no reference to this, no word either good or bad, saying to himself that it was unworthy to abuse men who had acted generously, and equally so to favour his enemies with praise in front of his own men. He contemplated making peace with them, knowing the Isle to be strongly defended both by nature and by the finest of men, and realizing that he could in no way prevent their coming and going there. So, summoning the magnates and counsellors, he explained to them what was in his mind, to make peace with those in the Isle, declaring that it would be very sensible to leave such men in the middle of the land at his rear, when they ought already to be marching against the Danish army and after that to go directly to Normandy.[59] Whereupon several of the leaders who were present and were most intimate with him, hearing this, hastily dissuaded the king from doing it, because the islanders had invaded many of their estates and taken their property, sharing it all out among themselves. They said: 'If you let them off with impunity – those who have rebelled against your sovereignty so forcibly and for so long – and are persuaded to make peace with them without their humbly begging and pleading for it, and even concede them privileges, then everyone will laugh at your supremacy and no one will be afraid to act likewise in your kingdom.' To this the king angrily replied that he could not take the Isle or any place so naturally fortified by the power of God. To which one of those present, Ivo de Taillebois by name,[60] indignantly answered: 'Well, for a long time now I've known a certain old woman who could by her art alone, if she were present, crush all their courage and defence and drive them all out of the island in terror.' And moreover he declared that he was willing to send for her, if the king agreed. On hearing this, all those who were present earnestly urged this on the king, saying that they should not oppose but rather assist such a work, and enrich with the greatest rewards anyone who could by art, invention or any way whatever, crush the enemies of the lord king. And so the king, complying with their words and arguments, ordered the hag to be brought directly; but it was to be done in secret though, not openly. Afterwards he had his army again gather to surround the Isle, guarding it closely on all sides, personally appointing sentries here and there and arranging a blockade, lest anyone should come out from the island and discover what action they were taking towards assaulting it, whereby they might contrive some opposing art or invention.

23

How Hereward dressed up as a potter and went to the king's court to spy out what they meant to do; and how he cheated them, and slew some in the king's court, and returned unharmed.

These matters being put in hand by the king therefore, the entrances to the Isle were so blocked up that it was quite impossible to enter or leave it. This was an unexpected cause for despondency and alarm to them, not knowing what action was to be taken against them, or what kind of attack, inasmuch as they heard that the king had learned of some new method of making war. So they decided that they ought, somehow or other, to send a man out to reconnoitre. Finding no one quite suitable however, at length it seemed best to Hereward to go out himself to reconnoitre in disguise, although everyone objected strongly, resisting his inclination. But in the end he set off, taking with him his mare called Swallow, who was perpetually drooping and awkward in appearance but whose great speed and willing endurance I have mentioned before. As he left he changed his clothes, cut his hair and beard and donned a greasy cloak. Coming across a potter, he took his jars and, pretending to be a potter,[61] made his way to the king's court at Brandon.[62] Arriving there the same evening, he happened to spend the night at the house of a widow where there lodged the witch whom I mentioned earlier had been brought in to destroy those who were in the Isle. There that same night Hereward heard them discussing in French how they were going to bring about the downfall of the Isle. (They supposed him to be a peasant and unfamiliar with the language.) Then in the middle of the night Hereward saw them go out silently to a spring of water which flowed to the east near the garden of the house. So he promptly followed them, and at a distance heard them talking, questioning some unknown guardian of the spring and awaiting replies. In the end he decided to deal with them on their return, but their lengthy delay prevented this plan, although leading to even greater and more daring adventures.

Early next morning Hereward took up his pots and left. Wandering all round the king's court, he called out in the manner of a potter: 'Pots, pots, good pots and jars! All first-class earthenware!'[63] Now in the course of this he was led into the king's kitchen by some servants so that they might buy some pots. And one of the town bailiffs coming in by chance immediately exclaimed on catching sight of him that he had never seen a man so much like Hereward in his appearance, nor so much like him in his bearing – insofar as a poor man could resemble a man of noble birth, or a peasant a knight. Hearing this, some people came to look at one who so resembled Hereward; and thus he was led into the king's hall among the knights and squires so they could see him. And looking at him closely, some of them declared that a man of such moderate height could scarcely boast so much bravery and valour as popular rumour attributed to him. And others asked him if he knew or had ever seen the scoundrel Hereward. To which he replied: 'Would that I had that limb of Satan here among us now; then I'd get my own back! He's more detested by me than anybody, for he stole a cow of mine, four sheep and everything I had, except for my pots and my nag, which up to now have been the livelihood of me and my two boys!'

Now in the meantime orders were given for the king's dinner to be prepared, and Hereward returned to the kitchen. Then after dinner the servers, cooks and kitchen-boys together plied themselves with wine and strong drink, with the result that they got drunk and made great fun of Hereward. In the end, sodden with wine, they tried to shave his head and pluck out his beard; and they blindfolded him and put his pots down on the ground all around so that he broke them. When he refused to submit to their buffoonery, one of them came up and hit him hard. But Hereward hit him back under the ear so that he fell to the ground insensible, as if he were dead. Seeing this, the man's friends all rose up and attacked Hereward with two- and three-pronged forks. So, snatching a piece of wood from the fireplace, he defended himself against them all, killing one of them and wounding many. This was immediately made known throughout the palace, with the result that he was seized and taken prisoner.

Then while he was in custody, the king having gone out hunting with his retinue, one of the guards approached, carrying in one hand iron shackles with which he intended to load Hereward, and in the other an unsheathed sword. Hereward promptly seized him and attacked him with his own sword, so that he tasted death; and after him he dealt out destruction to several others. And so, setting himself free, he went down over fences and ditches into the lower courtyard of the house,[64] where he found his horse. As he mounted, one of the king's pages caught sight of him and accosted him with foul language, warning his friends and the king's servants to give chase to him; but the pursuit of one and all was so slow, and Hereward's flight so effective that, crossing the island of Somersham and travelling throughout that evening and at night by the light of the moon, he came secretly to the Isle in the early hours of the dawn. Out of all those who had given chase, none heard any word of him, or saw any sign, except for one man who chanced to go deeper into the forest, where his horse unexpectedly succumbed to fatigue and he himself could hardly stand on his feet. Coming across him by chance, Hereward immediately asked him who he was, and he replied: 'One of the servants from the king's retinue who have been pursuing a fugitive peasant who by guile today killed his guard and one of the king's pages. So if you've seen or heard anything, for God's sake, and of your kindness, tell me!' 'Well,' said Hereward, 'since you ask for God's sake, and appeal to my kindness, let me tell you that I am myself the man you're looking for. And now, so that you'll know me better, and will the more truthfully declare to your lord the king that you've spoken with me, you can leave behind your sword and lance as a token and, if you want to keep your life, promise me that you'll tell them the way it was!' And so this aforesaid servant eventually got back and, as he had promised, told the king about Hereward. Everybody listened in amazement; and the king declared that Hereward was a generous and most remarkable knight.

24

How Hereward disguised himself as a fisherman, and cheated the king a second time; and how the king attacked the Isle, and about their means of defence.

Then when the war engines were prepared as he had arranged, and in furtherance of which he had travelled there, the king began the attack, leading his entire army to Aldreth. He had also brought heaps of wood and stone and all materials for building ramparts there. And he ordered all the fishermen in the district to come with their boats to Cottenham so that they could ferry across what had been brought there, and with it construct mounds and hillocks at Aldreth from the top of which they might fight. Among these came Hereward, like a fisherman with a boat along with the rest. They diligently ferried across everything that had been brought there. Finally on the same day – the sun not going down without some damage done – Hereward finished his work and before he left set fire to it. As a result it was entirely burnt, and several men killed and swallowed up in the swamp. He had shaved his beard and head so as not to be recognized, employing various disguises to encompass the death of enemies and the destruction of foes, preferring to look bald for a while and forego his finely styled locks, rather than spare his opponents. When it was learned that Hereward had again escaped with impunity, the king declared that it was shameful to be so frequently ridiculed by him. However, the revered king, among other things, gave instructions commanding his men that above all Hereward should be brought to him alive, and that they should keep him unharmed. And taking warning from the damage done on this occasion, they set a day-and-night guard over all their property and operations.

Thus struggling for a week, they just about completed one mound and set up four wooden bastions on which to site the war engines. But those in the Isle resisted vigorously, building outworks and ramparts to oppose them. And then on the eighth day they all advanced to attack the island with their entire force, placing the witch I mentioned earlier in an elevated position in their midst, so that being sufficiently protected on all sides she might have space in which to practice her art.[65] Once mounted, she harangued the Isle and its inhabitants for a long time, denouncing saboteurs and suchlike, and casting spells for their overthrow; and at the end of her chattering and incantations she bared her arse at them.[66] Well, when she had performed her disgusting act three times as she wished, those who had been concealed in the swamp all around to right and left among the sharp reeds and brambles of the marshland, set fire to part of it so that, driven by the wind, the smoke and flames surged up against the king's camp. Spreading for as far as two furlongs, the fire ran hither and thither among them, making a horrible sight in the swamp,[67] and the roar of the flames and crackling of twigs in the brushwood and willows making a terrible noise. As a result, stupefied and greatly alarmed, the king's men fled, each man for himself. But they could not go far along those watery paths through the wastes of the swamp, and they could not keep to the track easily. In consequence very many of them were suddenly swallowed up, and others overwhelmed with arrows drowned in the same waters, for in the fire and in their flight they were unable to use their lances against the bands of those who came cautiously and secretly out from the Isle to repel them. Among them the aforesaid woman who practised her abominable art, fell down in the greatest terror head-first from her exalted position and broke her neck.

And among the few who escaped – compared with the number of the fallen – the celebrated king himself carried right back to his men's camp an arrow stuck deep in his shield. Seeing which, his men were alarmed, thinking him wounded and bewailing the fact. To banish their hesitancy and fear, the king declared: 'I've no wound to complain of, but I am pained that I didn't adopt a sounder plan from all those that were suggested to me; for which reason almost all our men have fallen, deceived by the cunning of an abominable woman and encouraged by our ignorance as to her detestable art – even to listen to whom ought to be damnable! In fact, we've deserved what's happened to us.'

About this time Earl Ralph Guader, having secretly assembled a very large army, invited certain persons from among the English people to his wedding and by force and trickery compelled them to bind themselves to him by an oath.[68] And he laid waste and subjected to himself the entire country between Norwich, Thetford and Sudbury. Wherefore, thinking he was making a bid for the kingdom and nation, the three well-known earls and all those of high birth who were in the Isle now went off to join him, leaving Hereward and his men to guard the Isle alone.

25

How and why the men of Ely made an agreement with the king; upon which Hereward wanted to burn the church and town.

At length the king recognized that, despite all these preparations, his efforts to take the Isle by war or by force were to no avail. And considering how many of his men he had just lost on this one occasion, and also what great numbers he had lost previously, he decreed that the external lands of the church and the property of the monks should be divided among his more eminent followers, who only had to guard the Isle from outside. In consequence, therefore, several people expropriated the church lands in the vicinity, claiming them for themselves. Hearing this, the monks of the church in question adopted a more prudent plan in their activities; and upon the return of the abbot, who together with the aforesaid earls had fled in disguise to Bottisham with the ornaments and treasures of the church, asked the king for peace terms, on condition that he would freely and honourably restore to them all the lands of the church. This was done one day in secret though, so that Hereward should not know of it. They were received graciously by the king; and they arranged for the king to come to the Isle rapidly and secretly at a certain time when Hereward was out foraging with his men, in order that it might be managed without bloodshed and serious slaughter. However, one of the monks, Eadwine son of Ordgar, went to tell him that they had already been received by the king and had struck a bargain with him. He met Hereward already *en route*, marching with his men from the river bank, carrying brands to set fire to the church and town as a result of what they had heard. The monk with many prayers and entreaties stood out against him, warning him rather to look to his safety by flight, if he was unwilling to join them in securing peace, adding that the king with all his army was within a furlong at Witchford. [69] Eventually he yielded to his words and arguments because he had been a friend to him and a good comrade in war and of practical help in many of his needs. Thus he was persuaded. He decided upon immediate action and, with his boats which he had well defended with arms to guard the waters surrounding the Isle, withdrew to a certain mere called Wide near Upwell, a large expanse of water with ample channels and having an easy way out. And because he had dispatched some of his men to inflict damage at Soham and lay waste the land with fire there, he intended to wait there until the scouts that he secretly sent should lead them to him quickly to prevent their being captured. When at length they were found in a little island called Stuntney, they thought Hereward's messengers were chasing them, and hid themselves among the reeds some distance away in the swamp. In fact two of them lurking together, a certain Starcwulf and Broga, reckoned it might give them a better chance of safety if they had a tonsure like monks. And so they gave each other a tonsure as best they could with their swords. But in the end a shouted exchange brought mutual recognition, and assembled together they made their way back to their leader.

26

How Hereward was reduced to such straits that he slew with his own hands his excellent horse; and how next he overcame the army of five provinces.

After some respite from serious pursuit in the aforesaid mere, Hereward was more severely besieged by those in the region and by the king's men, and so hard pressed that in despair he slew with his own hands his splendid horse, so that no lesser man should boast that he had got Hereward's horse. But at length he escaped from this danger with his men, passed over Brunneswold and went to live in the great forests of Northamptonshire,[70] laying waste the land with fire and sword. Eventually, therefore, at the king's command an army was assembled from the counties of Northampton, Cambridge, Lincoln, Holland,[71] Leicester, Huntingdon and Warwick, which all came together on a pre-arranged day and with a host of soldiers tried to capture Hereward and his men, searching for him everywhere in the forests near Peterborough where he was staying at the time. And there, when surrounded by enemies and unable to avoid their hands, he moved about from place to place in the more remote parts of the forests in the district, waiting for his men and friends whom he had summoned to help him. Meanwhile, he had the shoes on his horses' feet put on back-to-front, so that it could not be discovered from their tracks where they were or where they were going.[72] He gave instructions that the friends and fellow soldiers for whom he had just sent were to do the same. These arrived one by one as best they could. Now that Hereward knew that there was no place to turn to, because warfare closed in on him on all sides, it seemed best to him to make an attack on his pursuers with a small number from the rear, front or flank, before they were prepared for battle, since he now had a hundred picked soldiers with him, and among them some of the toughest men, besides a few archers and slingmen. For in those days Hereward happened to have many men, both from that region and further afield, who came to him for military training and who, in order to be instructed in this, left their lords and friends and joined Hereward having heard of the fame of his men. Several even came from the king's court to find out whether what they had heard of him could possibly be true. Hereward received these with caution however, and with an oath of fidelity. For there was a very great number of knights and foot soldiers from the regions there, and Turold, Abbot of Peterborough,[73] and Ivo de Taillebois were leading the king's army to deal death to them all. Then Hereward and his men, not frightened by their numbers although they were seriously beset on all sides, made preparations. They concealed all their archers and slingmen positioned in the trees, standing unseen among the branches to discharge their missiles from above, so that when fighting they might be shielded from below and defended in this way lest they were unable to endure the force of a charge in any way. And thus they advanced from beneath the woodland trees under cover of their archers, Hereward always leading the way in everything. Immediately following him came Regenweald, steward of Ramsey, who always acted as standard bearer to his army. And other celebrated soldiers shared positions given them to right and left, the names and valour of which most distinguished men in so famous a battle it would be proper to record, in memory of what the few achieved against so many. And the most famous of them, and rightly held foremost both for warfare and courageous spirit, one Winter by name, was on the left flank. These had advanced on horseback, not without due consideration, to take the brunt of the attack. And becoming separated from the rest in the foray, these daring men charged the enemy, broke through their front line and killed many. And having inflicted some damage thus, they retired to the forest for protection, lest they should be unable to withstand the host of the enemy if they attacked in force. Finding their feet however, they retraced their steps again – and again and again, all day long, advancing and retreating, attacking great numbers, their friends continually covering them with missiles hurled from above and ensuring their safety in retreat. As they strove in this way into the afternoon, the horses of their adversaries as well as the heavily clad soldiers were greatly irritated, pursuing them in their flight, and waiting in armour all day long for them to come out again. Eventually they left off besieging the camp. And then Hereward with all his men immediately came on them from the rear in a single rush, engaging in a significant encounter, capturing and taking prisoner several men including five of some importance. Among these the aforesaid Abbot of Peterborough was captured, as well as others of great distinction. Then, learning of this, the enemy ceased fighting, although they were at close quarters, lest they should ill-treat or kill those whom they had taken. I have recounted the remarkable course of their battle up to this point. This last engagement proved a great blow and no little destruction to the enemy, who were completely worn down with fatigue; and being cut off from their camp, they now began to retreat.

27

How Hereward took vengeance upon the Abbot of Peterborough.

Afterwards the aforesaid Abbot of Peterborough was released from captivity by Hereward for a ransom of thirty thousand pounds. And one of Hereward's kinsmen called Siward the Blond set free the abbot's nephew and others whom they had captured, all of whom he had treated with honourable hospitality out of respect for the abbot. But remembering neither their kindness nor their agreement, they repaid Hereward by once more making war on him and his men. To this purpose, the aforesaid abbot distributed many of the estates of his church to knights on condition that they gave military assistance to subdue Hereward, on account of the trouble he had given the abbot. He arranged that they should attack Hereward as a duty in return for their lands. However, when Hereward heard reports of this, and that a punishment hung over him in return for his kindness, he did not long delay, but the same night went with his men to Peterborough to avenge themselves. And laying waste the whole town with fire, they plundered all the treasures of the church and pursued the abbot, although he and his men managed to escape by hiding themselves.[74]

28

Of a vision and a marvellous occurrence seen by Hereward.

In his sleep the following night, Hereward saw standing before him a man of indescribable appearance, in old age, fearsome of countenance, and more remarkable in all his clothing than anything he had ever seen or imagined in his mind, now menacing him with a great key which he brandished in his hand,[75] and with a fearful injunction that if he wished to ensure his safety and avoid a miserable death the next day, he should restore in their entirety all those possessions of his church which Hereward had taken the previous night. Indeed, on waking he was seized with holy dread, and that very hour carried back everything he had taken away, and then moved on with all his men. On their journey they unexpectedly went astray, losing the right path. A marvellous thing happened to them while they were astray thus – a miracle, if such things can reasonably be said to happen to flesh and blood. For while in the stormy night and gloom they were wandering hither and thither through the forests, not knowing where they were going, a huge wolf came in front of them, fawning on them like a tame dog and walking along in front of them down the path.[76] In the obscuring gloom they mistook it for a white dog because of its grey coat, and urged one another to follow the dog closely, declaring that it must have come from some village. This they did. And in the midst of the night, while they discovered that they had succeeded in getting out of the byway and recognizing the road, suddenly there appeared burning lights clinging to the soldiers' lances – not very bright, but like those popularly called will-o'-the-wisps.[77] No one could get rid of them, or extinguish them, or throw them away. Whereupon, greatly marvelling among themselves, although they were stupefied they could see their way, and went on led by the wolf. And then with dawning day they all eventually found to their astonishment that their guide had been a wolf! And while they were at a loss to know what had happened to them, the wolf disappeared, the lights vanished, and they had got to where they wanted, beyond Stamford. And realizing that their journey had been successful, they gave thanks to God, marvelling at what had happened to them.

29

Hereward had not been there more than three days when he heard that an enemy of his would be in the aforesaid town, a man who had often tried to ruin him and hand him over to those enemies who had lately broken faith with him. Whereupon to see if what he had heard was true, he set out with just two men. And when the fellow realized that Hereward was on his way, he immediately resorted to flight. Hereward hastily followed his track from house to house, from garden to garden, with a naked sword and a small shield in his hand, right into the great hall where many men from the man's own district were assembled at a club dinner. But having nowhere to turn, Hereward being so close on his heels, he left, fleeing into the interior of the house where, putting his head through the hole in a lavatory seat, he begged for mercy. And moved by a generous spirit, for he was always most gracious in all his ways, Hereward did not touch him there, nor inflict any injury in word or deed, but returned the way he had come, passing rapidly through the middle of the house. And being astonished, none of those feasting there ventured to grumble or upbraid him about what had happened, since they had nothing in their hands but just drinking horns and wine cups.[78]

30

How Hereward's wife assumed the habit of a nun at Crowland.

In the interval however, Turfrida, the aforesaid wife of Hereward, had already begun to turn away from him because at the time he was receiving frequent envoys from a woman asking him to marry her. She was the widow of Earl

Dolfin[79] and particularly powerful on account of her wealth. She should obtain a licence from the king which, as she had heard from the king's mouth, she could have for the asking if Hereward were peaceable and willing to pledge faith with him. For this reason therefore, charmed with the beauty of the woman, Hereward gave his consent, for there was nobody more lovely nor more beautiful in the realm, and scarcely anybody more eminent in their wealth. Consequently, he sent messengers to the king and asked for the aforesaid woman, saying that he was willing to be reconciled with the king's majesty. He received Hereward's messengers graciously and, accepting what he proposed, appointed a day to meet him, adding that he had for a long time been wishing to receive him into his favour. In consequence Hereward's own wife, about whom I spoke a little earlier, went to Crowland[80] and chose the better life, taking the holy veil. As a result of this, many unfortunate things happened to him later on, because she had been very wise and good with advice in an emergency. For subsequently, as he himself often admitted, much happened to him which would not have done in his rise to success.

31

How Hereward overcame a certain very eminent knight in single combat.

Once when Hereward was off on a journey across Brunneswold, he met with a certain Saxon soldier, a man of great courage and tall stature called Letold, who was well known and highly praised in many regions for his skill and valour in war. Highly courteous as usual, Hereward promptly first wished him well, and then enquired his name, rank and family. Not taking his words and questions in good part, Letold answered haughtily, calling him a simpleton and peasant. So finally moved to anger, they came to blows. And not only they but their soldiers grappled at the same time – five on the side of the aforesaid knight and three on Hereward's side, namely: Gærwig, Wennoth and Mæthelgar. As they fought, Gærwig soon laid low one soldier and turned to attack one of his comrades. Soon afterwards the other two also overcame their adversaries. Meanwhile, however, the aforesaid famous knight did not cease fighting with Hereward although his men were overcome. Nevertheless, Hereward would not allow any of his men to assist him, saying then as always when anyone was fighting with one of his men or with himself, that it was shameful for two to fight against one, and that a man ought to fight alone or else surrender. While these two continued to fight, the result of the combat between them being in doubt for some time, Hereward's sword unexpectedly broke off at the hilt, whereupon hesitating for a moment he stumbled over a helmet, the other standing thunderstruck. Immediately one of his soldiers, Gærwig, speaking in an amiable manner, asked him if he had forgotten what he had close by his side for such an emergency, adding that he wished Hereward would let him take over his place in the fight. Greatly encouraged by this, Hereward drew from its sheath a second sword which he had forgotten, and attacked his opponent more vigorously. And at the first blow, while feigning an attack on the head, he struck the man in the middle of his thigh. Still the soldier defended himself for some time on his knees, declaring that for as long as there was life in him he would never be willing to surrender or look beaten. Admiring which, Hereward praised his bravery and courage and stopped attacking him, leaving him and going on his way. And talking further about him to his men, he said: 'I've never found such a man, nor did I ever meet with his equal in courage! Nor have I ever been in such danger when fighting anybody, nor had so much difficulty in conquering anyone.'

32

How Hereward went to the king's court with his soldiers.

He was making his way to the king's court with these three men, but when at length he approached, he reflected that it would not be a distinguished way to meet the king, and immediately retraced his steps. And on his return he brought with him forty other most distinguished soldiers, all very big and tall in stature and proficient in warfare, and remarkable for their mere appearance and equipment in arms, if nothing else. He and his men were received by the king with great kindness and honour. However, the king would not allow Hereward's band to stay along with his courtiers, but gave instructions for them to be entertained at the next town, lest by chance any disturbance should break out between them and his own men. Nevertheless, he took Hereward with just three soldiers into the palace, so as to deal the next day with his proposal. On the following day, however, the revered king himself went to see Hereward's soldiers and had them stand and march before him, both armed and unarmed. And he was greatly delighted with them and praised them, complimenting their handsome appearance and stature, and added that they ought all to be really very distinguished in warfare. After this however, Hereward allowed them all to go home, except for two soldiers in addition to those already with him. And after having paid homage to the king, Hereward waited to receive his father's estate undiminished.

33

How he fought with a soldier of the king's court, and overcame him.

Now some of the king's soldiers at court, indignant at this, felt aggrieved that strangers and enemies should suddenly have come into favour with the king's majesty like this, and attempted to do him some harm. In fact they had a discussion in secret with a certain very eminent soldier of their company called Ogga,[81] and arranged that he should challenge Hereward to single combat, knowing that he could not keep his hands off anyone if impudently or haughtily provoked to a fight or test of courage. They were afraid to raise a hand against him in the presence of the king, but reckoned to get some remedy for their jealousy even if he refused, for they were optimistic that he would be beaten by such a soldier, since he was taller than Hereward and seemed very much stronger just from the look in his eyes. And so they incited this man against Hereward, as though he had been insulted. And he was to do it secretly, lest it should become known to the king before the combat took place. After being repeatedly abused, Hereward eventually consented. So they directly went some distance away to a woodland, together with just three companions on either side under agreement on oath that nobody should assist either of them but just stand by in case they wished for a truce or should prefer to fight it out. Thus they grappled and fought for a long time. Meanwhile Hereward repeatedly urged him to desist from the attempt, pointing out that it was a very stupid thing to do to go on fighting the whole day long for nothing. The soldier paid no attention to his words, but instead became more confident of himself, assuming that Hereward kept harping on this out of fear or feebleness of body, and resolved rather to see him defeated. And so he attacked him increasingly; at which Hereward over and over again gave way, so that the vain hope constantly deceived him. But finally unwilling to put up with this, Hereward made a stand. And as it was his custom in tournament and battle always to fight to a finish like a man, he stood bravely against him and did not stop until he had conquered him, his own right arm being seriously wounded.

34

How Hereward was accused by Robert de Horepol and put into prison.

When, therefore, these things came to the notice of certain of his enemies, jealous of his success, they came to court and made many false reports about him to the king, and deceitfully urged him not to have near him such men any longer, traitors and enemies of his realm; just so, they ought neither to be received at his court nor afforded a truce, but ought rather to be handed over to punishment or else be kept in perpetual imprisonment. The revered king did not take much notice of these words; nevertheless, in order to satisfy them, he gave orders for him to be taken into custody within the hour, making him over to a certain respected man, Robert de Horepol, at Bedford,[82] where he remained for nearly a whole year, merely bound with fetters. But the Earl de Warenne and Robert Malet[83] and Ivo de Taillebois remained hostile to him, dissuading the king from setting him free from custody, declaring that it was because of him that the country was not pacified. When they heard about this, Hereward's men dispersed. Nevertheless, they often sent in disguise to their lord a certain clerk of his called Leofric the Deacon, who was always astute in all his doings, and able to feign foolishness in place of learning – and cleverly so.[84] On one occasion there went with him Utlah the cook, a man who was cautious at all points yet very witty at the expense of the foreigners. In the presence of these men one day, Hereward's aforementioned warder, pitying him together with the rest, exclaimed: 'Alas, alas! Soon now, through the machinations of Ivo de Taillebois, this man once renowned for hosts of soldiers and the leader and lord of so many very eminent men, is to be taken from here and delivered into the hands of a detestable man and sent to the castle of Rockingham.[85] Would that those whom he formerly enriched with gifts and raised with honours, or who were on the Isle, would follow the tracks of their master and intercept us *en route*, so as to set their lord and master free!' Hearing this, and after receiving signs from their lord, Hereward's two men described what they had heard to his soldiers and all his men. So having secretly reconnoitred a forest through which the convoy would have to pass, they picked out a place and all assembled there on the day it was due to arrive. Upon their arrival, Hereward's men immediately rushed on them by surprise, overthrowing many of them before they could even take up their light arms. When they had recovered their arms, however, they resisted bravely, for there were a lot of them – in fact all of the soldiers from the castles round about. In the end it nearly proved the death of all of these; for when they could escape they wouldn't, and yet in the end they couldn't be seized. And then from the midst of several of them who still survived, Hereward shouted out that they should be careful not to injure the troops of his respected warder, and that Robert himself with his men should be allowed to go unharmed. Being set free from ten chains, Hereward moved here and there among those of his men who were still fighting, declaring that Robert had saved his life, so they immediately ceased from the pursuit. On the march Robert's men had come last, forming a rearguard, while Hereward was led in chains in the midst of those in front. At last his aforesaid warder wished to leave together with those of his comrades who survived, and Hereward returned him repeated thanks, for he had kept him in custody with courtesy and carefully treated him with honour. And Hereward asked Robert to make representations on his behalf to the lord king.

35

How Robert de Horepol made a good report of Hereward to the king.

After this the aforesaid Robert de Horepol immediately went to the court of the king, informing him of everything that had taken place, and how Hereward's men had set him free. Finally, he added the request he had carried: that Hereward might avail himself of the king's clemency, remembering how he had come to his court under his protection and safe conduct, and thus had been unjustly put in prison and into custody. However, if the king would even now carry out what he had then promised him, Hereward would in every way serve his most dear lord, knowing that this injury had not been perpetrated by him but through the persuasion and machinations of enemies. After reflecting on these words a little, the revered king replied that Hereward had not been justly treated. And when Robert realized that the king had taken his words well, he promptly recounted to the king many commendable things about Hereward and his men, adding that such a warrior in whom there might be found great sincerity and fidelity, ought not to be lightly banished from him and from his realm for so trivial a reason. And he declared that if there was any new disturbance in the country, Hereward would certainly prefer to rely on his former resources unless he could find favour rather than servitude in the king's eyes, and should in the king's kindness receive back his father's estates. At this the king instantly said that he ought by rights to have it, giving a document addressed to Hereward and the men of the district stating that he was to receive his father's estate and enjoy quiet possession of it;[86] but if he wished to retain the king's friendship hereafter, he must henceforth be willing to pursue peace rather than folly.

And so Hereward, the famous knight, tried and known in many places, was received into favour by the king. And with his father's land and possessions he lived on for many years faithfully serving King William and devotedly reconciled to his compatriots and friends. And thus in the end rested in peace, upon whose soul may God have mercy.[87]

3

EUSTACHE THE MONK

Thomas E. Kelly

INTRODUCTION

The Manuscript: Language, Date, Author

Written in Old French, with traces of the Picard dialect, the romance survives in only one manuscript, now Bibliothèque Nationale Fonds Française 1553 (fols 325v–38v), dated 1284. The author has been variously identified as Adenet le Roi or Gerbert de Montrueil, but neither thesis has been demonstrated convincingly. Present scholarship suggests that the anonymous poet, who composed his 2,307 verses in octosyllabic rhymed couplets, wrote the work sometime between 1223 and 1284 (see Conlon, pp. 10–11 and Burgess, pp. 40–5).

The Real Eustache the Monk

Eustache the Monk is based on the life of a real person, Eustache Busquet, who lived from about 1170 to 1217. The main facts of his life, as reconstructed by Conlon and Burgess, are as follows. Eustache was born at Course in the district of Boulogne in northern France in about 1170. He was the son of Bauduin Busquet, a senior baron of the Boulonnais. As a youth, it is likely that he trained as a knight because the *Histoire des Ducs de Normandie* lists him as a 'chevaliers de Boulenois' (Burgess, p. 8). As later evidenced by his seafaring skills, he also learned seamanship, possibly in Italy. The romance relates that he also studied necromancy in Toledo, Spain, but there is no evidence to support this claim. When he was about twenty, he entered the Benedictine abbey at Saint Samer near Boulogne, where he remained until the murder of his father by Hainfrois de Heresinghen. Eustache left the monastery to demand justice from Renaud of Dammartin, the Count of Boulogne. To settle the dispute, a judicial duel was arranged and Eustache's champion, Manesier, lost. In spite of this setback, in 1203 Eustache was appointed seneschal by the Count of Boulogne during his expedition with King Philip Augustus to win back territories in Normandy held by King John of England. Upon the count's return in early 1204, Eustache was accused of financial mismanagement by his enemy, Hainfrois, and suspecting treachery, Eustache fled into the forests surrounding Boulogne. The count retaliated by seizing his properties.

After his break with the count, Eustache undertook a campaign of outlawry against the count, his allies and soldiers. As Burgess notes, this long section of the romance, occupying verses 400 to 1,881, is the centre-piece of the entire work (p. 46), but in reality only three of the many episodes have any basis in history (pp. 14–15). Eustache's outlawry, moreover, actually lasted for only about a year, from early 1204 to early 1205. In 1205 Eustache left France for the English Channel, where, acting as a pirate, he captured English shipping. By November 1205 he was in England where he offered his services to King John as a mariner. Eustache proceeded to rove the Channel and captured the island of Sark, setting up his headquarters there (Burgess, p. 17). During this period of piracy he received two safe-conduct passes from King John, allowing him to return to England (Conlon, p. 17). As a reward for his services, he was given lands in Swaffam, Norfolk. In 1209 he was still in the service of King John as an English ambassador to the Count of Boulogne. When King Philip learned of his presence in France, he outlawed him (Burgess, p. 24).

Eustache was in London in 1212 when the Count of Boulogne negotiated there a charter of allegiance with King John. Fearing treachery, Eustache left England for France where he joined forces with King Philip. Whether or not Eustache was involved with the naval disaster at Damme in 1213 is a matter of speculation. Conlon suggests that Eustache lost the *Nef de Boulogne*, a huge ship in the shape of a castle, during the English attack on King Philip's fleet (p. 18). In 1214 the English barons began their rebellion against King John, and Eustache is recorded as supplying them with arms. As a result, his properties in Norfolk were confiscated. In 1215 Eustache continued to control the English Channel. In May 1216 the French fleet of 800 ships headed for England to support the Baron's War, and Eustache delivered King Louis to the Isle of Thanet. Finally, on 24 August 1217 Eustache sailed to England to support Louis, but his ship was attacked by four English ships and he was captured and beheaded on the spot.

Structure of the Romance

According to Burgess (pp. 45–9), the romance consists of four parts of unequal length: I, the prologue (vv. 1–38); II, the return from Spain (vv. 39–219); III, Eustache in the Boulonnais (pre-forest, vv. 220–399, forest outlaw, vv. 400–1,881); and IV, Eustache as pirate and mariner (vv. 1,882–2,307). It is clear from this arrangement that the poet's goal was 'to construct a story which is dominated by a description of Eustace's period as an outlaw' (p. 48). Unlike *Fouke fitz Waryn*, where the outlaw episodes are but part of the larger design of a 'family romance', *Eustache the Monk* focuses on the outlaw narrative itself. Looking at it in this way, we can readily identify the following structural and thematic elements:

1. Cause of the outlawry. Three events precipitate Eustache's decision to renounce his allegiance to the Count of Boulogne: the murder of his father; the loss of the judicial duel; and the accusation of financial mismanagement.
2. The outlawing. When Eustache refuses to appear before the count when summoned, he is outlawed. The count seizes his property and burns his fields.
3. The Greenwood. Eustache's base of operations is Hardelot Forest, but the typical seasonal details are lacking. There is one reference to venison, but no accounts of deer hunting or archery.
4. Outlaw activities. Employing a long series of disguises and tricks, Eustache avenges himself against the count, his allies and his soldiers.
5. Organization. Eustache is the leader of up to thirty well-armed men. However, there is no chief lieutenant, such as Little John or John de Rampaigne. Eustache frequently operates alone in disguise.
6. Supporters. While an outlaw, Eustache is supported by his friends and relatives among the nobility. When he is captured by the count, his supporters convince the count not to hang him on the spot. He is subsequently rescued by William de Fiennes.
7. Outlaw code. A premium is placed on loyalty and truthfulness. Those who betray Eustache are killed. Those who lie about the amount of money in their possession are robbed, but those who tell the truth get to keep their money. Eustache also displays chivalric conduct when he twice releases his adversaries unharmed.
8. Inlawing. Since the outlaw episodes are embedded in a larger narrative, there is no royal pardon. Eustache is executed by beheading at the Battle of Sandwich.

Eustache the Monk: Outlaw, Trickster or Devil?

Even a cursory glance at the outlaw narrative described above reveals a literary personage with strong connections to two important medieval motifs: the 'Outlaw in the Greenwood' and the 'Trickster'. Eustache's ties to the Robin Hood or 'Good Outlaw' legends, as well as to those of the 'Trickster' *par excellence*, Renard the Fox, are obvious, to say the least. Recent scholarship, however, seems to lead us down a less-travelled road, namely that of the 'Bad Outlaw'.

In a reading comparing the fabliau figure of Trubert and Eustache the Monk, Keith Busby persuasively argues that both are representatives of 'the diabolic hero in medieval French narrative':

Both texts date from roughly the middle of the thirteenth century, and both present a quickfire succession of unsavoury exploits concerning anarchic, and . . . diabolic heroes. Another feature they share which distinguishes them from outlaw tales is that their heroes are by and large downright bad. While it is true that the nemeses of Trubert and Witasse (Eustache) are nobles, they are foolish, gullible, and impotent rather than unscrupulously wicked, as is the case with, say, the Sheriff of Nottingham. The curious ambiguity with which we respond to the outrages perpetrated by these diabolic heroes bears more than a passing resemblance to the combination of distaste and admiration provoked by the master deceiver, Renart. (Busby, p. 415)

It is not difficult to list those passages in the romance which lend themselves to a such a 'bad guy' reading. Perhaps the most shocking episodes are those describing Eustache's various expressions of cruel revenge on those who cross him: the young man forced to twist his own rope before hanging himself (vv. 660–741); the four men whose feet he chops off in retaliation for the eyes of his own men gouged out by Renaud (vv. 742–75); his delight in burning down the count's mills (vv. 400–29); his sadistic pleasure in torturing Cadoc in the mud pit (vv. 1,954–2,125); the crudity and brutality in the passage where Eustache, disguised as a prostitute, humiliates the count's man and taunts him for trying to sodomize a Black Monk (vv. 1,186–283).

Busby (p. 423) finds that 'the gratuitousness of much of the violence in *Witasse le Moine* also underscores its fiendish nature. Having just deceived the count into believing he is a penitent and into giving him money, Witasse steals all the horses and burns down the town' (vv. 912–15). Seen from this perspective, the name chosen for Eustache in his final disguise as a *jongleur* during his escape from England toward the end of the romance is highly instructive: *'Sire, j'ai a nom Mauferas'* (vv. 2,160–7). *Mal* and *feras* equal 'you will do evil!' On this note Busby concludes his essay with a highly provocative suggestion: '. . . as Mauferas *does*, or perhaps *bears* evil, so his brother Trubert is resplendent (*bright*) with his own brand of trickery. Ultimately, Witasse and Trubert may be no more or less than incarnations of the bearer of the most deceptive light of all, *Luci-fer*, the Enemy, the Devil' (p. 426).

Perhaps too, the present translation of the *Romance of Eustache the Monk* will make a modest contribution in the direction of broadening the debate concerning medieval outlaws. This Black Monk from the Boulonnais is a fascinating 'Bad Guy'. His story, after remaining for many centuries ignored on dark and dusty library shelves, may in this present collection of outlaw tales begin again to twist his way into the company of his better known and more numerous 'Good Guy' relatives.

Translator's Note

The present translation into modern English prose attempts to render as accurately as possible the eventful career of the thirteenth-century outlaw, Eustache the Monk, as presented in the fast-paced narrative style of the original

Old French verse romance. Little attempt is made to focus the reader's attention on stylistic or linguistic nuances of the octosyllabic rhymed couplets. As a result, completely lost in translation is the sharp wit of a story-teller who never lets up on his word play, especially puns and *double entendre*. The word '*conte*', for example, offers frequent semantic shifts from the 'tale' to the 'Count' of Boulogne, to the settling of Eustache's '*comptes*' (accounts) with the count. In this same vein, one key expression in its various adjectival, verbal and noun forms, merits particular attention. From beginning to end the Devilish Eustache 'turns' the world around him upside down. Through a seemingly endless series of disguises the Monk sadistically twists his pitiful adversary, the Count of Boulogne, into endless contortions. One example among many similar instances is the passage where Eustache disguises himself as a leper (vv. 1,400–22). The narrator delights in frequent puns on the various meanings of '*tour*'/'*retour*': retraced tracks, turn, turn about, turn meaning trick or disguise. It is impossible to do justice to this dimension of the story in an English prose translation.

In order to provide context and flow for the modern reader, the translation consciously departs in many instances from the short sentences and pithy, frequently allusive nature of the narrative. In seeking the balance between literal and free renderings of meaning, the translator often takes the second path for the purpose of clarity.

For the name of the romance hero, the original Old French manuscript offers a number of variants: Witasse/Wistace/Wistasces/Uistasces/Uistasses. There is a note of conscious irony in the spelling chosen for the Devil-monk's name in this translation. In contrast to the normalized British form 'Eustace', the translator has substituted the modern French spelling of the name of a saint: Saint Eustache!

TRANSLATION OF *EUSTACHE THE MONK*

Eustache studies necromancy in Spain

Here begins the romance of Eustache the Monk. Concerning the Monk, I will briefly recount for you his exemplary deeds as best I know them. He went to Saint Samer in the Pas-de-Calais[1] some eight leagues distance from the sea where he became a Black Monk.[2] When he got back from Toledo, where he learned necromancy, there wasn't anybody in the kingdom of France who knew so much black magic or sorcery.[3] He played many tricks on lots of people. While in Toledo, for one whole winter and a summer, he lived down under ground in an abyss where he spoke to the Devil himself, who taught him black magic and unnatural tricks with which to fool and deceive everybody. He learned thousands of magic spells, evil tricks and charms. (1–18) [See plate 6.]

He learned the esoteric art of interpreting the scratches on a sword. He picked up the trick of turning the Psalter, that is reciting the psalms backwards, or worse, turning over the missal at a black mass. In order to return numerous lost objects to their owners, he learned the art of the haruspex, a diviner who knows how to read the ridges and grooves on the shoulder of a sacrificial lamb. Indeed he also practised water divination. By looking into a basin he was able to recover lost and stolen objects. He had the crafty power to bewitch women and cast evil spells on men. No other man from here to Santiago de Compostella knew as much about the zodiac, the firmament or the sphere of heaven.[4] He was able to take on the shape of that fabulous monster, the chimera, a beast whose tricks no normal human being can imitate. As for monks, he could make them fart in the cloister.[5] (19–32)

When Eustache had learned enough, he parted company with the Devil. The Devil told him his life would last long enough for him to accomplish a great deal of evil. He would fight wars against kings and counts and end his days struck dead at sea. (33–8)

Eustache casts magic spells in Montferrand

Eustache returned to France, where he subsequently performed many childishly mean exploits. One night he came to Montferrand,[6] where he accomplished a particularly devilish deed. The day after he arrived in town, before continuing on his journey, he had a huge meal prepared by a wealthy inn-keeper's wife, a very insolent and haughty woman. It was the wine-harvest season, and Eustache had with him three companions who were also returning from Toledo. The must from the grapes was stored throughout the house in some thirty barrels. Eustache ate and drank together with the inn-keeper's wife, and when they had finished eating, I believe, and it was time to pay the bill, Eustache didn't have any money from that part of the country, only coins from the cities of Tours and Paris.[7] The woman had brazenly overcharged them and refused their money to boot. For the three sous actually spent they had to pay six sous or more. Eustache, who was crafty as hell, cast a spell over the inn-keeper's wife before he left town. He threw down on to the door step a seed of grain over which he had made an incantation, and straight away the woman stripped to the waist and pulled out all the plugs from the first barrel she reached. She laid out all her wares for the market, as she shouted: 'Come on now, gentlemen!' (39–73)

The wine flowed all over the place and men and women came running. When they had crossed the door step, the men lowered their britches and the women stripped to the waist or the navel. You never heard the likes of it as all hell broke loose in that house. They removed the plugs from the barrels and the wine ran down all the streets. Everybody came running, but no one dared venture into the house without first showing their bare arse to everyone else who was going in. For that reason none of the outsiders just arriving dared enter. They all finally realized that the travellers who had eaten there were the cause of all this commotion. The townspeople rushed forward and started chasing after Eustache, catching up with the travellers about three leagues outside of Montferrand. The townspeople screamed at them: 'My lords, you're going to pay for this!' Eustache looked back in their direction and said to his companions, 'Someone is following us. What are we going to do about that?' In reply, a bearded old man who had spent twenty years in Toledo said, 'Don't worry. I'll take it upon myself to strike such fear into them that there isn't a cleric, townsman or priest who'd care to stay here, not even for five marks.' The old man cast a spell, whereupon a great wide river, deep and dark, wider than the Seine or the Loire, came gushing down between the clerics and the townspeople. The townsmen were so frightened they turned and ran, but the river kept coming, relentlessly hard on their heels. They fled backwards, being afraid of drowning, the travellers following them all the way. (74–118)

The townsmen went back to Montferrand, the travellers hard on their heels. Eustache no sooner got into the town than he started his tricks once again. When the townsmen sounded the alert Eustache winked at the old man, thereby giving him a sign to cast another spell to scare these folks. The town alarm bell started ringing and, as the people started to gather, the old man immediately set off his spell. People started grabbing each other by the hair as a great quarrel broke out among them. You've never seen the likes of such a mêlée, and all without even the use of clubs or swords. As each one arrived, he gave the first person he met a whack on the nape of the neck. Countless blows were exchanged, and all through the town of Montferrand some two thousand inhabitants came to blows with one another. Some were pushing, others pulling; one dropped like a cow, another one sent his buddy flying, and still another one shouted: 'Ladies! Gentlemen!' No one got into the mêlée without taking some sort of a whack. Eustache threw a kernel of grain on the ground between them, thereby separating them all. They instantly departed and peace returned at last. None of the wine was lost and everything returned to normal. Things were just as they had been before. All the women who had earlier taken off their clothes put them back on, and the men who had dropped their britches pulled them up again. Everybody went home, and Eustache went on his way again. Nary a one of them followed him. (119–59)

Eustache and the carter

Eustache overtook a cart driver in his cart pulled by four horses. The man was en route for a destination six leagues away where he was to pick up a barrel of wine. Eustache and his friends asked the driver how much he would charge to take them to the town he was heading for. 'For you, twelve pence,' to which Eustache responded: 'You'll have them with pleasure.' Now when the deal was done, they all climbed up and off they bounced at a good clip. The driver whipped the horses and they jolted forward down the road. In the process, Eustache's arse got scratched as a result of the cart's jerking movement up and down, taking them at too fast a pace. So he said to the driver, 'May God stop you by putting some obstacle on your path soon! You are driving us much too fast. My God, send this man some real misfortune, right away, today!' 'My dear sir,' said the driver, 'I'm in a terrible hurry, we can't slow down now. I have to finish my journey, and I think it's already past the hour of nones.' Eustache saw that it was useless to complain, but exclaimed anyhow: 'Slow down, you scoundrel. God damn you, you've taken the very skin off our butts!' (160–90)

The carter whipped his horses hard and the old man with the beard straight away started to cast a spell. Yet the more the driver tried to go forward the more it seemed that he was going backwards. No sooner had the old man begun his spell than the carter started to go in reverse. When he began to hit his horses they backed up angrily. He began to swear profanities against God and to threaten his horses: 'Come on, Martin! Fauvel, go ahead now! By the bowels and the brains![8] Get along! Get moving forward, by the teeth! I'm about ready to break all your bones. Get going! You stubborn old mare! I'm never going to get any help out of you.' The carter began to lose his wits, for he was convinced he was going backwards. 'My lords,' he said, 'get out of the cart, because from the moment you climbed on you brought me bad luck! So I will just cancel your fare entirely.' When they all saw that he was letting them off owing him nothing, they leaped out of the cart. At that point the carter realized that he had been duped and discovered that he had not gone backwards at all, but rather had been moving forwards all that time. (191–219)

Monk Eustache casts spells in his monastery

Eustache went off to the Boulonnais, to Saint Samer where he became a monk. There he did many devilish tricks before he left the abbey. He had the monks fast when they were supposed to have breakfast, and he made them go barefoot when they should have been wearing shoes. When they were supposed to be in bed he had them spreading scandal. When they were expected to recite the Office, Eustache made them curse, and he had them up to mischief when they should have been saying their grace. (220–31)

One day the abbot was in his room. He had been bled after returning from a trip and was sitting in front of a good supply of food and drink, pork and lamb, wild duck, venison. Eustache, who has since duped many a worthy man, went to see the abbot. 'Sire,' he said, 'here I am. Are you going to invite me to stay a while? If I thought I could get something to eat, I'd tell you what's on my mind.' The abbot replied: 'You're a fool. May I be cursed if you don't get a good beating tomorrow and if you're not held prisoner in the chapter house.' Eustache said,

'People who are threatened don't stop living! Among themselves they go on struggling for a long time.' Eustache went off to the kitchen where he spied a tub full of water. He fixed his gaze on it and began to cast a spell over it. The water began to change colour, turning as red as blood. Eustache sat down on a bench from which spot he saw half a pig hanging above him. Within earshot of everyone present, he cast a spell over the pig, first to the right, then to the left. The pig took on the appearance of an old hag, ugly, hump-backed and sour-pussed. The cooks turned and ran off to tell the abbot, who came back with them just in time to see the hideous old woman. So that all the monks could hear him the abbot yelled: 'In God's name, let's get out of here. This man is a devil.' Eustache broke the spell, grabbed the abbot's meat and carried it off to one of his neighbours, an inn-keeper who particularly liked this strange monk. He ate and drank at the tavern the whole night long and gambled away everything at backgammon. Eustache wagered everything, including the crucifixes and the statues, even the bell clappers. All the bells fell silent and there wasn't even a pair of monks' boots left. Eustache the Monk stole everything. (232–79)

I trust you won't be annoyed to hear this, as tonight I'll tell you something that will give you a good laugh. Just a minute now, and you'll hear me tell and relate it all. There are some people, I believe, who tell tales of Basin and Maugis.[9] Basin shook down many a town and Maugis pulled many a deceitful trick. For Maugis swiped the crown of France by necromancy, and also stole the swords Joyeuse, Courte and Hauteclaire, as well as old sparkling Durendal.[10] Basin also robbed Maugis and Maugis robbed Basin. But enough about Maugis; instead I'll tell you about Eustache the Monk, who was, I swear, much craftier than either Maugis or Basin. Neither Travers, nor Barat, nor Haimet ever knew so many tricks. So listen up and I'll tell you all about Eustache the Monk, who waged war against the Count of Boulogne for a very long time. (280–302)

Eustache's father is murdered

Here is how it all began. Eustache, whom I have been talking about, was born in Course in the Boulonnais region. We know for sure his father's name was Bauduin Busquet and that he was one of the peers of the Boulonnais. He was a man well versed in the law, especially concerning trial procedures, before he was killed near Bazinghen. Hainfrois de Heresinghen had Bauduin murdered at that spot, because he wanted to get his hands on his property. Bauduin Busquet was causing Hainfrois a lot of trouble concerning one of their fiefs. The case was being contested in court, on which occasion Hainfrois slapped Bauduin, a blow which turned their quarrel into a public dispute. Eustache had by that time already become a monk at Samer, near Boulogne, but when he learned of his father's death he left the abbey. He went in person to see the Count of Boulogne to whom he declared: 'My Lord, Hainfrois has murdered my father. I beg you to grant me justice.' Hainfrois was immediately summoned to court where Eustache rose to his feet and repeated his charge: 'Lord,' he said, 'listen to me. My father has been murdered, and Hainfrois is the one who had him put him to death. The man is now my mortal enemy.' 'I deny that charge,' said Hainfrois. 'I swear by God's name, the name of mankind and my own name, there was no eyewitness to this and no one here has heard anything about it. Moreover, I hereby call upon my friends to support my protest against such a claim.' (303–35)

Eustache seeks justice from the Count of Boulogne

Shortly thereafter commitments were made and pledges and hostages handed over. Along with thirty members of his family Hainfrois took an oath and formally stated his age. He swore he was sixty years old, perhaps even older than that, he thought. In that case it was immediately agreed that one of his relatives, or a man-at-arms, could fight on his behalf. But Hainfrois didn't have any relative or friend who dared take his place in the battle or one willing to defend his person. At that point someone suggested to him a certain individual named Eustache de Marquise, who was tall, bold, strong and handsome. So agreement was reached on the details of the trial by combat.[11] One of Bauduin Busquet's nephews, a young man named Manesier, stood up. He was a tall young man, a match for his opponent. For he too was tall, handsome, strong and bold. Straight off he accused Hainfrois of murdering his uncle and said that he would prove the fact of the assassination. So the dual combat was joined, Eustache against Manesier. Each man was cocky about his fighting skills. Both were strong and fierce. The battle took place at Etaples and the contest between the two vassals was ferocious. Then Eustache the Monk came before the Count of Boulogne: 'My Lord,' he said, 'I want you to know, and no mistake about it, that I disassociate myself completely from this battle. What's more, I'll never make peace, and I'll personally avenge my own father's death.' (336–69)

Eustache quits the count's service

No sooner had the Monk left the battlefield than his father's champion, Manesier, was killed.[12] Shortly thereafter the Monk entered the service of the Count of Boulogne and took complete charge of his affairs. He was made seneschal of the Boulonnais, and given the titles peer and bailiff, as rights pertaining to that office. It was not long before Hainfrois made false accusations against him to the count and plotted against him. As a result, the count quickly lost confidence in his seneschal. Without delay the count sent for Eustache to ask for an accounting of his stewardship of the offices he held and why he had discharged his duties so badly. Eustache came to see the count immediately and said, 'You have summoned me and now here I am, quite ready to explain myself before your peers and your barons. As you know, I too am a peer of the Boulonnais.' The count replied: 'You'll have to come to Hardelot to explain things to me there and give a formal accounting of your service. That way you won't be able to lie to me.' Eustache exclaimed: 'That's treason! You just want an excuse to have me put into prison.' The Monk left on the spot and quit the count's service on bad terms.[13] The count in turn quickly seized his former seneschal's lands and set fire to his fields. Eustache the Monk swore that the count would sorely regret having burned those fields and that it would cost him ten thousand marks. As you'll soon see, he was later to cause the count a lot of trouble on numerous occasions. (370–99)

Eustache burns the count's mills and is outlawed

One day Eustache came upon two mills which the count had built just outside the city of Boulogne. While his men stayed back he found a miller in one of the mills. He threatened to cut off the poor man's head unless he accepted to go at once to the city where they were celebrating Simon of Boulogne's wedding feast. The miller was instructed as follows: 'When you get there you shall say that Eustache the Monk has come to enlighten them, for they don't have enough light to see what they are eating. I'm going to set fire to the count's two mills so that they'll have two nice, bright candles to light up the festivities.' The miller set off. As instructed, he gave the monk's message to the count. The count leapt up from the table where he was sitting, and had great difficulty shouting instructions: 'Eustache the Monk . . . everyone . . . after him!' The mayor and the provost both jumped up too and in no time had the alarm bell ringing to signal Eustache's banishment as an outlaw. When Eustache heard the bell ringing he began his flight. The count's men began the chase but couldn't catch up with him. (400–25)

That's how it all happened on Simon of Boulogne's wedding day when Eustache set fire to the two mills you heard about earlier. And that's the honest truth![14] (426–9)

Disguised as a Cistercian monk, Eustache sits next to the count

One day, Eustache, a man of many tricks, was at Clairmarais Abbey. While there he discovered that the count was on his way to Saint-Omer. So he found a white cloak to put on, along with a broad-sleeved robe.[15] Thus disguised, he borrowed two monks from the abbot, and the three of them jumped on their horses. Eustache's horse had stirrups made of medlar wood. Somewhere between two valleys he caught up with the count, who was leading three ornery horses. The count greeted Eustache and the Monk bowed politely as they passed each other on the road. Shortly thereafter the count arrived at one of his residences. As he rode along Eustache screwed up his courage and decided to go back and speak to the count. He retraced his steps at once and arrived just as the count was getting down from his horse. Then Eustache the Monk sat down beside the Count of Boulogne. What an absolute fool he was to have done that, knowing that if he were captured he would be burned or hanged! 'My Lord,' he said, 'for God's sake, have mercy on poor Eustache the Monk. I beg you. You should pardon him and put an end to your anger.' The count replied: 'Please, don't say another word. If I get my hands on Eustache, I'll have him skinned alive. Eustache acted like a crusader when he burned down my two mills. Now he has started a real war against me. From here on I'll be on the lookout for him. If I ever get my hands on him, he'll die a horrible death. I'll either have him tortured or else hanged, burned alive or drowned.' (430–69)

Eustache said, 'I swear by my cloak! Peace would be a much better course of action. Since Eustache has become a monk and you are the Count of Boulogne, you should show him some mercy. In God's name, my lord, I beg you to stop being angry with him. If you do, I'm certain that he'll become your close friend. My lord, make peace with him; you must show some mercy on a sinner!' The count said, 'Hold your tongue and don't ever speak to me about this matter again. Get out of here, get going. I don't want to talk to you any further. I can't trust a monk to settle matters where Eustache the Monk is concerned.' The count stopped at this point and whispered to himself, 'By the Virgin Mary's bowels! I think this monk is spying on me. There's no worse tyrant on earth. I'm very much afraid he's going to cast a spell over me.' He then said, 'Lord monk, what's your name?' 'I'm called brother Simon. I'm a cellarer at Clairmarais Abbey. Eustache came to the abbey yesterday, along with thirty men, fully armed, and he petitioned the lord abbot to try to make peace with you on his behalf.' The count said, 'Your abbot had better not agree to give him lodging. If he did so, I'd go to the abbey and tear him to pieces. He'd be no friend of mine, if he housed my enemy. I would waste no time in having his tonsured head chopped off. Lord monk, where are you from, where were you born?' 'At Lens, my lord, I lived there for twenty years.' 'I swear', said the Count of Boulogne, 'you look just like Eustache the Monk in appearance and facial features. You have his body, looks and stature, the same eyes, mouth and nose. The only difference is the fact that you are tonsured. But your tonsure is broader, your face is pale, and you have on red shoes and a white robe. Were it not for my respect for God, I would have taken you and your two companions hostage. Get out of here! And make it quick!' (470–517)

Even though some of his relatives and his own people were there present, Eustache did not feel very safe. As for the other two monks with him, they were terrified. It so happened that the count had previously required all the peers in the Boulonnais to swear an oath that they would hand Eustache over to him if the occasion presented itself. They took that oath three times and promised they would not fail to do so merely on the grounds that they were Eustache's relatives. A man-at-arms came forward and pointed to Eustache the Monk. 'My lord,' he said, 'what are you waiting for? That's Eustache himself sitting there beside you. Seize him and you'll be acting wisely. I'm telling you the truth, it is he.' 'My lord, are you going to listen to this sergeant, this son of a whore,' said William de Montcavrel. 'That's not Eustache, the man is Dom Simon the cellarer from Clairmarais Abbey. I can recognize him as easily as I can a penny.' 'That's true,' said Hugh de Gannes. 'Eustache's skin colour is not so tawny.' 'No,' said Hugh de Belin. 'This man was born in Lens near Hénin.' 'I can also testify,' said Aufrans de Cayeux, 'that Eustache is not yellow or blue.' 'No,' said Walet de Coupelle, 'he is in fact rather reddish around the cheeks.' (518–43)

Eustache steals the count's horse

In the meantime the other two monks stood there trembling with fear, reciting their *miserere*. Each man's heart thumped. Eustache said simply, 'A lot of people look alike.' He then took his leave of the count. All three of them set off down the road, but first, Eustache, who knew so many devilish tricks, went into the stable. He had a stable boy saddle one of the count's finest mounts called Morel, a magnificent and comely horse. Then he mounted and rode off at great speed. Before leaving, he instructed the boy to tell the count that Eustache was taking off with Morel. The stable boy shouted out at once, 'Virgin Mary! Help, help!' The count and the rest of his household leapt to their feet. 'What's going on?' said the knights. 'There's a devilish, enemy monk riding out of here on Morel.' 'Get going,' exclaimed the count, 'by the brains, by the bowels, by the heart, liver and lungs! After him, and be quick about it. But with him riding Morel, there's little chance we'll ever get him. Morel runs like the wind and his rider has the Devil in his head. I know for sure I'll never manage to catch him.' 'My God,' said the count, 'why didn't I seize him when he was sitting right beside me?' The sergeant said: 'I told you so, but you didn't believe me.' (544–77)

Eustache disguises himself as a shepherd

The count ordered his entire household, his men-at-arms and his knights, to mount their horses. They all charged off after Eustache. As they were hot in pursuit, the Monk came to a hamlet. Realizing that he was being tracked he left Morel with a man he knew there. Then he took off the clothes he was wearing and changed into some others. He put on a light cloak, hung a club around his neck and in a shepherd's guise went off to guard a flock of sheep. They were grazing nearby on a stretch of moorland. The Count of Boulogne passed that way and inquired, 'Young man, did you by chance see which way a white monk on a black horse went by here?' 'My lord, he rode right up through that valley over there, and he was riding a horse as dark as a blackberry.' The count sped away without delay and continued his pursuit of Eustache, galloping off at a breakneck pace. Sensing that he was in grave danger, Eustache left his sheep and went back into the forest again. The count spurred his horse like a man possessed, leaving all his companions in his dust. When he spotted the two monks fleeing he yelled to them angrily, 'By God's legs, you won't get away from me this time. You'll never escape me now.' The monks implored God to save them from prison, and especially from probable cruelty and torture: 'Oh! Our Lady, Oh! Virgin Mary, make the count not desire to do us harm or shame! Eustache the Monk, the Devil, the Enemy, has most likely already been caught and now the count wants to take us too. We are frightened to death he'll have us both hanged. Here he comes, he's right on us now! He's here. In God's name, let's beg him for mercy'. (578–619)

The count captures two monks

You have never seen two monks in such a pitiful state, drained of all their strength. They were totally distraught and thought they had lost everything as they dismounted in a valley. The count followed suit and grabbed them by their cowls. The two of them went down on their knees. Dom Vincent begged, 'In God's name, have mercy on us.' 'By God's legs,' said the count, 'you won't escape me that easily. I'll have you hanged from a tree.' 'My lord, please have mercy! Lord, have mercy!' 'By St Honoré,[16] you won't escape me like that, your prayers are worthless,' said the count. 'For both of you are proven thieves. Now if you don't give me back my horse, Morel, you'll be put to death on the spot.' The count had them both tied up and left lying in a garden. During all this Eustache was in the forest nearby, carefully watching the count's equipment at a spot where a young boy was leading a packhorse. Eustache knocked the lad to the ground, cut out his tongue and sent him to give a full report to the count. The young boy went running to the count to tell him what Eustache the Monk had done. The poor mute tried to speak, but all he could do was stammer incoherently. 'What the Devil's the matter with you?' asked the count. With his tongue cut out, all he could reply was, 'Belu, belu.' He couldn't tell his story. A squire said, 'Sire, he's the one who was leading our packhorses. He has fallen into bad hands and, at the very least has lost his tongue while doing so. Eustache has obviously got his hands on the boy and he's the one now holding on to our packhorse.' (620–59)

Eustache is betrayed

Like a man possessed, the count and his men continued the relentless pursuit of Eustache. He followed him into the forest of Hardelot, pursuing in all directions. Eustache had two watchmen posted in the forest. Day and night the two men

were on watch, never taking any rest in any one place. The two young men had
been well taken care of by the Monk. He had in fact raised them both since
childhood. One day, as the count continued his hunt for Eustache, one of the two
lads came up to him and said, 'Sire, how much will you give me if I told you
where to find my lord? For I am Eustache the Monk's man.' 'In truth,' said the
Count of Boulogne, 'if you show me where he is you won't regret it. I'll take you
on as one of my retainers at court.' 'Sire, at this moment he's sitting at table
eating his meal. If you follow me I'll show you how and where you can capture
him.' 'Get going, then,' said the count, 'I'll follow you at a safe distance, but be
careful he doesn't suspect anything. I'm afraid he might try to trick you.' The
second watchman overheard the first and immediately sensed treason. His
comrade had betrayed his lord, biting the very hand that had fed him. In due
haste he came to Eustache and told him that the other watchman had sold out to
the count. Eustache said, 'You may take your leave, but as soon as my other
watchman arrives to betray and deceive me I'll string him up with a neck tie. For
he has served me ill and so he'll only be getting what he deserves.' (660–92)

Eustache hangs the spy

The young watchman left Eustache just as his former companion arrived to hear
Eustache say: 'Here, help me cut this willow branch.' 'Willingly, Sire,' said the boy
as he cut the sapling. 'Twist it well and make a cord out of it.' The young man very
fearfully twisted the strip of willow, after which Eustache looped it around his neck
and pulled it tight. 'For God's sake have mercy,' said the boy. 'Sire, why do you want
me hanged? Couldn't you at least wait until I've had chance to go to confession
first?' Eustache replied, 'You think you know something about evil tricks, but you
see I'm well informed on that score. You have fallen into evil hands, thinking
you could stall me here long enough for the count to capture me. I don't have much
time to spare for your confession of sins. Up there on the tree you'll have time
enough to talk to God. In fact, when you climb high up on that tree you'll be closer
to God for your chat. So go ahead, climb up there and tell me how you sold me out
to the count.' 'Sire,' he said, 'by Saint Remi[17] I did in fact sell you out and I
betrayed you. But tell me first, who in the Devil told you I did it? Now there'll be no
man to kill you, but you would do well to leave immediately and not tarry here any
longer.' Eustache answered, 'Before I leave I'm anxious to see you hanged. So climb
up there and get the job done.' The young traitor climbed up quickly into the tree
and hanged himself with the little rope he had himself prepared. (693–726)

Eustache mulitates the count's servants

Soon afterwards, the count arrived, spurring on his horse at breakneck pace. As
he remounted Morel, Eustache saw the count coming after him and declared,

'Sire, since I have no one else to watch over him, I'll go now, leaving this hanged man, my former watchman, in your care.' The count, like a mad man, along with his troops, immediately chased after Eustache. They succeeded only in stopping two of the Monk's sergeants. Their first reaction, in a fit of anger, was to put out the two men's eyes. When Eustache received news of the deed, he swore by the Holy Virgin that in retaliation for the four eyes put out, he in turn would maim four of the count's men by cutting off their feet. (727–41)

Being unable once again to catch Eustache, the count headed for Saint-Omer. In the meantime Eustache, not forgetting the oath he had sworn, started to keep watch in order to find any four of the count's men whose feet he could cut off. He watched everywhere, in all the woods, on roads and paths. A short while later he came upon five sergeants who were taking the two Clairmarais monks to prison. Eustache said to the count's men: 'Get off your horses; you won't be taking these two monks any further. If you think things are bad now, they'll soon be getting worse for you. Come over here where we can tell you what's going to happen next.' Eustache then stopped them in their tracks and cut the feet off four of them. To the fifth one he said, 'Now go and tell the count how Eustache the Monk has taken the feet belonging to four of his men in retaliation for those four eyes he put out.' 'Sire,' he hastily replied, 'most willingly, straight away.' He didn't forget he still had his own two trotters as he raced off. He went rushing to the count and wasted no time describing how, in exchange for the four eyes which his master had put out, Eustache in return had taken four men's feet. 'In truth,' exclaimed the count, 'I swear by the legs, body and bowels of this scheming, truant monk. Is there no end to the shame and humiliation he has brought on me?' Twenty knights were then sent out into the forest to pursue the chase. This organized search cost the count a lot of money, as the knights spent many days on their hunt through the forest. (742–75)

Eustache disguises himself as a robed bourgeois

One day as the went wandering through the forest Eustache the Monk put on a hairshirt and a rough homespun pilgrim's cloak. Thus woefully dressed, he came upon twenty knights along the way. He greeted them simply and they in turn responded joyfully: 'Say, where are you coming from and where are you going?' 'My Lords, I'm coming from Boulogne and am on my way at this very moment to see the Count of Dammartin to lodge a claim against a bad monk. He says he has a feud with the count and has stolen a hundred marks from me in this very land. The man is a scurrilous mendicant who refuses to give me even a piece of his bread in the morning or at supper. My Lords, tell me without delay where I might find the count.' One of the knights replied, 'In Hardelot. You'll do well to take my advice and go there.' (776–97)

Eustache entices the count into the forest

Eustache set off for Hardelot and, arriving at mealtime, exclaimed to one of the count's men, 'In God's name I seek justice against this devil! My good sir, which one is the Count of Boulogne?' The man answered, 'He's over there.' The Monk went straight up to the count. 'Sir,' he said, 'may God have mercy! I am a bourgeois from Les Andelys. On my way from Bruges in Flanders I was carrying woollen britches and a sum of money, some thirty pounds, when a drunken dimwit (he was tonsured like a priest, but looked too much like a monk to be truly one; he also said he was your sworn enemy), robbed me of all my gold and silver, my furs. He even took my horse and cloak. I beg you. Do me justice against this mad monk. He is nearby, not far from where we are standing.' (He was telling the truth, since it was in fact he who was talking to the count.) 'This false monk, son of a bitch, had me put on this pilgrim's cloak and made me swear that I would come to speak with you. You should know he's not very far from here. As a matter of fact, I saw the spot where he went into the woods.' The count asked, 'What does the man look like? Is he black or white, tall or short?' 'About my height,' Eustache replied. The count leaped forward immediately, shouting, 'Quick, take me to that spot and you'll soon have that revenge of yours.' Eustache said, 'Come on. I'll turn him over to you and you can take him prisoner.' The count, accompanied by seven of his men, followed Eustache, who had thirty of his own men with him. As Eustache led the count off, the latter became wary, surrounded as he was by Eustache's band.[18] When the count became frightened Eustache said to him, 'Don't be scared. All I'm seeking is reconciliation between the two of us. By God's mercy, my fair, sweet lord, let's talk peace.' But the count replied sarcastically, 'Leave me in peace! It's all for naught. Our differences are such that we can never reach accord.' Eustache responded, 'Get out of here, then, since things can't be otherwise. You came here in my safe conduct, so no harm will come to you.' The count returned home, and Eustache went off on another path. (798–853)

Eustache disguises himself as a hay man

One day the count armed himself and called together all his men. He had been told that Eustache had made his way into a fortified town. The count headed for the spot straight away. Eustache, however, still had many tricks up his sleeve. He started his usual scheming and planned an escape. First off, he exchanged his dark brown robe for a poor cloak with a man he happened to meet and thereby managed to get out of town. On the way he encountered another man carrying a heavy load of hay. Eustache quickly bought the hay and carried it over towards his enemies, shouting, 'Fodder for sale!'[19] He was staggering under the weight of his load, but kept one eye closed and the other open. He used the hay to hide himself as he went limping along past the Count of Boulogne. 'My good man,'

said the count, 'can you tell me if Eustache the Monk is still in there. I'm afraid
he may already have eluded me.' Eustache answered, 'I can tell you one thing for
certain, he spent last night at my house but left early this morning. You can
probably still catch him now that he is on the road again.' The count called to his
men: 'Get on your horses, go after him!' The horses were right nearby so they
were able to get going at once. Eustache, cunning as always, didn't waste any
time. He laid down his load of hay and set off after them. He soon came upon a
young lad leading one of the count's horses. Eustache snatched the reins from the
boy's grasp and leapt into the saddle. Within earshot of all present he yelled:
'Here's the Monk and he's just taking his leave.' As soon as the Count of
Boulogne heard him, he shouted: 'After him!' But the Monk escaped them all.
None of the pursuers was able to capture him or even catch up with him. The
count was fit to be tied when he realized that Eustache had eluded him again.
(854–99)

Disguised as a pilgrim, Eustache steals the count's horses

One day the count and his men headed towards Hardelot. This time Eustache
disguised himself as a pilgrim before setting off after them, along with ten of his
own companions. As the count dismounted Eustache came up to him begging,
'My Lord, I swear by the name of the Pope in Rome, we are penitents. We have
been sinners against many but have made repentance in God's name. We've now
undertaken a long period of suffering.' Once the count had heard this plea, he
was unable to refuse giving the pilgrim three sous. Then the count went into
the castle, leaving his horses outside. Eustache stole all the horses and set fire to
the town, after which he sent a sergeant to inform the count that the penitents
to whom he had given three sous were responsible for this. 'I swear', said the
count, 'I was a fool not to have seized those rogues, those scoundrels, those false
pilgrims! Now if I tried to leave here, I won't even have a horse to ride. One thing
for sure, he certainly is a master at what he does. No one has ever seen such a
devilish monk before! Now if I ever get my hands on him, he'll be dead in
a minute.' (900–29)

Merchant tells truth and keeps money

One day as Eustache was wandering through the forest he met a merchant on his
way home from Bruges in Flanders. The merchant was carrying forty pounds
and was himself from Boulogne, so he recognized Eustache the Monk
immediately. Knowing the Monk's reputation he was obviously worried about the
money he had on him. Eustache promptly asked, 'Tell me, how much money do
you have?' To which the merchant replied, 'Sir, I tell you truthfully without a lie I
have forty pounds in a belt and I also have fifteen sous in my purse.' Eustache

quickly took it from him and led the man into a thicket where he proceeded to count all the money. He immediately gave the merchant back his money, saying, 'Go! May God be with you! If you had in any way lied to me you would have left here without a cent. You would have lost all you have, keeping not even a penny.'[20] The merchant thanked him for his generosity. Eustache replied, 'Get going, but first give me your word that you'll go to the Count of Boulogne and take this palfrey to him. It represents one tenth of what I owe him. I'm planning to keep nine of his horses, the fat and comely ones. Yesterday evening, someone came and informed me that the count didn't have a mount to ride. Last night, before I left him, I took all his horses away from him. So now the least I can do is to give him back this tithe. That's why I'm requiring you to take him this one palfrey. You can also take him this small token of money. Three pennies and a farthing should pretty much cover another tithe based on the three sous of good Angevin money, which he threw to the pilgrims who then stole his ten horses and burned down his town.' (930–71)

After the merchant promised that he would indeed go to the Count of Boulogne, Eustache gave him three pennies, the farthing and one saddled palfrey. 'Tell him that Eustache's gifts represent the tithe from all his spoils.'[21] The merchant bade farewell and was delighted to leave at last. He went straight to the count and gave a full report of what had just happened to him. The count's immediate reaction was to have the merchant seized and held prisoner. He was completely convinced that this man was in fact Eustache the Monk. 'My lord,' exclaimed the merchant, 'I've come here to you from Boulogne. It was Eustache who made me swear that I would come and convey his message to you. My only reason for coming to you was in order to keep my word.' When the count heard what the merchant had to say, he finally changed his mind. 'I believe you,' he replied and immediately let the man go. Forthwith the merchant turned over to the count the horse, the three pennies and the farthing. (972–95)

Eustache disguises himself as a coal man

One day the count was out hunting. A spy came and told him that Eustache was in the forest. The count put on his heavy brown cloak, and he and his men followed the spy on foot. They set up an ambush in a ditch. One of Eustache's watchmen approached the group and recognized the count. He found Eustache and told him of the ambush. Eustache then approached a coal man and his donkey. The coal man's donkey was used to carry the coal to market. Without further ado, Eustache put on the coal man's clothes and black hood. He smeared coal dust on his face and hands, as well as around his neck. As a result, he was marvellously blackened. The donkey's back was loaded with sacks of coal. Goad in hand, Eustache set off with the donkey toward Boulogne. Not recognizing his foe, the count paid him no attention and didn't even deign to speak to him as he passed by. So Eustache shouted to them, 'My lords,' he said, 'what are you doing there?' The count was the first to answer, 'What's it to you, you scurvy fellow?' Eustache replied, 'By St Omer![22] I'll go lodge a formal complaint with the count telling him how shamefully we are treated by Eustache the Monk. I dared not bring my draft horse to carry my coal to market for fear that Eustache might steal it. Right now he is lying comfortably next to a good coal fire eating meat and venison. He has burned all my coal and has already cost me plenty.' 'Is he nearby?' asked the count. Eustache replied, 'He's in this very forest. Go straight down this road if you want to talk to him.' (996–1,041)

Disguised as a potter, Eustache escapes

Eustache struck Romer, his donkey, with the goad as the count and his men began to enter the forest. In the meantime, the real coal man had found it appropriate to put on the Monk's clothes. As a result, the poor man was mistaken for Eustache, beaten and mistreated. The count's men had thought, without any doubt, that he was Eustache the Monk. 'My lords,' he exclaimed, 'why are you beating me like this? You can have these clothes. But you need to know I have no money; this is the robe of Eustache the Monk who at this very moment is on his way toward Boulogne with my coal and my donkey. His hands, face and neck are well blackened with coal dust. He's also wearing my black cap. He made me take off my clothes and put on his.' In response, the count shouted: 'Listen to what I have to say, my lords! Catch him if you can. By God's teeth, I have been burned by this living Devil so many times! He was disguised as the coal man who spoke to us just a short while ago on this very spot.' The count added, 'Quick, after him!' The horses were nearby, so they mounted and rode off in haste after Eustache who, by that time had washed his face before meeting a potter. The potter was shouting, 'Pots for sale! Pots for sale!' And Eustache, who was no fool, knew he was being chased. So he immediately struck a deal with the potter. In exchange for his donkey and coal, he got pitchers, pots and vases. The swap was made and so Eustache became a potter and the potter became a coal man.[23] The latter was a fool for giving up his own trade. Eustache went off shouting, 'Pots for sale! Pots for sale!' Just at that moment the count came out of the woods and asked the potter if he had seen a coal man. 'Sir,' replied Eustache the Monk, 'he went down this road straight toward Boulogne, leading his donkey loaded down with sacks of coal.' (1,042–90)

The count dug in his spurs and he, his servants and knights caught up with the coal man. They proceeded to beat and mistreat the poor man. With their fists they beat him soundly, while tying him up hands and feet. They then threw him over the back of a horse, with his head dangling over the animal's rump. The poor fellow screamed, shouted and cried, 'My lords, in God's name, I beg you, have pity on me. Tell me why you have taken me thus. If I have done you any ill, I'll willingly make amends.' 'Aha! Aha! sir scoundrel,' said the count, 'you thought you could escape? I'll soon have you hanged.' One of the count's knights looked closely at the man and recognized him as the potter whom he knew well. This wise knight, who knew where the man was born, said, 'What devils have turned you into a coal man? You used to be a potter. No man will ever stay healthy who takes on so many different trades.' 'My lord, have mercy,' said the man, 'for this donkey and this coal I gave my pots to the coal man. May God strike him down, for it is because of him that I am tried this way. I think he probably stole the goods. By God's name I can truly say I didn't steal anything. I gave him my pots in exchange for the donkey. He rode off in haste into the woods, shouting, "Pots for sale! Pots for sale!"' The knight spoke to the count in these words: 'Eustache is a shameful fellow! Just a short while ago he was dressed as a coal man, now he has become a potter.' 'So I see,' said the count, 'by the pluck! Quick, after the man, let's go! Bring to me everyone you meet today and tomorrow. I'll never catch that Monk unless I take all of them as prisoners.' So they left the poor coal man and set off into the forest, once again on the chase. By this time Eustache had got rid of all his pots, having thrown them into a swamp. Besides, he had been carrying them too long in any event. (1,091–141)

Eustache imitates a nightingale

Eustache the brainless then climbed up into a kite's nest where he pretended to be a nightingale.[24] Because he considered the count to be a fool, the moment he saw him passing underneath, he let out a bird cry, 'Kill, kill, kill, kill.' Sure enough, Count Renaud responded, 'I'll kill him, by St Richard, if I ever get my hands on him.' 'Hit, hit,' said Eustache the Bird Monk. The Count of Boulogne in reply, 'I'll do it, I'll do it, but I won't seize him right here.' Thus reassured, Eustache let out another few words, 'He didn't get it, yes he did, no he didn't, yes he did!' When the Count of Boulogne heard that, he answered, 'He certainly did. He's taken all my fine horses from me.' Eustache shouted, 'Today, today!' 'You're surely right,' replied the count, 'today's the day I'm going to kill him with my own bare hands, if I can ever get hold of him. A man who takes a nightingale's advice', said the count, 'is nobody's fool. This nightingale has taught me how to take revenge on my foes, by calling out to me that I should hit him and kill him.' Then the Count of Boulogne rode off in pursuit of Eustache the Monk. The first thing he did next was to arrest four monks whom he took straight off to prison. Then he put into prison four merchants and a dealer. He seized three poulterers and two donkey drivers, after which he sent straight to his prison six fishermen along with their fish. Then four clerics and an archpriest were sent to the same place. In all, more than sixty companions found themselves together in his jail on that one day. (1,142–85)

Eustache disguises himself as a prostitute

The count went off to Neufchatel where he set up his new court. Eustache, who had many tricks up his sleeve, entered after him into the town. He dressed up in a woman's clothing, and his disguise was so good he did in fact look just like a woman.[25] He put on a linen dress, covered his face with a veil, and carried a distaff by his side. As he sat there spinning, a sergeant arrived almost immediately, riding one of the count's horses and leading another. Eustache exclaimed: 'Let me mount your horse and in return I'll let you fuck me.' 'Quite willingly,' said the sergeant. 'Climb up, then, on this good ambling palfrey, and I'll give you four pence if you let me fuck you. I'll also teach you how to arse play.' In reply Eustache said, 'Here and now, I declare, no man has ever screwed any better than this.' Eustache lifted a leg to the horseman; and, as he did so, let off a loud fart. 'Hah, damsel, you're farting!' Eustache responded, 'You're mistaken, my sweet handsome friend, don't let the noise bother you, it's only the saddle cracking.' Eustache the Monk climbed up on the second horse, and he and the young man rode off in haste into the forest side by side. 'Let's not go any farther. I'm riding my master's horse and you have his best palfrey.' The youth added, 'I'll be severely punished if this affair of ours isn't quickly finished. Let's do it right now.' 'Young man,' said the Monk, 'I too am aching for a good fuck. So let's get to our arse playing quickly. Come a little closer so that no one can spy on us.' 'Damsel,' said the young man, 'be careful there's no trickery. Should there be any, I swear by Saint Mary's bowels[26] I'd take your life.' In reply Eustache said, 'My dear friend, no need to get so upset, my lodge is just ahead. Come on, just a bit farther now.' The young man foolishly followed along as Eustache came upon his own band of men. He grabbed the poor wretch by the scruff of the neck as if he were mad. Here you have a good illustration of the truth in the popular saying: 'The goat scratches so much, it has a hard time to lie down.' (1,186–241)

Eustache ordered, 'Get down off the good horse, you won't ride it any farther. The palfrey too will stay here quite well. The count will never mount it again.' Both riders dismounted right there amid great bursts of laughter. 'My lords,' said Eustache the Monk, 'this young man will do his duty, for that I have his word.' He led the poor youth forward a bit, and took him to a mud pit, saying: 'Young man, don't let it trouble you. Quick, strip off all your clothes. I know how anxious you are to have a fuck.' The youth entered the mud pit for he dared not contradict Eustache. The latter exclaimed: 'Now, about that arse play! You can fuck at your leisure, all stretched out for some good arse play, or you'll be beaten so badly you'll never be able to leave. You thought you were going to fuck me. Aren't you ashamed for wanting to bugger a Black Monk?' The young man replied, 'May God have mercy, don't put me to such shame here. Sire, by Our Lady, I thought you were a woman!' Eustache, who was neither heretic nor buggerer, nor sodomite, answered, 'Well then, come forward before you leave.

You're going to have to promise to tell the count how I used you.' 'I will tell him straight away on your behalf,' said the young man as he set off in haste. In fact, his shame was such that he dared not return to tell the count anything about what had happened to him. Instead, he left the Boulonnais for a foreign land, never to return. Following this episode, the war between Eustache the Monk and the count lasted a long time. Eustache continued to put his adversary to even greater shame. (1,242–83)

Eustache is betrayed by a priest

One day, while Eustache was residing in the town of Coupelle, he found out that the count was looking everywhere for him in the region. He had thought he had found a safe haven for himself there, taking up residence with a priest who was rich and comfortably well off. His trust in this cleric was misplaced, for the priest soon betrayed him to the count. By way of reprisal Eustache caused his betrayer great humiliation. He tied the priest up hand and foot and threw him into a ditch.[27] (1,284–93)

Shortly thereafter the Count of Boulogne went to Genech on business, taking with him King Philip. The king had with him his whole army and was also accompanied by his son, King Louis.[28] The king had a fine company of men, as did Louis, and that night he decided to stay at Coupelle. From there, he was able to assemble his forces at Sainte-Marie-au-Bois, not far from Coupelle. Eustache the Monk, who had already done the count a lot of harm, now started to do the same to the king. He had his own fine company of men with him, one of whom he had posted outside the wood as a spy. Soon thereafter Eustache captured a man from the town of Corbic and left him with nothing other than his tunic. He sent this townsman to the king at Coupelle and proceeded to kill one of the king's knights. The king became enraged and exclaimed to the Count of Boulogne, 'Count, did you hear what Eustache the Monk, who robs and kills my men, has done?' The count replied, 'So help me God. I myself have been unable to take revenge against him. He's not only a warlike monk, he's a Devil, in fact.' The king gave orders to have Eustache pursued at once, but he never managed to get his hands on him. (1,294–321)

Eustache disguises himself as a peasant

From Coupelle the king headed to Sangatte. On his way back from there the count headed up the rearguard so that the king's men would have no cause for worry. Eustache, still full of tricks as usual, was staying in a town nearby. The Count of Boulogne learned from one of his spies that Eustache the Monk was waiting in that town so that he could keep watch on the king's army, which was passing that way. The count headed in that direction. Meanwhile, tricky old

Eustache, who had been warned of this by his own spy, caught sight of a new fence being built along the road. There was a peasant putting nails into this fence as Eustache approached him. The peasant was wearing an old cloak, which Eustache promptly ripped off his back, giving him in return his own good robe and ordering him off to his lodgings. The fence was very easy to nail, so Eustache immediately set to work hammering. He was wearing an old cap on his head and was holding a rough cloth, with which he was rubbing down the stakes and pickets. When the count emerged from a valley, he headed right for Eustache, furiously nailing away at his fence, 'Peasant,' said the Count of Boulogne, 'is Eustache the Monk in here?' Eustache answered, 'To tell you the truth, I don't know, my lord, and I wouldn't want to lie to you. A short while ago he headed out of town, taking flight because the king's army was coming. He was speeding away in great haste, right up there. So he can't be very far away yet. You can probably catch up with him in no time.' (1,322–58)

Eustache attacks King Philip's rearguard

The count dug his spurs into his horse, and Eustache, who could ask for nothing better, attacked the army's rearguard. In the process he captured five knights, six palfreys and five warhorses. He was able to pull that off because he had a large company of his own men nearby. Eustache and his men then fled into the woods where they found a safe hiding place. (1,359–66)

Eustache encounters Hainfrois

One day, just as they were sitting down to eat, Hainfrois, Eustache's mortal enemy, inadvertently came upon their meal. He had gone into the woods to take a piss, but once there he thought he would never get out alive. As he sat there on his horse, frightened to death, Eustache stood up and said, 'Well then, do dismount and join us for a meal.' Hainfrois got down from his horse, fearing for his very life. Little did he trust Eustache. When the meal was over Hainfrois began to beg for mercy. In reply the Monk said, 'Get out of here! You killed my father and my first cousin, bringing both to their end, not to mention the mess you have put me into with Count Renaud. But should anyone give me all of France I would not seek reconciliation with him. The same is not the case between you and me. Because you and I have eaten together, from this day forth you'll have nothing to fear from me. For you and I are quits. As for the count, you can tell him on my behalf that he spoke to me just a short while ago. I was the one nailing that fence when he asked me what direction the Monk had taken and whether he was still in there.' Hainfrois took leave of Eustache and ran to tell the count what had happened. When the count learned all that had been said, he immediately retraced the tracks, only to find that Eustache had taken still another turn. (1,367–99)

Eustache disguises himself as a leper

Eustache next turned up in the guise of a leper carrying his bowl, along with a crutch and a wooden rattle. As soon as he saw the count approaching he began to shake the rattle, with the result that the count and his knights put twenty-eight pence into the poor beggar's bowl. The troop passed by, but one of the men riding a fine warhorse had the misfortune to remain alone in the rear. Eustache the leper tripped the animal, knocked the rider out of his saddle, and rode away. The horseless rider came to the count and cried, 'Sire, upon my word, a leper stole your horse from me.' Furious, the count cursed, 'By the bowels, belly and legs, that damn Monk has tricked us once again. It was he disguised as a leper that shook his rattle at us. Yet, I could swear', so said Count Renaud, 'he really did look like a leper, with his fingers all bent over like claws and his face all pustulous.' And so the count continued his relentless pursuit of Eustache the Monk. (1,400–22)

Eustache disguises himself as a cripple

Eustache made himself look like a cripple. Having tied one leg to his buttock he knew exactly how to handle a crutch and walk one-legged with it. He also cut up a cow's lungs and tied them to his thigh with a blood-stained bandage before he made his way into the church. The prior was already singing Mass, with the Count of Boulogne in attendance along with many knights and men-at-arms. The church was full of people. Eustache approached the count and described his sad condition. He showed him his leg and his buttock and begged him to express his generosity toward such a sick man. The count held out to the beggar twelve pence and Eustache took the coins. Then he went right to the prior as he was taking up the offerings and raised his thigh, also showing him his buttock. 'Lord,' said Eustache, 'see what a sorry state I'm in. My poor thigh is completely withered. In God's name and the name of the Virgin Mary, do implore these knights to give me money so that I might have my thigh cured.' The prior said, 'Wait until all the offerings are collected and then I'll say a few words on your behalf. I'll be most pleased to ask them all to help you.' Once the offerings were all in, without delay the prior made a plea on behalf of Eustache the Monk, he who had already humiliated so many people. 'My lords,' said the prior, 'listen to my words. You can see that this poor man has a completely withered thigh. In the name of God and the Virgin Mary, he has a great need for others to do him justice. For walking he has only one foot and a crutch. In God's name, my lords, give him your alms. I beg you that above all else.' (1,423–65)

Eustache was nobody's fool. In addition to what the count had already given him he got eight more sous from the prior's appeal. With no desire to stay for the kiss of peace, he then quietly slipped out of the church before Mass was finished. He preferred war to peace anyhow. He found the count's horse and immediately mounted it with his crutch dangling down. Some children standing nearby shouted out loudly, 'The one-legged man is stealing a horse. Look at him go, spurring that horse on up through the valley!' All the knights dashed out and there was nobody left inside the church. Everyone present was astounded at the one-legged man, who had fled away on the magnificent Spanish horse. Eustache continued on his way, speeding through the countryside. 'Come on,' screamed the count, 'by the bowels! What a treacherous Monk. How can someone like him cause me so much grief and humiliation! Once again he has taken my horse. But there's no use my chasing after him. I'd never catch him in any event.' Then the count made everyone there swear that if they ever seized the Monk they would deliver him over as a prisoner, wherever it might be: in a wood, a town or on a road somewhere. (1,466–93)

Eustache tricks the count by reversing horseshoes

One day there was a heavy snowfall. Eustache had been spotted in a hamlet, where he was living, and the count went over there straight away with thirty fully armed men. Eustache would have soon been seized and taken prisoner had not William de Montcavrel sent a young boy to warn him. Eustache jumped on to his horse Morel, and fled along with two companions. He left in such haste that he didn't even have time to arm himself. The count followed his tracks, which showed up clearly in the snow. Eustache, however, found a smithy and had him turn the horse's shoes around.[29] Once the horseshoes were on backward, he rode off once again. The end result was that the further forward he went the more his tracks made it appear to the count as if he were retracing his steps. The count followed along the trail, but the tracks in the snow made it appear to him that Eustache was riding in the opposite direction. (1,494–515)

The count retraced his hoof prints, and the tracks led him to the smith who had earlier reversed the horseshoes. The smith would soon find himself in a sorry plight. The count summoned him and I think he fully intended to make the poor man suffer. Without further ado he demanded that he turn Eustache the Monk over to him. The smith exclaimed: 'I don't have him, so help me Virgin Mary.' The count said, 'You'll have to hand him over. These horseshoe tracks which have led us here are proof of your guilt.' The smith replied, 'My lord, have mercy! Three squires rode by here on horses that had their horseshoes turned round. But I don't know why they did that. They just left a short time ago taking the path by which you yourself came back here.' The count said, 'By the legs of the saints! This Monk is a treacherous devil. Because he has reversed the horseshoes we headed back in this direction. So my good smith, you who reversed the shoes, you're going to part with twenty pounds. Now, either you give me twenty pounds or I'll have you strung up high.' The smith quickly promised the twenty pounds and handed over guarantees as well as a hostage. (1,516–45)

Eustache disguises himself as a carpenter

The count continued to track Eustache through the forest of Hardelot. As he approached a ruined church Eustache was sitting there eating outside. Three carpenters were also there working on the construction of a new church. The count passed in front of their construction but one of his men-at-arms ran over towards the church. No sooner than he saw the man approaching, Eustache picked up some tools and quickly became a carpenter. With an axe hanging round his neck he hastened out the door of the church: 'May God protect you, my lord,' said Eustache, 'who's that riding past over there?' The man replied, 'Those men have taken an oath of private vengeance and are now in exile from their own land. They have come into this part of the country in search of a man very skilled in warfare. They've heard about a Monk, who was born near Boulogne, and have been looking for him far and wide, for he is reputed to be very brave and bold.' 'Brother,' said Eustache the Monk, 'you've all set out on a task which will turn out to be a waste of your efforts. The one you're seeking is a deceitful coward, an insolent bandit. In fact he's right over there, eating inside the church. May this devilish, enemy Monk suffer every misfortune he deserves! On his account we're all starving. If you dismount you can go and see for yourself the man sitting in a corner over there. He's your Monk, no doubt about it.' The man got down off his horse straight away, saying to the Monk: 'Hold my horse for me. There's no better charger from here to Monchy. But be careful he doesn't kick you. His rear hooves are very dangerous.' The Monk replied, 'You look like a trustworthy fellow and your horse won't kick me if I can help it.' The young man went inside the church, but he didn't see the Monk. When he didn't find him he soon realized that he had been tricked. His search was a wasted effort. Meanwhile outside, Eustache lost no time in climbing on to the horse, then shouted out in a loud voice, 'Carpenter, here's your axe. I commend you to God as I take my leave.' 'By God's teeth,' said the man, 'get off my horse and bring him back to me at once.' 'I'll do no such thing. Besides, he's such a fine-looking specimen. In fact I'm going to take this excellent horse for myself. That way you can be sure the count won't catch me today.' Eustache then added, 'Lord vassal, walk back on foot and advise the count from me that he'd have been well supplied and fed if he had chosen to stop over here.' (1,546–607)

Eustache rode off into the forest, and the squire whose horse was stolen set off on foot, angered and distraught. That day found him in a sorry plight. He stumbled frequently in the snow and became so hungry and thirsty he almost died. Groping his way along in such a pitiful state, his teeth couldn't stop chattering. The count was sitting at table eating when his squire abruptly appeared, all dirty, right down to his britches. The count said, 'You seem to have had a fine adventure! You apparently wasted no time and have followed close behind me. Did you catch the Monk?' The squire was so choked with anger he couldn't utter a word. So the count spoke up again: 'Say something, you devil! May you get a toothache!' 'My lord,' the squire blurted out sarcastically, 'what a fine knight the Monk of yours is. He often takes what's yours and certainly knows how to teach you your *paternoster*. He stole my horse and threatened my very life.' 'Go on!' said the count, 'by the legs, belly and bowels! By the throat and teeth! How can this man continue to deceive everyone like that! By God's legs, he'll not get away this time. My lords, men-at-arms, let me make this quite clear to all of you!' (1,608–37)

Eustache is captured by the count

Eustache was still in the forest and the count headed straight for him there. The count pursued his enemy like a madman. Eustache was riding Morel, but the horse did not have its saddle strapped on. It seemed certain now that the Monk would soon be caught! Eustache frantically spurred Morel and the horse darted forward. But as it did so the saddle slipped and Eustache fell off, allowing the count to seize him. He defended himself fiercely and threw the count's shield down in front of him. With his two hands the count quickly grabbed Eustache, but the Monk, who would have loved to humiliate his adversary once again, struck out wildly at the count. One pulled one way, one another. You have never seen such a tussle as there was when Eustache was finally captured, in spite of the great skill with which he defended himself. But in the end Eustache was taken and held prisoner. He was then restrained by force and guarded closely. They tied him up hand and foot and loaded him on to a charger. The count's immediate desire was to hang him on the spot. Eustache, however, had his supporters in the count's entourage. There would have been many blows exchanged had he been hanged or killed without a trial. 'My lords,' said the Count of Boulogne, 'I have finally captured Eustache the Monk. It is up to you now to advise me what I should do with him. Whatever you decide I'll follow your advice. Do you advise me to hang him or to turn him over to the King of France?' (1,638–69)

Eustache receives support from the count's vassals

William de Montcavrel said, 'We would not be pleased to see him killed. He's a relative of ours, as well as our friend. His death would bring you too many enemies.'[30] The count replied, 'I'll have him hanged at once and I'll soon see who'll try to take him from me! Or else I'll turn him over to the king and he'll have him hanged or drowned, or at the least have him severely tortured. There's no one on earth who'll stop me.' William said, 'Fair, sweet lord. Hold your anger in check just a bit. Surrender the Monk to us as a pledge against all that we owe you.' 'By the very bowels of God,' said the count, 'I won't do it! On the contrary it's my firm intention to finish him off right here and now.' Then Aufrans de

Cayeux spoke up, 'My lord, do try to curb your anger. You could easily cause great harm to his friends if you tried to kill him off.' 'My lord,' said Hugh de Belin, 'do you truly want his days ended completely?' 'Yes indeed, by St Peter of Rome. That way he'll never be able to deceive anyone again,' said the count. 'This treacherous Monk has already caused far too much harm.' Walet de Coupelle replied, 'By the brains, Eustache will not die today! My lord count, you're a very evil man. To act in this way won't be to your advantage. Don't forget that if he has acted in hostile fashion towards you, his behaviour was fully justified. After all, it was you who took his land from him. Now it's your duty to have him tried fairly in a court of law. Otherwise you're the one who'll come off badly. Should you have the Monk hanged, you'd immediately find yourself with a large number of enemies. What's more, if you don't treat him properly, you'll soon see many swords drawn.' (1,670–707)

'My lord,' said Bauduin d'Aire, 'in this matter you can just take my word for it. Send him off to Paris where the king will have him judged fairly by law.' The count replied: 'If he's allowed to go on living for even a single day, I'm certain he'll find a way to escape.' 'Well then, first have him so tightly bound that he won't be able to evade justice.' The count said, 'Very well then, I'll send him to the king in order to rid myself of him.' Each man present replied individually, 'That's my advice to you.' The count sent Eustache first to Hardelot. At nightfall he summoned a carter to take him to the king. The carter gave the count his word that he'd take the Monk to the King of France without anyone finding out about it. (1,708–25)

Eustache is rescued

Hugh de Gannes mounted his horse along with thirty other fully armed men. They were to be responsible for taking Eustache to the king. They preferred to help him, however, rather than to cause him any harm. Although his friends were grief-stricken, Eustache was lifted on to the cart and they set out by night. As they made their way past Montreuil, Hugh de Gannes alerted others to the fact that if they were ready and equipped to help Eustache the Monk they could rescue him just below Beaurain. So William de Fiennes armed himself and with thirty companions headed for Beaurain. There they rescued Eustache the Monk in spite of the Count of Boulogne. The Monk immediately crossed over the Canche River on the border of the Pas-de-Calais, having no desire to enter France. So before the count knew a word about it, he was paid back in full. (1,726–45)

Abbot lies and is robbed

Eustache soon spotted the Abbot of Jumièges and recognized him as he was coming down the road. 'Sir Abbot,' he said, 'stop where you are! What are you carrying? Come now, don't hide it.' The abbot answered, 'What's it to you?' At this, Eustache was ready to hit him, but instead replied, 'What's it to me, fat-ass! Upon my word, I'll make it my business. Get down, fast, and not another word out of you or I'll let you have it. You'll be beaten up so badly you won't be worth a hundred pounds.' The abbot thought the man was drunk, and said, more politely this time, 'Go away. You won't find what you are looking for here.' Eustache responded, 'Cut the bullshit and get off your horse, fast, or you'll be in for a lot of trouble.' The abbot got down, frightened now. Eustache asked how much money he had with him. 'Four marks,' said the abbot, 'in truth I only have four marks silver.' Eustache searched him immediately and found thirty marks or more. He gave back to the abbot the four marks he claimed to have. The abbot became duly furious; for, had he told the truth, he would have received back all his money. The abbot lost his money only because he told a lie.[31] (1,746–77)

Eustache disguises himself as a fishmonger

One day while the count was in Boulogne, Eustache the Monk went there and entered the town. He had previously bought some mackerel which he then sold to the count's men-at-arms. In order to receive payment and settle accounts Eustache went to eat at court, but he couldn't get a penny out of anyone there. He asked for payment of what was due him, but not a single drop of silver was forthcoming. The best he could do was get the men to set a date for payment. With that Eustache left. The count got ready to leave but first gave the order to have his horses saddled. Before the count came out, however, Eustache went over to the horses and took the reins of four of the very best, as if to lead them to water. He enlisted three serving boys to go with him and they led the horses for him. He took the horses along with the three boys out of Boulogne to a place where he had his own men stationed. He made the boys get down and his men took the horses away from them. The three youths had to find their own way back to town. In the meantime, Eustache informed the count, through a sergeant whom he met, that he was taking possession of the four horses by way of payment for his fish. The man came running to the count to give a full report on Eustache the Monk, who had sold him forty-four mackerel, or more. 'He has taken four good horses, I believe, in payment for his fish. To top it off he ate at your court.' 'By God's feet! He persists in keeping me on a short leash. By the Virgin Mary's bowels, I'll have his life shortened!' The count began once again to pursue his enemy, but never succeeded in getting his hands on him. He continued to be unable to see through the Monk's various tricks. Among other disguises Eustache became in turn a flan seller, a crêpe merchant and a cake vendor. (1,778–819)

Eustache disguises himself as a pastry cook

One day the count was in Calais. Eustache, full of evil and guile as ever, came there riding up at a gallop. Accompanied by a squire he made a big, blazing fire in a house just outside the town. The two of them set out to make waffles, tarts and some very fine dumplings. But their recipe called for unusual fillings. The tarts were baked with tow, pitch and wax. The bakers saw to it that all their pastries were masterpieces! Before they finished Eustache had written a note which he put into one of the tarts. It related the true story of his wicked joke. Eustache then carried in his wares himself and set them before the count who was sitting at table. He came over to the count and told him that one of his subjects, who held his fief from him, had a case to plead before him. For that reason the young nobleman was making him a present of the pastries and was going to come and eat with the count. The gift was duly accepted. But all present would come to rue that day. They would soon find themselves cruelly tricked. (1,820–45)

Eustache took his leave, and when the meal was finished the pastry gift was quickly presented to the count. They brought in the tarts, and the knight who had carried them in took one of them for himself. He happened to be the count's constable and one of his closest advisers. He no sooner bit into the tart than his teeth became stuck to the point that he couldn't even open his mouth or get his teeth free of it. Yet before he succeeded in extricating himself, he said to one of his companions, 'Here, have a taste. You've never eaten such tarts before nor tasted anything quite like them in all your life.' So his companion also took one of the tarts. The man's teeth were so large that they became severely stuck. In spite of all his efforts he couldn't get his teeth out of the pastry. He began to sweat with anguish before he finally managed to extricate himself. Once free his immediate reaction was to swear angrily, 'By God's teeth! I've been disgraced. I could swear I've eaten the Devil himself!' All those who had eaten the tarts were indeed badly tricked. No one was spared. As soon as anyone took a bite his teeth became inextricably stuck. At last in one of the tarts they found Eustache's message explaining that it was the Monk who had done this to them. 'I swear', said the Count of Boulogne, 'this Monk's treachery has no end. He continues to lead us a merry dance. May the Devil take him! For it seems none of us will ever catch or apprehend him.' (1,846–81)

Eustache goes to England and serves King John

Eustache fled to England and went to see King John. Once again in disguise, this time as a Hospitaller he prostrated himself at the king's feet, begging him for mercy.[32] When the king asked him why he was doing this, Eustache said only, 'My lord, have mercy.' 'Get up at once,' said the king, 'I can see you are a Hospitaller, so I'll willingly grant you mercy.' With that Eustache felt free to explain the matter which brought him here: 'Eustache the Monk has sent me to intercede on his behalf. With a plea for mercy, he wishes to become a retainer in your household.' The king replied without any hesitation, 'There's no problem for his becoming one of my retainers, provided that he's willing to swear to serve me always and in good faith. He must never let me down. But he will have to provide hostages.' Eustache said, 'If you so desire, you'll have my daughter as a pledge, or my wife, if you prefer her.' The king responded, 'Are you the Monk, you who are speaking to me about this matter?' 'Yes, my lord, Eustache is my name.' The king said, 'By St Edmund,[33] who is my true lord, I shall retain you willingly. You're very welcome in my household.' (1,882–910)

As King John's mariner, Eustache conquers the Channel Islands

So Eustache became one of King John's retainers and was given command of a fleet of ships. With some thirty galleys given to him by the king, Eustache then set sail. His first destination was the islands of Jersey and Guernsey. But as he approached one of these Channel Islands he found the islanders waiting for him there, armed and assembled with their leader Romerel, the lord of one of the island manors. As he saw Eustache's fleet approaching, the leader said to his men, 'Now wait until they've landed. The moment we see them coming ashore, we'll attack and destroy them at once.' When Eustache's ships landed, he was the first to disembark. All his companions jumped out after him and the inhabitants of the islands attacked them without delay. Eustache headed straight for the castellan, who was at the head of his troops. Marching well out in front, the leader tolerated no complaints. He boldly led all those under his command right up to the invader's ships. The combat began with an exchange of battle-cries: 'Godehiere!', 'Winchelsea!', 'God is with us here,' cried Romerel.[34] 'St Vincent help us,' cried Eustache. Heavy fighting broke out and many men were knocked off their horses. One side attacked fiercely and the other side defended itself very well. After the mêlée began, it soon became savage, violent and arduous. On the battlefield Eustache held a huge axe in his hands and with it he struck countless heavy blows. He smashed and split many a helmet, and more than one warhorse lost its shoulder. First to his right then to the left he struck blow after blow, making himself lord and master of the battle. Eustache shouted out, 'Don't stop striking your blows! They'll all take flight, as you'll soon see.' And so the great battle raged on ever more fiercely. That day many coffins were to be made. In the end, Eustache expelled everyone he found there. All the inhabitants of the Channel Islands were sent into exile. In fact, so complete was the destruction he wrought that there was nothing left to burn in any of the castles or manors. (1,911–53)

Eustache entraps Cadoc, the seneschal of Normandy

One day, as the tide was coming in, Eustache came to Harfleur, the place where the Seine River flows into the sea. He first anchored his galleys and then got into a small boat along with thirty of his closest companions. They began rowing up the Seine and in very short time landed at Pont-Audemer. After the craft was tied up Eustache went to stand on the bridge nearby. He had put on a surplice just in time to see Cadoc, the seneschal of Normandy, standing before him. Cadoc was in charge of three hundred men-at-arms in his household whose charge it was to guard the bridges along the Seine in order to prevent the Monk from getting past. While still on the bridge Eustache called for a barber and had himself shaved. He then said to Cadoc, 'What would you do to him if you ever caught the Monk?' Cadoc replied, 'I would make sure I turned him over to the King of France, who would have him crucified, hanged, burned or drowned.' Eustache then said, 'By St Winape![35] If you were to give me your cape, I'd soon provide you with information on his whereabouts and then I'd take you to where he's staying.' Cadoc replied, 'If you hand the Monk over to me you'll certainly have my cape.' Eustache said, 'Well then, take off your cape and give it to me. You'll see him soon enough.' (1,954–85)

Cadoc gave him the cape which was lined with grey squirrel fur. The garment would in fact soon be called an *es-cape*. As Eustache put it on he said, 'Get on your horse quickly! He's very near here, over in those meadows.' Along with thirty of his men Cadoc mounted and Eustache himself took them to the spot very near Pont-Audemer. It would not be long until Eustache would make Cadoc furiously angry. When they got to the meadows they found a reaper mowing one of the sections nearby. Eustache exclaimed, 'By St Winape! If that reaper gets away, you'll never catch the Monk.' At once, Cadoc and his men dug their spurs into their horses and rode over towards the man. As they did so they found themselves trapped in a huge quagmire and they all fell in. Every one of them became inextricably stuck and their horses sank right up to their bellies. In the meantime, Eustache came over to where Cadoc was struggling. He greeted the seneschal, saying, 'My lord, what are you doing in there?' 'By the bowels,' shouted Cadoc, 'you've tricked us cruelly by bringing us here! May God bring down some misfortune on you this very day!' From beneath his hood Eustache laughed heartily at Cadoc, who was thoroughly tricked when he fell into the quagmire. For now he and fifteen of his companions found themselves completely stuck. As they sat there on their horse flailing away, they all swore at Eustache like renegades. Eustache said, 'By St Remi! You'll never get out of this quagmire unless you do as I tell you.' Cadoc screamed, 'You son of a whore, you wretched swine! You're the one who got us into this mess! If I ever get my hands on you, you can be sure that tomorrow will be an evil day for you!' Eustache replied, 'As long as you're in this quagmire, I have nothing to fear from any of you. And so far as I'm concerned you can stay there until Easter. But you'll never get out of the mess unless you heed my advice. Now, all of you hold hands together and climb up on your saddles. By jumping up with your feet together, you'll ease the weight

on your horses and move more freely. Do it now, if you care to believe me.'
(1,986–2,039)

They took Eustache's advice and one after another they pulled themselves up
on to the horses' saddles. They held each other's hands and Cadoc jumped first.
So doing he fell into the mud all the way up to his armpits. The others held tight
on to their saddles but remained up to their waistbands in mud. Eustache was in
no way upset by any of this. He was so amused that he nearly fainted with
laughter, saying, 'You're definitely caught now and you'll never get out of here
unless someone pulls you out with ropes.' Cadoc exclaimed, 'By the thighs, the
belly and the bowels! By God's teeth! How humiliating this is for me!' Eustache
yelled to the reaper in a loud voice and called him to come help. The man rushed
over, taking a running jump into the mud landing next to Cadoc. He did so in
order to try to help him but he himself became stuck in it up to his waist.
Eustache commented, 'So, one more for the mud pit!' At that Cadoc became
absolutely convinced that the reaper who had attacked him thus was no other
than Eustache the Monk. In turn he immediately set upon the reaper, striking
him a stinging blow on the ear with his fist. The reaper was shocked by the attack
and his whole ear tingled from the blow. When Cadoc hit him on the ear a
second time, the reaper thought he was drunk and tried desperately to get away
from him. He had obviously fallen into bad hands and was being severely beaten
up and injured. (2,040–73)

Eustache shouted, 'Let him alone. He hasn't done anything wrong. He left his
reaping to come and help you. See how badly you're rewarding his good deed.
You're behaving shamefully and harmfully towards him. My name is Eustache
the Monk and I'm the one who has got you into this mess. As far as I'm
concerned, for now you can just stay there treading mud. To be sure you gave me
your cloak but have been poorly repaid by me for doing so. I'm leaving you in
this mess as I head off towards the sea. I had my beard trimmed as you watched
and now I'm watching as I force you to do some fishing here. So don't be stingy
with your efforts or hold back. There are a lot of eels to be found in this muck.
All you have to do is stomp around to get them. What a sorry plight you're in!
You've caught so many big fish and you won't be able to get them all ashore.'
Cadoc responded, 'If I were out of here, you'd soon be dead. You wouldn't live
long enough to deceive or trick anyone ever again.' Eustache replied, 'People
who are threatened don't stop living! They continue to struggle on for a long
time.' Then he left and returned to his boat. Cadoc was finally able to catch the
attention of the people on the bridge at Pont-Audemer. He called for them to
come and get him out of this muck, in which Eustache had forced him to go
fishing. (2,074–105)

At long last they were able to pull Cadoc out of the quagmire. The moment he
was set free he ordered three hundred men to arm themselves. Convinced that
he could trap Eustache there, Cadoc charged off towards Boulogne with his troops,

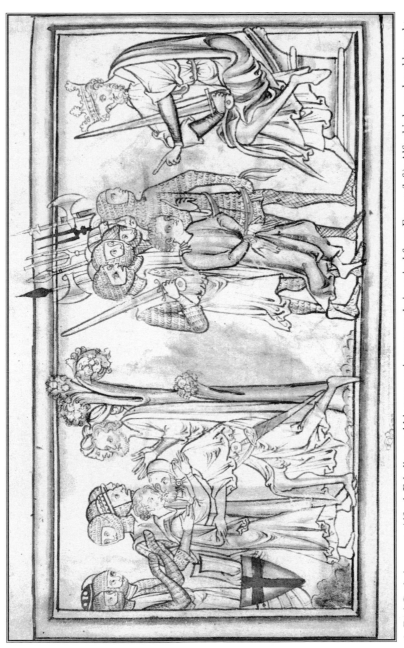

1. Earl Godwin greets Alfred Ætheling and his companions upon their arrival from France (left); Alfred is bound and brought before the king (right). A miniature from *La Vie du Edouard*, Cambridge University Library MS Ee. 3. 59, f. 5v.

ISLE OF ORKNEY

"BEYOND
NORTHUMBERLAND"

DUBLIN

FEN

LAND

MUNSTER

ZEELAND

CORNWALL

FLANDERS

Scale of 100 miles

NORMANDY

2. Major locations associated with the Hereward romance.

3. The Cornish princess gives the cup to Hereward, from the 1865 magazine edition of Charles Kingsley's *Hereward the Wake*.

4. Turfrida, Hereward's love interest, on horseback, visualized by Paul Gray for the *Good Words* magazine edition of Charles Kingsley's *Hereward the Wake*.

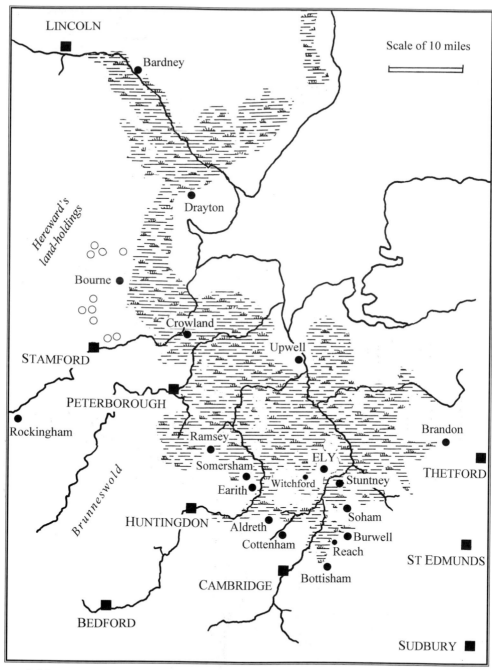

LINCOLN

Bardney

Scale of 10 miles

Hereward's land-holdings

Drayton

Bourne

Crowland

Upwell

STAMFORD

PETERBOROUGH

Rockingham

Brandon

Ramsey

Somersham

ELY

THETFORD

Witchford

Stuntney

Earith

Brunneswold

HUNTINGDON

Aldreth

Soham

Cottenham

Burwell

Reach

ST EDMUNDS

CAMBRIDGE

Bottisham

BEDFORD

SUDBURY

5. Map of the Fenland in the time of Hereward.

6. An historiated initial with Eustache the Monk receiving a magic book from the Devil, Paris, Bibliothèque Nationale de France MS FR 1553, f. 325ᵛ.

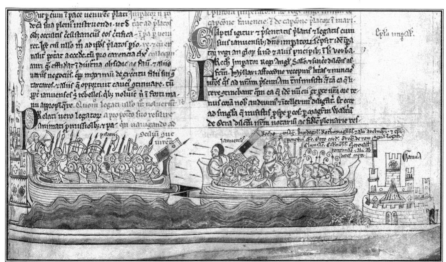

7. A sea battle, from Matthew Paris, *Chronica Majora*, Cambridge, Corpus Christi College MS 16, f. 146.

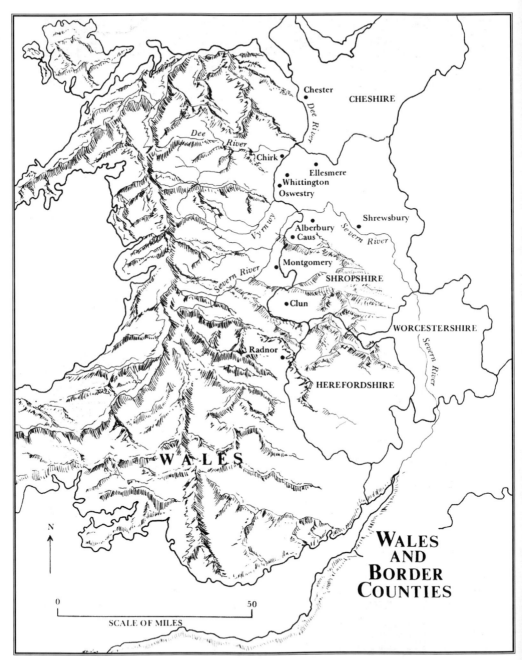

8. Map of Wales and border counties, from Janet Meisel, *Barons of the Welsh Frontier: The Corbet, Pantulf, and Fitz Warin Families, 1066–1272.*

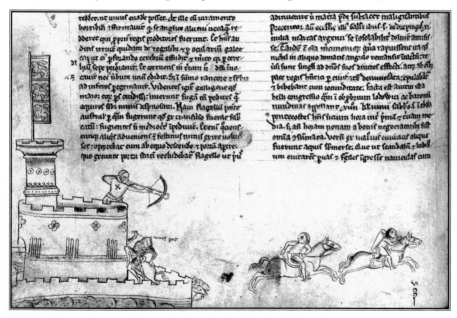

11. Atrocities perpetrated under King John, from Matthew Paris, *Chronica Majora*, Cambridge, Corpus Christi College MS 16 f. 44ᵛ.

12. A wrestling match, from Matthew Paris, *Chronica Majora*, Cambridge, Corpus Christi College MS 16, f. 58.

having first sent a hundred men on ahead. But, without further ado, Eustache had created a tidal wave to protect himself and was able to reach Barfleur safely.[36] He had previously extorted thirty marks as protection money from the Channel Islands and the rest of the region. When he got to Barfleur he received three thousand marks more in the same manner. Cadoc began to track him down, but couldn't catch him. He pursued him and his ships, but Eustache turned round and seized five ships from his pursuer. With that Cadoc lost all desire to continue the chase any further. He turned back, for the sea had treated him far too cruelly. (2,106–25)

As a pirate, Eustache captures a ship

Eustache raised his sail, and continued roving the Channel. He headed first toward the port of Croufaut. Near there he caught up with another ship which was sailing calmly directly ahead of him. He saw at once that it was a very fine ship and judged that it probably had a valuable cargo. With no delay he leaped on to the ship and attacked those whom he found on board. He proceeded to mistreat the crew and reduced them to such a state that he was able to extort two hundred marks from them. As they gave up that sum to Eustache, those on board the ship considered that they had just been defrauded by a pirate. (2,126–35)

Eustache builds a palace in London

From the sea Eustache continued on land his many evil deeds before he finally settled in England. Once there he went straight to see King John whom he addressed promptly: 'Sire, I want to make a formal request of you. I would like to have a place of residence in your land.' The king replied, 'Indeed you shall have one. You can take your pick of manors and reside wherever you desire. If you prefer to live in London I can give you a magnificent palace which is very well constructed.' Eustache accepted the gift and thanked the king for it. But no sooner had he moved in than he had the palace knocked down. A great number of workmen were set to work building new foundations which cost a good thousand silver marks. That amount was expended even before the building itself rose above ground level. When the King of England came for a visit he expressed his consternation, telling Eustache it was pure folly to have begun such a project. Nevertheless, the king proceeded to lend him four hundred marks to help him accomplish all his desires. Eustache had the work brought to completion and now had a magnificent, well-constructed palace. (2,136–59)

Eustache decides to leave England for France

While the Monk was living in England, the Count of Boulogne appeared on the scene. He had quarrelled with the King of France and decided to join forces with

King John. When he learned of the arrival of his nemesis, Renaud of Boulogne, the Monk decided his English palace was no longer a safe haven. And so he made up his mind to go back home. But getting there would now be a dangerous adventure, because he had worn out his welcome in England. Moreover, King John gave orders to have the sea watched in order to prevent Eustache from getting across to the French coast. (2,160–7)

Disguised as a minstrel, Eustache escapes to France

Eustache, who had a way with words, decided to set off disguised as a minstrel. He first found a bow and a vielle, then dressed himself properly for his new role. He covered up his short cloak and put on a hood with stripes of orphrey. Picking up a cane covered in leaves, he headed straight for the coast. Once there he saw a merchant ship about to set sail. Everyone had already gone aboard and Eustache waited near the ship, pondering what to do. At last he decided to chance it. He put his feet together and jumped on to the deck. The pilot said, 'Minstrel, you'll have to get off, so help me God'. Eustache replied, 'Yes, indeed, when the ship gets to the other side of the Channel. I don't think you're being very reasonable. To pay for my passage I'll give you the choice: either five silver pennies or my vielle.' 'And what other fables have you told?' 'I'm a very unusual *jongleur* and a minstrel; you'll find very few like me. I know all the songs. For God's sake, fair lord, take me across the Channel. Although I come from Northumberland I've spent the past five years in Ireland. I drank so much good ale there that my face has turned pale and wan. But now I'm going over to drink the wines of Argenteuil or Provins.' (2,168–97)

'What's your name, and no trickery?' 'Lord, my name is Mauferas.[37] God knows I'm an Englishman from Ganstead: Ya, ya, God-it-wot!' The sailor was dubious, saying, 'You an Englishman? I swore you were French. So now, do you know any *chansons de geste*?' 'Yes, of course, I know the ones about Agoulant and Aymon, as well as Blancandin. And I know all about the heroine Florence of Rome.[38] In fact there isn't a song on earth of which the tune or the melody is unfamiliar to me. I would have gladly entertained you well, but right now I wouldn't sing for anything. This sea has me frightened to death. Under these conditions I couldn't put my mind to singing anything worthwhile.' With that, no one asked anything further of him, so the Monk succeeded in worming his way out of having to perform. (2,198–216)

Disguised as a messenger, Eustache offers services to King Philip

It was evening when Eustache finally arrived in Boulogne. He immediately set off running, now in the guise of a messenger boy. He had with him a large box containing a letter which he was carrying to King Philip. He went straight to the king and showed him the letter. Once the king had read it he learned that the Monk had come to France and was sending his greetings. The letter also explained that the Monk was angry with King John on two counts. John not only killed Eustache's daughter, his cruelty was such that he also had her burned and disfigured. The other reason for his leaving England was because the Count of Boulogne was now there. So Eustache would never be at peace with King John again and that was the main reason why Eustache the Monk had come to France. In his letter he explained that he also had no intention of betraying King Philip, rather he wished to serve him as best he could. The king told the messenger: 'If he's on this side of the Channel, get him to come at once and speak with me. I promise that he can come and go in safety. He won't have any difficulty getting here, because no one will be on the lookout for him this far away.' With that Eustache spoke up saying, 'I'm already here!' 'Are you the Monk?' exclaimed the king. 'You don't look much like a Frenchman. You're so short! Yet from what I hear, in spite of your size, you're quite brave and bold. You also have a strong reputation for guile and cunning. So apparently you don't need any cat's grease to help you. But you need to be aware that you will not serve me unless you decide to lead a good life from now on.' Eustache said, 'By St Simon! I promise to serve you well by doing nothing other than good.' Thereafter, the Monk proved himself to be a good warrior. (2,217–50)

Eustache is blamed for naval defeat

Although the Monk was a great warrior, he was also very bold and cruel. Afterwards he did many devilish deeds in the islands on the other side. He led King Louis and a large fleet of ships across the English Channel, personally capturing the warship known as the *Nef de Boulogne* single-handedly.[39] He took the French king with him to the port of Damme. That was in AD 1213, the year the king lost his ships! They blamed Eustache for having betrayed the king's fleet and he was arraigned on that count. Eustache denied the charge completely and justified himself by claiming there was no man bold enough to furnish proof of such treason. And so they dropped the charges. (2,251–65)

Defeated in the Battle of Sandwich, Eustache is executed

Sometime later he again set out on the Channel with a great fleet of ships. With him there was Raoul de Tournelle, along with Varlet de Montagui. When Eustache, the courageous warrior, got out on the open sea he soon encountered more than twenty English ships bearing down on him. The enemy set out in small boats and attacked the ships with longbows and crossbows. [See plate 7.] The Monk's men guarded themselves against everything thrown at them in the chase by firing missiles and shooting arrows. They killed many Englishmen and defended themselves nobly. Eustache himself toppled many of them with the oar he wielded, breaking arms and smashing heads with every swing. This one he killed, another one he threw overboard. This one he knocked down, another he trampled under foot, and a third one had his windpipe crushed. But Eustache was assailed from all directions with no let up. Battle axes struck his ship on all sides. On the first wave the defenders were able to ward off the attack, preventing the enemy from coming on board. Then the English started hurling big pots of finely ground lime, smashing them to pieces on the ship railings, with the result that great clouds of dust covered the decks. That was what caused the most damage, against which Eustache's men could not defend themselves. To their misfortune the wind was against them, causing even further torment, for their eyes became filled with ash. In the confusion the English leaped on to Eustache's ship and mistreated his men badly, taking all the nobles prisoner. As for Eustache the Monk, he was slain, his head cut off.[40] With that the battle was over.

Epilogue

No man who spends his days doing evil can live a long life. (2,266–307)

4

THE OUTLAW'S SONG OF TRAILBASTON

Carter Revard

INTRODUCTION

The Outlaw's Rap

The *Song of Trailbaston* was written between April 1305 and February 1307, but the sole surviving copy of it was made in about 1341, by a scribe who lived and worked in Ludlow in southern Shropshire.[1] Composed in the Norman French then spoken by the upper classes in England, it is a passionate protest by a man who claims to have been wrongly indicted before the royal Trailbaston justices, and to be living as an outlaw in the 'Greenwood of Belregard'. He claims to have fought for the king in Flanders, Scotland and Gascony, presents himself as an expert archer who has practised that skill in the forest (which may hint at deer poaching), implies that he has considerable knowledge of legal matters, and threatens to break the backs and cut out the tongues of his judges. He ends by inviting all men – merchants, monks, clerics and others – who, like him, have suffered from these new statutes and these unjust judges, to join him in the woods where they can live in freedom and not be mistreated by the evil and bullying royal officials. He thus presents himself *exactly as Robin Hood is presented to us*: a virile but virtuous man, wronged by a powerful and unscrupulous gang of legal crooks, vows to avenge himself on the king's cronies who have mistreated him.

The Trailbaston courts before whom he has been summoned and indicted had only just been instituted by royal statute in 1304–5, officially to give local citizens a royal remedy against local corruption and violence, but according to one popular chronicle also to fill the royal coffers with their fines and forfeits.[2] *Baston* means 'club', so *trailbaston* meant something like 'club-wielder' – courts for dealing with thugs accused of violent crime or strongarm tactics against legal opponents, jurymen or judges. At the village level such a 'market-beater' is Chaucer's Simpkin Miller (*Reeve's Tale*) who with cutlass, sword, daggers, clubs and heavy fists, bullies and cheats the people of Trumpington. Such gangsterism at the baronial level was called *maintenance* – hiring armed retainers to intimidate juries and litigators and judges, to ride around extorting money or chattels from vulnerable householders, to oppress tenants on their manors.[3] In *The Outlaw's Song of Trailbaston* the speaker, though presenting himself as wronged and innocent, has been indicted as such a 'club-wielder', and in stanza 10 he threatens to club and knife his judges. Whether the anthologist who copied this poem believed such a speaker was protesting too much is a question to be asked.

The Poem as History: The Events of 1304–6

Some clues to the 1305 'historical meanings' are found in the poem itself, others come from study of the scribe, his likely patrons and probable audience. He worked as legal scrivener and probably as parish chaplain in and around Ludlow, near the Welsh border, from 1314 to 1349, and made the sole surviving copy of *Fouke fitz Waryn*, another 'outlaw' text preserved in a second manuscript containing this scribe's work, BL Royal MS 12.C.XII.[4] One hint that the nobles of Richard's Castle (3 miles south of Ludlow) were his patrons is that nearly half the surviving forty-one legal charters in his hand were written for tenants in their lordship, one of 1347 being a quitclaim from the lord of Richard's Castle, Sir John Talbot, to a Ludlow wool merchant, Philip Cheney, for a plot of land between Richard's Castle and Ludlow.[5] From 1328 to 1341, Sir John's widowed mother Joan (1291–1341) was the Lady of Richard's Castle, and the scribe may have been parish chaplain there from about 1316 to 1349.[6]

It is particularly relevant that a family scandal of 1304–6 involved Joan's mother, Maud Mortimer, and her chamberlain, William of Billebury. Maud 'accidentally' poisoned her husband Hugh, perhaps in complicity with William, and was indicted before the very judges of the Trailbaston courts who are named and execrated in the poem. It was no mere local scandal: Maud was lady-in-waiting to Princess Joan of Acre, favorite daughter of King Edward I and wife of Gilbert de Clare, Earl of Gloucester, and the marriage of Maud and Hugh had been arranged by Queen Eleanor herself.[7] While Maud was being held in the Tower for the poisoning, she was accused of sending William of Billebury to murder another man, for which William was indicted. But Maud had very powerful friends at court – the most powerful being Edward, Prince of Wales, who intervened on her behalf: he sent letters (still extant) complaining of her treatment, obtaining a change of venue and justices, and getting her pardoned within a year. William of Billebury, however, was indicted and would have been imprisoned, but fled and was outlawed. He too was eventually pardoned, but not until after he had been an outlaw for a year or so.[8] Could he have composed the poem while outlawed – perhaps while hiding out on an Irish manor called Belregard in the lordship of Trim? The flyleaves of Harley MS 2253 are fragments of an account-roll which records the visit of a large household to Trim and its manors at some time before Sir Geoffrey's death in 1314, so the scribe who copied *Trailbaston* knew, or knew of, those manors.[9]

From 1305 'History' to 1341 'Dramatic Monologue'

The *Song of Trailbaston* is a harsher version of 'Under the Greenwood Tree', the outlaw song in Shakespeare's *As You Like It* (a play based on the *Tale of Gamelyn*), and also resembles the Robin Hood poems. But unlike the Robin Hood poems, the *Song of Trailbaston* can be traced to its origins: we know certainly when (1305–6), probably where (among Marcher Barons of south-western England), and possibly even by whom it was first composed (William of Billebury). We must, however, distinguish what may have been the poem's 'real-life-outlaw meaning' when first written in 1305–6, from what may have been a 'bad example meaning' when it was copied into Harley MS 2253 in about 1341 – copied, perhaps, for the young Sir John Talbot, son and heir of the Lady of Richard's Castle, Joan, who died that year. How the scribe may have intended the poem to be heard in the 1340s must be inferred – as will be shown below – both from study of the manuscript's nature and intended audience, and from the historical circumstances of 1340–2, when the poem and its manuscript were being copied by the scribe.

The manuscript into which this scribe copied the *Outlaw's Song of Trailbaston*, British Library Harley MS 2253, contains most of the best Middle English lyrics from before Chaucer's time, as well as an astonishing variety of other texts in French, Latin and English. Its scribe, as I have elsewhere argued,[10] arranged many of its texts so as to bring out both the oppositions and the parallels between them. He certainly does this by placing the *Song of Trailbaston* between two other texts in a significant sequence.

In order, the three texts are *Urbain le Courtois*, *Trailbaston* and *The Man in the Moon* – the first two in French, the third in English. In each, a speaker advises listeners how to behave, but the advice varies wildly. Elsewhere in the two quires where these three texts are set we find similar oppositions: profane next to sacred, wise beside foolish, misogynist versus 'feminist', and so on. Perhaps the key text is that usually titled *Le Jongleur d'Ely* (fols 107v–109v), which might better be called *The King and the Wise Fool*.[11] It tells how the King of England meets a *menestrel* in the woods and asks a series of questions, to each of which the 'minstrel' gives nonsensical answers – but after this baffling wordplay the minstrel (like Shakespeare's Feste and other such fools) offers the king excellent advice: a king should not go to extremes, should neither too fiercely nor too gently rule his people, but hold the middle way, the golden mean.

As for the three dramatic monologues *Urbain le Courtois*, *Trailbaston* and *The Man in the Moon*, the speaker in *Urbain* is a wise and courtly father telling his son how to be nice and earn respect; the speaker in *Trailbaston* is a violent and reckless outlaw, reduced to living in the woods after having fled from the royal justices who have indicted him for some alleged crime or crimes which he never quite denies committing, advising his listeners to come and join him in the woods rather than live under the laws; in the third poem, *The Man in the Moon*, the speaker is a village peasant who looks up at the full moon, thinks he sees a fellow peasant who has stolen thorns from a neighbor's hedge to patch holes in his own, deduces that this thief has been caught by the manorial hayward (hedge-guard), and shouts advice on how to handle the indictment: invite the hayward home, get him drunk and have a pretty woman seduce him, then by hook or crook get back from him the pledge to appear in manorial court which the hayward (the speaker assumes) has taken from the Moon Man. This is a sequence made for the thinking reader: first, standard courtly advice; next, a Falstaffian invitation to become a Robin Hood; finally, a parody of good advice shouted up to a fictional Man in the Moon by a peasant who knows how to get round manorial law by pimping and bribery.[12] It is a sequence like that in Petrus Alfonsus's *Disciplina Clericalis*, where stories that illustrate wise behaviour are followed by those that illustrate folly, or stories of bad women are followed by stories of good ones. It would not be a wise reader who took a single text as offering the only road for a reader to follow in this uncertain and varying world.

And finally, we may consider the historical dimension of this poem as it was copied in about 1341. In the years 1339–41 England was gripped by a national crisis at the beginning of the Hundred Years War. In particular, the years 1340–1 saw much royal use of the Trailbaston Statutes in order to try to raise funds desperately needed for the nearly bankrupt king to continue the war.[13] Several other poems in Harley MS 2253 show how bitterly the taxation, purveyances and all legal and financial machinery, including especially the Trailbaston courts, were used to squeeze the populace for its money and its produce to allow Edward III to prosecute his claim to the throne of France.[14] In this perspective, copying the *Song of Trailbaston* was an act by which a scribe in the Ludlow area once again gave a voice to the men whom the king needed on his side for his wars – those archers and soldiers capable of brave and dashing warfare, but also capable of brutal and violent behaviour at home. Sometimes the outlaw of one year might be the brave soldier of the next – or vice versa.[15]

TRANSLATION OF *THE OUTLAW'S SONG OF TRAILBASTON*

I've got the urge to put this story in rhyme
About a scheme they've cooked up in this land –
They'd better put this off to some other time,
Or God help us we'll have a war on our hands.

What I mean is these Trailbaston Statutes, now –
Except for the king, may God damn everybody
That first let such a Commission be allowed,
Whatever their reasons this is just plain shoddy.

Mister, if I want to give my page-boy a whack,
Or a swift kick or two by way of correction,
He'll have me arrested before I can turn my back,
And to get out of jail I'll need a huge ransom.

They'll take a year's earnings from me for fine,
Then the Sheriff comes round for his payoff too
Or he'll put me down where the sun never shines.
I ask you, gents, is that how they ought to do?

So I'll stay in the woods under fresh cool shade
Where there's no treachery nor twisting of laws –
In the Fantastic Forest,[1] where the jay flies by day
And the nightingale sings with never a pause.

But those evil bastards, may they never see their Saviour,
With their lying mouths they've got me indicted
For strongarm robberies and other bad behaviour
So I don't dare go see my friends for even a night.

I've served my Lord King in peace and in war,
In Flanders, Scotland, in Gascony his own land –
But now I can't raise the funds[2] to live any more:
I've wasted my time trying to please such a man!

If these lousy jurors don't get things under control
So I can ride or go as I please back where I belong,
If I get my hands on them their heads are going to roll.
They think threats scare me, they couldn't be more wrong.

Judge Martin, Judge Knoville, they're nice enough guys,
They pray for poor folks and hope they do well –
But those sadists Spigurnel and Belflour I do despise –
If I had them in my power there'd be no more to tell.

I'll teach them the game of Trailbaston all right –
I'll break their backs and hand them their ass in a sling,
Arms and legs too, it's no more than right –
I'll cut out their tongues and hear how they sing.[3]

Whoever on these things was the first to begin,
His life's not long enough for him to do penance –

I'll tell you the plain truth, it's too great a sin.
Men'll have to turn thieves to keep out of prison.

Some will be robbers who never would have been,
Too afraid of being jailed to come in and settle;
A man can't live without food now and then.
The guy that did this, he was sure in fine fettle.

Now monks and merchants, they really ought to curse
The entire bunch that got this Trailbaston passed –
Letters from the king himself won't be any worth
Till they bribe guys his letters should get them past.

So you that've been indicted, come out here with me,
To this green Fantastic Forest, there's no legal hassle
But only wild game and the shade-play of trees –
What could be dumber than a common-law battle?

If you know Latin and got a priestly cut on your hair,[4]
You'll be dragged before judges and indicted as clergy,
They'll haul you to prison under the Bishop's care,
And keep you there till you find some jurors to purge you.

They'll make you do penance, oh yes indeed –
And maybe you'll never get yourself freed.

That's why it's better to come live in the woods
Than lie chained up in the Bishop's slammer.
Such a long hard penance does nobody good –
You can get out from under, why wait for the hammer?

I once was naïve, now I'm stupid, I guess –
That's what lousy laws make me, shafting me this way.
I can't come in with my kinfolks to settle this mess.
Rich people pay ransoms, poor folks just dwindle away.

It's tough to put up for bail what you'll never redeem,
I mean a man's life, the thing that's most dear,
And I've got nothing else that a judge would esteem –
If they got me in their grip they'd hang me I fear.

Still I'll wait for a pardon, and hear what people say.[5]

Those that badmouth me never dare come around me –
They'd be happy to beat me the worst kind of way,
But God can save me if a thousand devils surround me.

Would that He who's the son of Mary would save me,
Because I'm not guilty, it's envy got me indicted –
God damn the man that put me in this hard place!
To trust this unstable world I'd be out of my mind.

If I run with a bunch and can send arrows where I please,
My neighbor goes around saying, 'Those guys are hoods,
Hanging out in the forest doing target practice on trees.
He lives his life like a pig out there in the woods.'[6]

But they, if I know more law than these guys,
Say, 'The plot thickens, a conspirator's at work,'[7]
And I better not go nearer home than 30 miles.
Great neighbors, these guys – shame on such jerks!

I ask all good people that you please pray for me
That I might in some way get back to my home.
I was never a murderer, or never meant to be,[8]
Nor a thief out of malice to do people harm.

This rhyme was made in the woods, under a laurel tree,
Where blackbird & nightingale sing & sparrowhawk flies,
It was written on parchment to keep in memory,
And thrown on the highway where a reader might find it.

5

FOUKE FITZ WARYN

Thomas E. Kelly

INTRODUCTION

Fouke fitz Waryn survives in a single manuscript, British Library, Royal MS 12.C.XII, dating from about 1330. Written in Anglo-Norman prose, the romance is one of sixty pieces in this trilingual miscellany. The other texts range from liturgical pieces, hymns to the Virgin, prophecies, mathematical puzzles, cooking recipes and medical notes to longer works such as the *Short English Metrical Chronicle*, the poem *Ami et Amile*, the *Mireour de Seint' Eglise* and the astrological treatise *Liber Experimentarius*.[1] It is exactly the kind of collection that you would expect a young nobleman to possess. The editors of the Anglo-Norman edition suggest that the book's compiler 'might have been a tutor in a great baronial household' and that he 'was a priest, probably a canon of Hereford and a follower of Adam de Orleton, bishop of Hereford 1317–27'.[2] The compiler was, in addition, very likely the 'author' of the prose version of *Fouke fitz Waryn*. There is strong evidence that he recast a late thirteenth-century poem on the same subject, as remnants or snippets of the original verse romance, now lost, can be detected throughout, especially in the two verse prophecies at the beginning and end. The editors of the Anglo-Norman edition conclude that the *remanieur* or adapter was 'an idealistic young man, a medieval "high churchman", with a firm conviction of the need for resistence, exile, and martyrdom in the ecclesiastical cause'.[3] He was also intensely local to the baronial cause in his devotion to Thomas of Lancaster, who was executed by Edward II in 1322 as a political martyr. His strong anti-royalist sentiments are clearly seen in his unflattering portrait of King John in *Fouke fitz Waryn*: 'he was a man without conscience, wicked, cross, and hated by all good people'.

As the literary product of a bilingual Anglo-Norman culture, *Fouke fitz Waryn* would have been largely intelligible to an educated audience. However, a version in Middle English alliterative verse did exist, now unfortunately lost except for a prose synopsis or summary by John Leland, the sixteenth-century Tudor antiquary. This work, entitled 'Thinges excerpted owte of an old Englisch boke yn Ryme of the Gestes of Guarine, and his Sunnes', abridges the Middle English poem up to Fouke's adventures in Cartagena, at which point there was apparently a hiatus, which forced Leland to supply the ending from the same thirteenth-century romance used by the scribe/adapter of the prose version.[4] The existence of a vernacular version of the romance not only would attest to its popularity but would increase the odds that it was known by the yeoman minstrels of the Robin Hood tradition.

History of the Welsh March

The romance opens with a somewhat garbled account of how William the Conqueror attempted to pacify the Welsh borders 'by giving the March lands to his most valiant knights'. While it is historically accurate that he settled Roger of Montgomery in Shrewsbury (Shropshire) in 1071, the account of his distribution of lands to the Fitz Aleyns (Oswestry), Waryn de Metz (Alberbury) and the Peverels (Whittington) is erroneous – these grants were actually made in the reign of Henry I (1100–35).[5] The story then focuses on the two fortuitous marriages of the Fitz Waryns to landed heiresses: Waryn de Metz marries the Peverel heiress, Melette, thereby gaining Whittington, and his son, Fouke le Brun marries Hawyse, the daughter of Joce de Dynan, gaining the castle and town of Ludlow in the bargain. In order to win the hand of Melette, Waryn de Metz enters a 'love' tourney and defeats the field. Likewise, Fouke le Brun, an untested youth of eighteen, displays his prowess by rescuing Joce de Dynan from an attack by his enemy Walter de Lacy; as a reward he is given Hawyse in marriage. Due to the treachery of Marion de la Bruere, however, Lacy and Ernalt de Lyls escape imprisonment and attack the castle of Dynan, burning the town. Waryn de Metz then dies, leaving the task of recapturing Dynan to his son and Sir Joce. In the meantime, William de Lacy has joined forces with Yervard, the Prince of Wales, and they successfully counter-attack, capturing Sir Joce and wounding Fouke. Meeting King Henry I at Gloucester, Fouke asks the king to intervene, and he orders Lacy to release his prisoners. Fouke, as constable of the English army, then defeats Yervard and a truce between the English and Welsh is arranged by the King of France. Yervard returns all of the lands he had seized, but he refuses to give up Fouke's ancestral home, Whittington. When King Henry concurs, he gives Fouke Alveston instead. Whittington then passes into the hands of Roger de Powys. As complicated as these events are, they are important for setting the stage for the remaining two-thirds of the romance – Fouke III's revenge against his family's enemies and his attempts to regain his property and inheritance.

The Outlaw Narrative

If the first third of *Fouke fitz Waryn* concerns the Norman settlement of the Welsh March, the feudal rivalries among the English barons, their various allies and the Welsh princes, and the dynastic relations gained through marriage and war, the last two-thirds focus on the life and adventures of Fouke le Brun's son, Fouke III. This section constitutes the core of the outlaw narrative:

1. The childhood fight with Prince John over a chess game.
2. King John's granting of his ancestral home, Whittington, to Morys fitz Roger.
3. The break with King John and subsequent outlawing.
4. The exile abroad in Brittany, France and Spain.
5. The return to England where he forms an outlaw gang with his brothers, Baldwin de Hodenet, the Cosham brothers and his right-hand man, John de Rampaigne.
6. The bases of operation in various forests throughout England.
7. The outlaw activities: robbing the king's merchants; ambushing the king's knights; killing or wounding those who pursue him.
8. The covert disguises as a monk, merchant and charcoal burner.
9. The tricks: shoeing his horse backwards to deceive those tracking him; switching identities with a captured king's knight.
10. The eventual inlawing through a royal pardon and the restoration of his property and inheritance.

Fouke's outlawry resembles Eric Hobsbawn's paradigm of the 'noble robber' in that he is forced into the status of a 'wolf's head' as the victim of injustice, not as the result of some criminal act.[6] To be sure, he commits real crimes – robbery and homicide – but they are done either in revenge or in self-defence. Fouke avenges King John's betrayal by harassing and killing the king's knights, including Morys de Powys. He also robs a caravan of merchants, but only when he discovers that they are carrying the king's property. And he does not keep the goods for himself, but 'everyone of his followers received a liberal share'. Fouke not only rights the wrongs done to him and his family but he helps others: he frees Robert fitz Sampson and his wife from a gang of outlaws; he convinces Llewelyn, Prince of North Wales, to seek peace rather than war; he rescues seven damsels from the clutches of an evil hag and her seven robber sons; he converts the Saracen King of Barbary to Christianity; and he kills a giant in Ireland, aiding the Earl of Chester in his conquests.

The 'Good Outlaw'

Fouke clearly represents the 'good outlaw', which at first sight appears to be a contradiction in terms. As Ingrid Benecke observes, the concept of the good outlaw 'poses an almost paradoxical problem' because the outlaws are not treated as common criminals but as heroes 'who prove themselves far superior to their opponents, in battle as well as in moral conflict'.[7] Fouke fights to regain his feudal lands and rights against a corrupt monarch who illegally disinherited, outlawed and pursued him. The primary mission of the good outlaw is 'to reestablish moral order in feudal society through his victory over his unjust lord and king' (Benecke, p. 159). Fouke's actions, furthermore, reveal him to be an ideal vassal 'according to the moral code of feudal chivalry, a fact, which can be confidently stated after consulting the law books of the time or Magna Carta or even the much earlier *Policraticus* by John of Salisbury' (Benecke, p. 159). That King John's actions are illegal is clearly seen in article two of Magna Carta: 'If any of our earls or barons or others holding of us in chief by knight service dies, and at his death his heir be of full age and owe relief he shall have his inheritance on payments of the old relief, namely the heir or heirs of an earl £100 for a whole earl's barony . . .'.[8] As the editors of the Anglo-Norman edition point out, Fouke III revived the claims of his family for possession of Whittington upon the accession of King John by offering a fine of £100, but the king ignored the request, giving Whittington to Morys fitz Roger de Powys for 50 marks.[9] Thus, Fouke's rebellion against King John is 'perfectly legitimate, that is, in accordance with a vassal's right of insurrection against an unjust feudal lord' (Benecke, p. 157).

As evidenced by the two verse prophecies and the divinely-inspired vision in *Fouke fitz Waryn*, Fouke has a moral right to rebel as well. In the first prophecy, Geomagog, the demonic spirit, foretells that Payn Peverel's descendants will rule Whittington. He predicts that the Wolf (Fouke III) will drive away the Wild Boar (Morys of Powys) and as a result the Leopard (King John) will come into conflict with the Wolf. In the second prophecy, Merlin announces that the Wolf will chase the Leopard from Whittington. Fouke's superior moral status is further seen in the divine vision that he receives at the end of the work: 'God has granted to you, His vassal, a penance which is of greater worth to you here than elsewhere.' Implicit here is a theory of natural law concerning the limits of sovereignty and a justification for political disobedience and resistance. Although Fouke is guilty of rebellion against his secular lord, he is not obligated to obey King John because he has acted unjustly and against the common good. According to natural law theory as it was interpreted by the medieval canon lawyers, 'Politics are subordinate to Ethics.'[10]

Folklore

In addition to story elements concerning the history of the Welsh March and Fouke III's outlawry, there is a third layering of *matière* in *Fouke fitz Waryn*. The editors of the Anglo-Norman edition call it 'traditional folklore', but 'fairy romance' or 'marvels' would also be accurate. As John Stevens observes, the hero of romance must have worthy adversaries,[11] and, as seen above, Payn Peverel's defeat of the giant Geomagog not only enhances his chivalric reputation but marks him as God's favourite in his battle with supernatural evil. As the descendant of Payn Peverel, Fouke III is destined to be tested by many marvellous creatures when he sails in exile 'round the seven islands of the ocean'. Landing on an unnamed island beyond Scotland, he encounters an old hag and her seven churlish sons who have kidnapped and ravished seven damsels. After killing the churls and their robber gang, Fouke rescues the ladies and returns them safely to their home on Orkney. Fouke then sails for Sweden where he battles four-legged serpents and a venomous beast with a dog's head, goat's beard and hare's ears. Blown away by a storm at sea, Fouke then finds himself in Cartagena (Spain), a wasteland due to the devastations caused by a flying dragon, who has carried off the daughter of the duke of Cartagena. Upon locating the maiden Ydoyne imprisoned in the dragon's lair, Fouke battles the monster with great difficulty but finally subdues it. In another episode, Fouke, who is sleeping alone on his ship, is blown away by a wind to the land of Barbary in north Africa. Surrounded by the soldiers of the Saracen king of Barbary, Fouke bravely defends himself but is wounded and captured. His wound is tended by the king's sister, Isorie, who informs him that her brother is engaged in a war with the Christian queen of Cartagena, Ydoyne, daughter of the now deceased duke. To settle the dispute, Ydoyne proposes a battle of champions and she begs Fouke to undertake the challenge. Fouke agrees on the condition that the Saracen king renounce Islam, undergo baptism and become a Christian. During the fierce battle with the opposing champion, Fouke discovers that his adversary is none other than his brother, Philip the Red, and the fight is stopped. The Saracen king is then converted to Christianity and marries Ydoyne.

While these exotic encounters with fabulous beasts, hags and giants may seem incongruous in a work purporting to be 'historical', they serve several important thematic purposes – elevating Fouke to the status of a hero with supernormal powers and allegorizing him as the *miles Christi* or Christian knight defeating the powers of evil. The seafaring adventures are clearly indebted to medieval travel romances, such as *Mandeville's Travels*, whose roots are to be found in Greek and Roman literature such as Homer's *Odyssey*, Ctesias' *Indika*, the apocryphal 'Letter of Alexander to Aristotle on the Wonders of India' and Pliny the Elder's *Natural History*.[12] Several of Fouke's adversaries in fact reveal their ancestry as Marvels of the East. The dog-headed beast in Sweden, for instance, is no doubt related to the Plinian race known as Cynocephali or dog-headed carnivores. Likewise, the hideous giant, 'black and horrible, twelve feet taller than any other', Fouke defeats in Ireland is obviously related to the black Ethiopian giants in the Marvels tradition.[13]

Relation to Later Outlaw Tales

As Maurice Keen observes (p. 39), with *Fouke fitz Waryn* and *Eustache the Monk* 'Round Table romance' and 'stories of chivalrous brigandage' are beginning to part ways. In the later stories of Gamelyn, Robin Hood and Adam Bell 'chivalrous adventures in a world of enchantment find no place'. Gone are Merlin's prophecies, fights with marvellous beasts and rescues of damsels in distress. The Greenwood hero's world shrinks to more human proportions – counties instead of countries, *gestes* instead of *gestas* and commoners instead of counts. Despite these transformations, the core of the outlaw narrative remains pretty much the same. One can readily recognize the continuity of character types, incidents and themes. Some of the incidents in *Fouke fitz Waryn* and *A Gest of Robyn Hode* are, for example, too close to be accounted for by 'common tradition' or coincidence – the game of truth and consequences by which those who lie are robbed, while those who tell the truth keep their money; the trick of enticing the enemy into a forest trap by promising him a long-horned stag; the captured king or sheriff swearing an oath not to harm the outlaw and then breaking it; and the wounded sidekick begging the hero to kill him by cutting off his head. When we recall that a version of *Fouke fitz Waryn* existed in Middle English alliterative verse, it becomes easier to understand how these plot elements were known and repeated by later story-tellers.

Translator's Note

The present translation into modern English prose is based on the Anglo-Norman Text Society edition of the text established by E.J. Hathaway, P.T. Ricketts, C.A. Robson and A.D. Wilshire (Oxford, Blackwell, 1975). In order to provide context and flow for the modern reader, the translation consciously departs in many instances from the awkward sentence structure of the original. Many of the sentences are unusually long due to the author's predilection for co-ordinating conjunctions and redundant phrasing. The translation eliminates as much of the redundancy as possible without sacrificing meaning. In a number of instances sentence order is also changed for the purpose of narrative clarity.

TRANSLATION OF *FOUKE FITZ WARYN*

Introduction

Spring is the proper moment for us to remember the past. Especially appropriate are the months of April and May, when the meadows and the grass grow green again, and every living thing regains its power, beauty and strength.[1] When the hills and valleys echo with the sweet song of the birds, and all our hearts, moved by the season's beauty, soar upward with joy, that is the most fitting time for us to recollect the adventures and courageous deeds of our ancestors.[2] They toiled with honour, and loyalty guided their quest. To speak of such things now may be of great value to many of us.

William the Conqueror's expedition into Wales

My Lords, you have heard before now how William the Bastard, the Duke of Normandy, came to England with a large army and by sheer force of numbers conquered the whole country.[3] William slew King Harold [4] and had himself crowned in London. He then established peace and laws and divided the land among many of his loyal followers. At that time Owain Gwynedd was the Prince of Wales, a valiant warrior, much feared by King William.[5] This Owain had devastated all the March, and had laid waste to the countryside from Chester to Mount Gilbert.[6] The prince claimed the entire March as his own and appurtenant to the territory of Powys. This explains why, upon his arrival in Shrewsbury county, King William, dressed in full regalia, found all the towns from Chester to Shrewsbury burned to the ground.[7]

The prince retreated, for he dared not await the king. The king was very prudent, and decided he would give the March lands to the most valiant knights in his army. They could then be expected to defend the prince's March for their own benefit as well as for the honour of their lord the king. The king summoned Roger de Montgomery, to whom he very freely gave all the county of Shrewsbury, and at the same time naming him earl palatine, a title Roger retained all his life.[8] Just outside the city of Shrewsbury, Roger founded the Abbey of Saint Peter and endowed it very richly.[9] He also started construction on one castle at Bridgnorth[10] and another castle at Dynan;[11] but he did not finish them. [See plate 8.]

Subsequent grants by Henry the First

After the death of Roger, his son Robert de Bellême held the earldom of Shrewsbury; and his youngest son, Arnulf de Montgomery, had Pembroke.[12] These noblemen were overweening and very treacherous people who committed crimes against their lord, King Henry, son of William the Conqueror, brother of King William Rufus.[13] Contrary to the orders of King Henry, for example, they completed the castle of Bridgnorth. In retaliation, King Henry disinherited them, banished them forever and gave their lands to his knights. The castle of Ludlow and all the land thereabouts towards the River Corve, he gave to his knight, Sir Joce, who, as one of the honours related to the gift, took the surname of Dynan. Thenceforth he bore the title Joce de Dynan.[14] This Joce was a strong and valiant knight who finished the castle which Roger de Montgomery had begun in his time. The castle was built with three surrounding baileys, and Joce also had it encircled with a double ditch, one within and the other without. The town which is now called Ludlow was for a very long time called Dynan. Just below the town of Dynan, Joce had a limestone bridge built over the River Teme, on the high road which runs through the March from Chester to Bristol.

William the Conqueror's adventure at Castell Dinas Bran

As King William the Bastard drew near the mountains and the valleys of Wales he saw a very large town, formerly enclosed within high walls. Below the town, which was entirely burned out and in ruins, he set up his tents in a plain and stayed there that night. When the king queried a Briton as to the town's name and how it had come to be destroyed, the man replied: 'Sire, the castle was formerly Castell Bran, but it is now called La Vele Marche.[15] Long ago, Brutus, a very brave knight, came into this land along with Coryneus, from whom Cornwall derives its name, along with many others descended from the lineage of Troy.[16] At the time the only inhabitants in these parts were very ugly people, enormous giants, whose king was named Geomagog. When they heard of the arrival of Brutus, they set off in combat against him; but in the end all the giants were killed except Geomagog, who was wonderfully tall. The valiant Coryneus said that he would like to fight Geomagog himself, to test the giant's strength. At the first encounter the giant hugged Coryneus so tight that he broke three of his ribs. Coryneus became enraged and struck Geomagog so hard with his foot that he fell from a great rock into the sea where he drowned. The spirit of a devil forthwith entered into Geomagog's body, bringing him into these parts where his rule over the land was such that no Briton dared inhabit it for a long time. Many years after this King Bran fitz Donwal[17] rebuilt the town, repaired the walls, and cleared out the great ditches. He set up town life within the borough, including a great market-place; but the devil came by night and carried off all that was within. Since that time no one has dwelt there.'

Payn Peverel encounters Geomagog

Whereas the king was merely astonished at hearing the Briton's tale, Payn Peverel, the king's cousin, did more than just listen. This proud and bold knight declared that he would put the marvel to the test that very night. Payn Peverel armed himself very richly and took his shining gold shield with a cross of azure *dancetté*.[18] Accompanied by fifteen knights and other servants, he went to the highest palace and took up quarters there. When night came on the weather became so foul, so darkly overcast and there was such a storm of thunder and lightning that all who were there became terrified, to the point of being frozen by fear, unable to move either hand or foot. They lay flat on the ground like dead men. Payn, the proud, was scared too, but he put his trust in God, of whom he was wearing the sign of the cross. He could see that he would be aided by none but by God alone. He prostrated himself on the ground and prayed devoutly to God and his mother Mary, imploring them to defend him that night from the power of the Devil.

Payn's conversation with Geomagog

Scarcely had he finished his prayer when the Devil came in the shape of Geomagog. He was carrying a huge mace in his hand, and from his mouth he cast fire and smoke, thereby illuminating the whole town. Payn had deep trust in God; he signed himself with the sign of the cross and boldly attacked the evil spirit. The Devil raised his mace and aimed it at Payn, but he avoided the blow. By the power of the cross the Devil was filled with fear and he lost his strength, for he could not bear to touch the cross. Payn pursued him and struck him with his sword with the result that he began to cry out and fell flat on the ground, declaring himself beaten: 'Bold knight, you have overcome me, not by your own prowess, but by the virtue of the cross which you are holding.' 'Vile creature that you are, tell me', said Payn, 'who you are and what you are doing in this town. I charge you in the name of God and the Holy Cross.'

The evil spirit began to tell his story, word for word as the Briton had previously done. He said that after Geomagog died he gave up his soul to their lord Beelzebub, who entered immediately into the body of Geomagog. Under that guise he came into these parts to guard the great treasure which Geomagog had accumulated in this town and stored in a house which he had built underground. Payn asked him what kind of creature he was; and he said that he had formerly been an angel, but was now, as a consequence of his sin, a spirit of the Devil. 'Just what treasure did Geomagog have?' Payn inquired. 'He had oxen, cows, swans, peacocks, horses and all other kinds of animals cast in fine gold. There was also a golden bull, which in my opinion was his oracle, in whom he placed all his faith. This golden idol predicted for him all that was to happen. Twice a year the giants gathered to honour their god, that is the golden bull, for whom this great store of gold had been collected. Subsequently it came to pass that the whole of this country was called La Blanche Lande. I and my companions enclosed the plain with a high wall and a deep ditch, so that there was no entrance to it except through this town, which was inhabited by evil spirits. On this pasture land we regularly held jousts and tournaments; and many people came to witness these marvels, but not one of those spectators ever escaped. In due time a disciple of Jesus, named Augustine, arrived on the scene. By his preaching Augustine deprived us of many of our people. He baptized them, and had a chapel built in his name. Thereafter, great misfortune befell us'.

Geomagog's prophecy

'Now', said Payn, 'you shall tell me where the treasure which you have described is to be found.' Geomagog replied: 'Vassal, speak no further of that, for it is destined for others. But you yourself shall be lord of all this domain, and your descendants will continue to hold, not, however, without great strife and war.[19]

And from thy sleeve shall come forth
the Wolf who shall do marvels.
He shall have sharp teeth,
and shall be known by all.
He shall be so bold and so proud
that he will drive away the Wild Boar
from the *Blanche Lande*,
such shall be his great power.
The Leopard shall chase the Wolf
and shall threaten his tail.
The Wolf shall leave the woods and the mountains;
he shall remain in the water wherein we fish.
He shall cross the sea
and shall entirely surround this island.
Finally, the Leopard shall conquer.
by his craft and by his art.
He shall come into this plain
and shall take up his hiding place in the water.'

When the spirit had finished his prophecy he departed from the body. Such terror came to him that Payn thought death was upon him. When the fear finally passed, the night grew clear and the fine weather returned. The knights and the others who had been terrified rose to their feet again, much astonished at the adventure which had befallen them. The next day the affair was reported to the king and the whole army. The king had the body of Geomagog carried off and thrown into a deep well just outside the town. So great was this marvellous event, however, that the king kept the Devil's club and showed it for a long time thereafter to many people.

William's grants of lands in Wales

The king then set forth into the region adjoining the Blanche Lande.[20] A Briton named Meredith ap Bleddyn was the former owner of this land, within which there was a castle named Croes Oswallt, presently called Oswestry. The king summoned a knight named Alan fitz Flaald and gave him the castle as well as all the feudal rights connected with it. All the great lords of England who have the surname of Fitz Aleyn are descended from this same Alan, who afterwards greatly enlarged the castle.

The king crossed the River Severn, and saw that the surrounding country was beautiful. He summoned a knight, born in Lorraine, in the city of Metz, who was renowned for his strength, his good looks and his breeding. To this knight, whose banner bore two gold peacocks on red silk, the king gave Alberbury along with all the appurtenant rights.[21] Finally, the king called Payn Peverel and gave him

Blanche Lande, with its forest, waste lands, chases and all the surrounding country. On that spot there was a mound surrounded by marsh land and water. On that height, which was called the Berth, Payn built a tall, strong tower. A river named after Payn Peverel runs nearby. It was once called the River Peverel, but the name was later changed to the River Perry.

And so it was that the king gave all the lands, unenclosed hunting grounds and fiefs, from Chester to Bristol, to his best and most trusted knights. When the king had thus settled his lands he returned to London, and from London to Normandy, where he died. William the Red, his son, reigned after him in England, and after him Henry, his younger brother. The latter subsequently kept Robert Curthose, his elder brother, in prison all his life.[22] But for now I will not tell you the reason for Henry's action.

William Peverel and his two nieces

Afterwards it happened that Payn Peverel died in his castle in the Peak, and William Peverel, his sister's son, became Payn's sole heir.[23] This William by force of arms afterwards conquered the whole territory surrounding the River Morlas and as far as the River Dee, Ellesmere, Maelor Saesneg and Nanheudwy.[24] William also built a tower in the Blanche Lande, which he called Blanchetour, and the town nearby is still named Blancheville, or, in English: Whittington.[25] He built another tower in Ellesmere,[26] and a third over the River Ceiriog.[27]

William had two beautiful nieces: Eleyne, the elder, and Melette, the younger.[28] He married off Eleyne to one of the Fitz Aleyns. As a dowry he gave her all the land of Morlas as far as the River Ceiriog. Melette was by far the more beautiful of the two sisters. Because of her beauty she was much desired, William reasoned with his niece and asked her to tell him whether there were any knight in the country whom she was willing to take as her husband. If there were not one to be found, he promised he would help her to the best of his ability. She told her uncle that there was in fact no one acceptable to her as a mate. 'Surely, sire, there is not a knight in all the world whom I would take either for his riches or for the honour of his lands. But if ever I have a husband, he shall be handsome, courteous and accomplished, as well as being the most valiant in all Christendom. I care little for riches and I might add that the only true wealth is to have what the heart longs for.' When William heard this he smiled and said, 'My dear niece, you have indeed spoken well. I will do my best to find you just such a husband. Moreover, I will give you Blanchetour, with all that belongs to it, including all the feudal rights appurtenant to it. For a woman who has land in fee is always more desirable.'

A tournament at Peverel castle

Then William sent forth a proclamation throughout many lands and cities that all brave knights who wished to tourney 'for love' [*pour amour*] should come to castle Peverel in the Peak on the feast of Michaelmas (29 September). The knight who should perform the best and win the tournament should have as his prize the love of Melette of the Blanchetour. He would thereby also become lord and master of Blancheville and have all the feudal rights to the domain. This proclamation was published at once in many lands. A valiant nobleman, Waryn de Metz, had neither wife nor child; but he wrote to his cousin John, Duke of Brittany, concerning the full import of this proclamation, asking for his aid in this matter. This duke himself had ten sons who were all knights, the fairest and the most courageous in all Brittany. Roger was the eldest, and his brothers were named Howel, Audwyn, Urien, Thebaud, Bertrem, Amys, Gwychard, Gyrard and Guy. In response to his cousin's request, the duke sent all ten of his sons, along with one hundred knights, well mounted and all prepared with excellent equipment. Waryn de Metz received them with great honour. Aeneas, son of the King of Scots, came with the Earl of Murray and the Bruces, Dunbars, Umfrevilles and two hundred knights. Owain, Prince of Gwynedd came with two hundred knights, and the duke of Burgundy with three hundred. Ydromor, son of the King of Galloway, came with one hundred and fifty knights. As for the knights of England, they were reckoned at three hundred. [See plate 9.]

Waryn de Metz distinguishes himself

Waryn de Metz and his company pitched their tents in the forest, near where the tournament was to be held. They were well clad in red samite, and their horses were entirely covered to the ground in battle array. Waryn himself wore a helmet with a gold crest, in order to hide his identity. Then tabors, trumpets, pipes and Saracen horns blared forth, so that the valleys re-echoed with the sound, following which the tournament began in earnest. Knights were to be seen thrown from their warhorses, many a hard blow given, many a stroke to the neck.

Accompanied by many ladies the damsel had gone up into a tower, from which vantage point they could see this fine gathering of knights, and how each conducted himself. I do not care to describe the blows and the conduct of the knights, but Waryn de Metz and his company were that day regarded as the best, the handsomest and the most valiant. Of all of them Waryn was the most esteemed on all counts. It began to grow dusk; and the tourney could not continue into the night. The knights went to their quarters. Waryn and his company went secretly to their tents in the forest, where they disarmed themselves and made great joy. None of the other great lords knew what had become of them, or where they were, so quietly did they keep to themselves and remained unknown to all the others at the tourney.

The following day a joust was proclaimed throughout the land. Thereupon Waryn came out of the forest and went to the joust clad all in green with ivy leaves, like an adventurous knight, unrecognized by anyone. When the duke of Burgundy saw him he attacked immediately, striking him a great stroke with his lance. Waryn returned the blow, then struck a second and third time with the result that the duke fell from his horse in the midst of the place. Melette of the Blanchetour sent him her glove, and asked him to defend her. He said he would do his best. Then, having returned to the forest, he put on his red armour, and came with his companions into the field. He was the victor in the tournament, and held the field against all who came there. Thereupon it was decided among all the great lords, the heralds and the judges that Waryn, who was the adventurous knight, rightly deserved to have the prize for the tourney along with Melette of the Blanchetour. With great joy he took her, and the damsel took him. So they sent for the bishop, who in the presence of all married them. William Peverel gave a very sumptuous feast at the marriage.

When the feast broke up Waryn took his wife accompanied by all his men and they went to Blancheville. They remained there for forty days in great joy. Then the ten brothers and their hundred knights returned to Brittany. But Guy, the youngest brother, came back into England, and by the power of his sword won many fair lands. He was called Guy le Estrange, and from his lineage all the great lords in England who have the surname of Estrange are descended.

War between Waryn de Metz and the Welsh

Waryn de Metz held the lordship of Blancheville for a long time with great honour. But Yervard, son of Yweyn, Prince of Wales, did him great harm, slew his people and destroyed his lands.[29] They fixed a day for battle, in which many a good man lost his life. Finally, Yervard had the worst of it, for he lost many of his men. He left the field and fled in dishonour. Then Waryn sent a strong and brave knight, Guy, the son of Candelou de Porkington, to guard the honour of Blancheville and his other lands.[30]

Birth of Fouke le Brun

It so happened that the lady became pregnant. When she was delivered, at the time which God had appointed, they called the child Fouke. When the boy was seven years old they sent him to Joce de Dynan to be instructed and brought up, for Joce was an experienced knight.[31] Joce received him with much honour and great affection, and brought him up in his house with his own two children. The younger of his daughters was the same age as Fouke and she was called Hawyse. The elder was named Sibylle. At that time there was a great disagreement and war between Sir Joce de Dynan and Sir Walter de Lacy, who resided much of the time in Ewyas. Because of this strife many a good knight and many an honest man lost his life, for each of the two lords attacked his neighbours, burned their lands and robbed their people, and did much other mischief. When Fouke was eighteen years old he had grown up handsome, strong and tall.

Fight between Joce de Dynan and Walter de Lacy

One summer's day Sir Joce rose early in the morning. He climbed a tower in his castle in order to survey the country and, looking towards the mountain called Whitcliffe, he saw the fields covered with knights, squires, foot soldiers and fighting men. Some were armed and on horseback, others were on foot. He heard the horses neigh and saw the helmets shining. Among them he perceived the banner of Sir Walter de Lacy, shining with new gold, on which was a fess gules.[32] Then he summoned his knights, and commanded them to mount their warhorses, to take their crossbow men and archers, and to go to the bridge below the town of Dynan. They were to guard the bridge and the ford, so that none should pass. Sir Walter and his people expected to pass in safety; but Sir Joce's people drove them back; and many on both sides were wounded and slain. Then Sir Joce came with his banner entirely of argent, with three lions azure passant, crowned or. Accompanying him were five hundred knights and followers, on horseback and on foot, in addition to the townsmen and their servants, who were good men. Thereupon Joce crossed the bridge with great force, and the two armies engaged in hand-to-hand combat. With his lance Joce pierced Godebrand, who was carrying the Lacy banner, through the body. Thus Lacy lost his banner as the two troops attacked each other, and many were killed on both sides. But Lacy had the worst of it, for he fled in defeat, and he made his way alongside the River Teme.

Joce in great danger

The lady with her daughters and her other damsels had climbed a turret, from where they had a good view of the fight. They prayed devoutly to God to save their lord and his people from hurt and danger. Joce de Dynan recognized Walter de Lacy by his coat of arms, and saw that he was running away all alone, for he was greatly afraid of losing his life. He spurred on his horse, and passed mountains and valleys. In a short time he overtook Lacy in a valley beneath the woods near Champ Geneste,[33] where he ordered him to turn around. Seeing no one but Sir Joce, Lacy turned very boldly, and they exchanged fierce blows, for neither man thought of sparing the other. They exchanged great and heavy blows.

Joce, thinking that the fight was lasting too long, raised his sword angrily and gave Lacy such a blow on the shield that he split it in two, inflicting a severe wound on the left arm. Joce assaulted him eagerly, and had nearly taken him when Sir Godard de Bruz and two knights with him came to Lacy's aid. Sir Godard and his companions attacked Sir Joce on every side very boldly, and he defended himself like a lion against them.

Joce is rescued by Fouke le Brun

The lady and her daughters in the tower seeing their lord hard pressed, could scarce endure it. They cried, swooned and made great lamentation, for they never expected to see their lord alive again. Fouke fitz Waryn had been left in the castle, for he was only eighteen years old. Hearing the shouts in the tower, he went up in haste, and saw his lady and all the others in tears. He went to Hawyse and asked her what was the matter, and why she looked so downcast. 'Hold your tongue,' said she. 'You are very unlike your father. He is bold and hardy, but you are a coward and will always be one. Do you not see that my lord, who has always treated you kindly and brought you up gently, is in danger of death for want of help? And you, wicked young man, are running up and down here, without a care.' The lad grew quite red with anger at her reproof, and quickly left the tower.

In the hall he found a rusty old hauberk, put it on as he best could, and took a heavy Danish axe in his hand. He went into a stable near the postern which leads to the river, and there he found a packhorse which he mounted forthwith. Going out by the postern he quickly crossed the river, and came into the field where his lord had been knocked from his steed and was at the point of being killed had the lad not arrived in time. Fouke had only a shabby helmet, which barely covered his shoulders. The moment he arrived on the scene, with his axe he struck Godard de Bruz, who had seized his lord, and cut the spine of his back in two halves, after which he helped his lord to remount his horse. Fouke turned to Sir Andrew de Preez, and with his hatchet gave him such a blow on his helmet of polished steel that he split him down to the teeth. Sir Ernalt de Lyls saw that there was no way he could escape, for he was badly wounded; so he gave himself up to Sir Joce. Lacy defended himself, but in short order he too was captured.

Walter de Lacy and Ernalt de Lyls taken as prisoners

Now Sir Walter de Lacy was taken prisoner and Sir Ernalt de Lyls with him, and they were led across the river to the castle of Dynan. Then Sir Joce said, 'Friend burgess, you are very strong and valiant, and had it not been for you I should have soon been dead. I am much indebted to you now and for ever. You shall stay with me, and I will never fail you.' Joce believed that he was a burgess, for in fact the townsmen had taken up arms, and those which the lad was wearing were rusty and shabby. Then the youth answered and said, 'Sir, I am no burgess, do you not know me? I am Fouke whom you have reared.' 'Fair son, blessed be the day when I reared you, for the work done for a good man is never wasted.' Then they took Sir Walter and Sir Ernalt to a tower called Pendover, and their wounds were attended to there. They were guarded with great honour, and each day the lady and her daughters comforted and solaced Sir Walter and Sir Ernalt de Lyls.

Marion de la Bruere frees the two prisoners

Sir Ernalt was a handsome youth, and he became deeply smitten with love for Marion de la Bruere, a very gentle damsel, who was the principal waiting woman of the lady of Dynan castle. Sir Ernalt and the damsel spoke to each other frequently, for it was her daily custom to come into the tower with her mistress to comfort Sir Walter de Lacy and Sir Ernalt. When he saw the opportunity Sir Ernalt spoke with the damsel, and told her that he loved her more than anything in the world. So deeply was he taken with the love of her that he could have no rest, day or night, unless she would consent to him, for she could give him relief from all these miseries. If she would do this, he would of his own free will make a formal promise never to love any other woman except herself alone. As soon as he was set free he would take her for his wife. The damsel heard his fair promise and consented to do as he wished in all things, and took assurance from him that he would keep his promise to her. The damsel promised to help them secretly in all respects, so that they should be delivered from prison. She took towels and sheets which she carried to the tower where she sewed them together and with them she lowered Sir Walter and Sir Ernalt down from the tower. She asked them to keep faith and the promise which they had given her. They told her that they would behave faithfully towards her without violating any covenant, and they commended her to God.

Sir Walter and Sir Ernalt return to Ewyas

All alone and on foot Sir Walter and Sir Ernalt went their way. By daybreak they arrived at Ewyas, Sir Walter de Lacy's castle. When the people saw that their lord had returned safe and sound, there was no need to ask whether they were happy, for they thought they had lost him for ever.

Joce discovers the escape

Joce de Dynan arose in the morning and within the castle went to his chapel, which was built and dedicated in honour of Mary Magdalene, the day of the dedication of which is Saint Cyriac, with seventy days of pardon.[34] He heard God's service, after which he went up into the highest tower, the one within the third bailey of the castle, now called by many people Mortimer's Tower. It is called Mortimer's Tower because one of the Mortimers was held prisoner in it for a good while. Joce surveyed the country, and saw nothing out of the ordinary. When he came down he ordered the horn to be blown summoning the people to wash. He sent for his prisoner, Sir Walter, for he did him such honour that he would never wash nor eat without him. They searched everywhere for the prisoners, but all to no avail, for they had escaped. Sir Joce gave no indication that he regretted their departure and took no notice of it.

Joce and Walter are reconciled

Sir Walter determined that he would have his revenge or die, so he sent for his people from Ireland. He took on mercenaries, knights and others, with the result that between Sir Walter and Sir Joce hard battles and heavy fighting ensued. The earls and the barons of England saw the great toll in lives and the harm that had been committed, all of which went on day after day. So they fixed a love-day[35] between Sir Walter and Joce, with the result that all grievances were redressed and the parties finally reached agreement. The two enemies embraced each other in the presence of the great lords.

Fouke le Brun marries Hawyse

Joce de Dynan sent his letters to Fouke's father, Waryn de Metz, and Melette, his good lady. The child Fouke had dark eyes, and for that reason many people later called him Fouke le Brun. Waryn and Melette and other great people came to the castle of Dynan, and were received with great honour and joy. They remained there for a week. Joce spoke to Waryn very courteously, and said to him, 'Sir, you have here a son whom I have reared for you. I trust he will be a good and valiant man; and he will be your heir, if he survives you. I have two daughters who will be my heirs; and if it please you I should like that we be allied by marriage. In that case we need have little fear of any great lord in England, and our cause will be maintained by right and reason. If you will so consent, it is my wish that Fouke le Brun should marry Hawyse, my younger daughter, who shall be the heir of half of all my land.' Waryn thanked him greatly for his good offer, and said that he would freely grant everything he asked. On the following day they sent to Hereford for the bishop, Robert of ——. [36] The bishop came and married them with great honour. Joce held a great feast that lasted a fortnight.

Joce leaves Dynan Castle

When the feasting ended, Joce and Sir Waryn went to Hartland with their household, for they wished to remain there awhile.[37] Marion de la Bruere pretended to be ill and kept to her bed. She said that she was so sick she could not even turn herself except with the greatest difficulty. So she stayed behind in the castle of Dynan. Joce gave orders that she should be waited on according to her desires. For fear of Lacy and the others, he hired thirty knights and seventy soldiers and servants, and gave them his castle to watch over until his return to the country.

Marion invites Ernalt to visit her

The day after Joce's departure Marion sent her messenger to Sir Ernalt de Lyls, and asked him, for the great love which was between them, not to forget the agreements which they had made to each other. He was invited to come in haste to speak to her at the castle of Dynan, for the lord and the lady along with the greater part of their household had gone to Hartland. She added that he should come to the same place in the castle through which he had recently departed. When Sir Ernalt had heard his beloved lady's message, he immediately sent back the same messenger, and requested that Marion, for his love, measure the highest of the windows through which he had lately left the castle. She was also to send him back that information by the said messenger, as well as details as to how many and what kind of people the lord had left behind him in his household. Having no suspicion of treason, the damsel took a silk thread, and let it fall from the window to the ground. The measurement and all the other requested information concerning the castle were sent to Sir Ernalt. In turn, Sir Ernalt sent a message back to his beloved that on the fourth day, before the hour of midnight, he would be with her at the same window through which he had departed. He prayed her to await him there.

Ernalt induces Walter to join his plot

Sir Ernalt de Lyls had a ladder of leather made; it was of the same length as the silken thread which his lady had sent him. Then Sir Ernalt went to see his lord, Sir Walter de Lacy. He told him that Fouke, the son of Waryn de Metz, had married Hawyse, the daughter of Sir Joce de Dynan, and that Sir Waryn and Sir Joce, having left a garrison in the castle of Dynan, had gone to Hartland. They went there in search of soldiers, and to gather together an army and a countless number of people. 'And when all the army is assembled, they will immediately come to Ewyas, and will burn and seize your lands. If they catch you, you will be cut up into little pieces, and you and yours will be disinherited for ever. She who sent me this message is someone whom you know well, for she knows the truth, and has heard it.' When Sir Walter heard the news he became quite pale with anguish, and said, 'In truth I could not have believed that Sir Joce would do such treachery, since we have been reconciled, and have embraced each other in the presence of many people. I would hate to have our peers say that the accord had been broken on my part, while Sir Joce is considered a loyal knight.' 'Sir,' said Sir Ernalt, 'you are my lord, I am only warning you of the possible harm that can come to you, for I know the truth through her who heard the plan. Do not tell me afterwards that I knew of your danger and would not warn you of it, or that I have broken my pledge of loyalty.' Sir Walter became very thoughtful, and did not know what to do about the matter. Finally he said to Sir Ernalt: 'What do you advise me to do?' 'Sir,' said he, 'you will do well to follow my advice. I will myself go with my men, and we will take the castle of Dynan by ruse. When Sir Joce has lost his stronghold he will trouble you the less and will abandon his project. Consequently, you will have had your revenge for the disgrace which he has so often done us. And sir, remember that by right or by wrong it is a duty to avenge one's self on one's enemy.' Sir Walter placed himself entirely at the disposal of Sir Ernalt, believing that all that he had said was the truth. But he lied like a false knight.

Sir Ernalt got his large company ready. What with knights, squires and men-at-arms, he had more than a thousand in his company. He came to the castle of Dynan by night, and had one part of his company remain in the wood near Whitcliffe, and another part was to lie in ambush in the gardens below the castle. The night was very dark, so they were not noticed by the sentry nor anyone else. Sir Ernalt took with him a squire who carried the leathern ladder, and they went to the window where Marion was waiting for them. Never had she been so happy as when she saw them. She dropped down a cord and drew up the leathern ladder, which she fastened to a crenel of the wall. Ernalt went up into the tower easily and nimbly, and took his love in his arms and kissed her. They made great joy and went into another chamber, where they had supper and then went to bed. And they let the ladder hang there.

Dynan castle taken by Lacy's men

The squire who had carried the ladder went to fetch the knights and the main company who were hidden in the lord's garden and elsewhere, and brought them to the ladder. A hundred well-armed men went up by the ladder of leather, and descending from the tower of Pendover went along by the wall behind the chapel. There they found the watchman dozing off, for he had become cowardly on the approach of death. They quickly seized him and would have thrown him down from his tower into the deep ditch. He cried for mercy, and requested them to let him blow a note on his horn before his death, and they consented. But he did this in order that the knights inside the castle should be on their guard. All, however, was in vain. The more he blew his horn the more the knights and men-at-arms were cut to pieces. They screamed and cried in their beds that God might have pity on them. But Sir Ernalt's companions were without pity, for all that were within they put to a cruel death. Many a sheet which had been white in the evening was dyed red with blood. As a final deed they threw the watchman into the deep ditch and broke his neck.

Marion de la Bruere kills Sir Ernalt

Marion de la Bruere lay in bed beside her lover Sir Ernalt, and knew nothing of the treason which Sir Ernalt had done. Hearing a great noise in the castle she arose from her bed and looked down into the castle. She heard the noise and the cry of the wounded and saw armed knights and shining helmets and hauberks. She immediately perceived that Sir Ernalt had deceived and betrayed her. At that she began to weep very tenderly and said piteously, 'Alas, that I was ever born of mother, for by my misdeeds my lord, Sir Joce, who has brought me up so gently, has lost his castle and his good men. Had it not been for me, nothing would have been lost. Alas, that I ever trusted this knight, for by his flattery has he deceived me, and alas, my lord also, which means even more to me.' Weeping, Marion, drew Sir Ernalt's sword and said, 'Awake, sir knight, for you have brought a company of strangers into my lord's castle without permission. If you, sir, and your squire had been sheltered by me, the others who have been let in by your means would not have been here. Since you have deceived me, you cannot reasonably blame me if I pay you back according to your desert. You shall never boast to any other woman friend of yours that by my treachery you got possession of the castle and lands of Dynan.' The knight sat up; and Marion, with the drawn sword held in her hand, ran him through the body. The knight died immediately. Marion well knew that if she were taken she would be delivered to an evil death. Not knowing what to do she threw herself from a window which opened out towards Linney and broke her neck.

The town of Dynan sacked and burned

The knights within the castle unfastened the gates and went into the town. They opened the gates of Dynan towards the river and let all their people come in. At the end of every street in the town they placed a number of men and set the town on fire. In each street they made two fires. The inhabitants and the guards of the town, when they saw the fire arose from their beds, but did not know what to do. For all of them were nearly out of their wits. Lacy's knights and squires fell upon them and hacked them to pieces and killed them in great numbers. The townspeople could not defend themselves. All of them who were found were cut down or burned alive in the fire. As they went up the alleys the young girls saw their fathers and their brothers lying murdered in the streets. They knelt, they asked for mercy, they begged for their lives. All this was for naught, as the story tells us; men, women and children were all killed, young and old, either by sword or by fire. At last day came, and then they sent for their lord to come with all his armed forces to the castle of Dynan. And so he did, he who had once been a prisoner there. He placed his banner on the Pendover tower as a sign of the victory he had gained, but the town and all that was in it was burned to black cinders.

Sir Joce and his friends try to recover the castle

When the news came to Sir Joce and Waryn de Metz they were very sorrowful, sad and dejected. From everywhere they summoned their relatives, friends and their own people, with the result that within a month they had seven thousand well-armed troops. They came to Castle Key, which is built upon a hill, one league away from Dynan. But at that time Castle Key was old, and the gates were rotten, for no one had inhabited it for the past hundred years. Key, the seneschal of Sir Arthur the king, had built it, and the whole area belonged to it. The place name still remains, for the people of that country call it Keyenhom. The next day Joce and Waryn and Fouke le Brun, with their troops, came to the castle of Dynan and attacked it very eagerly on all sides. Sir Walter and his knights very boldly defended the crenels and the walls. Afterwards Sir Walter and his Irish men came out of the castle and made a bold attack on those who were outside. Joce, Waryn and Fouke assailed them on all sides and slew them in great numbers. The Irish men lay cut down in the meadows and gardens, so much so that Sir Walter and his men had the worst of it. He and his people withdrew and entered the castle and defended the walls. If they had remained outdoors longer they would have soon heard very unpleasant news. Sir Joce and Sir Waryn returned to their lodgings and disarmed themselves; and when they had eaten they rejoiced among themselves. The next day they attacked the castle very eagerly on all sides, but they could not take it. As many as they encountered on the outside, however, they cut them down. This siege lasted for a long time. [See plate 10.] Then afterwards it happened that by the consent of a king of England, the gates of the castle, which were triple, were set fire to and burned. The fire was fed with bacon and grease, and the tower over the gate was burned on the inside. The high tower in the third bailey of the castle (which was so strong and so well built that up to that point in time no one knew any stronger or better one in existence) was in great part demolished, and that bailey almost completely destroyed.

Death of Sir Waryn de Metz

Sir Waryn became ill and took leave of Sir Joce, and with only one squire went to Alberbury, where he died. When his father was dead Fouke le Brun came to Alberbury, and took the homage and fealty of all his father's tenants. After taking his leave of Melette, his mother, and Hawyse his wife, he returned to Sir Joce and told him what had become of his father. Joce was very sad at the news.

Walter de Lacy asks for help from the Welsh

Sir Walter was very sad and angry that he had lost his troops, and he was in great fear of being conquered and vanquished. So he carefully planned a scheme. He sent a letter to Yervard Droyndoun, Prince of Wales, as his lord, friend and relative.[38] In that letter he told him that 'William Peverel, who holds Maelor in Ellesmere, is dead.' He said further that 'these lands are of his lordship and appurtenant to Powys. And Sir William holds them wrongfully as a gift of the King of England, but the king will seize them for his own. If he does this he will be a very bad neighbour to you, for he has no great love for you. Sire, come, therefore, and claim your right. And if you please, have the goodness to send me help, for I am harshly besieged in the castle of Dynan.'

Prince of Wales besieges Sir Joce

Yervard, when he had heard this news, assembled more than twenty thousand Welsh, Scots and Irish, and hastened towards the March. He burned the towns and robbed the people; and his troops were so great in number that the country could not withstand them. Joce was wary and caught sight of the approach of Yervard. He and his people, along with Fouke, armed themselves and boldly attacked Roger de Powys and his brother Jonas, who came in the vanguard of Yervard's army. They killed many of them. Roger and Jonas could not withstand the attack and fell back. Thereupon Yervard came armed (his arms were or and gules quartered, and in each quarter a leopard) and assailed Sir Joce and Fouke. They defended themselves for a long time and killed many of their people, but their assailants were in such great numbers that Sir Joce could not sustain the attack. He returned to Castle Key, a league's distance from Dynan. But it turned out badly for him, for he had lost many of his people.

Yervard and Lacy, who were thus delighted, pursued Sir Joce and Fouke, besieged them in the castellet and attacked them vigorously. Joce, Fouke and their knights defended their weak and old castellet, without food or drink, for three days against the entire army. On the fourth day Sir Joce said that it would be greater honour for them to leave the castle and die on the field with honour than to die of hunger in the castle with dishonour. They came into the field forthwith, and on their first approach they killed more than three hundred knights, squires and foot soldiers. Yervard Droyndoun and Lacy, with their people, assailed Sir Joce and his followers, who defended themselves like lions. But so many set upon them that they could not hold out for long. For Sir Joce's horse was killed and he himself was badly wounded. As for his knights some were taken prisoners and some killed.

Sir Joce taken prisoner and Fouke wounded

Then they took Sir Joce and his knights and sent them to be imprisoned in the castle of Dynan, there where he used to be lord and master. When Fouke saw Sir Joce taken and led away he nearly went mad with sorrow and anger. He goaded his horse with his spurs, and with a lance struck one of the knights who was carrying Joce away, piercing the knight through his body. Then Owen Cyfeiliog, a bold and proud knight, came and, with a lance of ash, struck Fouke through the pit of his stomach. The lance broke and the stump remained in his body; the bowels, however, were not damaged. Fouke felt himself severely wounded and could no longer defend himself. He took to flight, and the others chased him for two leagues or more. When they could not overtake him they returned and seized all the lands which Fouke had. Then they captured Guy, the son of Candelou de Porkington, who was Fouke's constable, and sent him to prison in Rhuddlan, and his seven sons with him.

Fouke goes to see King Henry at Gloucester

Fouke greatly lamented his lord. So, when he heard that King Henry was staying at Gloucester, he went there at once. As he drew near the town the king was going to disport himself in a meadow after supper. He saw Fouke coming armed on horseback, riding painfully, for he was weak and his horse was worn out. 'Let us wait,' said the king, 'we shall now hear some news.' Fouke came on horseback to the king, for he was unable to dismount. He told the king the whole affair, from beginning to end. The king rolled his eyes very angrily and said that he would take vengeance upon such criminals within his realm. He asked him who he was and where he was born. Fouke told the king where he was born, and of what people, and that he was the son of Waryn de Metz. 'Fair son,' said the king, 'you are welcome to me, for you are of my blood, and I will help you.' [39] The king had his wounds attended to, and sent for Melette his mother, and Hawyse his wife, and the rest of the household. So he had them stay with him, and had Hawyse and Melette lodged in the queen's chambers. Hawyse was great with child, and when she came to term was delivered of a child, whom they named Fouke. The latter was very renowned in his time, and rightly so, for he had no peer for strength, daring and goodness.

Lacy compelled to deliver Sir Joce

When Fouke le Brun's wound was healed, King Henry sent a letter to Sir Walter de Lacy and commanded him, upon pain of life and limb, to deliver to him Joce de Dynan, his knight and the other knights whom he wrongfully held in his prison. If he did not do so, moreover, he himself would come to get them, and would do such justice that the whole of England would speak of it. When Sir Walter had heard the message he was much alarmed by it. So he released Sir Joce and his knights, clothed them and mounted them honourably, and brought them by the postern gate towards the River Teme. They were led across the ford of the River Teme and beyond Whitcliffe, until they came to the high road towards Gloucester. When Sir Joce came to Gloucester the king received him with great delight, and promised him law and justice. Joce stayed with the king as long as he pleased, then he took his leave and went to Lambourn, where he took up residence. Soon afterwards he died and was buried there. May God have mercy on his soul!

War between Fouke and the Welsh settled

King Henry summoned Fouke and made him constable of all his army, and entrusted him with all the forces of his land.[40] Furthermore, he directed him to take a sufficient body of men and go to the March. He was to drive Yervard Droyndoun and his armed forces out of the March. Thus was Fouke made master over all, for he was strong and courageous. The king remained at Gloucester, for he was ill and could hardly travel. Yervard had completely taken over the whole of the March from Chester to Worcester, and had disinherited all the barons of the March. With the king's army Sir Fouke made many a fierce assault upon Yervard. In a battle near Hereford at Wormesly he forced him to flee and abandon the field. Before doing so, however, many were killed on both sides. The war between Sir Fouke and the prince continued fierce and hard for four years until, at the request of the King of France, a love-day was held at Shrewsbury between the king and Yervard the Prince. There they embraced each other and were reconciled.

Joce de Dynan and Fouke lose Whittington and Maelor

The prince gave back to the barons of the March all the lands that he had taken from them, and restored Ellesmere to the king. But for no amount of gold would he give up Whittington nor Maelor Saesneg. 'Fouke,' said the king, 'since you have lost Whittington and Maelor Saesneg, in their stead I give you in perpetuity Alveston with all the feudal rights appertaining to it.'[41] Fouke thanked him warmly. King Henry gave to Llewelyn, the son of Yervard, a seven-year-old child, his daughter Joan; and he gave them Ellesmere and many other lands in marriage. He then took Llewelyn to London with him. Prince Yervard and his followers took leave of the king and set off for Wales. The king also gave Whittington and Maelor to Roger de Powys. Afterwards Roger gave Maelor to his younger brother, Jonas.

You have now heard how Sir Joce de Dynan, Sybil his elder daughter and Hawyse, his younger daughter, were disinherited of the castle and feudal rights to Dynan, which Sir Walter de Lacy held wrongfully. Afterwards the town of Dynan was restored and rebuilt, and was called Ludlow. And you have heard how Sir Fouke, the son of Waryn de Metz, was dispossessed of Whittington and Maelor.[42] Sybil, the elder sister, was afterwards married to Payn fitz John, a very valiant knight.

Family of King Henry II

Fouke le Brun and his wife Hawyse remained for some time with the king, long enough in fact to have five sons: Fouke, William, Philip the Red, John and Alan. During the same period King Henry had four sons: Henry, Richard the Lionhearted, John and Geoffrey, who later became duke of Brittany. Henry was crowned during his father's lifetime, but died before his father. Richard then reigned after his father's death, followed in turn by his brother John who, all his life, was wicked, contrary and spiteful. Fouke the younger was brought up with King Henry's four sons, and he was much loved by all of them except John, with whom he quarrelled frequently.[43]

Quarrel between Fouke and Prince John

It so happened that one day John and Fouke were sitting all alone in a room playing chess. John picked up the chessboard and struck Fouke a great blow with it. Feeling the pain, Fouke raised his foot and delivered a swift kick to the chest. John's head struck the wall so hard that he became dizzy and fainted. Fouke's immediate reaction was fright, but he was glad there was no one else in the room with them. He rubbed John's ears, and he regained consciousness. John immediately went to the king, his father, and lodged a complaint. 'Be quiet, you good-for-nothing,' said the king, 'you are always squabbling. If Fouke did all you said he did, you most likely deserved all you got.' He called the boy's master and had him soundly whipped for his complaint. John was very angry with Fouke, and from that day forward never again had any true affection for him.

King Richard favours Fouke

When King Henry died his son Richard became king. Richard held Fouke le Brun, the son of Waryn, in very high esteem because of his loyalty. At Winchester the king summoned the five sons of Fouke le Brun – Foket, Philip the Red, William, John and Alan – and their cousin, Baldwin de Hodenet.[44] With great pomp all six men were dubbed and raised to knighthood. Sir Fouke the younger, along with his brothers and their troops, crossed the sea to seek honour and distinction. There was not a single tourney or joust at which they did not wish to be present. And so highly were they esteemed everywhere that it became a common saying that they were without equals as to strength, bounty and bravery. For they had such good fortune that they came into every combat being considered and praised as the best.

Following the death of Fouke le Brun, King Richard sent letters to Sir Fouke to come to England to receive his father's lands. Fouke and his brothers were deeply saddened to learn that Fouke le Brun, their good father, was dead, and they all returned to London. King Richard was very glad to see them, and he restored to them all the feudal holdings which Fouke le Brun possessed at his death. The king was preparing for his journey to the Holy Land, so he entrusted all the March to the keeping of Sir Fouke. The king loved and favoured him much for his loyalty and great reputation. Fouke stood well with the king during the whole of the life of King Richard.

King John grants Morys the property of Fouke

After Richard's death, his brother John was crowned King of England. Soon thereafter, John sent for Sir Fouke to come and talk with him about various matters concerning the March, and said that he was coming there himself on a visit. He went first to Baldwin, now called Castle Montgomery. When Morys, the son of Roger de Powys, Lord of Whittington, perceived that King John was approaching the March, he sent to the king a handsome steed, and a molted gyrfalcon. After John thanked him for the gifts, Morys came to speak to the king who asked him to stay and to be of his council, making him warden of the entire March. When Morys saw the time was ripe he asked the king, if it were his pleasure, to confirm by royal charter the honour of Whittington to him and his heirs, as King Henry his father had formerly confirmed it to his own father, Roger de Powys. The king knew full well that Whittington belonged to Sir Fouke by right, but he also remembered the blow that Fouke had given him when they were young. He delighted that he now had an excellent opportunity for revenge. So he granted that whatever Morys should put into writing, he would seal it. For the favour, Morys also promised John one hundred pounds cash.[45]

Fouke renounces his homage to King John

There was a knight nearby who had overheard all that the king and Morys had said. He came in haste and told Sir Fouke how the king had confirmed by his charter to Sir Morys the lands which of right belonged to Fouke. With his four brothers Fouke came before the king and asked him that they might have the benefit of common law, whereby these lands were theirs by right and reason as Fouke's inheritance. And they pleaded with the king that he would have the goodness to accept one hundred pounds, on condition that he would grant them the award of his court for gain or for loss. The king told them that he would maintain the grant which he had already made to Sir Morys, whether Fouke was angry or not. Then Sir Morys spoke out saying to Sir Fouke: 'Sir Knight, you are very foolish to challenge my lands. If you say that you have right to Whittington, you are a liar. Were it not for the king's presence, I would prove it upon your body.' Before any further words were spoken Sir William, Fouke's brother, stepped forward, and with his fist gave Sir Morys such a blow to the face that it was covered with blood. The knights came between them so that no more damage was done. Then Sir Fouke said to the king: 'Sire, you are my liege lord, and I have become bound to you by fealty since I have been in your service, and because I hold lands from you. In return you ought to afford me reasonable support, but you fail me both in reason and in common law. Never has a good king denied law in his court to his free tenants. Therefore, I renounce my allegiance to you.' Having said this, he departed from the court and went to his house.

Fouke defeats King John's knights

Fouke and his brothers armed themselves immediately, and Baldwin de Hodenet did the same. When they had gone half a league from the city they encountered fifteen well-armed knights, the strongest and bravest of all the king's retainers, who ordered them to return. The knights said they had promised the king that he should have their heads. Sir Fouke turned round and exclaimed: 'Fair sirs, you were very foolish when you promised to give what you could not get.' Then they attacked each other with lances and swords, and four of the king's most valiant knights were soon killed. All the others were wounded to the point of death, save one, who seeing the peril took to flight. When he came to the city the king inquired of him whether Waryn had been taken prisoner. 'Not at all,' he replied, 'nor was he even injured. He and all his companions have escaped, and all of our men, excepting myself, were slain. I alone escaped with great difficulty.' 'Where', said the king, 'are Gyrart de France, Pierre of Avignon and Sir Amys le Marchys?' 'Slain, my lord.' Then ten knights arrived, all on foot, for Sir Fouke had made off with their horses. Some of these knights had lost their noses, some their chins. All ten were a piteous sight. The king swore an oath that he would take revenge for them and all their lineage.

Fouke seeks refuge in Brittany

Fouke next went to Alberbury [46] and told dame Hawyse, his mother, how he had travelled to Winchester. Fouke took a great sum of money from his mother and left with his brothers and his cousins for Brittany, where he remained for some time. King John seized all the lands which Fouke had in England and did much harm to all his relatives.

Fouke returns to England

Fouke and his four brothers, along with two cousins, Audulph de Bracy[47] and Baldwin de Hodenet, bid adieu to their friends in Brittany and returned to England. In the daytime they rested in woods and moors and travelled on only at night, for they dared not face an attack in daylight. They did not have sufficient manpower to engage the king's troops. At length they came to Higford (Shropshire), to Sir Walter de Higford, who had married dame Vylene, the daughter of Waryn de Metz.[48] Her true name was Emmeline, and she was Sir Fouke's aunt. When he arrived at Alberbury, the next stop on his journey, the local people told him that his mother had recently been buried. On her tomb Fouke deeply grieved his mother's death and prayed compassionately for her soul.

Fouke attacks Morys

That same night Sir Fouke and his people went into a forest called Babbins
Wood, near Whittington, to watch for Morys fitz Roger.[49] A valet passing nearby
spotted them and ran to tell Morys what he had seen. Morys armed himself in
full regalia, taking his shield, green, with two wild boars of beaten gold (the
border was of argent, with fleurs-de-lys of azure). He had in his company
the nine sons of Guy de la Montaigne and the three sons of Aaron de
Clerfountaygne, so that there were thirty men well mounted and five hundred
foot soldiers. When Fouke saw Morys he raced out of the forest. A sharp fight
was begun between them, with Morys being wounded in the shoulder. After
many knights and foot soldiers had been killed, Morys finally fled towards his
castle with Fouke in pursuit. Fouke thought he had struck Morys on the helmet as
he was escaping, but the stroke fell on the saddle of his charger. Then Morgan
the son of Aaron shot forth from the castle, and with a crossbow bolt he struck
Fouke through the leg. Fouke was angry that he was thus unable to finish the
battle and avenge himself upon Sir Morys. As for the wound in his leg, he took
no heed of it. Sir Morys made his complaint to the king that Sir Fouke had
returned to England and had wounded him in the shoulder. The king became
enraged, and appointed one hundred knights with their retinue to go through all
England to search for Fouke, capture him and bring him back, dead or alive. The
king was to pay all their expenses, and in addition he promised to give them
lands and rich fees if their search were successful. The knights went throughout
the whole of England in search of Sir Fouke. But wherever they heard that
Sir Fouke might be located, they avoided going to that place; for they feared him
beyond measure. Some loved him, but many feared his noble chivalry,
apprehending the danger that might happen to them should they test his strength
and daring.

Fouke robs the king's merchants

Sir Fouke and his company came to the Forest of Braydon[50] where they remained
in hiding. They dared not venture forth openly, for fear of the king. One day,
more than ten merchants arrived carrying through the forest expensive cloths,
furs, spices and dresses for the personal use of the King and Queen of England.
These men were merchants who had purchased the rich goods with the money of
the King of England, and were travelling to deliver their purchases to the king.
They were followed by twenty-four foot soldiers charged with guarding the king's
treasure. When Fouke saw the merchants he called his brother John and told him
to go and speak with these people, and find out what country they were from.
John spurred on his horse, and rode off to speak with the merchants. When he
inquired from what land they might be, a spokesman for the group, a haughty
and proud person, came forward and asked what business it was of his to have

such information. John replied politely by inviting them to come and speak with his master in the forest. If they would not go willingly, he said, he would have to use force. A man-at-arms came forward and struck John a great blow with his sword. In return John gave him such a stroke on his head that he fell senseless to the ground. Then Sir Fouke and his company arrived on the scene and attacked the merchants. They defended themselves very vigorously, but at length they surrendered, for they could not do otherwise.

Game of truth or consequences

Fouke took them into the forest, where they told him that they were the king's merchants. When Fouke heard this he was delighted, and said, 'Sir merchants, if you lose this property, on whom will fall the loss? Tell me the truth.'[51] 'Sir,' they said, 'if we lose it through our cowardice, or by our own carelessness, we ourselves are responsible; but if we lose it otherwise, by danger of the sea, or by force, the loss will fall upon the king.' 'Are you speaking the truth?' 'Assuredly, sir,' they replied. When Fouke understood that the loss would be the king's, he then measured out the rich cloth and the expensive furs with his lance.[52] He clothed all who were with him, tall and short, in this rich cloth. To each he gave according to his degree. Everyone of his followers received a liberal share, and of the other goods, each took what he liked. When evening came and the merchants had dined heartily, he bid them Godspeed, and asked them to salute the king in the name of Fouke fitz Waryn, who thanked him heartily for all this fine clothing. During the entire time that he was a banished man neither Fouke nor any of his followers did damage at any time to any one, save the king and his knights.

At last the merchants and their foot soldiers arrived before the king. Wounded and maimed, they repeated to him all that Fouke had charged them to convey, describing how Fouke had taken the king's property. He became enraged, and in his fury sent out a proclamation throughout the realm. Any person who would bring Fouke to him, dead or alive, would receive a thousand pounds. The king would, moreover, add to this cash reward all the lands that belonged to Fouke in England.

Fouke meets the king's messenger

Fouke next journeyed into the forest of Kent. Leaving his knights in the thick of the forest, he went riding alone along the highway. There he met a messenger, wearing a wreath of red roses around his head, who was singing merrily. Fouke asked him politely for the chaplet of flowers, and if he would be so kind would pay him double for it. 'Sir,' said the messenger, 'he is very niggardly of his property who will not give a chaplet of roses at the request of a knight.' And he gave the wreath to Fouke, who, in return, gave him twenty shillings. The messenger recognized Fouke, for he had seen him often. When the messenger later arrived in Canterbury, he met the hundred knights who had been searching for Fouke through all of England. 'Sirs,' he said to them, 'where have you come from? Have you yet found the man you have been seeking by the order of our lord the king and for your own advancement?' 'No,' they replied. 'Then what will you give me', he said, 'if I take you to the place where I have seen and spoken with him today?' The knights' reply, in both goods and promises, was so generous that the messenger told them where he had seen Fouke. He also described how he had received twenty shillings in exchange for the chaplet of roses which he had graciously given.

Fouke is hunted by one hundred knights

The hundred knights immediately sent out a summons through the countryside. They hastily rounded up knights, squires and foot soldiers, in sufficient numbers to encircle the whole forest. As if this were an animal hunt, beaters and receivers were placed at strategic points. Others were positioned throughout the countryside with horns to give warning the moment Fouke and his companions came out of the forest. Fouke, however, remained in the forest, unaware of all this activity. At length he heard a horn sounded by one of the attacking knights. He became suspicious, and ordered his brothers to mount their horses. William, Philip, John and Alan immediately mounted, as did Audulph de Bracy, Baldwin de Hodenet and John Malveysyn.[53] The three Cosham brothers, Thomas, Pieres and William, who were good crossbowmen, and all the rest of Fouke's followers were soon ready for the assault.

With his companions Fouke came out of the forest, and saw, before all the others, the hundred knights who had been hunting him throughout England. In the first rush of battle Fouke's men killed Gilbert de Mountferrant, Jordan de Colchester and many other knights. They made several passes back and forth through the hundred knights, knocking them down in great numbers. At length, however, many knights, squires, burgesses, foot soldiers and people in great numbers joined in the battle. Fouke wisely perceived that he and his men could not continue thus. Finally, after his brother John received a bad head wound, he decided to return into the forest. Fouke and his companions spurred their horses. But before they left, many a good knight, squire and foot soldier were slain. People from all over then began to sound the cry, and they were pursued by the populace everywhere they went. At length they entered into a wood and saw a man raising his horn, about to sound the warning. In an instant, one of Fouke's men shot him through the body with a crossbow bolt. That put a quick end to the warning blast.

Fouke seeks refuge in an abbey

Fouke and his companions were soon forced to leave their horses, and fled on foot towards a nearby abbey. When the porter saw them coming he ran to shut the gates. Alan, being very tall, quickly got over the wall, and the porter began to run away. 'Stop,' said Alan, and ran after him. He took the porter's keys from him, and gave him a blow with the chain from which the keys hung. The porter thus had good reason to regret his attempted flight.[54] Alan then let all his brothers enter the abbey. Once inside, Fouke grabbed the habit of an old monk and quickly put it on.[55] Taking a large staff in his hand, he went out of the gate. After he had shut the gate he walked on, as if lame of one foot, supporting his whole body on his big stick. Shortly thereafter the knights and foot soldiers arrived followed by a great mob. One of the knights shouted: 'Old monk, have you seen any armed knights pass here?' 'Indeed, sir, and may God repay them for all the mischief that they have done!' 'Just what have they done to you?' 'Sir,' he replied, 'I am old, and I cannot help myself, so worn out am I. Seven came on horseback, and with them fifteen others on foot. Because I could not get out of their way quickly enough, they did not spare me. They had their horses trample over me, and took little account of my protest.' 'Say no more,' replied the knight 'you shall be well avenged this very day.' The knights and all the others rode off in such haste to pursue Fouke that they quickly left the abbey a full league behind them. Meanwhile, Sir Fouke was left there in peace to see what would happen next.

Fouke, disguised as a monk, tricks the knights

Sir Gyrard de Malfee soon arrived accompanied by ten well-mounted knights. They had come from a distance, and were riding horses of great value. Gyrard said mockingly, 'Well, here is a fat and burly monk. He has a belly big enough to hold two gallons of cabbage.' Fouke's brothers were still inside the gate, from where they could see and hear all of Fouke's proceedings. Without a word, Fouke raised his big staff and struck Sir Gyrard such a blow beneath the ear that he fell senseless to the ground. Fouke's brothers, when they saw this, immediately rushed out of the gate and subdued Sir Gyrard and the ten knights. After tying up their prisoners very tightly in the porter's lodge, they took all the harnesses and the good horses, and rode off non-stop until they came to Higford, Shropshire. Once there, John's wounds were able to be healed at last.

Fouke disguises himself as a merchant

During their stay at Higford a messenger arrived who had been seeking Sir Fouke for some time. He greeted him on behalf of Hubert, Archbishop of Canterbury.[56] The archbishop wanted to speak with Fouke as soon as possible. So Fouke led his men to a place near Canterbury, in the forest where he had been before. There he left all his company, except his brother William. The two dressed themselves like merchants, and went into Canterbury to meet with the archbishop, Hubert Walter. 'Gentlemen,' said the bishop, 'you are very welcome. You no doubt know that Sir Theobald Walter, Butler of Ireland,[57] my brother, is now deceased. Before his death he married dame Matilda de Caus, a very rich lady, and the fairest in all England. King John himself desires her for her beauty and it is with great difficulty that she guards herself from him. She is here in Canterbury under my protection, but you shall see her presently. My dear friend Fouke, it is with some urgency that I pray and command you to take her for your wife, with my blessing.' Fouke soon met with the lady, seeing for himself how good, as well as beautiful she was, not to mention her excellent reputation. As for her possessions in Ireland, she had fortresses, cities and lands, plus rents and great fiefs. So with the assent of his brother William and on the counsel of Archbishop Hubert he married Dame Matilda de Caus. Fouke remained in Canterbury two days, and then bid his farewell. He left his new wife there in the care of the archbishop, before returning to join his companions again in the forest. When he told them all that he had done, they made fun of him, laughed at him, and called him 'husband'. They also asked him just where he would put the fair lady, in a castle or in the forest. Yet, while they often joked together in this way, they also did more serious mischief to the king everywhere the opportunity presented itself. But they did such to none other than the king, excepting those persons who were openly their enemies.

Adventure with Pieres de Brubyle

A knight named Robert fitz Sampson was residing in the march of Scotland. The knight frequently received Sir Fouke and his company, and he entertained them with great honour. He was a man of great wealth whose wife's name was Dame Anable. She was a very courteous lady. At that time also there was a knight in the country named Pieres de Brubyle. This Pieres was in the habit of gathering together all the gentlemen's sons of the country who were addicted to thieving and other debauchery. It was their custom to go through the country, killing and robbing decent people, merchants and others. Whenever this Pieres led his company out to rob people, he assumed the name of Fouke fitz Waryn.[58] As a result, the real Fouke and his companions had acquired a very bad reputation for matters in which they were blameless.

Fouke's fear of King John was such that he dared not tarry too long in one place. So it was by night that he came into the March of Scotland, very near the court of Robert fitz Sampson. As he approached he saw a light within the court, and could hear people talking. He heard his own name mentioned often in the conversations. After telling his companions to remain outside, Fouke himself boldly entered the courtyard from where he made his way into the great hall. Once inside he could see Pieres de Brubyle and some other knights sitting at supper. Robert fitz Sampson and his good lady and all their household were bound with ropes, laid out on the floor off to one side of the hall. Sir Pieres and his men were all wearing masks. Those who were serving the meal, when they knelt before Sir Pieres, called him their lord Sir Fouke. The lady, who lay bound near her husband in the hall, said very pitifully, 'Oh, Sir Fouke, for God's sake have mercy. I never did you any harm, but have loved you as best I might.'

At this point Sir Fouke had kept quiet, listening to everything that had been said. But when he heard the lady speak, she who had done him much kindness, he could bear no longer. Alone, without any of his companions, he stepped forward with his sword drawn and said: 'Silence, I order you, stay where you are. Let no one move hand or foot.' And he swore that, if any one were so bold as to move, he would cut him into small pieces. Pieres and his companions felt trapped. 'Now', said Fouke, 'which of you here calls himself Sir Fouke?' 'Sir,' said Pieres, 'I am a knight and I am called Fouke.' 'Well, Sir Fouke,' he shouted, 'by God, you had better move quickly. Tie up and all your companions tightly. If you do not, you shall be the first to lose your head.' Pieres, terrified by the threat, got up and unbound the lord and the lady and all the other members of the household. He then tied all his companions well and firmly. Next, Fouke made him cut off the heads of all those whom he had bound. After he had beheaded all his companions he heard a voice say: 'You recreant knight, you who called yourself Fouke, you are a cowardly liar. I am Fouke, and you will now pay dearly for having falsely caused me to be charged with theft.' Forthwith he cut off Pieres' head, after which he called his companions inside to join him in supper. All made themselves very comfortable. Thus did Sir Fouke save Sir Robert and all his treasure, so that nothing was lost.

King John pursues Fouke

Very often King John did great harm to Sir Fouke, but Sir Fouke was no less wise and crafty than he was strong and bold. The king and his people very frequently pursued Sir Fouke by tracking the footprints of his horses. Fouke countered on many occasions by having his horses shod with the shoes put on backwards.[59] In that way the king was deceived in his pursuit. Sir Fouke was to suffer many a hard fight before he finally regained his inheritance.

Disguise of John de Rampaigne

Sir Fouke took leave of Sir Robert fitz Sampson and went to Alberbury where he set up camp in a forest near the river. Fouke called on John de Rampaigne, saying to him: 'John, you know a lot about minstrelsy and juggling. Do you have you the

courage to go to Whittington and perform before Morys fitz Roger to discover
just what they are up to?' John agreed to do it.[60] He prepared himself by first
crushing a herb and putting it into his mouth. As a result, his face began to swell
so badly that it puffed out. His whole face became so discoloured that his own
companions scarcely knew him. John dressed himself in poor clothes and he took
his box with his juggling equipment and carried a great staff in his hand When
he arrived in Whittington he told the porter that he was a juggler. The porter
brought him before Sir Morys fitz Roger, who asked him where he was born.
'Sir,' he replied, 'in the March of Scotland.' 'And what news do you have from
there?' 'Sir, I know none, other than the recent death of Sir Fouke fitz Waryn. He
was killed in a robbery which he was committing in the house of Sir Robert fitz
Sampson.' 'Are you speaking the truth?' 'Yes, certainly,' he said, 'people from all
over the countryside say it is so.' 'Minstrel,' he said, 'I will give you this cup of
pure silver for your news.' The minstrel took the cup, and thanked Sir Morys for
his generosity.

John de Rampaigne was very ugly of face and body, and consequently the
scoundrels of the household mocked him. They treated him like a fool, and
pulled him by his hair and his feet.[61] He raised his staff, and gave one of the
scoundrels such a blow on the head that his brains flew into the middle of
the room. 'Wicked rascal,' said the lord, 'what have you done?' 'Sir,' he replied,
'by God's mercy, I cannot help myself. I have a malady which is very grievous, as
you may judge by my face, which is so swollen. This malady takes entire
possession of me for certain hours of the day every week. It is not within my own
power to contain myself.' Morys swore that, were it not for the good news which
John had brought with him, he would have beheaded him forthwith. The juggler
thus hastened his departure, for he had no desire to tarry further. So he returned
to see Fouke, and described word for word what he had heard and done at the
court in Whittington. One important item of news was the fact that Sir Morys, in
his function as keeper of the march, was planning a trip. Along with fifteen
knights and his entire household, he was to leave the very next day for the castle
of Shrewsbury. Sir Fouke was delighted to learn this news, and so were his
companions.

The next morning Fouke was up early. He and his men armed themselves well
for the events to follow. Morys and his fifteen knights set out towards Shrewsbury.
Also in the company were the four sons of Guy fitz Candelou of Porkington,[62]
and the rest of the household. When Fouke caught sight of his enemy, he was
very pleased. At the same time, he was also much incensed, because Guy
was unlawfully keeping his heritage from him by force. Morys looked off in the
direction of Great Ness, where he quickly recognized the heraldic markings on a
shield: quartered with gules and argent *dancetté*. By this coat of arms he
immediately knew that it was Fouke. 'Now I am certain', said Morys, 'that
jugglers are liars. For there stands Fouke, very much alive.' Morys and his knights

fought bravely. Boldly they attacked Fouke and his companions, and called them thieves. They said that before evening came many heads would be placed on the high tower of Shrewsbury. Fouke and his brothers defended themselves with such vigor, however, that Sir Morys, his fifteen knights, and the four sons of Guy fitz Candelou of Porkington were all quickly slain.[63] Fouke had that many fewer enemies!

Fouke takes refuge with the Prince of Wales

From there Fouke and his companions went towards Rhuddlan (Flintshire) to speak to Sir Lewys, the Prince of Wales who had married Joan, the daughter of King Henry and the sister of King John.[64] The visit was prompted by the fact that Sir Lewys had been brought up together with Sir Fouke and his brothers in the court of King Henry. The prince was very glad that Sir Fouke had come, and asked him what agreement he might have with the king. 'None, sir, for I cannot have peace with the king no matter what I do. I have, therefore come to you and to your good lady to make peace with you both.' 'Truly,' said the prince, 'I grant and give you my peace, and you shall have a good reception from me. The King of England doesn't know how to have peace with you, or me, or any other.' 'My deepest thanks, sir,' said Fouke, 'for I have great trust in you and in your great loyalty. But since you have granted me your peace, I must tell you something else. Morys fitz Roger is dead, and it is I who killed him.' When the prince learned that Morys was dead he became very angry. He exclaimed that had he not just given his peace to Fouke he would have had him drawn and hanged, for Morys was his cousin.[65] At that moment Princess Joan stepped forward to confirm the peace made between her husband and Sir Fouke. They embraced each other and all ill will was pardoned.

At this time there was great discord between Prince Lewys and Gwenwynwyn, son of Owen Cyfeiliog, to whom a great part of the country of Powys belonged. Gwenwynwyn was very proud, haughty and fierce. He refused to submit himself to the prince for any reason. Instead, he brought great destruction to his land. By force the prince had totally beaten down the castle of Metheyn, and had taken possession of Mochnant (Montgomeryshire), Llannerch Hudol (Montgomeryshire) and other lands which belonged to Gwenwynwyn. The prince assigned Fouke to act as overseer of all his land holdings, commanding him further to attack Gwenwynwyn and destroy all his lands. Fouke, however, was prudent and very wary, for he knew that the prince was in the wrong. So he told him very courteously: 'Sir, for God's sake, you should pardon Gwenwynwyn. If you do what you have planned, you will be much blamed in foreign countries by all people. And please do not be annoyed with me for what I am telling you. Every one says, in fact, that you have sinned against him. Sir, for God's sake, therefore, have mercy on him. He will most surely reform himself in his dealings with you, and will serve you to your satisfaction. Do not lose sight of the fact that you don't know when you will need your barons.' Fouke preached and talked to the prince at length and so convinced him to change his strategy. Shortly thereafter, Lewys and Gwenwynwyn were reconciled with each other when the prince gave back all the lands which he had previously taken.

King John wages war on Fouke

King John was at Winchester when the news came to him that Fouke had killed Morys, Roger's son. He learned further that Fouke was staying with Prince Lewys, the husband of his [John's] own sister. His immediate reaction was a moment of thoughtful reflection. For a good while he did not utter a word. Then he shouted: 'Hey! By Saint Mary, I am the king. I rule England. I am duke of Anjou and Normandy, and the whole of Ireland is under my lordship. Yet I cannot find a single man in all my jurisdiction, who, no matter how much I offer to give, will avenge the damage and the disgrace which Fouke has done me. But you can be certain that I will not desist until I avenge myself upon this prince.' He then sent forth a summons to all his earls and barons and his other knights that they should on a certain day be at Shrewsbury with all their people.[66]

When all those summoned got to Shrewsbury, Lewys was warned by his friends that King John was planning to wage war against him. At that he called Fouke and told him the bad news. Fouke in turn assembled thirty thousand trusted men at castle Bala in Pennlyn (Merionethshire). Gwenwynwyn, the son of Owen, also came with his troops, all strong and bold men. Fouke was a very crafty strategist in war, and was familiar with the terrain over which King John must travel, including all the narrow passes. One in particular, called the ford of Gymele, was a very tight passage.[67] It was very narrow, enclosed with woods and marshes, so that the only way to pass was by the highway. Fouke and Gwenwynwyn, when they reached the ford with their troops, dug out beyond the highway a long, deep and broad ditch. They filled the ditch with water, so that no one could pass, partly because of the marsh on one side, and partly because of the ditch. Beyond the ditch they built a well-fortified palisade. To this day that ditch is still to be seen.

King John with his army finally reached the ford, which he expected to pass safely. Then he noticed just beyond it more than ten thousand armed knights, who were guarding the passage. Fouke and his companions had passed the ford by a hidden path that they had made, and found themselves on the same side as the king. Gwenwynwyn and many other knights were also with them. The king immediately recognized Fouke, and ordered his knights to attack from all sides. Fouke and his companions defended themselves like lions. They were often knocked off their horses, but quickly remounted, killing many of the king's knights in the process. Gwenwynwyn, however, took a bad blow to his helmet and received a serious head wound. When Fouke saw that neither he nor his men could long remain on the outside of their ditch, they returned by their hidden path to defend their palisade and the ditch. From that position they were able to shoot crossbow bolts and light spears against the king's troops, killing many and wounding an immense number in that manner. This fierce struggle lasted till the evening. When the king saw so many of his people killed and wounded, he was so sorrowful that he did not know what to do. He finally returned to Shrewsbury.

King John's character

As for King John's character, he was a man without conscience, wicked, cross and hated by all good people. In addition he was lustful. Whenever he heard described any fair lady or damsel, he wished to have her at once, either to entrap her by promise or gift, or to ravish her by force. It mattered little whether she was the wife or daughter of an earl, or a baron, or of any other for that matter. That was why he was the most hated. For this reason too many great lords of England had renounced their allegiance to the king, which in turn led to his being less feared by many. [See plate 11.]

Prince of Wales restores Whittington to Fouke

John le Estrange, Lord of Knokin and of Ruyton-of-the-Eleven-Towns (Shrop-shire), remained faithful to the king, and continued to bring harm to Prince Lewys and his people. For this reason the prince had the castle of Ruyton overthrown. When King John learned that this entire garrison was captured and imprisoned, he was very upset. Soon thereafter, the prince summoned Sir Fouke to castle Bala for the purpose of restoring to him not only Whittington, his heritage, but also Ystrat Marchell (Montgomeryshire) and Dinorben (Den-bighshire). After first expressing his thanks to the prince, Fouke went to Whittington with his own people, and had the castle restored and thoroughly repaired.

King John attacks Fouke again

John le Estrange came to the king, and told him that Fouke had done great harm to his people by taking the castle of Ruyton. Since he was in very good standing with the king, he took the liberty to request royal troops in order to avenge himself. To that end the king summoned Sir Henry de Audley, who was lord and first conqueror of the Red Castle.[68] He commanded Sir Henry to take ten thousand knights, the most valiant of England, and ordered that the lord and his knights should be obedient to Sir John le Estrange in all matters. Sir Henry and Sir John and their knights set out for Whittington. Along their way, they slew whatever men and women they found and pillaged the countryside. A cry of panic was raised everywhere.

Fouke remained in Whittington, where he had assembled a large contingent of men to defend his newly acquired lands. The company included seven hundred Welsh knights and many foot soldiers. When the news came that Sir John and Sir Henry were coming towards Whittington, Sir Fouke and his men armed themselves forthwith, going secretly to Middle Pass. The moment Sir John saw Sir Fouke he spurred on his warhorse with lance down. He gave Sir Fouke such a blow with his lance that it flew into splinters. Sir Fouke in turn repaid Sir John by a blow to the face that sliced through his helmet and knocked him to the ground. The scar left by this blow was to be visible for the rest of John's life. In an extraordinary act of valour, however, John quickly leaped up from the ground and cried out: 'Now, my lords, all of you attack Fouke.' Fouke proudly answered: 'By all means, and here comes Fouke to meet you all.' Then the knights from both camps struck out at each other. Fouke, Sir Thomas Corbet[69] and their other companions slew many; but Alan fitz Waryn, and Philip his brother, were wounded. When Fouke saw his brothers wounded, he became so enraged that he slashed out at all around him. Whomsoever his sword hit had no chance to escape from death. Unfortunately Sir Fouke's troops were vastly outnumbered. In the battle he had only seven hundred knights, while the others were ten thousand or more. Seeing that he could not win this skirmish, Fouke returned towards Whittington. In the press Sir Audulph de Bracy was knocked from his horse. Although he had boldly defended himself, he was finally taken prisoner and carried off to Shrewsbury.

Sir Henry and Sir John were much delighted with the capture. They came to the king at Shrewsbury, where they delivered up Sir Audulph de Bracy. The king argued heatedly with his prisoner, swearing boastfully that he would have him drawn and hanged, because he was both a traitor and a thief. He had killed his knights, burnt his cities, and overthrown his castles. Audulph in reply answered the king boldly, saying that neither he nor any of his kindred had ever been traitors.

John de Rampaigne, disguised as a minstrel, rescues Sir Audulph de Bracy

Back in Whittington, Fouke saw first to the care of his brothers and his other troops. When their wounds had been cleaned and their injuries attended to, it came to his attention that Sir Audulph was missing. He searched everywhere, but when he realized Audulph was nowhere to be found he thought he would never see him again. No one ever expressed sorrow at the loss of a friend more movingly than did Sir Fouke on this occasion. At length John de Rampaigne, seeing the depth of Fouke's grief, came forward and said: 'Sir, have done with this lamentation. If it please God, before tomorrow at prime, you shall have good news of Sir Audulph de Bracy. For I myself shall go to speak to the king.'

John de Rampaigne was a fairly skillful musician and juggler. He could play the harp and vielle, as well as the psaltery.[70] He dressed himself in fine clothes worthy of any earl or baron, and stained his hair and the whole of his body jet black. In fact, there was nothing left white except his teeth. Around his neck he hung a beautiful tabor, before mounting a handsome palfrey. Once inside the town of Shrewsbury he rode through, as far as the gate of the castle, and was stared at by many as he rode along. John presented himself to the king, kneeling before him and saluting very courteously. The king saluted him in return, and asked him whence he came.

'Sire,' said he, 'I am an Ethiopian minstrel, having been born in that country.' In reply the king inquired further. 'Are all the men of your land the same colour as you?' 'Yes, my lord, men and women alike.' 'What do they say of me in foreign realms?' 'Sire,' said he, 'you are the most renowned king in the whole of Christendom. It is your great renown that explains my visit to your court.' 'Sir,' said the king, 'you are very welcome.' John thanked him briefly, then added quietly that the king was renowned more for his wickedness than his goodness. Of course the king did not hear the last remark. So John spent the remainder of the day just playing his tabor and other instruments. When the king had gone to bed, Sir Henry de Audley sent for the black minstrel to be brought to his chamber. All present joined in the singing, and when Sir Henry had drunk a great deal he said to a valet: 'Go get Sir Audulph de Bracy, whom the king intends to put to death tomorrow. He shall at least have a pleasant night before his death.' The valet quickly brought Sir Audulph into the chamber, where all were talking while the music continued. John began playing a song which Sir Audulph was accustomed to singing. Sir Audulph raised his head, and looked the minstrel straight in the face. With some difficulty he finally recognized John. Then, when Sir Henry asked for drink, John obligingly leaped to his feet, and served the cup to everyone in the room. John acted very cunningly, sprinkling a powder into the cup in such manner that no one perceived him. He was, after all, an excellent juggler. All those who drank became so drowsy that very soon afterward they lay down to go to sleep. When they were all asleep, John dragged one of the king's fools over and placed him between the two knights who had been assigned to guard the condemned prisoner. John and Sir Audulph then found some towels and sheets which were in the chamber, and escaped by a window facing the Severn River. They immediately headed towards Whittington, which was twelve leagues from Shrewsbury. The matter could not long be hidden. Early the next morning, when he was told the details of the escape, the king was furious. That same morning Fouke had risen early, for he had slept little the preceding night. As he looked in the direction of Shrewsbury he saw Sir Audulph and John approaching. No need to ask whether he was glad when he saw them. He ran out to embrace and kiss them both. Sir Audulph told him all that John had done and how they escaped. Fouke, who until shortly before had been sad, rejoiced greatly at this good news.

Fouke's wife and children

Now let us return for a moment to speak of Fouke's wife, Dame Matilda de Caus. When the king, who had lusted after Matilda, learned for certain that she was married to Sir Fouke, his enemy, by the counsel of Archbishop Hubert, he did great harm to both the archbishop and the lady. He wished to have her carried off by violence, but she was able to find refuge in the church. There she gave birth to a daughter, Hawyse, who was later to become Lady of Wem. The archbishop himself baptized the baby.

Somewhat later Fouke and his companions came to Canterbury under cover of night. From there they took his wife to Higford, where she remained for some time. It then came to pass that the lady was again with child. During this pregnancy she remained in hiding in Alberbury. She soon discovered, however, that she was under surveillance by the king's men, so she fled secretly to Shrewsbury. At that point, she was so big with child, that she could travel no farther. So she took refuge in the church of Our Lady at Shrewsbury, and there she gave birth to another daughter. At her baptism this baby was given the name Joan, and later in life she was married to Sir Henry de Pembridge.[71] Subsequently, Matilda had still another child, this time a son. He was born in Wales, up in the mountains, and was baptized in a stream which flowed from the Maiden's Well.[72] The mother and child were very weak, for the child was born two months before term. In their weakened condition both had to be carried down from the mountain to a farmhouse, nearby Carreg-y-nant.[73] When the child was later healthy enough to be confirmed by the bishop, he was called Fouke.

Prince Lewys plots the betrayal of Fouke

When the king saw he could in no way avenge himself upon Fouke, nor disgrace or take his wife, he sent a letter to his own brother-in-law, Prince Lewys. In the letter he begged Lewys to remove from his household his mortal enemy, the felonious Sir Fouke. Should he comply, John promised in return that he would restore all the lands which the king's ancestors had ever taken from his lordship. The single condition was that he must deliver Sir Fouke's body. The prince called his wife Joan into his chamber and showed her the letter which the king, her brother, had sent him. When the lady had heard the letter, she immediately sent a full report of it to Sir Fouke, thereby informing him that the king wished to come to terms with her husband. Fouke was distressed at this news, and feared treason. His first reaction was to protect his wife, Dame Matilda. In the company of Baldwin de Hodenet she was sent secretly to the bishop of Canterbury. Following that mission, Baldwin was to meet him again at Dover.

Fouke and his four brothers, along with Audulph de Bracy and John de Rampaigne, armed themselves fully. They set out with all their men for castle Bala to speak to Prince Lewys. Fouke said to him: 'Sir, I have served you loyally to the best of my ability, but these days a man does not know whom to trust. For, on the mere promise made by the king, you wish to abandon me. I am all the more fearful, sir, since I know that the king has sent that promise in a letter which you have concealed from me.' 'Fouke,' the prince replied, 'stay with me. Assuredly, I plan to do you no treason.' 'Indeed, sir,' said Fouke, 'even though I can believe your word full well, I will not remain on any account.' At that he and of all his companions took leave of the prince. From castle Bala he journeyed night and day until he arrived in Dover. There he met up with Baldwin, who had taken his wife Matilda to stay in safety with the archbishop. They put to sea and arrived in France at Whitsuntide.

Fouke's adventures in France

When they got near to Paris, Fouke and his men saw a tournament underway. King Philip of France had come into the fields to watch his French knights in action.[74] Fouke himself was still disguised, as were his companions. When they saw such a fair assembly, they tarried to see the jousts. Noting the presence of some English knights, the Frenchmen exerted themselves much the more to do well. Then Sir Druz de Montbener, a very proud Frenchman, sent word to Sir Fouke asking that he come joust with him. Fouke immediately accepted the invitation.

Fouke and his brothers armed themselves and mounted their horses. John de Rampaigne was richly attired, mounted on a fine charger. At the entrance to the tilting fields John gave a drum beat on the tabor he was carrying. The beat on the tabor was so loud that the hills and the valleys resounded, causing the horses to caper. Then, when the king saw Sir Fouke in full battle dress, he said to Sir Druz de Montbener: 'Take heed, sir, for it is quite obvious that this English knight is very valiant.' 'Sire,' he replied, 'there is not a knight in all the world whom I would not dare to take on man-to-man, either on horse or on foot.' 'May God be with you!' said the king.

Fouke and Sir Druz spurred their horses and engaged the combat. Fouke pierced his opponent's shield with his lance, which also sliced through the knight's hauberk and into his shoulder. The blow hit with such force that the lance flew into pieces. Sir Druz ended up flat on the ground. Fouke then led the riderless horse back to Sir Druz and offered it to him as a present. For

Sir Fouke had no desire to keep the horse as a prize of battle. A second French knight immediately came forward ready to avenge Sir Druz. He struck such a blow with his lance that it went clear through Fouke's shield. Fouke struck back, hitting his attacker on the helmet with such a blow that his lance splintered into fragments. The knight also lost his balance and fell from his saddle. Fouke's brothers and companions stood ready to joust, but the king would not permit it. Instead, he spurred his horse in Fouke's direction. 'English knight,' he said, 'a blessing upon you; for you have done exceedingly well.' The king then graciously requested that Fouke remain with him. He was very thankful for the offer, and consented to stay at the king's pleasure. Fouke had such grace that he was held to be the finest of knights and without peer. From that day forward the English knight was held in highest esteem by many in France, and was praised everywhere he went for his courage, chivalry and prowess.

Fouke remained for some time in France, and was loved and honoured by the king and queen and all the gentry. When the king asked him what his name was, Fouke told him that he was called Amys del Boys. 'Sir Amys,' said the king, 'do you know Fouke fitz Waryn, of whom so much good is spoken everywhere?' 'Yes, sire, I have seen him quite often.' 'And what is his stature?' 'Sire, in my opinion, he is about the same height as I am.' 'That he may well be, for you are both valiant men.' Fouke travelled all over France to jousts and tourneys. Everywhere he was praised and honoured for his prowess and largesse.

King John discovers Fouke's residence in France

The King of England finally learned that Fouke was residing with King Philip of France. He sent a letter to the king respectfully requesting that Sir Fouke fitz Waryn, his mortal enemy, be expelled from Philip's household. When the King of France heard the letter read, he swore by St Denis[75] that no such knight was in his retinue. This was in effect the answer he sent back to the King of England. Sir Fouke in turn heard the news, and went directly to see the King of France to announce his imminent departure. 'Tell me what prompts your sudden decision,' said the king. 'I will make full amends for any failing on my part which might have occasioned your desire to leave me.' Fouke replied simply: 'Sire, I have heard news that compels me to set out with all due haste.' At these words the king understood immediately his real identity. 'Sir Amys de Boys', said the king, 'I believe that you are in fact Fouke fitz Waryn.' 'Yes, my lord, I am indeed.' The king then pleaded: 'Stay here with me, and I will give you richer lands than any you have ever had in England'. 'With due respect, my lord,' he responded, 'a man who cannot reasonably hold those which are his own by right heritage is unworthy to receive lands as a gift from someone else.'

Fouke meets the mariner Mador

Fouke took leave of the king and headed toward the coast. As he approached he saw some ships afloat on the sea, but there was no wind in the direction of England, although the weather was fair. Fouke saw a mariner, who appeared to be bold and hardy. He called out to him: 'Sir, is that your ship?' 'Yes, indeed, sir,' came the reply. When asked his name the mariner answered: 'Sir, I am Mador of Mont de Russie, where I was born.' 'Mador,' said Fouke, 'how well have you mastered your trade? Are you able to take passengers by sea into various regions?' 'Frankly sir, there is no land of any worth in all of Christendom to which I do not know how to take a ship safely.' 'Assuredly,' said Fouke, 'yours is a very perilous trade. Tell me, brother Mador, of what death did your father die?' Mador answered that he had drowned at sea. 'How did your grandfather go?' 'In the same way.' 'How about your great-grandfather?' 'In like manner, as did all my relations, to the fourth generation, as far as I know.' 'Truly,' said Fouke, 'it is very foolhardy of you to venture out to sea.' 'Why indeed, sir? Every creature shall have the death that is destined for him,' said Mador. 'Now then, if you please, answer my question. Where did your father die?' 'In his bed, of course.' 'Where did your grandfather die?' 'In the same place.' 'And your great-grandfather?' 'Certainly, all of my lineage, as far as I know, died in their beds.' 'Assuredly, sir,' said Mador, 'since all your kindred have died in their beds, I am much astonished that you dare go near any bed'. At that Fouke was forced to concede that the mariner had told him a simple truth. Every man shall have such a death as is appointed him, and he does not know whether it shall be on land or on sea.

Fouke orders a ship to be built

Judging that Mador well understood the business of ships, he contracted with him to have a ship planned and built, and promised to meet all the expense involved. Mador agreed and the ship was made in a forest near the sea, according to the mariner's own specifications. All the ropes and other tackle with which Mador outfitted the vessel were of exceptional quality. It was an exceedingly well-provisioned ship.

Fouke defeats an English ship at sea

Fouke, his brothers and all his retinue put out to sea and drew near the coast of England. Mador saw a well-manned ship coming towards them. When the ships drew near each other a knight on board called out to Mador: 'Mariner, who owns the ship which you are steering, and what is her provenance? For it is an unfamiliar vessel in these waters.' 'The ship is my very own, sir,' said Mador. The knight retorted: 'In no way is that so. You are thieves, and I know it by the quartered sail, which bears the arms of Fouke fitz Waryn. He must be on board the ship, and this very day I will deliver his body up to King John.' 'Well indeed,' said Fouke, 'you will do no such thing. Should you, however, want some of our provisions, you are welcome to them gladly.' 'I prefer instead to take all of you', he said, 'and whatever belongs to you, with or without your consent.' 'On that account you are sadly mistaken,' said Fouke. Mador, who was an excellent mariner, let out his sails and steered his ship directly into the path of the other vessel. He cut the other ship cleanly in two, so that the sea poured into its hold. Fouke and his companions immediately boarded the ship after it was struck. They plundered the contents, including all the food, and carried the booty back on to their own ship. The enemy vessel was destroyed, but many a hard blow was struck first. The other ship then disintegrated and sank to the bottom.

Fouke's ship is driven beyond Scotland

For an entire year Fouke continued sailing just off the coast of England. He sought to bring harm to no one other than to King John. On many occasions he seized the king's property and whatever else of his he could find. Finally, the ship set sail for Scotland, but a strong west wind forced them to continue on for three additional days journey, well beyond their intended destination. A very beautiful island appeared in the distance, and as they drew near it they found a good port.[76] Fouke and his four brothers, along with Audulph and Baldwin, went ashore to see the country and find food for their ship. Their first encounter was with a young shepherd, who came forward to greet them in very bad Latin. Fouke asked him if he knew whether there might be any provisions for sale in the country. 'Truly sir, none at all,' he said. 'For this is an island inhabited by very few people, and those who do reside here live only off their animals. But if you will please come with me, such food as I have, I am willing to share with you.' Fouke thanked the lad and followed along as he led them down into an underground cavern, which was very beautiful. The shepherd asked them to sit down and otherwise received them graciously. He then told them he had a servant on a nearby hill. 'Please, do not be annoyed', he said, 'if I blow my horn to summon him. That way we will be able to dine more quickly.' 'Please do so, in God's name!' said Fouke. The young man went outside the cavern and blew six blasts before returning into the cavern.

Fouke confronts six peasants

Forthwith six tall and fierce peasants arrived, dressed in coarse and dirty tabards. Each one was carrying a strong, hard club. When Fouke saw them he immediately suspected mischief. The six peasants went into a chamber, took off their dirty tabards and replaced them with much richer cloth of a fine green colour. Their shoes were ornamented with gold, and in all their attire they were as richly dressed as any king might be. Returning to the hall, all six respectfully greeted Sir Fouke and his companions. Their first request was that rich chessboards with pieces made of fine gold and silver be brought to them. The guests were all invited to play. Sir William played a game, but he lost it immediately. Sir John played another, and in no time he too lost. Philip, Alan, Baldwin and Audulph, one after the other played, and each in turn lost the game. Then one of the haughtiest shepherds said to Fouke, 'Will you play?' 'No', he answered. 'Indeed, sir,' said the shepherd, 'you shall either play chess or you will have to wrestle with me. You have no other choice.' 'By my faith,' said Fouke: 'you are a villainous shepherd and a liar. Since I am forced either to wrestle or to play chess despite myself, I choose instead to play the game I know best.' So he leaped up, drew his sword, and struck such a blow that the shepherd's head flew into the middle of the room. A second, then a third one met a similar fate. Fouke and his companions ended up killing all those peasant scoundrels.

Fouke rescues seven damsels

Fouke then entered a chamber where he found an old woman sitting. She was holding a horn which she tried repeatedly to put up to her mouth, but she had not the strength to blow it. When she saw Fouke she begged for mercy. He asked her of what use the horn might be if she could blow it. The old woman answered that if the horn were blown, help would come immediately. Fouke took the horn from her and went into another chamber. There he found seven beautiful damsels, dressed very richly, who were doing fine handwork. When they saw Fouke they threw themselves on their knees and cried for mercy from him. Fouke asked them where they were from, and one of them said: 'Sir, I am the daughter of Aunflor of Orkney. My father is resident in one of his castles in Orkney, called Castle Bagot, which is in a very beautiful forest near the sea. One day I and my maidens, with four knights among others, took a boat and went for a pleasure ride on the sea near my father's castle. As we were sailing the seven sons of the old woman, whom you just saw with her horn, attacked us from a well-manned ship. They killed all our people and brought the survivors here. Against our consent they have repeatedly ravished our bodies, and heaven is our witness! Wherefore we pray, in the name of the God in whom you believe, to save us from this misery. Please, help us to escape from here, if you can. Judging by your appearance, I perceive that you are not from this country.' Fouke comforted the damsels, assuring them that he would help them to the best of his ability.

During their search for provisions Fouke and his men also found great treasure, including armour. Fouke kept for himself a rich *haubergeon* (short coat of mail) which he came to love so much that he often wore it secretly. During the rest of his life he would neither give it away nor sell it at any price.

Fouke fights the robbers

Fouke first provisioned his ship liberally and placed the damsels on board, comforting them as best he could. Then he commanded all his men to arm themselves quickly. When all were ready, Fouke sounded the little horn that he had taken from the old woman. More than two hundred robbers from all over the countryside came running through the fields. For there were no other inhabitants on the whole island except robbers and thieves. They lived there as pirates venturing forth from their haven to kill whomsoever they could reach upon the sea. Although they defended themselves vigorously, Fouke and his company immediately fell upon these robbers and killed more than two hundred of them.

Fouke sails for Orkney

Fouke asked Mador whether he could take them by sea to the kingdom called Orkney. 'Yes, certainly, it is only an island, and Castle Bagot is very near the port.' Fouke said, 'That's the castle where I want to be.' 'Sir, you shall be there this very day.' When Fouke arrived he asked the damsels whether they recognized the country. 'Indeed, sir,' one of them replied 'it is the realm of my father Aunflour.' Fouke went straight to the castle where he delivered to the king, his daughter and the other damsels. The king received them with great honour, and gave rich gifts to Fouke.

Fouke encounters serpents and beasts

Fouke sailed so far to see wonders and adventures that he had gone round the seven islands of the ocean: Brittany, Ireland, Gothland, Norway, Denmark, the Orkneys and Sweden. There are no human inhabitants in Sweden, only serpents and other foul beasts. It was there that Fouke saw four-legged serpents with very sharp horns. They were able to fly like birds. One of these serpents attacked Fouke, striking him with its horn that pierced through his shield. Fouke was astonished by the blow, but noticed immediately that when the serpent struck the shield it could not easily withdraw its horn. So Fouke had time to pierce it through the heart with his sword. Then Fouke saw a venomous beast which had the head of a dog, a thick beard like a goat and ears like a hare. The many other beasts here were those that St Patrick had driven from Ireland. By the power of God the good saint had shut them up in this land from which he himself came. Still to this day, no venomous beast inhabits the land of Ireland, excepting tailless lizards.

Fouke's ship caught in a storm

Fouke set sail on the North Sea, beyond the Orkneys. There was so much cold and frost that no one could bear it, nor could the ship make headway in the sea due to the ice. So Fouke returned towards England. A horrible tempest arose, whereupon they all thought they would perish. They cried out devoutly to God and to St Clement[77] to deliver them from the storm. The tempest raged for fifteen days before they finally spotted land, but they did not know where they were.

Fouke lands at the Castle of Cartagena

Fouke went ashore to discover a very beautiful castle; and, noticing that the gate was open, he ventured in. Once inside the castle, he found no one living there, neither humans nor animals. He was astonished to find such a beautiful place uninhabited. The whole surrounding countryside, moreover, was similarly deserted. Upon his return to the ship he told his followers what he had seen. At that Mador advised that they all go ashore. 'Let's leave the ship here with a few men to guard our provisions, and we will perhaps soon find someone to tell us what's going on in this place.' Once ashore, they met a peasant. Mador asked him what land this was, its name, and why it was not inhabited. The peasant told them that it was the kingdom of Iberia and the name of the land was Cartagena, held in fief by the King of Iberia. The castle here belonged to the duke of Cartagena, who had a daughter, the fairest maiden in the realm of Iberia. One day this damsel unfortunately climbed to the top of the castle's main tower, from which she was carried off by a flying dragon. The beast took the damsel to a high mountain in the sea, and there ate her. This same dragon had devastated the land, killing everyone in sight, with the result that no one dared inhabit the place. Because the dragon was so horrifying the duke himself didn't dare enter the castle.

Fouke and the others returned to the ship and again set sail. As they approached a high mountain in the sea Mador exclaimed: 'It's the mountain where the dragon lives; now we're all in real danger.' 'Hold your tongue, Sir Mador,' said Fouke. 'So far you haven't spotted anything to cause us harm here. Do you wish to die of fright? We have already seen many dragons, and God has delivered us from frequent dangers. Never yet have we been in any peril from which, thank God for it, we were unable to escape safely. Your cold comfort would put a coward to death.'

Fouke discovers the damsel

Fouke took Audulph de Bracy, and the two of them climbed the steps leading up the high mountain. When they reached the mountain top they saw many hauberks, helmets, swords and other arms lying there. Scattered near the arms they observed human bones alongside a large and beautiful tree. There was also a fountain below, running with clear, placid water. Looking around further, Fouke noticed a cave carved inside a hollow rock. He drew his sword, and very boldly went inside, like one who entrusts himself entirely to God. Before doing so, however, he first raised his right hand and signed himself in the name of the Father, the Son, and the Holy Ghost. Inside the cave he found a very beautiful damsel weeping and wailing. In answer to Fouke's question as to her homeland she replied: 'Sir, I am the daughter of the duke of Cartagena, and I have been here for seven years. The only Christians I have ever seen here have all come unwillingly. If it's in your power, for God's sake, leave here at once; for if the dragon returns you will never escape.' In reply Fouke exclaimed: 'I will not leave this place before I hear and see more. Damsel, how does the dragon treat you? Has he caused you any harm?' 'Sir, the dragon is wild and powerful, and he can easily carry an armed knight into these mountains after he catches him in his talons. As you can judge by all the bones outside the cave, he has already carried and eaten many knights. He prefers human flesh to any other kind. In the process of killing he smears his hideous face and his beard with the blood of his victims. He then comes to me and makes me wash his face, beard and breast with clear water. When he wishes to sleep he goes to his couch made of fine gold; for his nature is such that he is excessively hot. In contrast, gold is very cool by nature; so in order to cool himself he sleeps on gold. Before going to bed, however, he takes a large stone, such as the one you see over there, and blocks the door with it. Because he possesses the senses of a human being he fears me greatly, and he is especially worried that I will kill him while he is asleep. I, for my part, am convinced that he will end up killing me first.' 'God forbid,' said Fouke, 'I promise you he shall not do so.'

Fouke fights the dragon

Fouke took the damsel by the hand and entrusted her to Sir Audulph for her protection as they left the rock cave. They had scarcely come out into the open air when they saw the dragon flying in the sky above and heading straight towards them. From its hot mouth the beast belched forth smoke and horrible flames. It was a very ugly creature, with a large head, square teeth, cruel claws and a long tail. As soon as the dragon spotted Fouke it swooped down and struck at him with its claws, delivering such a blow on the shield that it tore it in two. Fouke raised his sword and, with all his strength, struck at the dragon's head. Given the hardness of the creature's outer shell and the horny matter on the front side of its body, the sword blow did no harm whatever to the beast, nor did it even cause it to waver in its flight. The dragon began his flight from afar in order to strike harder. Fouke, who could not stand the blow, dodged behind the tree which was beyond the fountain. He saw that he could not harm the dragon from the front side, so he waited until it made a turn. Then Fouke struck a convincing blow to the body near the tail, thereby cutting the beast in two. The dragon began to scream and yell. It rushed for the damsel with the intention of seizing her and carrying her away, but Sir Audulph defended her. The dragon clasped Sir Audulph so tightly in its claws, that he would have been crushed if Fouke had not come so quickly. After cutting off the beast's paw, Fouke was able to free Sir Audulph with great difficulty. Its sharp talons had already cut through the hauberk. Fouke struck the dragon squarely in the mouth with his sword, and in this way he finally killed it. Fouke was very weary, and rested a while before going to the dragon's lair. He took all of the gold he found there, and carried it to his galley. John de Rampaigne examined Sir Audulph's wound and dressed it, for he knew a lot about medicine. [See plate 14.]

Fouke and the damsel return to Cartagena

Mador turned his ship towards Cartagena; and they arrived in the country, and surrendered to the duke his daughter, who was overjoyed to see her again. The damsel told her lord what kind of life she had led, and how Fouke killed the dragon. The duke fell at the feet of Fouke, thanked him for saving his daughter; and begged him, if such were his pleasure, to stay here. He offered to give him all Cartagena along with his daughter in marriage. Fouke thanked him from the heart for his fine offer. He told the duke that he would take his daughter willingly, if only his Christianity would permit it. Unfortunately, he was a married man. Having said this, Fouke tarried there only until Sir Audulph's wounds were healed. To each of Fouke's men the duke gave rich gifts. He gave them many fine and beautiful jewels, as well as fair and fiery warhorses. At last Fouke took leave of the duke, who was very sorrowful at his departure.

Fouke returns to England

Fouke and his companions at last sailed towards England. When they came to Dover they went inland, but first making certain that Mador remained with the ship at a safe location where they could find him whenever they might need him again. Fouke and his companions had learned from the peasants that King John was presently at Windsor, so they made their way secretly in that direction. During the day they slept and rested themselves, and during the night they went on until they came to the forest. Since they were already very familiar with the area, they easily found a place to hide, for Fouke knew well every part of Windsor Forest.[78] When they heard a horn sounded, Fouke and his companions armed themselves for a skirmish, for they realized immediately that the king's hunters and beaters were getting ready for a hunt. Fouke swore an oath that fear of death would not deter him from taking revenge on the king, who by force had wrongfully disinherited him. He would thus challenge the king to restore his rights and his heritage. Fouke decided to act on his own, so he told his companions to remain where they were. Having said this, he set out alone to seek adventure.

Fouke disguises himself as a charcoal burner

Fouke's first encounter was with an old charcoal burner carrying a shovel, dressed all in black, as becomes a collier. Fouke kindly asked him to give him his clothes and his shovel. 'Willingly, sir,' he said. In exchange, Fouke gave him ten bezants [Byzantine gold coins], and asked him to tell this to no one. The charcoal burner went his way; Fouke stayed there and immediately put on the clothes which the collier had given him.[79] He then saw to his coals and began to stir the fire. There was a large iron fork that he used to arrange the logs on one side and the other.

Fouke entices King John into the forest

King John soon arrived on foot accompanied by three knights and saw Fouke tending the fire. Fouke immediately recognized the king; and, throwing down his fork, saluted his lord by falling humbly to his knees before him. The king and his three knights laughed and made great sport over the politeness and demeanour of the charcoal burner. After standing there for a long time, the king said: 'My good peasant, have you seen a stag or doe pass this way?' 'Yes, my lord, some time ago.' 'What kind of an animal did you see?' 'One with long horns, my lord.' 'Where is it now?' 'Sire, I can very easily lead you where I saw it, but I ask your permission to allow me to take my fork. For if it were stolen it would be a great loss to me?' 'Yes, peasant, if you like, go on and we will follow you.' Carrying his big iron fork, Fouke conducted the king to an excellent place from which to shoot. The king was a very good bowman. 'My lord,' said Fouke, 'would you like me to go into the thicket and direct the animal to come this way?' 'Yes, indeed,' said the king. Fouke leaped into the thick of the forest, and summoned his band hastily to take King John. 'Be quick, for I have led him here with only three knights. Come while all of his retinue is still on the other side of the forest.' Fouke and his band rushed out of the thicket and quickly captured the king.[80] 'Now, sire,' said Fouke, 'I have you at last in my power. Shall I pass such a sentence upon you as you would upon me if you had taken me?' The king trembled in fear, for he greatly dreaded Fouke. Fouke swore that he should die for the great harm and the disinheritance that he had inflicted upon him and upon many a good man in England. The king cried for mercy, and in God's name, begged for his life. He promised that he would restore to Fouke his entire inheritance and whatsoever he had taken from him and all his friends. Moreover, he would grant him his friendship and peace for ever. To that end, John pledged to abide by whatever guarantees of security Fouke himself might decide appropriate. Fouke accepted the king's offer on one condition. In the presence of all the knights here present, he would have to give his solemn word to keep this covenant. The king pledged solemnly that he would keep faith with Fouke. He was overjoyed to be able thus to escape so easily.

King John breaks his oath

Upon his return to the palace, King John assembled his knights and his retinue, and told them in detail how Sir Fouke had deceived him. Since his solemn oath was made under duress, he had no intention whatever to keep it.[81] He therefore commanded all to arm themselves in haste and capture these felons while they were still in Windsor Forest. Sir James of Normandy, who was the king's cousin, requested that he be placed in the vanguard. He claimed that the English, at least all the nobles, were cousins to Sir Fouke, hence they were most probably traitors to the king, and would not help take these felons. Randolph, the Earl of Chester, protested vehemently.[82] 'In faith, sir, with due respect to the king, but not to you, that is a bold lie.' He would have punched him in the face, had the Earl Marshal not restrained him. He claimed that they were not now nor ever had been traitors to the king or to anyone else. Furthermore, he reminded Sir James firmly that many nobles here present, including the king himself, were cousins to Sir Fouke. The Earl Marshal interrupted, saying: 'Let us go after Sir Fouke, then the king will see for himself who might be holding back for reasons of family ties.' Sir James of Normandy and his fifteen knights armed themselves splendidly all in white armour and nobly mounted on white steeds. This nobleman hastened forward with his company in quest of fame.

Fouke fights Sir James of Normandy

John de Rampaigne had overheard all these proceedings, and reported them back to Sir Fouke, who concluded that there was no means of escape open to him other than to fight. Sir Fouke and his companions thus armed themselves well, and boldly took on Sir James in battle. They defended themselves vigorously, and killed all their opponents except four, who were seriously wounded. Sir James himself was taken prisoner. Sir Fouke and his men immediately put on the arms of Sir James and the other Normans. They also mounted the Normans' healthier white horses, for their own horses were tired and lean. Tying his mouth so that he could not speak, they dressed Sir James in the arms of Sir Fouke, including the helmet, and rode towards the king. When the king saw them approaching he immediately recognized them by the arms. He believed that Sir James and his men were bringing back Sir Fouke.

Fouke deceives King John

Sir James was delivered to the king, with the prisoner being identified as Sir Fouke. At this news, both the Earl of Chester and the Earl Marshal were deeply saddened. Assuming that he was in fact addressing Sir James, the king presently commanded him to kiss him. Sir Fouke replied that, because he was in such haste to follow the other Fitz Waryns, he had not time enough even to take off his helmet. So the king dismounted from his good horse and ordered James (i.e., Fouke) to mount it, for it was a swifter one for pursuing his enemies. Sir Fouke got down from his own horse and mounted the king's steed. When he finally rejoined his companions, they all fled to a spot some six leagues farther away. Safe at last, they disarmed themselves in a thicket and tended to their injuries. They bound up the wounds of William fitz Waryn, whom they considered as dead, for he had been severely wounded by one of the Normans. All his companions shared Fouke's deep grief over his brother's fate.

Meanwhile, the king proceeded to order that Sir Fouke be hanged. Sir Emery de Pyn, a Gascon, who was a relative of Sir James, stepped forward and said that he would see to the hanging himself. He took charge of the prisoner and, leading him off a short distance, made him take off his helmet. He saw immediately that it was not Fouke. With his mouth unbound, Sir James was at last able to explain what had happened. Emery brought Sir James back to the king, and reported what Sir Fouke had done. When the king realized that he had been thus deceived he was furious. He swore an oath that he would stay armed in his hauberk until such time as he had taken these traitors. Fouke knew nothing of the king's oath.

King John pursues Fouke

The king and his nobles pursued Fouke's band by following the tracks left by their horses until they reached the wood where Fouke was hiding. When Fouke saw them coming, he stood disconsolate, lamenting for his wounded brother, William. He felt that all was lost. William begged them to cut off his head and take it with them.[83] That way, when the king arrived, he would not be able to identify William's body. Fouke refused the request. With warm tears streaming down his face, he prayed for God's mercy and help. No one has ever seen greater sorrow than that shared between these two brothers.

Fouke and the Earl of Chester parley

Randolph, the Earl of Chester, led the assault. Upon seeing the Fitz Waryns, he commanded his troops to halt. He went on alone to beg Fouke, for the love of God, to surrender himself to the king. If he did so, Randolph gave his word of guarantee for safe passage, assuring him further that he would be reconciled with the king. Fouke replied that he could not do so for all the gold in the world.

'My dear cousin,' said Fouke, 'for the love of God I beg your help for my brother lying here near death. Promise me that after he dies you will make certain that his body is buried, so that wild beasts do not devour it. Please do likewise for the rest of us when we too are dead. For now, go back to your lord the king, and do his service without hesitation or regard for us who are related to you by blood. We will stay to face the destiny that awaits us here.' Very sadly, the earl returned to join his companions. Fouke remained there weeping greatly, out of pity for his brother, whom of necessity he would be compelled to leave there to die. He could do little more than pray that God come to their aid.

Fouke is wounded in battle

The earl ordered the assault, and his men attacked in full force. Randolph himself fell upon Sir Fouke, but lost his horse in the attack, during which most of his retinue was killed. Fouke and his brothers defended themselves doggedly. Sir Berard de Blois came up behind Fouke and struck him with his sword on the side, thinking that he had killed him. Fouke, however, turned on his assailant and struck back, hitting him on the left shoulder with his sword grasped in both hands. Cut through to the heart and lungs, Berard fell dead from his horse. Fouke had bled so much, however, that he slid down upon the neck of his horse, and the sword fell from his hand. Saddened by this turn of events, the Fitz Waryns rushed to the aid of their wounded brother. John leaped behind Fouke on the horse, and held him up so that he could not fall. They all then took to flight, for their forces were overwhelmed. The king and his men rode in pursuit, but were unable to overtake them. All that night they went on thus, till in the morning they came to the spot on the coast where they had left Mador and his ship. When Fouke revived, he asked where he was and whether he had been taken prisoner. His brothers comforted him as best they could, and put him to bed in the ship. John de Rampaigne tended his wounds.

William fitz Waryn taken prisoner

After the fighting, the Earl of Chester looked out on the field of battle. He saw that he had lost many of his own people, but he also remembered Fouke's earlier request. So, when he came upon William fitz Waryn nearly dead, he had the body sent to a nearby abbey to be nursed. At length William was discovered there. Forthwith the king had him transported in a litter to Windsor Castle, where he was promptly thrown into a dungeon. King John was exceedingly angry with the Earl of Chester for having concealed his charitable action. 'Fouke too is mortally wounded,' said the king, 'but at least I have one of his family here now. The other Fitz Waryns will be my prisoners too before they know it. To be sure, pride is at the heart of the matter, for had not it been for his excessive pride

Fouke would still be alive. While he lived, there was no better knight in the whole world, hence his death is an even greater loss.'

Fouke sails to the island of Beteloye

In the sea near the coast of Spain there is an island called Beteloye.[84] It is closed in with high rocks and there is only one entrance. Neither man nor beast dwells on this island, which measures half a league in length and an equal distance in breadth. On the seventh day of their voyage Fouke and his companions arrived at this island. Fouke was at last able to find rest. For the six days of the sea voyage he had been unable to sleep. While his brothers and the others went off to explore the land, he himself remained alone asleep on the ship. Suddenly, a terrible wind came up and broke the ship's mooring ropes, even though it was firmly anchored to a rock. The ship was carried out on to the high sea. When Fouke finally awoke he saw the stars in the night sky. He called his brother John and his other companions, but no one answered. Slowly he became aware that he was alone on the sea and began to curse his cruel destiny. As he wept for his lost brothers, sleep overcame him at last. Soon afterwards his ship arrived in the land of Barbary at the city of Tunis.

Fouke drifts alone to Barbary

At that time Messobrin was the King of Barbary. In the company of four other kings and six emirs, who all were Saracens, he was standing in a tower overlooking the sea. When he saw this amazing galley approaching his land, the king ordered two soldiers to go and see what it was. The soldiers boarded the ship, finding nothing except one knight asleep. One of them kicked Fouke and ordered him to awake. The frightened knight leaped up and struck the soldier such a blow with his fist that he fell overboard into the sea. The other one fled to report to the king what had happened. A hundred knights were promptly dispatched by the king to take this ship and bring the knight to him. Well armed, the hundred knights surrounded the ship, and assailed it from all sides. Fouke, even though badly outnumbered, defended himself bravely, but at last was forced to surrender. This, however, he did under very favourable conditions. For, when he was brought to the palace, Fouke was taken to one of the royal chambers. There, by order of the king, he was to be well attended.

Fouke's adventures with Isorie

Isorie, the king's sister, was a very beautiful and gentle damsel. She often came to visit Fouke and bring him comfort, because she had noticed that he had a bad wound in his side. She graciously asked him to tell her his name and where he was from, as well as how he had come to be wounded. He told her his name was Lost Sailor (*Maryn le Perdu*) of France. He was deeply in love with the daughter of an earl in his home country. The lady seemed to return his affection, but she apparently loved another even more. 'And it happened that one day she and I met for an amorous tryst. As she was holding me in her arms very closely, the other man whom she loved more arrived. He struck me with his sword here, in my side, and put me on to a galley for dead. The ship set out to sea and brought me to these parts.' 'This damsel was certainly not very courteous,' Isorie remarked, as she picked up a richly ornamented harp. Her songs and melodies were her way of bringing solace to this handsome knight, whom she could see was of truly courtly bearing.

Isorie issues a challenge to Fouke

Fouke asked lovely Isorie what was all the commotion before the king in the great hall. 'I will tell you, indeed,' she said. 'In the province of Murcia in Iberia there lived a nobleman, the duke of Cartagena, who had a very beautiful daughter, Ydoyne. While her father was alive, she dwelt with him in his castle in Cartagena. One day a dragon came and carried her to a high mountain in the sea. There he kept her for more than seven years, until a knight of England, called Fouke the son of Waryn de Metz, came to the mountain and slew the dragon, thereby restoring the maiden to her father. Shortly afterwards the duke died, and his daughter ruled over the duchy. My brother, the King of Barbary, sent messengers to her offering to take her as his wife, but she refused him. Feeling shame at the refusal, the king reacted by assembling an army which destroyed Ydoyne's cities and overthrew her castles. The damsel fled abroad to seek reinforcements. She has now returned with her own large contingent of troops and has begun fiercely to wage war upon my brother. To end this struggle she proposes rules of battle whereby two champions, to be chosen from the two armies now set against each other, will square off against one another. If her chosen knight is conquered, she accepts to give up her duchy and go with Messobrin to Barbary. If ours is beaten, however, my brother the king must entirely restore to her all the land he has taken. That was the context of the deliberations you overheard earlier today in the great hall, upon the arrival of some messengers sent by Ydoyne. Would that it pleased the God Mahomet that you were such a one as dared undertake the battle on the part of my brother the king! For you would earn great honour in doing so.'

Fouke accepts Isorie's challenge

'My lady, I am greatly indebted to my lord the king, and especially to you; but I could never undertake battle for a Saracen against Christians. I would rather die first. But if the king would renounce his law, be baptized and become a Christian, on such conditions I would, however, accept to undertake the battle as his champion. If I succeed, this land and its people will be saved. The King will, moreover, finally have this damsel of whom you have spoken.' Isorie ran immediately to report to her brother Messobrin, the King of Barbary, all that Fouke (who called himself Maryn le Perdu of France) had told her. The king accepted the generous offer unconditionally, promising to follow any orders Fouke might give. If he could but accomplish all that he had promised!

Fouke engages in battle and discovers his brother

The day of the battle was appointed. The king and his emirs, along with the Berbers and all his other people, came forward, very well armed to face Ydoyne and her troops. Sir Fouke had been provided with rich arms, and Isorie herself graciously attended him. When all was ready, the king put forward his champion knight (Fouke) to do battle, and the duchess put forward hers. The two bold knights spurred on their horses, and exchanged lance blows such that the splinters flew all over the field. Then they drew their swords and had go at each other bravely. Fouke struck his opponent's horse such a blow that it fell dead, although he would have preferred to hit the knight instead. When the knight hit the ground he shouted: 'Wicked heathen, evil Saracen of pagan faith, may the God of Heaven curse you. Why have you killed my horse?' Fouke dismounted, and the two knights continued their fierce combat well into the evening.

At last the knight asked Fouke: 'You, sir, may be a pagan, yet you are strong and noble. Please tell me where you were born.' 'If you want to know my country of birth I will not tell you, unless you tell me first about yours. Only then will I reply to your question.' The knight said that he was a Christian born in England, the son of Waryn de Metz. His name was Philip the Red. He recounted his whole life and that of his brothers in great detail, telling how the duchess had come in a ship to the island of Beteloye and had rescued them. They had been stranded on that island half a year or more. Almost to the point of starvation, they were even forced to eat their own horses. 'And when the countess saw us, she knew immediately who we were, and provided us with all the food we needed. She told us that she had just come from England, where she had gone in search of us to help her carry on her war against the King of Barbary. So, there you have a full account of the hard life we have led.' At that point Fouke interrupted: 'Dear brother, Philip the Red, do not you know me? I am your brother Fouke.' 'You, sir, are a Saracen, you cannot be my brother. You are trying to deceive me. By God, you shall not do so!' Then Fouke showed him something, saying: 'Here is a sign.' Philip recognized it at once. There was great joy all around, and the battle was adjourned till the following day. Philip explained to the duchess that it was his brother Fouke with whom he had been fighting. Then Fouke, Philip and their other brothers took counsel with Messobrin. He and all his household were baptized, and the king married the duchess with great honour.

Fouke returns to England

Fouke, his brothers and their men stayed for some time with the king in order to make proper preparations for their return voyage to England. The king gave them gold, silver, horses, arms and all the luxury goods which they might desire. They filled their ship with such riches that it was a wonder to behold. When they arrived secretly in England, Fouke arranged to have John de Rampaigne go disguised as a merchant to locate King John and find out whether his brother William were alive or not. John dressed himself in the clothes of a rich merchant and went to London.[85] There he made the acquaintance of the mayor and all his household. He gave them such rich gifts that he was even invited to live in the mayor's house, where he was attended to as a wealthy guest. Taking advantage of this privileged status, John asked the mayor to arrange an audience with the king so that he might seek royal favour in allowing his ship's cargo to be unloaded in England. Although he spoke bad Latin, the mayor understood him very well. So the mayor brought the merchant before King John at Westminster. He greeted the king very courteously in his own language. The king understood his words and asked him who he was and his country of origin. 'Sire, I am a merchant from Greece. I have been in Babylon (i.e., the medieval city of Old Cairo), Alexandria and India. I have a ship laden with heavy merchandise, including rich cloths, jewels, horses and other valuables, which might be of great value in your realm.' 'It is my pleasure', said the king, 'that you and your people should be free to land in my country. I grant you my surety.' The merchant, together with the mayor, was invited to remain and eat at the king's table.

Two sergeants-at-mace soon entered, bringing into the hall a tall knight with a long black beard and poorly clothed. They led him to the middle of the room and gave him some food. When the merchant asked the mayor who this was, he was told that it was a knight named Sir William fitz Waryn, and was given the poor man's full story and that of his brothers. Upon hearing the man's name, John was overjoyed to see him still alive, yet very troubled at heart by the poor man's wretched condition. As soon as it was feasible for him, the merchant hastened to Sir Fouke to report on William's plight. Later he had his ship brought as near to the city as he could.

The following day the merchant took a palfrey, the like of which there was none so handsome in all the kingdom, and presented it to King John, who gladly received this marvellous gift for its beauty. In fact, the merchant gave so liberally that he won his way into everyone's graces. As a result, he was allowed to do whatever pleased him at the king's court.

John de Rampaigne rescues William

One day John went to the court at Westminster accompanied by his men, who had first put on sailors' tunics and armed themselves well. After they were nobly received, they noticed William fitz Waryn being led by his keepers to the prison. The merchant and his companions took William by force from the guards and carried him toward their boat, which was moored very near the palace. The keepers immediately sounded the alarm and followed in pursuit. But the merchants were well armed and defended themselves bravely. They escaped to their galley, placed William on board, and headed out to sea. No need to ask whether Fouke was delighted to see his brother William and John de Rampaigne, still dressed in his merchant garb. The brothers embraced and each one told the other a tale of adventures and misfortunes. When the king heard that he had been deceived by the merchant, he thought himself ill used.

Fouke captures King John and is pardoned

Fouke and his companions arrived in Brittany, where they remained with relatives more than six months. At last he made up his mind that nothing would deter him from returning to England. When he got to England, he went straight to New Forest in Hampshire, where he had often spent time.[86] There he met the king, who was hunting a wild boar. Fouke and his men captured him, along with six of his knights, and brought them back to their galley. The king and all his followers were very frightened by all this. Many heated words were exchanged, but at length the king pardoned them his ill will, and restored all their inheritance. He also promised them that he would proclaim a truce throughout all of England. As a token of good faith that he would indeed fulfill his promise, he left his six knights as hostages until the peace could be proclaimed.

King John proclaims the peace with Fouke

The king returned forthwith to Westminster, where he assembled earls, barons and the clergy, and told them openly that he had willingly granted his peace to Fouke fitz Waryn and his brothers, and to all their followers. He ordered that henceforth the Fitz Waryns should be honourably received throughout the realm, since he had decided to grant them once again their entire heritage.[87] Hubert the Archbishop was delighted at this news. He promptly sent letters to Fouke, to the Earl of Gloucester, to Randolph, Earl of Chester and to Hugh Bigod, Earl Marshal, to come immediately to Canterbury. When they were all assembled, it was appointed that Fouke and his companions should surrender themselves to the king in London.

Fouke's lands are restored

Fouke with his brothers and the three earls, along with all their forces, equipped themselves as richly as they could and set out for London in noble apparel. They knelt before the King at Westminster, and surrendered themselves to him, upon which the King returned to them all their rightful possessions in England. They were given a royal reception, and were invited by the king to stay awhile with him at court, which they did for an entire month.

Then Fouke took his leave, and went for a visit with the Earl Marshal, who surrendered to him Ashdown and Wantage in Berkshire, and other lands as well. Fouke and his brothers put on full armour and next went to Abingdon (Oxon.), where they removed whatever they could find. These possessions were then taken on to Wantage which was later to become a market town. The fair that Fouke set up in the town has been held there ever since.

Fouke goes to Ireland with the Earl of Chester

Fouke took leave of the Earl Marshal, and went to see Earl Randolph of Chester, who was assembling an army to go to Ireland to defend his rights there. When they got there a great troop of their enemies was waiting for them. The earl commanded his men to take up their arms. Fouke himself set off with three young brothers whom the earl had brought with him. The three young men were of great valour and strength, well armed and mounted on fine horses. Among the enemies facing them stood a hideous giant.[88] He was well armed, black and horrible, twelve feet taller than any other. The giant stepped forward and shouted out: 'Earl of Chester, in order to defend your rights, send me the most valiant knight you have.' The three youths heard the shout and rushed to engage the giant. He killed them swiftly, one after the other, with the hatchet which he was wielding. Then Fouke charged forward on his steed and tried to pierce him with his lance. The giant dodged the blow, striking Fouke instead, such that he almost disabled him. Fearful now, Fouke became very cautious, until he was finally able to smite his opponent through the body with his lance. As he was falling down, the giant struck Fouke's horse, severing its two legs. Fouke himself fell to the ground, but quickly leaped up again. He drew his sword and cut off his enemy's head. After the battle, Fouke was later to take this giant's hatchet to his castle at Whittington. For now he helped the Earl of Chester in his conquest of all these lands and castles in Ireland. Sir Randolph stayed long enough in that country to restore his lands, after which he returned to England.

Fouke returns to Whittington

At long last Fouke came to his stronghold at Whittington, the beautiful castle he had built on marshy ground. There once again he found Matilda, his wife, and his children, who greeted him with great joy. Fouke proceeded to have all his treasures brought to Whittington. He gave lands and horses to his servants and friends very liberally, and maintained his land in great honour.

Fouke founds an abbey

Fouke reflected on the fact that he had sinned greatly against God by killing many men, not to mention his other great misdeeds. So, in order to gain remission for his sins, he founded a priory in honour of Our Lady, of the order of Saint Mary of Grandmont, near Alberbury, in a forest on the River Severn. It is called the New Abbey.[89] Shortly thereafter, Fouke's wife, Dame Matilda de Caus, died and was buried in this priory. A good while after the death of this lady, Fouke married another very noble woman, Dame Clarice d'Auberville. Both of his wives bore him fair and healthy children.

Fouke's daughter marries the Prince of Wales

Fouke's reputation for prowess and goodness was such that his children benefited greatly from their father's renown. The hand of his daughter Eve, for one, was granted upon formal request of the Prince of Wales (Llewelyn the Great). She was married with great honour and solemnity to the prince after the death of his first wife, Dame Joan, who was herself the daughter of King Henry of England. But Llewelyn lived only a year and a half after the wedding. He died and was buried at the Cistercian abbey of Conway (Caernarvonshire). Eve, who had no children from Llewelyn, was afterwards married to a worthy knight, the Lord of Blancmostiers (either Oswestry or Whitchurch, Shropshire).

Fouke's repentance, vision and blindness

One night Fouke and his wife, Dame Clarice, were lying in bed in their chamber. The lady was asleep, but Fouke kept awake reflecting upon his youth, and he repented deeply in his heart for his misdeeds. Suddenly, he saw a wonderful brightness in the room. He wondered what it could be. Then he heard a thundering voice in the air say to him: 'God has granted to you, His vassal, a penance which is of greater worth to you here than elsewhere.' At these words the lady awoke and saw the great brightness. She covered her face for fear. Then this brightness vanished, after which Fouke never saw anything again. He was to remain blind for the rest of his life.[90]

Merlin's prophecy of Fouke

This Fouke was a good and generous host. He had the path of the royal road changed so that it passed nearby the hall at his manor in Alveston. That way, no stranger should travel by without being offered food, lodging or other honours which it was his to give. Merlin says that:[91]

> In Great Britain
> A wolf shall come from the Blanche Lande.
> Twelve sharp teeth shall he have,
> Six below and six above.
> He shall have such a fierce look,
> Such strength and power,
> That he shall chase the Leopard
> From the Blanche Lande.
>
> But now we know that Merlin
> Said this about Fouke fitz Waryn;
> For each of you must know well
> That in the time of King Arthur
> The place called Blanche Lande
> Is now named Whittington.
>
> For in this country was located the beautiful chapel of
> Saint Augustine [of Canterbury],
> Where Cahuz the son of Yvain dreamed
> That he stole the candlestick,
> And that he met a man
> Who wounded him with a knife,
> And wounded him in the side.
> While asleep Cahuz cried so loud
> That King Arthur heard him.
> And when Cahuz awoke from his sleep
> He put his hand to his side;
> There he found the knife
> Which [in his dream] had wounded him.
>
> This is all recounted in the Grail story,
> The book of the Holy Vessel.
> We also learn therein how King Arthur
> Recovered his health and his valour,
> When he had lost all
> His chivalry and his power.
>
> From this very country came the wolf,
> As the sage Merlin said,

And by his shield
We have known the twelve sharp teeth.

He bore a shield *dancetté*,
As the heralds have devised:
On the shield there are twelve teeth
Of gules and of argent.
It is well understood that King John
May be known as the Leopard,
For he bore on his shield
Leopards of beaten gold.

Fouke remained blind for seven years, suffering his penance gladly. Dame Clarice died, and was buried at the New Abbey. After her death Fouke lived only one more year. He died at Whittington, and he too was buried with great honour at the New Abbey. His body lies near the altar. May God have mercy on his soul!

And may God have mercy upon all, the living and the dead! AMEN.

6

THE TALE OF GAMELYN

Stephen Knight

INTRODUCTION

The Tale of Gamelyn only survives today because it was added very early to one version of *The Canterbury Tales*. It follows the unfinished *Cook's Tale*, and often has a new link to make it his second tale. Some think Chaucer himself placed *Gamelyn* among his papers, planning to use it in this way – others think he might have set it aside for rewriting as *The Yeoman's Tale* since it does deal with some forest activities suitable to that character. There can, however, be no proof that Chaucer ever saw the poem, intriguing though it may be to speculate what he might have made of it.

Of the surviving manuscripts most have little value as a record of *The Canterbury Tales* and one of the misfortunes of *Gamelyn* in the past was that it has been printed from the heavily edited and quite unauthoritative Harley 7334 and from the error-prone Corpus manuscript. This translation, like the edition found in Knight and Ohlgren,[1] is taken from the Petworth manuscript, the best of *The Canterbury Tales* manuscripts that include *Gamelyn*.

Gamelyn differs from many other outlaw tales in this collection through the fairly low social status of the hero, the limited local nature of the action, and of course by being written in English – though there was a lost English verse *Fouke fitz Waryn*, which was certainly a parallel to this story and may perhaps have influenced it, if it was available early enough. Most commentators have thought *Gamelyn* was written fairly early: Lindner improbably suggested the thirteenth century,[2] while Skeat placed it about 1340 on the basis of its events and legal structures.[3] That would still be an early date for a secular and satirical English poem of this kind, and later commentators have moved it slightly forward – about the middle of the fourteenth century for the historians Keen and Holt[4] and for Dunn it belonged to 1350–70.[5]

Genre

Another unusual feature of *Gamelyn* is its genre: it falls between the martial epics of the alliterative revival and the full-length English romances that look to French sources. It is, however, much longer and weightier in narrative than a ballad, and is often given a hybrid name such as 'ballad epic' or 'epic romance'. There are, though, other lengthy and action-filled poems of the later Middle Ages that are not entirely unlike it in direct and vigorous, even violent, response to difficulties, like *A Gest of Robyn Hode, Adam Bell* and lengthy battle ballads of the sixteenth century such as *Chevy Chase* or *The Battle of Otterburn*.

Many commentators have found the legal and historical context that shows through the adventures of Gamelyn to be the most interesting thing about the poem, and the fullest account of its context is to be found in essays by Kaeuper and Scattergood.[6] Those features are, however, only in support of the narrative and might better be seen as a strong context for a story, which often appears in folklore, about the maltreatment of the youngest child – here in 'male Cinderella' form.

The place of origin of the poem can only be assessed by dialect: there are no place names, and Gamelyn's father's surname 'of Boundys' just means 'of the borders', which could mean anywhere. The underlying dialect appears to be from the north-east Midlands, and the small but noticeable number of words of Scandinavian origin (including 'Lithes' – Listen – the first word of the whole poem) suggests an origin in the more Danelaw-oriented part of the region, such as Lincolnshire, Leicestershire or Nottinghamshire – which need not suggest that the outlaws' forest is Sherwood.

Audience

Audience has, as with many poems of this kind, remained a problem, perhaps because it, like the Robin Hood texts, appeals to a wide range of interests. In the poem there is a range of positions which might appeal to different social groupings: dispossessed landholders like Gamelyn himself; the falsely accused – like Gamelyn, Ote and the king of the outlaws; upper servitors like Adam who have to decide whom to serve; and even the humble bondsmen who resist the pressures imposed by Gamelyn's vicious eldest brother. While the physical directness and brusque satire would seem to preclude an audience of courtly sophistication like that of Richard II, the poem, in its concern with defending a rightful position and defeating grasping wrongdoers, would certainly appeal widely in a century of rapid and bemusing social change and the frequent rise of self-made men.

Style and Structure

The style of *Gamelyn* has, like its content, been seen as direct rather than subtle, though it is often treated sympathetically as a plain treatment of a vigorous story. A similar effect is created by the unadorned diction of the poem, and the frequent use of fillers and semi-proverbial statements of the 'as I may thrive' and 'to tell the truth' kind – some thirty of these occur. They, like the quite common verbal repetitions, are elements of a style that most commentators have felt to be at least in part oral: clarity and communication are the central elements of the discourse.

Yet these features can have an effect capable of some subtlety in a context of dynamic meaning. In the opening sequence, as Sir Johan of Boundys lies on his death bed, the text keeps repeating how he lay increasingly 'still' and 'sick'. At the same time the poem keeps returning, as he does, to the question of his lands. In performance the passage has considerable power: as the man grows weaker, his lands become mobile, more and more a matter of obsession for him and, as it transpires, others. The identity of landowner and land, the difficult dissolution of that bond and the crucial nature of its re-formation – these issues are central to the period and the land-holding classes, and they lie behind the emphatic language of this highly effective opening passage.

If repetition of language can have such a marked effect, the use of imagery, though a rare feature, can also strike deep. In general this feature is highly stylized and proverbial, of the 'like a wild lion' or 'as still as a stone' kind. But in the central fight scene, where Gamelyn and Adam wreak their revenge on the clerical visitors, a biting irony frames their violent acts with a quasi-religious signification – Gamelyn respects their enemies' 'orders' by laying them out 'in order', and he pays special treatment to their tonsures with his huge club.

In terms of structure the poem has quite complex resources within an apparently plain and effective exterior. It is not simply a well-told story in the sense of a modern coherent narrative. The plot is in fact shot through with incoherencies and improbabilities. Why did Gamelyn take so many years to grasp his sorry position – it appears to be sixteen? Why did his brother suddenly lock him out when he went to the wrestling? Why on earth did Adam not set Gamelyn free as soon as they became allies, rather than wait for a public brawl? What precisely makes Gamelyn at the end suddenly return to court to rescue Ote rather than remain free? And what, most of all, leads Gamelyn to give up his quest for his own lands and accept from Ote the position of heir – which had been unacceptable when offered by his brother?

It is possible to imagine answers, or at least discussions, relating to these points, but the text does not consider them as important. Rather than a coherent novel-like sequence of action and reaction, the text in fact arranges a series of dramatic encounters, much like the melodramatic surges of action and rhetoric in romance. Adam does not free Gamelyn early simply so there can be a splendid brawl with the clerics. Gamelyn returns to court so he can break the judge's arm and then hang the whole jury – to dry in the wind, in another of the poem's brusquely ironic images.

Theme

If the structure in this way prepares high moments of ethical melodrama, the theme is accordingly directed towards such strongly flavoured moments of violent frustration of the forces of evil. Most commentators have related Gamelyn's rugged sense of equity to the real processes of medieval law (Kaeuper provides the fullest account), but there is in fact a strong fictional and ideological structure of ethics at the heart of the poem. The disinherited younger son is a common figure in the Middle Ages, and in romance this hero will win both a lady and a land with his prowess and his courtesy. However, Gamelyn's social standing is less aristocratic, his trajectory less fantastic, and women play no part at all. And whereas the fair unknown will reveal his birth, like Sir Gareth or Lybeaus Desconus, and all will fall into his lap, Gamelyn's late birth, inscribed in his name ('old man's son') is the problem from the beginning. In this moderately realistic context, the author derives a resolution for this 'male Cinderella' story not from the fantastic resources of romance but from another uncomfortable reality of medieval life, the outlaws who challenged settled law through the period.

Though stripped of his true familial base, with this new band of supporters Gamelyn is able to exercise lordship and rescue the true elder brother Sir Ote from the corrupt legal hands of the false elder brother Sir Johan. Family is reconstituted with outlaw help, just as the knight's world is rectified in *A Gest of Robyn Hode*. Then, however, follows a remarkable shift in the story, unnoticed by commentators. In this new familial context, both Gamelyn and the story go quietly. With good lordship in place, the younger son's problems are managed without the partition of inheritance that the wise men at the beginning tried to avoid. Old Sir Johan's wishes never come true. For all his heroism and violence, Gamelyn fits back into the family when it is purged of its evil leader: primogeniture is restored and all in the family is again well.

Not only does the text arrive at this consoling conclusion by a series of melodramatic and violent events, these actions also reveal the sub-textual operations of a structure of social and ethical forces that in fact define the ideology of the text. Gamelyn is attended by four categories of value, and it is only at the end that all are benevolent to him and fully at his service: they are strength, family, honour and law. Through the action he negotiates with these forces as one or the other is either taken from him or made hostile to him. At first a child without strength, having lost his familial role with the death of his father, Gamelyn has no honour and, through his elder brother, law is turned against him. Steadily he regains control over each component of value – though some, like law, are thoroughly elusive. It is only at the very end, when he and Ote reform their family, when he is honoured by the king and made an agent of a true law, that his tremendous strength and powerful outlaw support are no longer agents of social and narrative disruption but belong to and strengthen traditional society.

But there remains a distance between this text and those others where the outlaw life is central to the theme rather than, as here, merely instrumental to the resolution. Of the gentry rather than a yeoman, seeking land rather than occupying the potent spaces of the forest, having no trickster characteristics nor being close to natural imagery, Gamelyn is very different from Robin Hood, and his text survives from a period when it seems that the Robin Hood ballads were still entirely oral in medium. It is of course tempting to think that the nameless 'king of the outlaws' is in fact Robin Hood, and is unnamed in order not to draw attention away from the hero of this poem. The direct action, the interest in wrestling and the hostility to the established church all seem much like the mood and events of the early Robin Hood texts, but *Gamelyn*'s concern with the transmission of property and resistance to family betrayals appears more like the interests of more aristocratic outlaws like Eustache the Monk and Fouke fitz Waryn.

Gamelyn is the first English language link in the chain between the early distressed gentleman sagas of Eustache and Fouke and the plainer English heroes of forest resistance like Robin Hood and Adam Bell. It is a text whose robust and direct qualities have always been visible, while its subtleties have largely been overlooked on behalf of its simpler status as historical and legal corroboration. But if, as the author repeatedly asks, we 'Hear and listen and harken closely' there will be heard something more literary, more imaginative, more resonant through time and the outlaw tradition.

TRANSLATION OF *THE TALE OF GAMELYN*

Part I

Hear and listen and harken[1] closely, and you shall hear the story of a brave knight, whose name was Sir John of Boundes.[2] This knight, who knew about good breeding and sport, begot three sons. The eldest, Sir John the Younger, was a great wicked rascal, and he soon began to show it. His two brothers Sir Ote and Gamelyn loved their father well, and were in awe of him; but the eldest deserved his father's curse and got it in the end. His father, the good knight, lived so long that his death was approaching and tormented him bitterly. Lying on his sick bed, Sir John worried about the welfare of his children after he died. He had been far and wide, and he was not a farmer. Since all of his lands had been acquired by true purchase during his lifetime, he was eager to divide them equally among his sons, so each had an appropriate part.[3] He then sent for wise knights in the shire to help him evenly divide his lands. He asked them by letters to hasten quickly if they wanted to speak to him while he was still alive.

When the knights heard that he lay sick, they didn't rest night or day until they came to him where he lay still on his death bed, to await God's will. Then the good knight said, where he lay ill, 'Lords, I warn you truly, without denial, I may no longer live in this time because, through the will of God, death draws me to the ground.' There was not one of them who heard him that didn't have pity for that same knight, and they said, 'Sir, for the love of God, do not be dismayed, for God may work a remedy for evil that now is wrought.' Then spoke the good knight, where he lay ill, 'God may send remedy for evil, I know there is no denying it, but I beseech you knights, for the love of me, go and divide my lands among my three sons. And, for the love of God, do not divide wrongly and forget Gamelyn, who is my young son. Pay attention to that one as well as to the others [i.e., Sir John the younger and Sir Ote, the middle son]. Seldom do you see any heir help his brothers.'

Then they let the knight, who was not in good health, lie, and went into council in order to divide his lands. Their intent was to deliver all the lands to one, and since Gamelyn was the youngest he should have none. They divided in two all the land and let Gamelyn go without any land. And each of them loudly said to the other that his brothers might give him land when he [Gamelyn] knew right from wrong. And when they had divided the land according to their will, they came to the knight where he lay still and told him at once what they had done. And the knight liked it not.

Then said the knight, 'By Saint Martin,[4] in spite of what you have done, the land is still mine. For God's love, neighbours, delay all action, and I will divide my lands as I want. John, my eldest son, shall have five plough-measures, which was my father's heritage when he was alive.[5] And my middle son, Ote, shall have the 5 plough-shares that I won with my right hand.[6] And all my other acquisitions of lands, tenants and good horses I bequeath to Gamelyn. And I beseech you, good men who know the law of the land, let my bequest stand, for the love of Gamelyn.' Thus the knight divided his land while he was alive on his death bed where he lay ill. And soon afterwards he lay stone still and died when his time came, according to Christ's will.

As soon as he was dead and buried under grass, the elder brother, Sir John the Younger, beguiled the young boy and took his land and tenants into his hand. He took under control his land and tenants and clothed and fed Gamelyn badly and wrongly. And he let his lands, houses, parks and woods go to ruin; he did nothing well! And afterwards he paid for it with his own skin. As long as Gamelyn was the strongest one in his brother's hall, they all feared him. There was no one there, neither young or old, that would anger Gamelyn, were he ever so bold. One day Gamelyn stood in his brother's garden and began to stroke his beard.[7] He thought about his unsown lands, his fine oaks that were pulled down, his parks that were broken into, his deer stolen, his good horses missing, and his unroofed and poorly repaired houses. Then thought Gamelyn that nothing went aright.

Afterwards his elder brother came walking there, and said to Gamelyn, 'Is our meal ready?' Then Gamelyn grew angry and swore by God's book, 'Go bake thyself, I won't be thy cook!' 'What? brother Gamelyn, how did thou answer? Thou never spoke such words as thou do now.' 'By my faith,' said Gamelyn, 'now it seems to me necessary. I never yet took notice of all my harm. My parks have been broken into, my deer have been stolen, and none of my weapons and horses are left. Everything my father left me has gone to shame, and therefore you shall have God's curse, brother in name only!'

Then spoke his brother who was quick to anger, 'Stand still, base bastard, and hold thy peace! Thou should be glad to have thy food and clothing. What are thou saying, thou lowborn, about land and tenants?' Then said Gamelyn, the boy so young, 'Christ's curse may he have who calls me bastard! I am no worse bastard or no worse fellow, but I was born of a lady and begotten of a knight.'

Sir John didn't dare go one foot nearer to Gamelyn, but he called to his men and said to them then, 'Go and beat this boy and rob him of his wits, and let him learn to answer me better the next time.' Then said the young boy Gamelyn, 'Christ's curse may thou have, if thou are my brother! And if I must be beaten anyway, Christ's curse may thou have unless thou be the one.'[8] And at once his brother in great anger made his men fetch staves to beat Gamelyn with. When every one had taken a staff, Gamelyn was wary when he saw them coming. When Gamelyn saw them coming, he looked everywhere and saw a pestle[9] leaning against the wall. Gamelyn was light of foot and leaped to it, and drove all his brother's men at once into a heap. He looked like a wild lion and laid on a good number of blows. When his brother saw that, he began to leave and fled up into the loft and shut the door tight. Thus with his pestle Gamelyn terrified all of them. Some out of affection and some for awe [of him], they drew themselves on one side or the other when he began to 'play'.[10]

'What now!' said Gamelyn, 'May you prosper ill! Will you begin the combat and so soon flee?' Gamelyn sought out his brother where he had fled, and saw where he looked out of a window. 'Brother,' said Gamelyn, 'come a little nearer and I'll teach thee to play at the buckler.'[11] His brother answered him, and swore by St Richard,[12] 'While that pestle is in thine hand, I will come no nearer. Brother, I will make peace with thee, I swear by Christ's mercy. Throw away the pestle and don't be angry any more.' 'I must avenge myself at once', answered Gamelyn, 'because thou ordered thy men to break my bones. If I didn't have the power in my arms to defend myself, they would have done me harm.'

'Gamelyn,' said his brother, 'don't be angry, because I'd hate to see thee harmed. I only did it as a test to see whether thou were strong for one so young.' 'Come down to me', Gamelyn replied, 'and grant me my request of the one thing I will ask thee, and we will soon be reconciled.'

Down then came his brother, who was deceitful and cruel, and was very much afraid of the pestle. He said, 'Brother Gamelyn, ask me thy request, and look to it

thou blame me unless I grant it at once.' Then said Gamelyn, 'Brother, indeed, if
we are not to quarrel thou must grant me everything my father bequeathed to me
while he was alive: thou must give it me if we are not to fight.' 'Thou shall have
that, I swear by God's grace! All that thy father bequeathed thee, though thou want
to have more. Thy land that lay untilled, it shall be sown well, and thine houses
rebuilt that are laid low.' Thus said the knight to Gamelyn with his mouth,[13] and
planned falseness as well as he could. The knight planned treason, but not
Gamelyn, who went and kissed his brother. And when they were reconciled, alas,
young Gamelyn didn't realize at all with what treason his brother kissed him!

Part II

Harken, and listen and hold your tongue, and you shall hear about Gamelyn the
young. Nearby there was announced a wrestling match, and a ram and a ring
were set out as prizes. Gamelyn wanted to go there to prove his might, to show
what he could do. 'Brother,' said Gamelyn, 'by Saint Richard, thou must lend me
tonight a swift horse that is fresh to the spur for me to ride. I must go on an
errand a little way from here.' 'By God!' said his brother, 'go and choose thyself
the best of steeds and coursers that stand nearby, and don't spare any of them.
And tell me, good brother, where will thou ride?' 'Near here, brother, a wrestling
match has been announced, and a ram and a ring shall be the prizes. It would be
a great honour to all of us if I might bring home the ram and the ring to this
hall.' A steed was quickly and swiftly saddled, and Gamelyn put a pair of spurs
firmly on his feet, set his foot in the stirrup, mounted the horse and the young
squire rode towards the wrestling.

When young Gamelyn had ridden out of the gate, the false knight his brother
locked it after him and begged Jesus Christ, who is heavenly king, to let Gamelyn
break his neck in the wrestling match. As soon as Gamelyn came to the place, he
dismounted from his horse and stood on the grass. And there he heard a franklin
cry 'Woe is me' and begin to bitterly wring his hands.[14] 'Good man,' said
Gamelyn, 'why art thou carrying on so? Is there anyone who can help thee out of
thy grief?' 'Alas', said this franklin, 'that I was ever born! I fear that I've lost two
sturdy sons. The champion is here who has caused my sorrow. Unless God save
them, my two sons will be slain. I would give ten pounds and more if I found a
man to handle him [the champion] roughly!' 'Good man,' said Gamelyn, 'do me
a favour and hold my horse while my servant takes off my boots, and help him
guard my clothes and horse. I will go into the arena to see if I can win.' 'By God!'
said the franklin, 'it shall be done. I will myself be thy man to take off thy boots.
And while thou go into the arena, Jesus Christ make thee succeed, don't worry
about thy clothes or thy good horse.'

Barefoot and bare chested, Gamelyn came in, and everyone there took notice
of him and how he dared to challenge him, to try the power of the champion,

who was so strong in wrestling and fighting. The champion jumped up quickly and began to approach young Gamelyn. He said, 'Who is thy father, and who is thy lord? Truly thou art a great fool to come here!' Gamelyn then answered the champion, 'Thou knew well my father while he was alive, by Saint Martin! Sir John of Boundes was his name, and I am Gamelyn.'

'Fellow,' said the champion, 'so may I thrive, I knew your father well while he was still alive. And thyself, Gamelyn, listen to me, when thou were a young boy thou were a great mischievous fellow.' Swearing by Christ's grace, Gamelyn said, 'Now I've grown older, thou'll find me a greater rogue!' 'By God!', said the champion, 'welcome may thou be! Come thou into my hands, thou will never thrive.'

It was well into the night and the moon was shining when Gamelyn and the champion came together. [See plate 12.] The champion tried various holds on Gamelyn, who was ready, and Gamelyn stood firm and bade him do his best. Then Gamelyn said to the champion, 'Thou are trying hard to bring me down, but I have withstood thy many holds. Now thou must withstand one or two of mine.' Gamelyn went quickly to the champion, and showed him one of his many holds, and threw him on his left side, breaking three ribs and also his arm, which gave a great crack. Then said Gamelyn suddenly, 'Shall it be considered a throw, or not?' 'By God!' said the champion, 'whichever it be, he that comes into thy hands will never prosper!'

Then said the franklin who had the sons there, 'Blessed be thou, Gamelyn, that thou were ever born!' The franklin said to the champion, of whom he stood in no fear, 'This is young Gamelyn who taught thee this play.' Again answered the champion, who was very displeased, 'He is master of all and his play is very cruel. Since I first wrestled a very long time ago, I was never in my life handled so sorely.'

Gamelyn stood in the place without his shirt and said, 'If there be any more, let them come to work. It seems by his demeanour that the champion who worked so hard doesn't want any more.' Gamelyn stood in the place as still as a stone to await more wrestling but no one came there. There was no one who wanted to wrestle with Gamelyn because he handled the champion so severely.

Two gentlemen, who had charge of the place, came to Gamelyn – God give him good grace! – and said to him, 'Put on thy hose and thy shoes because, truly, at this time this fair is over.' And then Gamelyn said, 'So may I fare well, I have not yet sold my wares by half.' Then the champion said, 'As I may use my neck, he is a fool who buys your wares because thou sell them so dearly.' Then said the franklin, who had been in much care, 'Fellow, why find fault with these wares? By Saint James of Galicia, whose shrine many man has visited, it is a bargain that which thou have bought.' The wardens of the wrestling match came and brought Gamelyn the ram and the ring, and he thought it was a fair thing and went home with much joy in the morning.

His brother saw where he came with a great company, and he ordered the gate to be shut and him to be kept outside. The lord's porter was afraid and started quickly to the gate and locked it fast.

Part III

Now harken and listen, both young and old, and you shall hear sport of bold Gamelyn. He came to the gate in order to enter, but it was shut fast with a strong bolt. Then said Gamelyn, 'Porter, open the gate because many good men's sons are standing there.' The porter answered and swore by God's beard, 'Thou shall not, Gamelyn, come into this yard.' 'Thou liest,' said Gamelyn, 'as I may use my chin!'[15] He struck the gate with his foot and broke away the bolt. The porter saw then that it might be no better, and he set his foot on the earth and began to flee. 'By my faith,' said Gamelyn, 'that effort is lost, because I am as light of foot as thou even if you swore to the contrary.' He overtook the porter and avenged his anger, and struck him on the neck, breaking the bone. He took him by one arm and threw him in a well that was seven fathoms deep, as I have heard tell.

When young Gamelyn thus had played his play, all of Sir John's men in the yard drew away from him. They feared him greatly for the deeds that he did and for the fine company that he brought thither. Gamelyn went to the gate and had it opened wide. He let in everyone who wished to walk in or ride, and said, 'You are welcome without reservation because we will be masters here and ask no man permission. Yesterday I left five barrels of wine in my brother's cellar, and I will not let this company part from each other while any mouthful of wine is in there, if you will follow my desire. And if my brother grumble or complain foully about the cost of food or drink we are spending here, I am our caterer and shall bear the purse for all of us. Let him have Saint Mary's curse for his grumbling! I swear by God's grace, my brother is a skinflint, and we will spend generously that which he has long saved. And whoever complains while we stay here, let him join the porter in the well.'

Gamelyn held his feast seven days and seven nights with much merriment, and there was no quarrelling. His brother lay hidden in a little turret and saw him wasting his goods, but he dared not speak a word. Early in the morning on the eighth day, the guests came to Gamelyn and wished to go on their way. 'Lords,' said Gamelyn, 'why do you want to hurry away? If I can use my eye,[16] all the wine is not yet drunk.' Gamelyn's heart was very sad when his guests took their leave to go from him. He wished that they had stayed longer, but they declined, commending him to God and saying goodbye. Thus Gamelyn made his feast and brought it to a good end, and his guests received permission to depart.

Part IV

Harken and listen and hold your tongue, and you shall hear sport of young Gamelyn. Harken, lords, and listen attentively how Gamelyn was treated after all the guests were gone. All the time that Gamelyn held his feast, his brother thought about how he would be avenged by treachery. When Gamelyn's guests had ridden away, he stood all alone without any friends. It then happened shortly that Gamelyn was taken and tightly bound. Out of the upper room the false knight came out and went very close to his brother. He said to Gamelyn, 'Who made thee so bold as to waste the goods of my household?' 'Brother,' said Gamelyn, 'don't anger thyself, since many days ago it was paid for. By Saint Richard, thou hast had fifteen plough-shares of land for the last sixteen years, and thou bred from all the animals that my father left to me on his death bed. I give thee the profits of these sixteen years in return for what we have spent now on the food and drink.'

Then said the false knight – may he have ill luck! – 'Listen, brother Gamelyn, to what I will give thee. Since I have begotten no heir, brother, from my body, I will make thee my heir, I swear by Saint John.' 'By my faith!' said Gamelyn, 'if it be that thou act as thou say, God reward thee!'

Gamelyn knew nothing of his brother's deceit. Therefore he soon beguiled him. 'Gamelyn,' said he, 'one thing I tell thee, when thou threw my porter in the well, I swore in anger in the assembly that thou should be bound both hand and foot. This must be done in order to trick my men to hold to my vow as I promised thee.' 'Brother,' said Gamelyn, 'as I may prosper! Thou shall not break your oath for the love of me.' Then they made Gamelyn sit and not stand until they bound him foot and foot. Gamelyn's brother, the false knight, was frightened and he sent for fetters to shackle him fast. To those who came in, his brother told lies and said that Gamelyn was insane. Gamelyn stood bound to a post in the hall. All of those who came in looked at him, and all the time Gamelyn stood rigidly upright! He had no food or drink by day or night. Then said Gamelyn, 'Brother, by my neck, I have now discovered that thou art a false person. Had I known the treason that thou conceived, I would have given thee blows before I had been bound.'

Gamelyn stood bound, still as any stone, two days and nights without any food. Then he said, 'Adam Spencer, it seems to me I have gone without food too long. I now beg thee, for the great love my father gave thee, release me from my bonds if thou can come upon the keys. I will divide my free land with thee.' Then said Adam, who was the officer in charge of provisions, 'I have served thy brother for sixteen years, and if I let thee go out of his chamber, he would say afterwards that I was a traitor.' 'Adam,' said Gamelyn, 'as I use my neck! Thou wilt find my brother false in the end. Therefore, brother Adam, free me out of my shackles and I will share with thee my free lands.' 'Upon such an agreement,' said Adam, 'certainly I will do all that I can.' 'Adam,' said Gamelyn, 'as I hope to thrive, I will hold covenant with thee if thou will with me.'

As soon as Adam's lord went to bed, he took the keys and released Gamelyn at once. He unlocked both his hands and feet in hope of the advancement that he was promised. Then Gamelyn said, 'Thanks to God's Providence my hands and feet are free. If I could eat and drink now, there is no one in this house who could bind me tonight.' Adam took Gamelyn, who was quiet as a stone, and quickly led him into the pantry and set him down to eat in a private place. He bade him to enjoy himself and so he did.

As soon as Gamelyn had eaten well and also drunk well of the red wine, he said, 'Adam, what is thy advice now? Shall I go to my brother and strike off his head?' 'Gamelyn,' said Adam, 'it shall not be so. I can teach thee a plan that is worth two of thine. I know we are going to have a banquet here on Sunday, and abbots, priors and other men of Holy Church will be here, as I tell thee. Thou shall stand up by the post as if thou were bound tightly, and I shall leave the shackles unlocked so thou can cast them away. When the men have eaten and washed their hands,[17] thou shall beg them all to release thee from the bonds. And if they are willing to go bail for thee that would be a good game. Thou would be out of prison and blame. But if all of them say to us "nay", I shall take another course, I swear by this day! Thou shall have a good staff and I will have another, and Christ's curse have the one of us who fails the other!'

'Yes, by God,' said Gamelyn, 'I say for myself, if I fail on my side, evil may I thrive! If we shall "absolve them of their sins", warn me, brother Adam, when we should begin.'[18] 'Gamelyn,' said Adam, 'by Saint Charity, when it is time for thee to go, I'll warn thee by winking: cast off thy fetters, and come to me at once.' 'Adam,' said Gamelyn, 'bless thy bones! That is good advice given for the occasion. If they forbid thee to release me from my bonds, I'll set good strokes on their loins.' When Sunday arrived and people came to the feast, both high and low were finely welcomed. As they entered the door of the hall, they cast their eyes on young Gamelyn. His brother, the treacherous false knight, told all the guests at the banquet all he could about the harms and shame of his brother Gamelyn.

When they were served two or three courses, then Gamelyn said, 'Am I to be served? By God that created us all, I am not well served, who sits here starving while other men are enjoying themselves.' The false knight told all the guests that Gamelyn was insane. And Gamelyn stood quietly and didn't answer, but he remembered Adam's words. Then he began to speak dolefully indeed to the great lords who sat in the hall. 'Lords,' he said, 'for Christ's Passion, help to bring me out of prison.' Then said an abbot – may there be sorrow on his cheek! – 'He shall have Christ's and Saint Mary's curse who begs to free thee or stands bail for you. Ever may he prosper who causes thee much sorrow.' After that abbot then spoke another, 'I wish thy head were cut off even if thou were my brother! May ill luck befall them that go bail for you!' Thus they all said who were in the hall. Then said a prior – evil may he thrive! – 'It is a great sorrow and care, boy, that thou are alive!' 'Oh!', said Gamelyn, 'as I use my bones! – I have discovered that I have no friends. Cursed may he be of flesh and blood who ever does a prior or abbot any good!'

Adam the spencer took up the cloth and looked at Gamelyn and saw that he was angry. He didn't care about his work in the pantry, but brought two good staves from the pantry to the hall door. He looked at Gamelyn, who was aware at once, and he cast away the fetters and began to act. When he came to Adam he took one staff and began to work and gave good strokes. Gamelyn and Adam came into the hall and looked around as if they were angry. Gamelyn 'sprinkled holy water with an oak twig'[19] so that some who were standing upright fell in the fire. There was no layman in the hall who would do Gamelyn anything but good. They stood aside and let them both 'work' because they had no pity for men of Holy Church.

'Gamelyn,' said Adam, 'for Saint Charity, pay a liberal allowance of blows for the love of me, and I'll guard the door, as sure as I ever hear Mass! No one will pass until he has been "absolved".' 'Fear not,' said Gamelyn, 'as long as we stay together. Thou guard the door and I'll "work" here. Stir thyself, good Adam, and don't let any flee, and we'll count fully how many there are.' 'Gamelyn,' said Adam, 'do them nothing but good. Since they are men of Holy Church, don't draw any blood from them. Respect their tonsures and do them no harm, but break both their legs and then their arms!'

Thus Gamelyn and Adam worked very fast, and sported with the monks and terrified them. They came there riding jauntily with their servants and were carried away home in carts and farm wagons. When they had all gone, then a grey friar said, 'Alas! Sir abbot, why did we come here? When we came here, it was a fatal choice. We had better stayed at home with bread and water.'

While Gamelyn 'made orders' of monks and friars, his brother stood by and acted distraught. Gamelyn raised his staff, which he knew how to use, and struck him in the neck and he fell down. The backbone broke a little above the waist. And Gamelyn set him in the shackles where he sat before. 'Sit there, brother,' said Gamelyn, 'to cool thy body as I did mine.' As soon as they had avenged themselves on their foes, they asked for water and washed themselves at once. All the servants served them in the best manner, some out of love and some because of fear. The sheriff was distant only five miles, and everything was told to him within a short while, how Gamelyn and Adam had made a grievous attack, had bound and wounded men against the king's peace. And the sheriff went about to capture Gamelyn.

Part V

Now harken and listen, as God may give you a good ending! And you shall hear good sport about young Gamelyn. Twenty-four young men, who considered

themselves very bold, came to the sheriff and said that, by their faith, they
desired to fetch Gamelyn and Adam. The sheriff gave them permission, the truth
to tell, and they hurried fast, and wouldn't tarry, to the gate where Gamelyn was
within. As they knocked on the gate, the porter, who was close at hand, looked
cautiously out of the peep-hole. Looking at them for a little while, the porter, who
loved Gamelyn, was afraid of trickery, so he fastened the small window and asked
them outside what they wanted. One spoke for the large company, 'Undo the
gate, porter, and let us go in.' And the porter said, 'As I may live and breathe, you
shall tell me your errand before you come in.'

'Say to Gamelyn and Adam that, if it be their will, we want to speak two or
three words with them.' 'Fellow,' said the porter, 'stay there and I will go to
Gamelyn to know his will.' The porter went in at once to Gamelyn and said, 'Sir,
I warn you, your foes have come here. The sheriff's men are at the gate to take
you both, and you can't escape.' 'Porter,' said Gamelyn, 'as I may thrive! I'll
praise your words when I get a chance. Go again to the gate and dally with them
for a while, and thou shall very soon see, porter, a trick.'

'Adam,' said Gamelyn, 'get ready to go. We have many foes and not one
friend. The sheriff's men have come hither, and they have sworn together that
we'll be taken.' 'Gamelyn,' said Adam, 'hasten thee quickly, and if I fail thee
today evil may I thrive! And we'll so welcome the sheriff's men that some of
them will make their beds in the mud.' Gamelyn went out at a rear gate and
seized a good cart-shaft in his hands. Adam seized another large staff in order to
help Gamelyn, and he gave good strokes. Adam knocked down two men and
Gamelyn felled three. The others set their feet on the earth and began to flee.
'What,' said Adam, 'as I ever hear Mass! I have for you a draught of good wine
[i.e. the staff] before you go!' 'Nay, by God,' they said, 'thy drink is not good – it
would cause a man's brains to lie within his hood.'[20]

Gamelyn stood still and looked around, and said, 'The sheriff is coming with a
large troop. Adam, what do you suggest we do now? Here comes the sheriff who
wants our heads.' Adam said to Gamelyn, 'My advice is this now: let's not stay
here longer lest we are treated badly. I suggest we go to the woods before we are
found. It is better for us to be free there than be bound in town.' Adam took
young Gamelyn by the hand, and after taking a draught of wine, they departed
and went away. Then the sheriff found the nest but not the eggs.[21] He
dismounted from his horse and went into the hall, where he discovered the lord
[Sir John] firmly fettered within. The sheriff quickly released him and sent for a
doctor to heal his backbone.

Let us now leave this false knight lie in his grief and talk about Gamelyn and
how he fares. Gamelyn walked cautiously into the woods, and Adam Spencer was
not pleased. Adam swore to Gamelyn, 'By Saint Richard, now I see it is merry to
be a spencer; it would be more pleasant carrying my keys than walking in this
wild forest tearing my clothes.' 'Adam,' said Gamelyn, 'don't be alarmed, for

many a good man's child is brought to sorrow.' As they stood talking together, Adam heard men conversing very near them. When Gamelyn looked through the trees, he saw seven score well-armed young men. All of them were sitting in a circle eating their meal. 'Adam,' said Gamelyn, 'now I have no fear, through the might of God good will come after evil. It seems that I can see food and drink.' Adam then looked through the tree boughs, and when he saw food he was very glad, because he hoped to God to have his share and he was sorely longing for a meal.

As he said that word, the master outlaw saw Adam and Gamelyn under the thicket in the woods. 'Young men,' said the master, 'by the good Cross, I'm aware of guests that God sent us. Yonder are two well-armed young men, and perhaps whoever looked carefully might see more. Arise, young men, and fetch them to me. It is good that we find out who these men are.' Seven men rose up from their dinner and went to meet Gamelyn and Adam Spencer. When they reached them, one of them said, 'Young men, yield up your bows and arrows.' Then said Gamelyn, who was young of age, 'Much sorrow may they have who yield them to you! I curse no other man but myself: though you fetched five more to add to your seven men, then you would be twelve, and we would still not be afraid of you!' When they heard from Gamelyn's mouth that there was pith in his arm, none of them wished to do him any harm, but they spoke mildly and quietly to Gamelyn, and said, 'Come before our master and tell him your will.' 'Young men,' said Gamelyn, 'by your truth, what kind of man is your master who is with you?' Without deception, all of them answered, 'Our master is the crowned king of the outlaws.' 'Adam,' said Gamelyn, 'let's go in Christ's name. He may neither deny us food and drink for shame. If he is courteous and comes of gentle blood, he will give us food and drink, doing us some good.' 'By Saint James!', said Adam, 'whatever the harm I may get, I will venture so I might have food.'

Gamelyn and Adam went forth together, and they greeted the master that they found there. The master, king of the outlaws, then said, 'Young men, what are you searching for in the wood thickets?' Gamelyn answered the crowned king, 'He must walk in the forest who cannot walk in town. Sire, we are not walking here to do any harm. But as men who have been hard beset under the linden wood, we are hungry, and having found no food we will shoot at a deer if we find one.'

The master outlaw took pity on Gamelyn's words, and said, 'You shall have enough food and drink, God may have my pledged word on that!' He invited them to sit down and rest and eat and drink of the best. As they ate and drank excellently, one said to the other, 'This is Gamelyn.' The master outlaw was then taken into council and told that it was Gamelyn who had come there. As soon as he heard how it had happened, he made Gamelyn master under him of them all. Within the third week tidings came to the master outlaw that he should return home because his peace was made [i.e., he was pardoned]. And he was very glad about that good news. He then said to his young men, to tell the truth, 'Tidings have come to me, and I can no longer stay.' Then was Gamelyn without delay made the master outlaw and crowned their king.

When Gamelyn was crowned king of the outlaws and had walked for a while under the forest trees, his brother, the false knight, was appointed sheriff and lord and, because of hate and anger, had his brother [Gamelyn] indicted. Then were Gamelyn's tenants sorry when he was cried wolf's head,[22] and sent out his men to seek Gamelyn in the forest, wherever they might find him, in order to tell him the news about how the wind had changed and how all his property had been despoiled and all his men badly treated. When they found him, they set themselves on their knees, drew down their hoods, and saluted their lord. 'Sire, don't be angry, by the good Cross, for we have brought you tidings, and they are not good. Thy eldest brother, Sir John, is now sheriff and holds the bailiff's office. And he has indicted thee and declared thee wolf's head.' 'Alas!' said Gamelyn, 'that I was ever so careless by not breaking his neck when I broke his back. Go, tell my tenants and their wives that I will go to the next shire court, God protect my life!'

Gamelyn came ready to the next meeting of the shire court, and his brother, lord and sire, was there. Gamelyn came boldly into the moot hall and lowered his hood [to reveal his identity] to all the lords there. 'God save you, lords, that are here! But broken-back sheriff, may thou thrive badly! Why hast thou done me shame and villainy by indicting me and declaring me an outlaw?' Then the false knight Sir John thought to be avenged: Gamelyn was not allowed to say anything, nor given any mercy, but finally was thrown into prison and soundly shackled.

Gamelyn had another brother, called Sir Ote, who was as good and courteous a knight as any who walked on earth. At once a messenger went to that good knight and told him how Gamelyn was treated. As soon as he heard that, he was very sorry and not at all happy. He had his horse saddled, took his way, and came right away to his two brothers. 'Sire,' said Sir Ote to the sheriff, 'we are but three brothers, we shall never be more and thou hast imprisoned the best of us all. May evil befall such a brother as you!' 'Sir Ote,' said the false knight, 'give up thy curse. By God, he shall fare the worse because of thy words. He has been taken to the king's prison and there he shall wait until the justice comes.' 'By God,' said Sir Ote, 'it shall be better than that. I demand that thou grant bail for him until the next sitting of the court of deliverance and let Gamelyn appear to answer that charge.' 'Brother,' replied the sheriff, 'I agree to commit him to thee, but by thy father's soul, if he is not ready when the justice sits thou shall bear the judgement in spite of thy great wisdom.' 'I agree indeed', said Sir Ote, 'that it be so. Have him freed and give him to me.'

Gamelyn was then delivered to Sir Ote, his brother. And that night each dwelt with the other. On the morning Gamelyn said to the courteous Sir Ote, 'Brother, I must in truth go from thee to see how my young men are leading their lives, whether they live in joy or else in strife.' 'By God,' said Sir Ote, 'that is a bad plan. I see that all the responsibility shall now fall on my head. If thou cannot be found when the justice sits, I shall be taken at once and bound in thy place.' 'Brother', said Gamelyn, 'don't be dismayed, for by Saint James in Galicia, whom many men have sought, if Almighty God protect my life and wisdom, I will be ready when the justice sits.' Then said Sir Ote to Gamelyn, 'God shield thee from shame. Come when it is time and bring us out of blame.'

Part VI

Harken and listen and be quiet, and you shall hear how Gamelyn had all his desire. He went under the forest branches and found his worthy young men sporting there. When he found his men under the wood boughs, Gamelyn was very glad. And talking together, they had a good time listening to their master. His men told him about the adventures that they found, and Gamelyn told them how he had been captured and bound. While he was outlawed, no one criticized him. Nobody feared the worst from him, except for abbots, priors, monks and canons: he left them nothing when he could catch them.

While Gamelyn and his men amused themselves, his brother, the false knight – evil may he thrive! – was busy both day and night bribing the members of the inquest to hang his brother. One day Gamelyn stood and beheld the woods, groves and wild fields, and he thought about how he had promised his brother Sir Ote that he would be ready when the justice sat in the law court. He thought he would go without delay to keep his day before the justice. And he said to his young men, 'Make yourself ready because when the justice sits we must be there. Since I am under bail, my brother Sir Ote must be taken to prison in my place unless I come.' 'By Saint James!' said the young men, 'if you so advise, ordain how it shall be, and it shall be done.'

While Gamelyn was on his way, the justice took his seat on the law bench. His brother, the false knight, Sir John, had not forgotten to bribe the men of the jury to hang his brother. If they couldn't have one [Gamelyn], they would have the other [Sir Ote]. Then Gamelyn came from under the forest boughs and brought with him his worthy young men. 'I see that the justice is sitting,' said Gamelyn, 'Adam, go and see what is happening.' Adam went into the hall and looked around. He saw lords, great and proud, standing there, as well as Sir Ote strongly shackled. When Adam rushed out of the hall as if he were terrified, he said to Gamelyn and to his fellows, 'Sir Ote is fettered in the moot hall!' 'Young men,' said Gamelyn, 'all of you hear this: Sir Ote stands fettered in the moot hall. If God gives us grace to succeed, he shall pay for it, who brought it about.' Then said Adam, who had grey hair, 'May he have Christ's curse who bound him so sorely! And if thou act, Gamelyn, according to my plan, there is no one in the hall who shall leave with his head.' 'Adam,' said Gamelyn, 'we will not do so. We will slay the guilty, and let the others go. I'll go into the hall and speak with the justice. I will be avenged on those who are guilty. Let no one escape through the door, take heed, young men. For I will be justice today and hand down verdicts. God help me at my new work today! And, Adam, come with me for thou shall be my clerk.' His men answered him and told him to do his best, and said, 'If thou hast need of us, thou shall find us ready. We will stand with thee as long as we may endure, and unless we perform as men, pay us no wages.' 'Young men,' said Gamelyn, 'as I may thrive, a dependable master you shall find in me!'

Gamelyn went in among them all where the justice sat there in the hall, and had his brother released from his shackles. Then his courteous brother, Sir Ote, said, 'Gamelyn, thou had almost stayed away too long, because the verdict was that I should hang.' 'Brother,' said Gamelyn, 'may God give me good rest! Today they shall be hanged who are on the jury, and also the justice who is the judge, and the sheriff who began it all.' Then Gamelyn said to the justice, 'Thy power is now finished, so thou must leave. Thou hast rendered verdicts that were unjustly given. I will sit in thy seat and arrange them correctly.' The justice sat still and did not rise at once, and Gamelyn broke his cheekbone. Taking him in his arms, Gamelyn, who said nothing further, threw him over the bar and broke his arm. No one dared to say anything but good to Gamelyn, terrified of the company who stood without.

Gamelyn sat down in the justice's seat, with Sir Ote his brother at his side and Adam at his feet. When Gamelyn was seated in the justice's place, just listen to his jest! He had the justice and his false brother fettered and made them come together to the bar of justice. When Gamelyn had done thus, he had no rest until he found out who on the jury had judged his brother Sir Ote to hang. Before he discovered which ones they were, it seemed to him a long time. But as soon as he knew who they were, he had them shackled together and brought them to the bar and set in a row. 'By my faith,' said the justice, 'the sheriff is a villain!' Then Gamelyn said to the justice, 'Thou hast given judgements of the worst court of law. And the twelve jurors who were on the inquest shall be hanged today if I ever have good peace!' Then the sheriff said to young Gamelyn, 'Lord, I beg thee mercy, thou art my brother.' 'Therefore,' said Gamelyn, 'may thou have Christ's curse! If thou were master I would have worse.'

To make the tale short, and not too long, he ordained an inquest of his strong men. They hanged both the justice and the sheriff as well as the twelve jurors. Misery to anyone who cares! They were all hanged by the neck. Thus ended the false knight with his treachery, who led his life with falseness and folly. He was hanged by the neck and not by the purse. [23] This was the reward that he got for his father's curse.

Sir Ote was eldest and Gamelyn was young. They went with their friends straight to the king. They made peace with the king in the best legal manner. The king loved well Sir Ote and made him justice. And afterwards, the king made

Gamelyn, in the east and west, the chief justice of his free forest. The king forgave the guilt of all his bold young men, and afterwards appointed them to good offices. Thus Gamelyn won back his land and his tenants and avenged himself on his enemies and gave them their reward. And his brother, Sir Ote, made him his heir. And afterwards Gamelyn married a fair and good wife. They lived together while Christ willed it. And afterwards Gamelyn was buried under the earth. And so shall we all be, may no man escape it. God bring us to that joy that ever shall be!

7

THE SAGA OF ÁN BOW-BENDER

Shaun F.D. Hughes

INTRODUCTION

Manuscript and Date

Áns saga bogsveigis is preserved in an Icelandic vellum manuscript, AM 343a, 4to, from the third quarter of the fifteenth century and in at least forty-five paper manuscripts.[1] Because *Áns saga* has yet to appear in a scholarly edition, many important questions concerning the relationship among the surviving manuscript versions remain unanswered. Carl Christian Rafn published the only serviceable edition of the saga in 1829[2] basing his text on AM 343a, 4to, and the following translation is based on Rafn's text as it appears in the edition of Guðni Jónsson.[3]

Áns saga is clearly composed in Iceland and written in imitation of the style of the thirteenth-century Icelandic family sagas (*Íslandinagasögur*), but is itself unlikely to be that early. It may date from as late as the third quarter of the fourteenth century which would make it not far removed in time from the composition of the metrical romance (*rímur*) based on the saga. Ólafur Halldórsson dates the poem to the first quarter of the fifteenth century and it survives in three Icelandic vellum manuscripts, the oldest dated to the fourth quarter of the fifteenth century.[4] The numerous differences in detail between *Áns rímur* and *Áns saga*, especially towards the end of the narrative, suggest that the former is based on a version of the saga at least one or two removes from that found in AM 343a, 4to.

Genre

Áns saga is one of a group of fifty-five late Icelandic prose narratives to which Rafn gave the designation *fornaldar sögur Norðurlanda*[5] (sagas of the northern countries in ancient times, i.e., before the settlement of Iceland, AD 874). Under this classification were collected a large number of miscellaneous narratives from different periods and of different types whose only unifying feature is that their setting is Scandinavia rather than central or southern Europe. *Áns saga* is further distinguished as one of four sagas sometimes known as *Hrafnistumannasögur* ('sagas of the people from Hrafnista, an island off what is the modern district of Nord-Trøndelag in central-north Norway'). These sagas concern the descendants of

Hallbjörn *hálftröll* ('half-troll') of Hrafnista, his son Ketill *hængur* ('jack-salmon'), his son, Grímur *loðinkinna* ('shaggy-cheek'), and his son Örvar-Oddur ('Arrow' – Oddur) and Án bogsveigir. Án as a great-great-grandson of Hallbjörn *hálftröll* is not a direct male descendant of Hallbjörn, for he traces his lineage back through his mother, Þorgerður who, in a detail not confirmed by *Gríms saga loðinkinna*, is said to be the daughter of Hrafnhildur, the daughter of Ketill hængur and his wife Sigríður Bárðardóttir.[6]

There is one detail which distinguishes *Áns saga* from all the other *fornaldarsögur*: it is the only one in which the chief protagonist is an outlaw. Because of this some scholars have tried to link it with the medieval Icelandic outlaw tradition, particularly the sagas that have outlaws as chief protagonists, *Gísla saga Súrssonar*, *Grettis saga Ásmundarsonar* and *Harðar saga Grímkelssonar*.[7] Connections between these Icelandic outlaw narratives and the medieval English outlaw tradition have long been suspected.

Áns saga and the English Outlaw Tradition

In 1916 Henry Goddard Leach wrote an article on outlaws in Icelandic literature, medieval and modern, at the close of which he observes that 'England has borrowed the word "outlaw", the institution of outlawry, and the motif in literature' from the North.[8] This article was expanded into the chapter 'Outlaw Legends' in his 1921 volume, *Angevin Britain and Scandinavia*,[9] where it was suggested that there might be some connection between the medieval Icelandic outlaw sagas and the medieval English outlaw narratives of Hereward, Gamelyn and Robin Hood. Specifically, Leach adduces a number of fairly minor parallels between *Grettis saga* and the *Gesta Herwardi*, sufficient at least for him to claim that the two are 'cognate developments'.[10] He also asserts that both Gamelyn and Robin Hood 'can lay claim to Scandinavian descent',[11] although the evidence he brings forward to substantiate this claim is even more tenuous than the links he finds connecting the stories of Grettir and Hereward.

It was up to the Dutch scholar, Joost de Lange to take this hypothesis one step further. In his *The Relation and Development of English and Icelandic Outlaw Traditions* (1935) de Lange took Leach's observations and used them as the starting point for a radical and daring thesis which claimed that the connection between the two outlaw traditions was anything but casual. De Lange surveyed the outlaw traditions first of England (the narratives of Hereward, Fouke fitz Waryn, Gamelyn and Robin Hood) and then of Iceland (the sagas of Gísli Súrsson, Grettir Ásmundarson and Hörður Grímkelsson)[12] before turning his attention to *Áns saga*. After giving a detailed synopsis of the saga, de Lange discusses the points of contact between *Áns saga* and other surviving texts in Old Icelandic including *Grettis saga Ásmundarsonar* and *Egils saga Skalla-Grímssonar* (see footnotes 10 and 12 to the translation). He then turns to consider what is known of Án bogsveigis from sources outside his saga, principally the story of Ano Sagittarius in the twelfth-century *Gesta Danorum* of Saxo Grammaticus,[13] before turning to what he sees as direct parallels between episodes in *Áns saga* and incidents from English outlaw narratives. These can be summarized as follows (retaining de Lange's numbering but paraphrasing his text):

1. The relationship between Án and Þórir parallels that between Gamelyn and his brother.
2. Like Án, Hereward and Gamelyn perform youthful feats of strength.
3. The fight between Án and Björn parallels that between Hereward and Ogga.
4. Án's punishment of Ketill for calling himself Án has a parallel in Fouke fitz Waryn's punishment of Pieres de Brubyle for passing himself off as Fouke.
5. Án's rough treatment of the king's hired killers has parallels in the English outlaw tradition from Hereward to Robin Hood.
6. Án has a loyal female companion in Jórunn as Hereward in Turfrida.
7. Án as a leader in the forest when Ívar is condemned parallels Robin Hood's position in Barnsdale or Sherwood Forest.
8. Án uses bow and arrows except in his last battle with the king when he uses a cudgel. Gamelyn is armed with a club, but uses bow and arrows when a member of an outlaw band.

De Lange does not claim that there is any direct connection between the English outlaw narratives and *Áns saga*, but rather that there is an underlying Norse tradition of outlaw life which has given rise to both. This leads him to make the following five claims:

1. Comparison between *Áns saga* and the Ano Sagittarius episode in *Gesta Danorum* proves the existence of an earlier saga about Án.
2. Those features which *Áns saga* and the English outlaw tradition have in common belong to the underlying Norse tradition even if not initially associated with Án.
3. The Norwegian setting of *Áns saga* forecloses the possibility that the saga originated in the Danelaw and travelled from there to Iceland. Rather the English outlaw tradition contains Norse elements introduced by the vikings which subsequently underwent their own separate development.
4. *Áns saga* as it was brought to Iceland contains a kernel of historical memory since Án is someone attested to in the Icelandic genealogies.
5. A preliterate complex of outlaw traditions existed in Norway before the settlement of Iceland which was characterized by the following features: '*a*, enmity between king and subject; *b*, the outlaw is strong as well as cunning and always outwits his opponents; *c*, the outlaw is the leader of a community

or band of outlaws; *d*, the outlaw is ridiculous and clumsy in his youth; *e*, the test-fight; *f*, feats of strength at an early age; *g*, the trusted wife.'[14].

De Lange then discusses elements of the preliterate Norwegian outlaw tradition which are to be found in the Icelandic outlaw tradition before proceeding to the following conclusion:

> Our ultimate conclusion is then that we must assume the old Norse outlaw-tradition, as embodied in the Án-saga, to represent the trunk of which the Icelandic and English outlaw-matter as the branches. Each branch has developed in its own way and has been strongly influenced by social and national conditions, without ever losing altogether the inherent Scandinavian impress of the original tradition.[15]

In 1938 Jan Spoelstra published the most comprehensive introduction to the Icelandic outlaw traditions to date. The discussion of *Áns saga* is first concerned with the historicity of Án, but most of the remainder of the section is devoted to a critique of de Lange's thesis on the connection between the Icelandic and English outlaw traditions. Spoelstra criticizes each of de Lange's eight points of comparison between *Áns saga* and the English outlaw narratives as being insufficiently specific (many are common *märchen* motifs) to support the claims that are made for them. Rather, what de Lange has shown is that there are connections between Old Norse popular literature and West European *Chansons de Geste* and romances.[16]

Subsequent scholarship agrees with Spoelstra's conclusions. For example, Ingrid Benecke summarily dismisses de Lange's hypothesis in her study of the English outlaw tradition:

> Leach [*Angevin Britain*, pp. 35–55] treats the British *Outlaw Legends* together with the Icelandic sagas of the outlaws Hardar [*sic*], Gísli and Grettir. The sympathy of their respective authors – it is stated – was on the side of the Nordic outlaws as well as the British [*Angevin Britain*, pp. 339, 355]; in this however the connection between them is exhausted [350, 355]. J. de Lange is not able to convince the reader that a single Old Norwegian source, the Saga of Án bogsveigir is the foundation of the British and the Old Norse Outlaw-Literature [*Relation and Development*, pp. 108–31, esp. 129ff.].[17]

Benecke argues that the narratives of Hereward and Fouke fitz Waryn concern a good retainer who, being wronged by an unjust monarch, is eventually able to restore feudal order by his resistance, whereas the narratives of Gamelyn and Robin Hood concern individuals who remain loyal to their monarch, resisting the abuses of aristocrats such as the sheriff who have local authority, while at the same time displaying both a readiness to help and 'courtly' behaviour towards their opponents.[18] On the basis of this research it has been suggested that *Áns saga* could be grouped along with the narratives of Hereward and Fouke fitz Waryn.[19] However, the very different social structure of early medieval Iceland which lacked both the institutions of monarch and sheriff[20] makes problematic the application of Benecke's insights to the other medieval Icelandic outlaw narratives.

As can be seen there has been little support for de Lange's thesis almost from the moment it appeared, and the passage of time has done nothing to warrant a resurrection of his conclusions, virtually every one of which is difficult in its own way. But the chief structural flaw in his argument is his assumption that this ancient outlaw tradition remained somehow hermetically sealed from outside influences in the 'oral tradition', barely influencing the family sagas that have outlaws as chief protagonists, to appear in its pristine and archaic form in *Áns saga*. Besides, *Áns saga* is not an ancient text. While Torfi Tulinius argues that one of the *fornaldar sögur*, *Hervarar saga og Heiðreks* in something close to its surviving form, was composed in about 1200 and was known and used by the composer of *Egils saga Skalla-Grímssonar* some thirty years later,[21] there is general agreement that the date of the composition of *Áns saga* is much later. For the early Norwegian outlaw tradition to remain intact over the centuries to appear in about 1400 in *Áns saga*, de Lange's thesis requires the existence of an oral tradition that is more faithful to its 'text' than the literate tradition of preserving texts in manuscripts. While the oral tradition is capable of preserving traditions over long periods of time, it is by its very nature dynamic, and de Lange's formulation of the working of that tradition is no longer tenable. As Gísli Sigurðsson explains:

> They [earlier academics] were wrong when they thought that the oral tradition would necessarily preserve information accurately for centuries, they were wrong when they equated oral with historical, they were wrong when they thought that artistic composition would exclude oral origins, they were wrong when they stated that stories could not survive for two or three hundred years among people and families who lived on the same turf for that period of time. And if all these conclusions were wrong we are bound to arrive at the conclusion that everything which has been based on them will have to be revised.[22]

Áns rímur and *A Gest of Robyn Hode*

But the relationship between the narrative of Án bogsveigir and the English outlaw tradition is not to be entirely dismissed even with the rejection of de Lange's hypothesis. There remains a point of comparison not in terms of content or theme, but on the strictly formal grounds of the genre of *Áns rímur* and *A Gest of Robyn Hode*.[23] The recent editors of the *Gest* tacitly accept the theory that that poem is the result of drawing together shorter ballads to achieve an extended narrative,[24] while often emphasizing its structural and thematic integrity.[25] Barrie Dobson and John Taylor wrestle with the genre of the *Gest* and come to the conclusion that '[w]hat seems most probable is that the *Gest*, like other Robin Hood stories defies precise categorization'.[26] David Fowler's suggestion that the *Gest* is the original form from which the ballads were later excerpted had not won critical acceptance.[27] Stephen Knight in his *Robin Hood: A Complete Study of the English Outlaw* discusses the *Gest* in his chapter 'Robin Hood in the Ballads', while recognizing that '[a]part from its mode and extent, there are other features in which the *Geste* seems quite different from the ballads'.[28]

The *Gest* is not a ballad, but the sole surviving English example of a 'ryme', a long narrative poem broken into fits or chapters and originally having a more formal rhyme scheme than the ballad. The 'ryme', however, did not flourish in England but was supplanted by the shorter and more flexible narrative form of the ballad. The 'Middle English' forms found in the *Gest* in its printed version suggest that the genre was already archaic and non-productive by 1500. On the other hand, the numerous printed fragments suggest that there was still a market for this form of poetry. What happened to the other 'rymes'? Why is there no further trace of them? We know that there was at least one other dealing with Randolph, Earl of Chester, but it has completely disappeared without even leaving behind a ballad to signal its existence. The survival of the *Gest* was pure chance so the disappearance of all other traces of the 'rymes' is not a necessary argument against the existence of such a genre. The fate of the 'ryme' was probably determined by the changing taste of its primary audience whatever it may have been, for the difficulty of determining this question can be seen in the continuing debate over the primary audience of the *Gest*.[29] In Iceland the fate of the 'ryme' was the exact opposite. The *rímur* flourished as a genre while the ballad never really took root.[30] Nor was the existence of 'rymes' restricted to English or Icelandic literary traditions, for they are also found in the Faroe Islands, although the discussion of this complex matter lies outside the scope of the present introduction.

The earliest surviving *ríma* (sixty-five stanzas) is found in an Icelandic manuscript from no later than the last quarter of the fourteenth century and the poem shows every indication that it is already part of a well-established poetic genre. Its author, Einar Gilsson (*fl.* 1360), is an exact contemporary of the composer of the B-Text of *Piers Ploughman*. There in the fifth passus Sloth explains to Repentance that even though he does not know his Paternoster, yet he does know 'rymes of Robin Hode and Randolf Erl of Chestre'. This knowledge would hardly be singled out for the poet's wrath if it were not something particularly time consuming – the time taken to recite a poem the length of an *Áns rímur* or *A Gest of Robyn Hode*, for example. In fact the two poems are somewhat similar in terms of the number of fitts and total number of stanzas as the following demonstrates:

A Gest		Áns rímur	
Fitt	**Stanzas**	**Fitt**	**Stanzas**
1	81	1	61
2	62	2	65
3	61	3	68
4	76	4	63
5	36	5	63
6	37	6	89
7	64	7	79
8	39	8	57
Total:	456		545

Metrically *Áns rímur* is far more complex than *A Gest*, but fitts 1, 3, 5 and 8 are in *ferskeytt* ('squared meter'), a form similar to numerous stanzas in *A Gest*. It has four stresses in lines 1 and 3 (seven syllables) and three stresses in lines 2 and 4 (six syllables), rhyming ABAB. By a conservative count, omitting those stanzas where lines 1 and 3 end in the same word, seventeen stanzas of *A Gest* qualify as *ferskeytt*[31] although the majority of the stanzas are in 'ballad metre . . . a quatrain that rhymes ABCB with A and C being four stresses and the B lines three-stressed'.[32]

Conclusion

Áns saga bogsveigis did not necessarily have a direct influence on the English outlaw tradition as was once claimed, nor did *Áns rímur*. But that does not mean that there were no points of contact between the popular literatures of England and Iceland. There was regular contact between the two communities throughout the Middle Ages. The question of influence and cultural exchange between England and Iceland remains open and is likely to have extended far beyond their respective outlaw traditions.

TRANSLATION OF *THE SAGA OF ÁN BOW-BENDER*[1]

Án's family and his growing up

This saga begins in the time when there were regional kings in Norway. At that time a father and son ruled jointly over one region. The elder was called Ólafur and the younger Ingjaldur; however, Ingjaldur was fully grown-up when this saga took place. Father and son were quite unlike each other. King Ólafur was popular, but Ingjaldur was the most deceitful of men. Their retainers were called Ketill and Björn, who was called Björn 'the Strong'. They were of a like temper to King Ingjaldur, extremely overbearing and aggressive. King Ólafur had a daughter who was called Ása, the most good-looking of women and very gifted. Father and son ruled over the region called Naumudalur.[2] [See plate 13.]

King Ólafur was already an old man at the time of this saga. He had had two queens, and both were dead. His second wife was called Dís. King Önundur 'the Denier' from the region of Firðir[3] had been previously married to her and had two sons by her, both of whom were called Úlfur.[4] They now ruled over the region of Firðir, and Ingjaldur thought that he ought to share half that domain with his brothers as an inheritance from his mother. He had two battles with them and had been defeated in both.

There is a farmer named Björn. He lived on Hrafnista which is an island off the coast of Naumudalur. Björn was counted among the more prominent farmers there in the north. His wife was called Þorgerður. She was the daughter of Böðmóður Framarsson and Hrafnhildur, the daughter of Ketill 'the Jack-Salmon'.[5] She and Björn had a daughter who was called Þórdís. Gautur from Hamar,[6] a man worthy in his own right, had married her. They had a son called Grímur. As a youth, he was both large and strong. Björn and Þorgerður had more children. Their elder son was called Þórir, a handsome man, civilized in manner and gifted in all things. He was a retainer of King Ólafur who had a high regard for him. As a token of this regard, King Ólafur gave Þórir the sword that he and his family had owned for a long time and which was regarded as a great treasure by them. It was called Þegn ('Thane'). Thrice-polished, it was both long and broad and bit the best of all swords. For a long time Þórir spent one winter with the king and the next with his father.

Björn's younger son was called Án.[7] He grew early to be large in size, not handsome and somewhat backward. Concerning his strength men were quite in the dark because he never put it to the test. Rather he seemed foolish. His father had little affection for him, but his mother loved him greatly. It did not seem to people that Án bore any resemblance at all to the earlier members of his family such as Ketill hængur and the other people of Hrafnista except in size. Án did not lie around the kitchen,[8] but nevertheless he was called a simpleton by some people. He took no pains to acquire any skills. So it went on until he was nine years old. He was then no smaller than Þórir, his brother. He was somewhat unattractive to be with. Also he was poorly dressed, for he went around with both his knees and elbows showing through.

When he was twelve years old, he went away for three nights so that nobody knew what had happened to him. Án went into a forest clearing. He saw a large stone standing there and a man by a stream. He had heard mention of dwarves, together with the fact that they could be more skillful than other people. Then Án went between the stone and the dwarf and spells the dwarf away from the stone. He said he would never make it back inside to his home again unless he made for him a bow so large and strong that it might be suitable for him and along with it five arrows. They should have the quality to allow him to hit whatever he wished. This should be completed within three nights and Án waited there in the meantime. So the dwarf who was called Litur, did that which had been agreed upon and did not put any curses on the weapons. Án gave him some loose money which his mother had given him. The dwarf gave Án a handsome chair.[9] Afterwards, Án went home and carried the chair on his back. People laughed at him a good deal. Án gave the chair to his mother and said that he ought to reward her the best.[10]

Án settles matters with Þórir, his brother.

Then when Án was eighteen years old, he was larger than all people there to the north. Nor, however, had intelligence or civilized manners yet developed any further in him. That winter Þórir had remained in Hrafnista, and had by that time been given an appellative on account of his sword, and he was called Þórir Þegn. And in the spring Þórir made ready to go to meet the king. Án asks to go with him, but Þórir flatly refuses him. But when he went out to his ship, Án came heading in the same direction. Þórir asks what he wants then. Án says he intends to travel with him whether he would give his permission to him or not.

Þórir says that he should never go, 'you don't know how to behave in the company of chieftains,' he says, 'you who by your conduct are scarcely able to be fit company here at home'.

Then he took Án and tied him rather firmly to an oak tree. Án did not struggle. Then Þórir left and it was not long before he saw that Án was coming in his direction and dragging the oak tree after him; he had wrenched it up roots and all.

Then Þórir spoke: 'You're a marvellous fellow, kinsman, in so far as your strength is concerned, but it doesn't seem advisable to me, however, that you should go to meet the king with such a disposition as you have.'

Þórir then cut the bonds from him and spoke: 'You don't want to respect my words very much.' He then drew the sword Þegn and threatened Án with it. 'This sword will teach you a reasonableness which you've had none of before, and it'll not think you much of a match and stop this journey of yours.'

Án spoke: 'You'll not frighten me like a child who can still be whipped, and so that you know what I can do with you, then you'll now see what that is.'

Án grabbed hold of Þórir and tossed him up into the air and shook him like a child and spoke: 'See now, what you risk on your part if our minds don't run along the same path.'

Án then let him go free, and Þórir saw then what stuff there was in the man. They then went out to the ship and thereupon Án considered where he should thus find a place for himself that might seem to have the greatest drawbacks for everyone.

The merchants asked one another who this person might be. Án spoke: 'Why don't you ask me that? I can tell you. I am called Án and my lineage is from Hrafnista, the brother of Þórir Þegn', and they said that they didn't believe it.

He said it was true what he had said. They said he would be welcome among them. Án was poorly clad. Þórir asked for some of the merchandise to be cut up to clothe Án so that he might not be of such an odd appearance, and so it was done. This was not that much use to him because he put it on himself in an awkward fashion and there was no improvement in his dress as a result. The sailors were friendly toward Án. He did not know anything better than to be friendly in return.

Án accepts winter lodgings with King Ingjaldur

Án and Þórir came to the Naumudalur region and heard there the news that King Ólafur was dead, and Ingjaldur was sole king over the territory which they had both ruled.

Þórir spoke then: 'There died who was the more prominent, and I'd not have journeyed from the North if I'd known this change of fortune.'

Þórir comes now to the king's dwellings. Án had his bow with him, and when they came to the hall, Án bends his bow which was incredibly strong. Þórir asks what that might mean. Án replied that it would soon become evident. He placed the bowstring across his chest and the bow about his shoulders, his arrows he had in his hand. When they came to the hall doors, the door-keepers gave way to Þórir, but Án's approach caused a great uproar because he had not made any adjustments to his appearance. Then he went close to the doors, and the bow jutted out around his shoulders, and there was not sufficient room for it in the doorway, so that the bow had either to break or bend a great deal, because the doors were equal to the onslaught. Then Án went into the hall; the bow bent but did not break. Án sat down near the entrance and Þórir went up to the king and greeted him.

The king was very pleased to see him and told him to go to the high seat opposite him. 'You're welcome here among us, and who was that accompanying you, and why did this man part company with you so quickly?'

Þórir spoke: 'That man is my brother and has barely the level of the manners of the common people.'

The king spoke: 'He'll be welcome here, and let him sit next to you. We'll do that for your sake, and we've heard mention of Án, and he is a marvellous fellow in many respects.'

Þórir meets Án and tells him the king's words 'and turn this to your honourable advantage, kinsman'.

Án replies: 'We shall not share a place, and of course, it benefits me the more to receive winter-lodgings.'

Þórir said he thought that it would be ready at hand. All the same, Þórir went before the king, and spoke: 'I want to request winter lodgings for my kinsman, Án, at his request, even though his seating will remain unchanged.'

The king spoke: 'Winter lodging is at hand for him, but what other seat is better for him than beside you?'

Þórir said that he was not able in any way to have the slightest influence on him 'this is not the first time that he has wanted to have his own way, and therefore I was reluctant to have him come with me, because I knew that he would behave strangely'.

Þórir told Án the king's words. Án spoke: 'This has now turned out well and off you go, brother, to your place.' Þórir does so.

Án was reserved and unsociable; he stayed in his place much of the time except when he went to relieve himself. The retainers laughed at him a great deal and Ketill was the leader in this. Án turned a deaf ear to it all, and so it went on until Yuletide. Then the king announced that he would give Yule gifts as his father had done, said he also wished his men to pay homage to him. On Yuletide eve all the men came to accept their gifts except Án.

The king asked why Án did not come to accept a gift: 'shall he not accept gifts as the others?'

That was told to Án. Then he rose up and spoke: 'It seems to me good to accept gold'.

The man was not an attractive sight when he pushed his way up to the king. He was amazing large to see.

The king spoke: 'What twanged so loudly, Án, when you came in here through the doors the first time?'

'My bow,' said Án, 'because your hall-doors were so narrow, sire, that it bent all together when I had it on my shoulders before I came in and it sounded loudly when it sprang back.'

'You shall', said the king, 'be called Án "Bow-bender".'

'What are you giving me for a name-fastening?' said Án.

'Here have a gold ring as a combination name-fastening and Yule gift', said the king, 'because I heard what you spoke before and indeed you must be a very strong fellow being as big as you are.'

'I suppose', said Án, 'that I'm very strong, but I do not know to what extent.'

Án took the ring and did not thank the king for it. He played with the ring and placed it on his coat of mail. He juggled it in his palms and on one occasion the ring shot away. He went to look in an antechamber where the men relieved themselves, and when he came back he looked as if he had bathed in night soil. His bench companions asked him why he was so hideous.

He said scarcely anything to the questioning, but later on saying to one of them: 'but I'll tell you if you keep it secret'.

He said he would keep it secret. Án said: 'Here that has been proved true what is said: "Wealth that people envy is eager to be off;" the ring is now lost.'

His bench companion spoke: 'Let's keep quiet about this.'

Án spoke: 'So it shall be, but that ring is not intended for me, and I'll give it to him who finds it.'

This came to the notice of the retinue, and each told the other, and Ketill laughed greatly at it and said it had turned out as might be expected in giving this idiot gold. He went then and searched for the ring with the retinue. They crawled about together in the antechamber.

Án spoke then: 'How come that people are going on their hands and knees and busying themselves in the night soil or, on the other hand, is there a scuffle going on here?'

He was told that people wished to make good his misfortune by finding the ring. Án spoke: 'I'm not one to remember things. Here's now the ring on my arm, and now I've paid you back one time for you've often imposed upon me.'

The retainers said they'd been made a great deal of fun of. Án said that was the way it would have to be. After this there was a pause in the mocking of Án, and yet it returned to the same level as before and Ketill was the most involved in it.

Concerning the great achievements of Án

One day it happened that the two brothers were both outside by the hall. Then the retainers came out and spoke: 'You must be a strong fellow, Án.'

He replies: 'It may well be that such is the case, but I've not put it to the test.'

They spoke: 'Will you wrestle with Björn?'

He replies: 'There'll be certain conditions for you to fulfill. Do as I say and build a huge fire for me.'

They did so and told him to warm himself. He said there would be a greater need for him to take it easy when he comes back from the bout. Next they made ready for the wrestling match in the hall. Án had then arrived dressed in a fur cloak which his mother had given him. He did not have a belt around himself and the cloak was so long that it dragged after him for more than a yard; the sleeves hung down over his hands. Björn then leaped out at Án and he stood still in the face of this. Björn was the strongest of all men. He picked Án up and threw him farther out into the fire, so that he came down with his shoulders into the fire, and his feet banged to the ground farther out on the partition. There was a great burst of laughter. Án stood up slowly. The fire did not harm him on account of the fur cloak.

The king spoke then: 'You don't seem to me, Án, quite as strong as you pretended.'

Án spoke: 'He seems to me the stronger, sire, who falls first.'

Then the king laughed. Án looked for a belt for himself and girded himself up and rolled back the sleeves. They leaped at each other for a second time. Then Án drew Björn to him, swung him as a child and then next flung him farther out into the fire and so let him go. The retainers leaped to and snatched him from the fire, and Björn was badly burned. People said this fellow to be remarkably strong. That suited Án's disposition well, that he should be called strong, and he said that now one could see that he wanted Björn to warm himself by the fire and said that he had a greater need for it than himself. Án said then said a verse:

> A factious fellow, as he shouldn't have,
> Flung me at the partition.
> I couldn't come in the way of it,
> Damned be that man.
> It occurred during the encounter,
> I added some wood to the blaze;
> Denied him distinction;
> Damned be ever that man.

It now drew toward winter and one day the two brothers were once again both outside. Then spoke Þórir: 'Aren't you dissatisfied with your journey to this place, here where you've suffered scorn and mockery?'

Án said that he was not dissatisfied: 'I've received gold here, good winter lodging and I take no notice of their mockery.'

Þórir said, 'I'll give you an idea of how it seems to me. I'll give you the sword Þegn, so that you may kill any two of the king's men, and settle the matter yourself.'

Án spoke: 'I want to look at the sword and I'll accept it, but I'll not promise them a payback.'

Another day during the drinking time, Án rose up and turned and peered at the person sitting next to him, and did the same with everyone in the hall; he stood the longest before the king. Next he went before Þórir and laid the sword on the table in front of him and said that he did not want to have it. There was a great burst of laughter, and Þórir was extremely displeased with this.

One time the two brothers both met together and Þórir asks, 'Why did you behave in such an outrageous manner, brother, and do totally the opposite of what I had intended?'

Án said: 'I thought about it, what revenge there seemed to be for me as far as the king's men were concerned, and there didn't seem to be any for me. But anyway I looked longest at the king, because there I wavered the most over whether or not I would come to any decision.'

Þórir spoke: 'You are too stupid, because the king is well disposed toward you.'

Án said: 'We don't need to deliberate about him, because I think that no worse man will grow up in Norway than this king.'

Then they broke off their conversation, and it drew on to spring. Then King Ingjaldur had called together a council. He stood up in the council and spoke: 'It is known to people that my father is dead and I own this territory, and I wish to proclaim that I wish to make atonement to all those I have wronged and will give them, and you all, good laws. And I intend to go on an expedition with you, my thanes, and seek a meeting with my brothers, and we should be able to put our territory to rights in a peaceable manner, and I shall provide food and ale for my men.'

This was loudly applauded. Then Án spoke: 'The king must seem to you to speak well, brother.'

Þórir said that remained to be seen. Án said: 'I can tell you this, that he is now the worst disposed towards them and he thinks in this way he can bring about the greatest harm to them.'

Þórir said that he had not turned his mind away from the king. After that they make themselves ready.

Án asks Þórir whether or not he wished that he should go with the retainers 'and you and the king. It's also no big deal if I go on this trip as I am, and it's quite unclear what I'd do here for food and lodging in the meantime. I'm therefore the more ready to go with you; that will last for the longest time and turn out the worst.'

Þórir said that he wanted him to go and they made their way North with the king and hove to the lee of some islands. Then the king said that they should raise a harbour mark. [See plate 15.] Then Án said a verse:

> Well for you, sallow
> You stand near the sea
> Leafed rather well;
> A man shakes from you
> Morning dewdrops.
> And I on a thane
> Think night as day.

Þórir spoke: 'You'll not stand in need of this, because I'll give you the sword Þegn.'

Án says: 'I'm not thinking on that thane.'

Ketill said then: 'I suppose that you are thinking on some man or other and that you want to bugger him.' And they made great mockery and sport at this.

'It's not so,' said Án, 'I'm not thinking on such a thane, I'm thinking on Þórir þegn, my brother, because he is so shallow minded that he trusts this king, and I know that he will bring about his death.'

Next they came to the region of Firðir. Then King Ingjaldur said: 'I think we should now have come into the territory of my brothers, and I've heard that they don't wish to come to terms with us, and it seems to me the best choice for us that we should fight and so free us from their opposition.'

Many wished then rather to have stayed at home than to have come there. And when the two brothers heard that, they gathered an army to go against King Ingjaldur. And King Ingjaldur commanded drink be given to the men so that they might be more eager to set out. Then a great ox-horn came to Án. He said a verse:

> Much better it seems to me
> If bodies should fall
> That faster we force
> Feet to the spears' meet;
> Let us drink a draught
> Deep from oxen forehead spears.
> Will be the sword's swinging
> Swifter, if I shall prevail.

The king spoke: 'That's well composed and he is not without a shield when you go along beside him.'

Án spoke: 'I don't think that this will prove to be of help today although I know how to provide support.'

The king said he didn't know what sort of thane he was. Án allowed that both possibilities must appear to be the case. He rested himself in the ship when the others went up to fight.

Þórir spoke: 'Your part in this is really bad, to have first come here and to lie now in the ship when there is need of assistance; I'd thought that courage might make you more attractive.' Án said that he didn't care about his words.

The king went inland and the land levy came against them. They met by a certain forest and fought. Án stood up and went into the forest and up on a stump. From there he saw over both armies and the two standards carried in front of the brothers of King Ingjaldur.

Án spoke to himself: 'Why shouldn't that be an idea to offer assistance to King Ingjaldur and do so even though on the one hand he has the least need of it and yet on the other it is something he himself desires? I'll shoot and I've more expectation than not of success because he who gave me the bow and these arrows said that I would be an accurate shot. He was the dwarf whom I met earlier in the forest on Hrafnista, although people thought I was lost at the time the dwarf and I made this exchange. And now I shall test the craftsmanship with which he freed himself and his head when I earlier spelled him away from the stone. He made these so that I'd be able to shoot three shots which would become famous and one time with each arrow.' [See plate 16.]

He shot and aimed at the second of the Úlfurs, and the arrow flew through him and into a thicket behind him. Then immediately the standard fell. Án took the arrow and dashed off to the ship. And when the men saw that they told the king that he must have been brought low by a javelin or an arrow shot.

In the evening the men came to the ship. The shot was talked about by everyone. Án heard that and said that they should now be pressing the attack 'if now it is half over'.

In the morning the king exhorted the men to go ashore and said he expected victory. Án remained behind, and nobody asked him to go ashore. He got the idea that King Ingjaldur might be in need of support. He shot a second arrow. It entered Úlfur's breast and Án was on this occasion a weaker shot than before as the arrow stuck firmly there. The men recognized the arrow and guessed as was the case, that one man must have owned both arrows, even though no one saw him.

The king spoke: 'I've known for a long time that Án would be a man of great accomplishments.'

The king sent after him and says that he would have a splendid reward on account of this. The messengers see that Án had then gone into a ship's boat and was not at all near to them. They told him the king's words and greetings, and that he would receive honour on account of his valour.

Án spoke: 'I'll not go to meet the king because he'll desire the gallows for me on account of my effort.'

The men came back and told the king. He says: 'He was not far from the truth for I desired that he should not perform any more secret manslaughters against men of honour, and I had intended to let my brothers live and to have the territory under their control.'

Þórir spoke: 'You're behaving very badly; you'd rather have done it yourself. It's not been a long time that you've not wished them marked out for death.'

The king answers: 'Had he gone up with us he'd have been worthy of praise but on account of these secret manslaughters he's worthy of death.'

Þórir says he thought that he could look to receive an equal reward from him. Ingjaldur took the possessions of his brothers and set men over the region. Next a barrow was built over them which was called Barrow of the Úlfurs. The king was on board and made ready to depart.

Ketill says he wishes to go and meet a friend of his who lived a short distance away from there. The king answers: 'Make sure you are not late because we sail soon.'

Ketill had Án's arrow in his hand. He came to the house of a farmer a short distance from the ships. He was not known to him. The farmer greeted him and asked him his name.

He answers: 'I'm called Án Bow-bender and you'll have heard tell by now of my shots.'

The farmer answers: 'Your shots have been *Án*-welcome[11] to us here, because our chieftains were steadfast and friendly. But be with us tonight.'

Ketill said that he would accept that. There were no more people inside other than the farmer's wife and his daughter. She was called Drífa.

Now there is to say about Án that he rows up a hidden inlet and came to the same farmhouse and took up now a position and listened to the mens' talk.

The guest began to speak: 'Is that your daughter, farmer?'

'That's right,' he said.

'I intend to settle in bed with her tonight and nothing better will be offered to you.'

The old man did not say much to that. Ketill said he had done more great deeds than to get into her bed. And when Án hears this he banged on the entry frame and went in to the entry passage. A servant came to the door and quite a long way farther out down the passage before he saw the man. He asks him his name. He says he is called Án.

The servant said, 'Here's a great coming and going–*Án* for so is he called who has come inside.'

Án said that may well be the case and went in and sat down opposite Ketill. The farmer asks him his name. He said his name was Án.

The farmer said, 'This is a great *Án*-convenience but will you stay with us?' He said he would accept that 'and I must delay for a little while before I have a meal, and has he Ketill called himself Án?'

He said, 'I did that in jest.'

Án spoke: 'I've borne such well from you in our meetings. Both of us had accepted food and lodging under the same roof, and there you inquired into certain aspects of my ability and you seemed to see nothing in it, but rather that I was an idiot, and I'm nevertheless a man renowned for my accomplishments. And I know a remedy to properly take care of your hankering after women. I heard before that you sought after the farmer's daughter with a mind to taking her to bed.'

Án took him by the hair on his forehead and roughly shoved him outside and said a verse:

> That will you discover
> When you dung out the cowshed
> That you aren't ever
> Án Bow-bender;
> You are Bread-bender
> Rather than Bow-bender
> Cheese-bender
> Rather than Weapon-bender.

Án tied him up and shaved the hair off him and smeared on tar, and said that any creature which was feathered should be able to fly. He put out one of his eyes and next he gelded him. After that he let him go free and fetched him two staves, 'And I'll take back my arrow.'

Án said, 'People call that the treasure of a king if something surpasses all other things. Now you are somewhat altered and therefore I'll send you now so prepared to King Ingjaldur. And I'll pay compensation to him with you for one of his brothers whenever recompense is made for one of them.'

Ketill made his way to the ship and told the king, and his staves bore him witness that he had become crippled while the sight of him was a more powerful tale concerning his eye and his testicles that both were missing.

'You're unfit for me', said the king and drove him away from him.

Concerning the exploits of Án and his taking a wife

Now there is to report of Án that he spoke with the farmer: 'You've given me a hearty welcome and you'll not suffer any harm on my account. Let us abandon the farm and go into the forest because the king's men will quickly come here,' and so they did.

Án was in this guessing near the truth because the king sent men immediately during the night and they burnt down the farmstead and afterwards went back.

The king spoke to his men: 'If Án has escaped then I'll place three marks of silver on his head and will make him an outlaw throughout all Norway.'[12]

That became now widely known. The king went home to his own district. Án remained with the old man and rebuilds his farmstead during the summer.

Án was thus dressed for everyday wear, that he was in a white fur coat; it was so long that it went down to his heels. Then he was in a shorter grey fur coat; it went down to the middle of his calf. Then he was in a red tunic; it went down to his knees. Outermost he wore a wretched cape of common wadmal. It reached down to the middle of his thighs. He had a hat on his head and a woodsman's axe in his hands. The man was amazingly large and masculine but not very handsome.

It was one day that Án met outside with Drífa, the old man's daughter. Three women were walking with her. She was the most beautiful of women and well dressed. She was in an unflared red tunic with long sleeves, long in the body and tight at the waist. She had a lace fillet around her forehead and had hair such as the best of women. The women laughed a great deal at Án and mocked his apparel.

Drífa spoke then: 'Where are you coming from now, four-fold?'

'From work,' said Án.

At this moment the farmer came along and told the women not to mock Án. Án said then a verse:

> Maids enquired,
> When me they found,
> Fairhaired females;
> 'From where come you, four-fold?'
> And I shot back
> To Silky-Gunnur,[13]
> Followed up flipantly:
> 'From where comes the calm weather outside?'[14]

'It doesn't seem to me', said Án, 'that your tunic looks any better than my cape, because it falls below the back of your cloak.'

Next they parted company for the time being. And when the rebuilding of the farmstead was finished, the farmer says to Án during the autumn that he would be permitted to stay there during the winter 'and you have well earned this'.

Án said he would accept this. He felt a considerable attraction to the old man's daughter even though she might have made fun of his fashions in clothing, but he was indulgent towards her in that.

And in the spring he made it known that he would go away and set another task for himself. 'But if it so happens as I suspect that your daughter is with child there are few men here to put the blame on, and I'll own to being the father. And if it's a boy send him to me when you have found out a little more about my permanent place of residence, and let this ring follow as proof of his parentage, and if it's a girl you can take care of her yourself.'

Then he went away and eastward into a forest. [See plate 17.] There was a footpad out there called Garan and during the day when Án was walking down a forest path, he saw that here was a man circling in on him.[15] He had a black shield and a helmet on his head and bow in his hand, a quiver on his back. He saw the newcomer and shot immediately a spiked arrow at his shield which barely went through it. Án took aim in return and shot through his shield and the arrow entered his biceps muscle so that he was wounded. The footpad said that it seemed to him a need to be harder shooting in this and he laid down his weapon and met Án and asked him his name. He said he was called Án.

Garan says that he has heard his name 'and you are famous'.

Án said: 'I've also heard of you and always to the bad.'

Garan said: 'You'll get something good from me. I'll invite you home to my place and let's have a partnership together, and we'll accomplish much.'

Án said: 'That'd be a potent combination if we wish to do evil.'

They came to a hall which stood in the forest, and the door was closed on the latch. They went in and there was no lack of wealth, weapons and armour. Án saw there two stones one higher than the other. Án asks what they might be.

Garan said: 'There I have tested the backbone strength of various men who have visited me.'

Án said: 'You've behaved cruelly towards your guests, and which of the two would to you be the more fitting stone to be laid over?'

He said that he had not given any thought to it but that nevertheless he declared the higher one to be the better suited to him on account of its height. By then had passed most of the day.

Garan said: 'Now let's prepare food, and which would you rather, fetch water or make the fire?'

Án said that he himself preferred that he should make the fire, because he said he was accustomed to that job. And when he had bent down, then he turned the sword with which he was armed round to his back. He heard a swish up above him; the footpad hacked at him, and the blow landed on the sword and that protected him.

Then Án leapt up and spoke: 'You're not now to be trusted, and you'll quickly want to change partners, and I've moreover done little to deserve this. It may be that now you'll spend this evening with the high farmer stone.'

There was a hard fight, and each wished to avoid the stones. Then Garan came close to the stones. Án stood on his instep, and drove his hands to his chest and bent him over the stone; then his backbone broke asunder. Án left him dead. He hacked the head off him, and dragged him outside, and stuck his nose in the cleft of his thighs so that he would not walk about dead. The night wore on. Án was there during the summer and did no harm to anybody and allowed no one to see him. When it became autumn, he locked up the hall and went away for he wished to have other winter lodgings.

Late in the day he came to the place of a certain wealthy widow, who was called Jórunn. He was there during the night and concealed his identity. But when the mistress of the house came into the hall, she asked the guest his name. He said such as seemed fit to him.

She went away and turned back and spoke: 'Why did you come here? It's my suspicion that you must be Án Bow-bender.' He allowed that to be true.

'Why did you come here?' she says. 'There's no protection here for you from the king.'

Án said that he thought that he would not need that any more 'I'll risk it to be here, if you'll give your permission.'

She spoke: 'I'll not withhold food from you.'

He was there for a time and was busy and attended to her farmstead and that was with great mutual agreement. Án spoke: 'Here I want to be this winter with you but I'll not commit myself completely to be a permanent resident.'

She said that it was not suited to him there 'where the king is looking for you; we can do little for you here'.

He allowed that he thought King Ingjaldur would not do him harm.

'I'll not withhold food from you,' and she allowed that he himself should take care of his own affairs.

He made himself a most active man. Later a conversation takes place between them. He says that he is of a mind to propose marriage to her. She said it would have to be done with the consent of her kinsfolk and that such was close to her own inclinations, but no one objected, and they got married. Án was the greatest of managers and very skillful. He had a boat shelter in the forest not far from the farmstead, and he built a ship there. He added greatly to their store of wealth and honour. He had four large farmsteads, and there were thirty men in fighting condition with him at each place. The men of the region who were there had him for their leader. He was popular and generous. King Ingjaldur hears about this and searches for him. Þórir his brother went often there to the east with offers of terms and the two brothers were on a friendly footing. By then their father Björn was dead in Hrafnista and Gautur their brother-in-law and Þordís their sister looked after the farm. Grímur their son was large, handsome and strong and said none of his kinsmen to be equally agreeable in temperament to him as was Án. He went to meet him. Án received him well, and he lived there for a long time. He was popular.

Þórir often told Án that he should give in to the king 'and do not hesitate, brother, because I see clearly his disposition is ill disposed toward you'.

'Fate must settle things between the king and me,' said Án, 'and you trust him too much. I'd rather you looked after our farm.' But this did not happen.

Concerning the hired killers[16] of the king

Ívar was the name of a man, from the Upplönd[17] in family and of good stock. He came to the retinue of King Ingjaldur and he received him well; he was not there when Án was with the king. Ívar was an able man. He was very attracted to Ása and made an offer of marriage to her. The king responded to this unenthusiastically. They discussed the matter among themselves.

The king spoke then: 'You press this matter resolutely, and I'll give you an option. You shall go to meet Án and bring me his head and when you come back, you can have an expectation of the match you request, because you'll be called a powerful man and a deserving brother-in-law of a king.'

Ívar said that would not be easy to perform 'and do you give, king's sister, consent to this matter?'

She answers: 'I intend to be under the authority of my brother if you should succeed in this errand.'

With that he went to the east and met Án and pestered him for winter lodgings.

Án asks who he might be and said for himself he was hardly able to know with what kind of intentions anyone might be, but indicated that he was unaccustomed to deny food: 'I request also no payment in return for the food before I know how it is accepted or is appreciated.'

Ívar was a eager follower to him in building and other work.

It was one evening when they were going home that it entered Ívar's mind what he had to take care of. He leapt then at Án and hacked at him. Án walked more quickly than Ívar calculated and was taking great strides and Ívar drove his axe into the earth and all the way into a tree root. Now Án was aware of his attack and he turns back and said it did not seem to him that the payment in return for food and lodgings was very good. Án bound him with a bowstring and drove him homeward before him. He placed Ívar in fetters during the night. And when people found that out they begged Án to kill him and they say he has deserved this.

Án said that such should not be. 'That would then be said that I was making myself an opponent of the king if men did not know the true story. I'll have a council called to be attended by a large number of people and let the king's man say his story and bring this problem out into the open in front of everyone.' And so it was done.

Án came to the council and leads Ívar after him. Án spoke: 'Now tell everything concerning your errand.'

Ívar did so. Then everybody said that he had condemned himself to death.

Án spoke: 'No,' he said, 'that shall not be. I know whom he had at home to visit, as you have heard.'

He had his legs broken all the way up to his knees and next had them heal and turned the feet opposite to the way they were before; his toes then pointed backwards.

Án spoke: 'Stand now in front of me,' and so he does.

Án spoke: 'Now you are a king's treasure, as you're different from that which other people are.'

Then he altered his face a bit and spoke: 'Now are you at both ends surpassing other people, handsome in personal appearance and in addition with feet different from those of other people. Go now and meet King Ingjaldur; I'll pay compensation to him with you for the second of his brothers, and further, he has now in this direction nothing on which to base a claim.'

Ívar met the king and said that his journey had not been smooth. The king spoke: 'I've been aware that people have struck down others, one in return for another, but I really don't know of such mutilations having been done and to call that result a king's treasure. And it seems to me that there's nothing of a treasure in you, and go to your estates.'

The king's sister spoke: 'Will you not now grant him the marriage contract with me?'

The king said that it was not the same thing, and allowed that Ívar had overconfidence in himself, that he might be able to bring such a thing about 'and has, therefore, no refusal in this matter been applied to your case'.

Þórir had then not long since gone home.

After this the king sent twelve men after Án's head and spoke thus: 'I'll send you with this in mind to meet Án, that you'll ask him for winter lodgings, and he's very generous, and will ask why so many of you travel together. You'll say that you own property all together and that you don't trust anyone to divide it up among yourselves except him. And if he takes up with you, entice to your cause an equal number of others from among his men with bribes and I consider it then in your power for you not to let him escape.'

Next they went to meet Án and the words went so between them as the king had suggested. Moreover, he took them in and they were there from then until after Yule.

One evening Jórunn spoke with Án: 'What sort of guests do you think they are who have visited you?'

He said: 'I think that they are good men and we can expect things from them to this end.'

She says she doesn't think that they would be able to be called trustworthy men 'and I suspect that either they have performed evil work or they intend to, because each time you go from your bed they look after you and their faces flush'.

He said that he had not noticed that. 'I'm more worried about you than I intended,' she said. 'I want you to go from the house tomorrow and if they make no suspicious moves against you then there is nothing in it. Say you'll be home in the evening and you want to travel alone and if they make any suspicious moves against you we will know who they are.'

Án said that that would be done. In the morning Án went from the house and when the winter guests saw that they thought that they then had a chance at Án, and they went from the house to two spots, six in each spot and six were at home of the spies and six of the household retainers who had taken money for the head of Án. There six of these two groups in the ambush. They placed themselves beside Án's path.

Jórunn meets Grímur and said that their journey seemed to her suspicious looking 'and go now to spy'.

He says that he is ready to do this and went into the forest with many men so that the others knew nothing and they did not see them at all. Evening drew on and it seemed to them the greatest urgency to return home and to pay attention to the time so that nothing would happen to their plan for an attack. They came home. Án had then come into the high seat and was frowning. Grímur had also then come home.

Án spoke: 'It would be appropriate for our winter guests to make known their errand and how they intended to kill me today. I know now your plan and for a long time I have known of your treachery toward me, and I do not have a trustworthy choice of servants.' They became anxious to leave.

Án spoke: 'I'll not kill my servants and they may go away. But I'll give the king's men over into the hands of Grímur, my kinsman, and he may have fun with them today.'

Grímur said such was well spoken. He went to the forest with them and strung them all up together on a single gallows.

King Ingjaldur heard of this and it pleased him not at all. Þórir was at that time come to the retinue. He was quiet and the matter seemed to him extremely oppressive.

The king enquires why he should be so quiet 'we wish to act as well toward you as before'.

Þórir says: 'I'm not complaining about that but it is difficult to be comfortable about this.'

The king enquires: 'What is lacking here compared to what my father did?'

'I'm not blaming anyone on that account,' said Þórir, 'but your father gave me more, such as this sword.'

The king said: 'Is that a great treasure?'

'Have a look,' said Þórir. The king took hold of it and drew the sword and spoke: 'This is not the possession of a common man.'

Þórir said: 'You take it then, your highness.'

The king said: 'I don't want to do that; you shall have it and it will accompany you the longest.'

He attacked Þórir from the high seat and thrust the sword through him and let the sword remain there in the wound. He said: 'Án and I will make an exchange of various gifts between each other.'

Then he prepared a ship and there were sixty men on it and he told them to go meet Án, and lie at his anchorage and entice him on to the ship 'and say that Þórir, his brother, has arrived there and wishes to try and effect a reconciliation. And if he should come into your clutches, then kill him, and then some compensation will have been paid for my brothers if this comes to pass. Come early in the day to Án.'

This deed was very badly spoken of by everyone and he was now called Ingjaldur 'the Evil' by everyone.

Next they went on their way. And during the night when they came close to the land then Án had a dream and said to Jórunn, 'It seemed to me that Þórir came here, very dismal, and he's always come when I have dreamed about him. I don't want them to come in vain who bring him here in such a manner as my mind tells me, because he appeared all bloody to me with a sword thrust through him.'

She said that it might be so that his dreams were straightforward. Án sprang up and said that the men should come. He had four ships made ready, and two were alongside an outlying island and the other two in a secret inlet by the anchorage opposite the farmstead. Án sent men into the neighbourhood after people to drink at a welcoming feast to greet Þórir if he should arrive cheerful and healthy, and otherwise to test their weapons. Án was at the farmstead and his men on the ships, and he waited thus prepared for whatever would happen to come to hand.

After that they saw that a ship glided into the anchorage opposite the farmstead and it had red shields on it. The crew sent a message to Án that he should come over to them and meet Þórir, his brother, who had come there to try to effect a reconciliation.

Án spoke: 'Often had he not considered it a bother to walk to the house but he may now fall a little short in it.'

They said that he was drowsy. Án said that he would go over to the ship and no farther. They did not trust themselves to attack him and they hoisted Þórir up out of the ship and told Án to accept the friendly gift of King Ingjaldur.

Án took Þórir up and spoke: 'You've paid for your credulity when you trusted the king too much and something else is now more pressing than to rebuke you.'

He hurriedly placed him in a hollow under some protruding rocks and leaped out on to the ship and snatched up a red shield. He attacks them now and they fought and almost all of the men of King Ingjaldur fell. One man fought on his knees. Grímur advanced toward him, and the man hacked at his hamstrings and took off his calf along with his heel bone and it made him become stiff legged before it healed. They killed every man's child of them.

Án had a barrow built and a ship placed in it and Þórir placed in the cabin and the king's men on both sides so that it might seem that they all attended upon him. Grímur was healed. The king now heard tell of this news and it seemed to him that this had not greatly added to either his honour or his credit.

Concerning Þórir Ánsson and the killing of Ingjaldur 'the Evil'

That was one morning when Án was at home at his farmstead that he spoke: 'I think', he said, 'that there are a great many people in the forest and it may be that it's come to the point as it is said, that great is a king's power and great is a king's good luck.'

Án now wakes up the household retainers and spoke: 'It's often been commented upon that I am well married. Jórunn has often warned me that I should not remain here in the face of the dislike of the king but I wished to let the struggle develop in whatever way it might turn out.'

Next he took a beam and hacked it in half and shaped hand grips on both pieces.

Án said: 'Then when we come out a circle will be thrown around us but it seems to me bad to flee. But Grímur and I shall not use weapons,' and he told him to take the other club and so they made ready.

They turned now towards the sea. Then the king had arrived with a great host of men. Án and Grímur blazed a path for themselves and lashed out on both sides. It seemed to the king's men not a good thing to have to put up with and the household retainers advanced after them and were many killed, but the women had gathered under Jórunn's protection. Án and Grímur come upon a rowing smack and they saw the king's fleet all around them and in the middle of the sound was a reconnaissance vessel.

Án said that it seemed to him a good thing if they played some malicious trick on them 'who are situated to harm us'.

Án flung a two-pronged boat-hook that was fitted with iron into one of the planks fastened to a mid-rib and it came about that the dark blue sea entered at that place and the men called out to the king's ships that they should help them. Án escaped out between them. Án said that Grímur would be more useful in rowing if both his legs were even. He said nothing should be lost on account of that. Án noticed nothing until the handles of the oars banged him between the shoulders and Grímur had died of exhaustion at the oars. Án now stepped overboard and wanted that least of all that the king's men lay hands on him. They saw that a man had stepped overboard and that a second lay dead in the bilge water.

They tell the king this. He said: 'It's to be expected that Án would begrudge our laying hands on him but it shall, however, all come to the same thing for him and let us place guards all along the coast so that he cannot return to the land.'

Án had thought about this and he turns away towards an island which lay out from the coast, and came ashore there and was then totally worn out. Erpur was the name of him who dwelt there and his wife. There were no other people there. Erpur was checking out the foreshore and went with a draught animal and saw that a large man lay on the strand. The farmer thought that he was dead and it had gone badly for him. Án told him to approach boldly.

Erpur said, 'You would have had a softer bed at home beside Jórunn.'

He carts him now home and Án's feet stick out of the wagon. The old woman told him not to cart dead men home. Erpur said matters stood another way and told her. She said it would be good for a reward if he were dealing with a good fellow. Án now much recovered his strength there. King Ingjaldur thought Án was dead and he went home. Án was with the old man and when he was healthy, Erpur took him over to the land. Án said they had done well and gave the old woman gold and Erpur the island and made it known that their reward would be more when he had free time. Next Án came home. Jórunn had improved things somewhat in the meantime and she was, however, still lacking a great deal in order to be able to keep up a level of appearances.

People welcomed Án heartily and he replies to the mistress of the house: 'We've not been fair with you up to this time concerning money matters.'

She says she would not object to it if he remained. It now entered his mind that it would not be an ill-advised step to fetch the wealth in Garan's hall because it seemed to him now to fit the need.

He had it now brought home and said to Jórunn: 'Here you may gaze on my wealth,' and tells everything connected with it. He appeared not as poor as people had thought. They were now come to the same situation concerning their wealth as before or more.

Án now places spies on all the roads from his place. King Ingjaldur learned that and had a bodyguard placed around himself and slept in the hall beside his retainers. Án carried out his tasks as before.

And one evening as he went from work he saw a fire burning on one of the islands. It came to his mind that the king might again visit him or robbers had laid hands on his livestock. He became curious about it and went to the sea all alone, took a boat for himself and rows to the island. He saw a man sitting there by a fireplace, youthful and large. He was dressed in a shirt and linen trousers. He was eating. A silver plate was in front of him. He had a knife with a handle of walrus tusk and stuck it in and up out of the pot and ate such as he felt like and threw the rest back in when it got cold and took another bit out. Án thought that he was not particularly alert about himself. He shot at him and the arrow hit the piece of meat he had lifted out of the pot and it dropped down into the ashes. He places the arrow down beside him and continued to eat as before. Án shot a second arrow and it hit the plate in front of him so that it broke in two pieces. The man sat and paid no attention to this. Then Án shot a third time and the arrow hit the handle of the knife which stood out from the back of his hand and the handle of the knife flew into two pieces.

Then the young man spoke: 'This man has done me an injury, and there was little advantage in it for him when he damaged my knife.'

He snatched up his bow and it came to Án's mind that it was not known for certain in what direction a badly shot arrow might go off in. He went to the other side of an oak tree and let it be between them. Then the young man shot the first arrow so that Án thought that it would have entered his midriff if he had waited for it; the second it seemed to him would have entered the lower part of his chest, and the third into his eye, and thus they all stood there in the oak tree, there where Án had taken up position.

Then the young man spoke: 'It's advisable for him who shot at me to now show himself and we can meet one another if he has any complaints against me.'

Next Án went out to him and they began to wrestle and their attack was most vigorous. Án became weary more quickly because the other was strong legged and powerful. Án asked then to take a rest and the young man professed himself ready for either alternative and yet Án had his way.

He asks: 'What's your name?'

He said that he is called Þórir and said his father is called Án 'and who are you?'

'I'm called Án,' he said.

The young man said: 'That must be true, that you are *Án*-aware of what of your property you are missing, because you are the *Án*-er of this wether which I took now.'[18]

Án said: 'Let's not bandy around belligerent words and that sheep's of little value, but what do you have as a proof if you meet your father?'

'I may intend to make available the true token of my story, but however I'm not obliged to show it to you,' said Þórir.

Án said that it was the more fitting to show what there might be as a token concerning his paternity. Þórir shows him the ring.

Án said, 'True is this token because your father recognizes its validity and let us go home and find better lodgings.'

They now do so and come home and his men sat and waited for him with apprehension and fear because they did not know what had happened to him. Án sat down in the high seat and Þórir beside him. Jórunn asks who the young man might be. Án told him to say his name for himself.

He said: 'I'm called Þórir and I'm the son of Án.'

She spoke: 'It now turns out as it is spoken that each person is wealthier than it may seem. You did not tell me that you had this son and nevertheless I don't think that he'll prove to be conceived without any good purpose, and have his wet clothes off him, and how old are you?'

'Eighteen years,' said Þórir.

She said: 'I think that I'll call you "Long-leg", because I've never seen anyone taller up to the knees.'

He said: 'This name is pleasing to me and will you give me something for a name-fastening so that men may call me this.'

She said that would be done and gave him a large gold ring. Án asks Þórir about his upbringing with the old man. He said that the word had been put out that a daughter was being brought up there, 'because King Ingjaldur would have wanted to kill me and therefore I fled from there North when I was able to do so.' Þórir was there during the winter.

One time Án spoke: 'I'm not inclined to bring you up sitting down for long if you do not make some sort of show for yourself.'

He says that he doesn't have any valuables except the ring. Án said it would seem better for him to accept some sort of errand, 'It seems to me that you might be obliged to revenge your namesake on King Ingjaldur. I think that it most falls to your lot of our kin, because it's proven that the king and I can never lay hands on each other. And you had no reason to visit here except to carry out vengeance whether you were related to me or not. You shall own the sword Þegn, and if you accomplish this deed then the sister of the king is there. Take her with you and yield her a son for her brother.'

Þórir said this would be done and he set out with a ship completely equipped for raiding and by the autumn he had five ships well prepared. He was a very daring man and strong and the greatest war viking. He came to the dwelling of King Ingjaldur in the darkest part of the night and carried fire to the hall. People woke with the smoke. King Ingjaldur asks who was in charge of the fire. He says Þórir Long-leg to be the one.

The king says, 'It may be, that this spark has flown from Drífa, the old man's daughter, because there it has long been my suspicion, and it may be now, that in the end it would become very hot for us.'

Þórir says that he is desirous that he should abate his evil deeds. King Ingjaldur then had the inside walls broken up and carried to the hall doors and said he did not wish to burn inside. Then the people leaped out. Þórir was near the place where the king came out and struck him his death blow.

He took Ása away and had her with him and a great treasure and sent both to his father. He received Ása well and Þórir went off plundering and performed many exploits. He was a excellent man and seemed like his father. Þórir returned after that to Án when he had become extremely wealthy and he had there a good reception. He was there during the winter.

And in the spring Án said to him that he had decided to go away, 'and I shall hand over to you all the property, but you will not want that property which King Ingjaldur had owned because that will not be long before the regional kingships will be declared done away with. It will be better to tend to one's own honour than to set yourself in a higher place and so diminish from there. I'll go north into Hrafnista to my property. You'll take care of Erpur and your foster-father and your mother.'

Next Án went north and Þórir became a great man. Án went to an island and had there a daughter who was called Mjöll, the mother of Þorsteinn, the son of Ketill 'Oaf', the father of Ingimundur 'the Old' in Vatnsdalur. Often Án had to fight the skin-clad people to the north of there and he seemed by his own actions the greatest of people. Þórir's son was Ögmundur 'Destroyer-of-fields', the father of Sigurður 'Bald-bowl', an excellent man in Norway.

And here ends the saga of Án Bow-bender.

8

A GEST OF ROBYN HODE

Thomas H. Ohlgren

INTRODUCTION

As depicted in film and television, the modern Robin Hood contrasts markedly with the late medieval yeoman outlaw from the West Riding of Yorkshire, who, together with his three comrades – Little John, Will Scarlock and Much the Miller's son – waylay and rob travellers on the road from Doncaster to Ferrybridge. While they spare 'gode yeman', they vow to 'bete and bynde' rich churchmen and the Sheriff of Nottingham. The four commit real crimes: deer poaching, jail breaking, theft, extortion, armed robbery and murder. And, although they are threatened with capture, imprisonment and execution by corrupt local officials, they invariably escape unharmed or are pardoned by 'Edwarde, our comly kynge', who recognizes in them their dynamic energy, intense loyalty and essential goodness. The early rymes of Robin Hood develop a series of thematic contrasts between forest and town, natural law and man's law, yeoman and aristocrat, secular and religious.

Of the thirty-eight Robin Hood ballads collected by Francis James Child, three are considered the earliest in date: *Robin Hood and the Monk* (Child, # 119), *Robin Hood and the Potter* (Child, # 121), and *A Gest of Robyn Hode* (Child, # 117).[1] The first two survive in manuscripts dated about 1450 and 1500 respectively, while *A Gest of Robyn Hode* exists only in five printed or black letter texts of the sixteenth century.[2] The two earliest versions are those of Jan Van Doesborch of Antwerp around 1510 and Wynkyn de Worde around the same time or earlier. Although no manuscript survives, most scholars agree that the poem was compiled in the fifteenth century from pre-existing sources and material of the poet's own devising.

Genre

The genre or story type has been variously described as a ballad, tale, *ryme* or *talkyng*. Since traditional ballads were sung, the *Gest* is not a ballad in the conventional sense; instead, it was orally recited or chanted by a minstrel. It is, as David C. Fowler observes, recited minstrelsy, characterized by such features as the opening formula to 'lythe and lysten', the division into eight parts or fitts, the use of narratorial transitions ('Let's leave that monk in silence, and speak about the knight . . . '), and the use of direct address to the audience ('You will hear some good mirth!'). Moreover, it represents a transitional form of poetry that was developing in the fifteenth century 'when the metrical romance tradition of the later Middle Ages joined the mainstream of folksong to create a type of narrative song which we now call the ballad'.[3]

Dating

The precise dating of the *Gest* is complicated by the fact that it is a compilation of pre-existing sources, including earlier ballads (now lost) a miracle of the Virgin Mary and unidentified romance elements. Both internal and external evidence point to the mid-fifteenth century (during the reign of Henry V, 1413–22, or Henry VI, 1422–61) as the probable time of its composition/compilation.[4] The historical time depicted is, however, about a hundred years earlier in the reign of Edward III (1327–77). A close reading of the allusions, the genre of one of the eight sections or fitts, and the military, feudal and social practices in the poem all suggest the 1330s and 1340s as the historical time being depicted.[5]

Structure

The 1,824 verses, arranged in 456 four-line stanzas, are divided into eight parts or fitts. It cannot be determined if this arrangement is due to the early sixteenth-century compositor or to the fifteenth-century poet-compiler.[6] The presence of oral formulas, narratorial transitions and direct addresses to the audience all suggest oral performance at some stage, but we must be careful in assuming that the printed texts represent faithful transcriptions of their manuscript copy texts. Parts 1, 3, 5 and 6 all open with the poet-minstrel calling the audience to attention ('Lythe and listin, gentilmen'), indicating perhaps an original four-part structure. Moreover, the use of transitions (i.e., 'Now is the knight gone on his way.'), repeated words linking two parts (i.e., 'our comly king', last line of part 6, and 'The king came', the first line of part 7) and coda-like summarizing comments at the end of some parts (i.e., 'God, who sits in high Heaven, Grant us to fare well') reinforce the original four-part structure (parts 1–2, 3–4, 5, 6–7). This arrangement, however, disrupts the dramatic continuity, isolating part 5 by itself, when its matter – the sheriff's attack on Sir Richard's castle – is continued at the beginning of part 6.

Audience

If the identification of the historical context is correct, we can then ask: by whom and for whom was *A Gest of Robyn Hode* created? Earlier critics are sharply divided on the issue of production and consumption. R.H. Hilton argued that the poems were created for peasant yeomen, expressing their discontent about intolerable social and economic conditions.[7] By contrast, J.C. Holt located the popularity of Robin Hood among the household retainers and dependents of the northern aristocracy and landed gentry.[8] Disagreeing with both of these views are R.B. Dobson and J. Taylor, who posited Robin Hood as a new type of hero for a new social group: 'the greenwood legend can and should be seen as an expression of social aspiration based on the real economic progress achieved by many Englishmen in the years before and after 1400'.[9] The new social group – yeomanry – emerged following three waves of bubonic plague in 1348–9, 1361–2 and 1369. The resulting population decrease produced a labour shortage, which affected wages, prices and farm production, and led to a population shift from the rural manors to villages and towns, where freemen, in spite of the repressive measures of the Statute of Labourers (1351), sold their services to the highest bidders. The more enterprising yeomen, particularly those possessing skilled crafts, quickly rose in social and economic standing, and by the end of the fourteenth century, 'the wealthier freeholders were not easy to distinguish in their way of life and their social prestige from some of the knightly class'.[10]

The status term 'gentlemen', which previously designated 'gentle' or noble birth, now replaced the older term 'franklin' and marked the social position next below knights and esquires.[11] The *Gest* poet addresses his audience directly as 'gentlemen' who are 'of freeborn blood' (ll. 1, 574, 1,126, 1,266). Robin Hood, in addition, is clearly identified as 'a good yeoman' (l. 3). The status term 'yeoman' encompassed a broad spectrum of the Third Estate or bourgeoisie, ranging from, as witnessed by Chaucer's *General Prologue*, the Yeoman, the Guildsmen and their Cook, and the Merchant.[12] The Yeoman, with his 'cote and hood of grene' and his 'myghty bowe' and 'shief of pecok arwes' represents the the 'old' yeomanry – servitor to the landed aristocracy. The five Guildsmen – 'An Haberdasshere and a Carpenter, A Webbe, a Dyere, and a Tapycer' – represent the 'new' merchant yeomanry, which was achieved by becoming a free citizen of a town, owning property and a business, being elected a master or alderman of a guild and serving the economic needs of the king, lord or municipality. Their ostentatious dress and silver knives, their wives' demands to be called 'my lady', and their personal servant, the Cook, all mark these craftsmen and proprietors as urban *nouveaux riches*. They no doubt would insist on being called 'gentlemen'. Their Cook later tells the incomplete tale of a victualler and his 'riotous servaunt' Perkin Reveller, who, as an apprentice, resides at the lower end of the mercantile scale. Apprentices were not admitted to the guilds until they had served their apprenticeships, which usually lasted from seven to ten years. Some of these indentured workers formed their own organizations, called yeoman fraternities. By contrast, the London Merchant, who deals in importing and exporting, represents the most powerful and important group, the Merchants of the Staple (exporters of wools, woolfells and skins) or the Merchant Adventurers (dealers in cloth and wine). These burghers steadily gained political power, and in 1374 they were given the right to elect all of the City officials, including the Mayor.[13] Thus, as a status term, 'yeomanry' covered a broader spectrum of the 'middle' class, while 'gentlemen' designated the upward mobility made possible by education, marriage, inheritance, achievement and service. When we consider the themes and underlying ideology of the *Gest*, it becomes clear that the poet is appealing to a range of people, from apprentices, day labourers and journeymen to small proprietors and liveried merchants.

Themes and Ideology

I am using the term 'ideology' in Martin Seliger's sense of 'sets of ideas by which men posit, explain, and justify ends and means of organized social action, and specifically political action, irrespective of whether such action aims to preserve, amend, uproot or rebuild a given social order'.[14] The *Gest* then can be seen as promoting and legitimizing the interests of one social group in the face of opposing interests. Earlier scholars have seen the main opposition in terms of the forest versus the town, church and court. The forest has been enshrined as the imagined refuge, the securely collective world and the fully natural state to which the oppressed underclass has escaped in order to reconstitute the 'liberties of the greenwood'. Simon Schama characterizes the forest as 'a place where the conventions of gender and rank are temporarily reversed in the interest of discovering truth, love, freedom and, above all, justice'.[15] The forest encapsulates the virtues of an ideal realm: loyalty, fidelity, honour, chivalry, brotherhood, solidarity, magnanimity, hospitality, ceremony and courage. Opposed to the forest are the engrossing negative values of the dominant social, political and economic powers – the court, church and town, so marked by statutory law, cash nexus, oppression and corruption.

While these oppositions are powerfully present in the *Gest* and the other outlaw narratives, there is another subtext at work that has been largely unnoticed by previous commentators. The world of the forest has already been penetrated by the values of the town market-place, revealing what Michael Nerlich calls a 'change of consciousness' from the courtly-knightly ideology of adventure to mercantile self-awareness and self-fashioning.[16] The virtues celebrated in courtly romance – martial prowess, voluntary daring, quest for unpredictable risk, loyalty to a revered lady, solidarity of the group and largesse – have been conserved, imitated and appropriated by the urban merchant and artisan classes, who are the producers and consumers of the Robin Hood poems. The outlaw of Sherwood, then, fulfills the need for a mercantile hero to replace the knightly hero of the aristocratic romances. Robin Hood's imitation of courtly behaviour and forms in the *Gest* is not mere flattery but dialectical: imitation – appropriation – domination, if only in imaginative terms.

Robin Hood, who is clearly identified as a yeoman, imitates knightly behaviour by giving liveries and fees to his retained men; by acting in a courteous manner (the word 'curteyse' is used seventeen times); by refusing to eat until he is visited by an unknown guest (like King Arthur in *Sir Gawain and the Green Knight*); by showing respect to his social superiors in lowering his hood and kneeling; and by granting a boon to the wife of Sir Richard at the Lee, the impoverished knight. Indeed Robin exhibits all of the courtly virtues enumerated by Michael Nerlich, but he also personifies the concomitant commercial virtues of the guildsman or merchant. In the first section of the poem, Robin offers to help the bankrupt knight, Sir Richard, by *lending* him £400 to pay off his loan to the rapacious Abbot of St Mary's. Moreover, Little John suggests that they give him a 'lyveray' because his clothing is 'full thynne'. Robin can well afford the gift because there is 'no *marchaunt* in mery Englond/ So ryche in scarlet and grene' cloth (my italics). Before agreeing to lend Sir Richard the money, Robin asks for a 'borowe' or guarantor, and when the knight pledges God Himself, Robin turns him down flat, demanding 'a better borowe . . . Or money getest thou none'. The fact that Robin offers a loan to be repaid and not a gift is made clear when he states that the money is to be repaid in twelve months to the day. In addition to being cast as a money lender (Robin replaces the Jewish money lender in the source, 'The Merchant's Surety'), he also plays the role of cloth merchant in another scene when King Edward asks him if he has any green cloth to sell. Robin replies that he has 'thyrty yerdes and thre'. Although the actual sale is not depicted, the story implies that a deal was made and coin exchanged for Lincoln green cloth.

Beyond these scenes in which commercial activity is described, there are many other examples of mercantile ideology. The entire poem, in fact, reflects guild policies and practices as preserved in records from the fourteenth and fifteenth centuries. There were some 600 merchant and craft guilds scattered throughout England at this time, and many records survive in the form of royal charters, statutes, licences, by-laws, ordinances and writs.[17] Some of the shared features are:

1. Patronage by the Virgin Mary;
2. Adulation of the monarch;
3. Organization and officers of the fellowship;
4. Recruitment of new members by offering them liveries and fees;
5. Election feasts;
6. Entertainments;
7. Charity to the poor;
8. Penalty for perjury;
9. Processions or 'ridings'.

A Gest of Robyn Hode registers a crucial moment in the social and economic transformation of late medieval England, when the merchant adventurer replaces, if not opposes, the feudal petty nobility. We are, in short, witnessing the birth of capitalism, albeit in imaginary terms.

Translator's Note

The translation is based upon the edition of the *A Gest of Robyn Hode* in Knight and Ohlgren, *Robin Hood and Other Outlaw Tales*, pp. 80–168.

TRANSLATION OF *A GEST OF ROBYN HODE*

Part 1

Attend and listen, gentlemen, who are of freeborn blood, I shall tell you about a good yeoman,[1] whose name was Robin Hood. While he was alive, he was a proud outlaw,[2] and no outlaw was found who was as courteous. Robin stood in Barnsdale,[3] leaning against a tree, with the good yeomen Little John, Will Scarlock, and Much the Miller's son, who was every inch a man. [See plate 18.]

Little John spoke to Robin, 'Master, it would do you much good if you dined early.' Then Robin replied to him, 'I have no desire to eat until some bold baron, strange visitor, lord or sire, or knight or squire will come to pay for the meal.'[4]

Robin's custom was to hear three Masses everyday before he dined: one in honour of God the Father, another of the Holy Ghost, and the third of Our Dear Lady, the Virgin Mary, whom he loved the best of all. For fear of deadly sin, Robin loved the Virgin.[5] He would never do any harm to a company that any woman was in.[6]

Then said Little John, 'Master, if we shall spread our table, tell us where we shall go, and what life we shall lead? What shall we take, and what shall we leave behind? Where shall we wait behind? Where shall we rob, and where shall we despoil? Who shall we beat and tie up?'

'No matter,' then said Robin, 'we shall do well enough, but look that you do no harm to any small farmer, who tills with his plow. Nor shall you harm any good yeoman who walks by the greenwood thicket, or a knight or a squire who would be a good fellow. However, you should beat and tie up bishops and archbishops, and don't forget the Sheriff of Nottingham.'[7]

'Your wishes will be kept', said Little John, 'and this lesson we will learn. It is far on in the day – God send us a guest – so we can have our dinner!'

Robin replied, 'Take your good bow in your hand, and let Much the Miller's son and William Scarlock go with you, and no man stay with me. Walk up to the Saylis and to Watling Street and look for some unknown guest.[8] If he is an earl, baron, abbot or knight, bring him to stay with me – his dinner will be waiting for him.'

The three yeomen went up to the Saylis, but when they looked east and west, they didn't see anyone. But as they looked towards Barnsdale, a knight came riding through a secret way, and at once they met him. His appearance was sad and little was his pride. One foot was in his stirrup, while the other dangled beside. His hood hung over his eyes as he rode in plain clothing. A sorrier man never rode on a summer's day! [9]

Little John went down on his knee courteously and greeted the knight, 'You are welcome, gentle knight, welcome you are to me. And welcome to the greenwood, noble and courteous knight. My master has awaited you without food for three hours.'

'Who is your master?' asked the knight. Little John replied, 'Robin Hood.' 'He is a good yeoman,' said the knight, 'about him I have heard much good. I agree to accompany you, my fellows, although I had planned to dine today at Blyth or Doncaster.'[10] This gentle knight went forth with a sorrowful expression as the tears ran from his eyes and fell down his face.

When Robin Hood saw him arrive at the door of the hut, he courteously took off his hood and knelt down on one knee, saying, 'Sir knight, welcome, I have been waiting for you without my dinner for three hours.' The knight then answered with fair and noble words, 'God save you, good Robin and all your fair company.' After washing and wiping their hands, they sat down to dinner.[11] They had bread and wine in plenty as well as deer sweetbreads. They also had fine swans, pheasants and river-bank birds. They lacked not even the smallest bird that was born on a branch. 'Eat well, sir knight,' said Robin. 'Thank you, sir,' replied the knight, 'I haven't had such a dinner in three weeks, and if I come this way again, Robin, I shall make you as good a dinner as you have made me.' 'Thank you, knight,' said Robin, 'when I have that dinner, by God, I won't be as ravenous as you were! Oh, by the way, I think it is only right that you pay me before you leave. You know, it was never the custom, by God, for a yeoman to pay for a knight.'

The knight replied, 'I'm ashamed I have no money in my money chest.' 'Little John,' Robin orders, 'go and look and don't delay. By God, sir knight, tell me the truth.'[12] 'As God is my witness,' the knight replied, 'I have no more than ten shillings.' 'If you don't have any more than that, I'll not take a penny', said Robin, 'and if you have need of more I'll lend it to you. Go ahead Little John, tell me the truth. If there isn't any more than ten shillings, I won't touch a penny.'

Little John spread the knight's mantle on the ground, and found there just half a pound. He let it lie alone and went to his master. 'What is the news?', Robin asked. Little John replied, 'Sir, the knight is telling the truth.' Robin said, 'Let's fill our cups with the best wine, and let the knight begin. Sir knight, tell me why your clothing is so threadbare? Tell me in a word, and I'll counsel you. Were you

13. Map of the northern countries, from Olaus Magnus, *History of the Northern Peoples*, Rome, 1555.

14. A knight battles a serpent, from Olaus Magnus, *History of the Northern Peoples*, Rome, 1555.

15. A northern seascape, from Olaus Magnus, *History of the Northern Peoples*, Rome, 1555.

16. Archery practice, from Olaus Magnus, *History of the Northern Peoples*, Rome, 1555.

17. A forest of pine trees, from Olaus Magnus, *History of the Northern Peoples*, Rome, 1555.

18. The title page of the Wynkyn de Worde edition of the *Lytell Geste of Robin Hode*, Cambridge University Library MS Sel. 5. 18, *c.* 1515.

19. An old 'Gray-headed' oak in Sherwood Forest.

20. Sherwood Forest at dawn.

21. An early portrait of Robin Hood, *c.* 1510–15, from the Lettersnijder edition of the *Gest of Robyn Hode*, Edinburgh, National Library of Scotland.

ADAM BELL,
CLIM of the CLOUGH,
AND
WILLIAM of CLOUDESLE.

Clim of the Clough.   Adam Bell.   William.

LONDON,

Printed by *A. M.* for *W. Thackeray,* at
the *Angel* in *Dnck-Lane,*

22. The frontispiece to *Adam Bell, Clim of the Clough and William of Cloudesley.*

23. Map of Scotland in the time of William Wallace.

24. Sir William Wallace,
Scottish patriot, *c.* 1272–1305.

25. An outlaw being dragged to the gibbet: accused of killing Richard, Earl Marshall, in 1234, William de Marisco was outlawed, captured and executed in 1242. After being dragged behind a horse, he was hanged, disemboweled and dismembered into four pieces, which were displayed in four cities, from Matthew Paris, *Chronica Majora*, Cambridge, Corpus Christi College MS 16, f. 155ᵛ.

made a knight by compulsion or else by yeomanry?[13] Or were you a miserable farmer and lived in conflict and strife? Were you a usurer, or else a lecher', asked Robin, 'who wrongly led your life?' 'By God who created me, I am none of those,' said the knight. 'My ancestors have been knights for one hundred years. It often happens, Robin, that a man is deprived of his status, but God, who sits in heaven above, may amend his state. Within the last two years, Robin, my neighbours know it well that I had £400 of good money to spend, but now I have no possessions. May God, who shaped such an end, amend my difficulties for the sake of my wife and children.' 'How did you lose your riches?' Robin asked. The knight replied, 'By my great folly and my kindness. Robin, I have a son who in truth should have been my heir. When he was twenty years old, he killed a knight from Lancaster and his bold squire while jousting in a tournament. To save him I sold my goods and pledged my lands as security for a loan from the rich abbot of St Mary's Abbey in York'.[14] 'Tell me the truth, what is the sum due?' asked Robin. 'Sir,' the knight answered, 'the abbot counted out to me 400 pounds.' 'If you lose your lands, what will happen to you?' Robin asked. 'I will have to hurry over the ocean', the knight answered, 'to see where Christ lived and died on the mount of Calvary. Farewell friend and goodbye, it may not be otherwise.' As tears fell from the knight's eyes, he wished to go on his way, saying, 'Farewell, friend, and have a good day, I have no more to pay.'

'Sir knight,' Robin asked, 'where are your friends?' 'Not one will recognize me,' said the knight. 'While I was rich enough at home, they boasted that they knew me, but now they run away from me like scared beasts. They pretend that they had never seen me before.' Little John, Will Scarlock and Much wept together for pity. 'Fill your cups with the best wine', said Robin, 'and let's put on a cheerful face. Do you have any friend who will guarantee my loan to you?' The knight replied, 'I have none but God who died on the Cross.' 'Do away with your jokes,' then said Robin, 'do you seriously believe that I would accept God, Peter, Paul or John as guarantors? No, by God who made me and created both sun and moon, find me a better securer of the loan, or you won't get any money from me.' 'To tell the truth,' said the knight, 'I have none other than Our Dear Lady, who has never failed me before this day.' 'By dear worthy God,' Robin replied, 'searching throughout England, I never found better security for my money.[15] Little John, come forward now, go to my treasure box, and bring me £400 – and make sure that it is accurately counted.'

Little John and Scarlock went and counted out £400. Little Much asked, 'Is it counted correctly?' And Little John replied, 'What's the matter with you? It is charitable to help a noble knight who has fallen into poverty. Master, because the knight's clothing is threadbare, you must give him a livery to wrap his body in. You have plenty of fast-dyed scarlet cloth and many rich clothes. I dare say that there is no merchant in merry England as rich as you.'[16] 'Little John, give him three yards of every colour', says Robin, 'and make sure it is properly measured.'

Using his bow stave as a measure, Little John added three feet to every handful of cloth. Little Much exclaimed, 'Who do you think you are, the Devil's draper?' Standing still and laughing, Will Scarlock said, 'By Almighty God, Little John is giving him good measure because it isn't costing him anything.' Then said Little John to noble Robin Hood, 'Master, you must give the knight a horse to carry home these goods.' 'Give him a gray courser and a new saddle', said Robin, 'because he is Our Lady's messenger, and God grant that he is true.' 'And a good saddle horse', said Little Much, 'to maintain him in his right.' 'And a pair of boots for he is a gentle knight,' said Scarlock. 'And what will you give him, Little John?' asked Robin. 'Sir, a pair of gilded shining spurs and a prayer from all this company that God will deliver him from sorrow.'

Then the knight asked, 'Robin, when shall I repay you,' and Robin answered, 'Twelve months from this day under this greenwood tree.' [See plate 19.] Robin then said, 'It would be a great shame for a knight to ride alone without a squire, yeoman, or page to walk by his side. I'll lend you Little John, my man, to be your servant. If you have great need, he will serve you as a yeoman.'

Part 2

Now the knight is gone on his way, and he thought the arrangement was good. When he looked back towards Barnsdale, he blessed Robin Hood. And when he thought of Barnsdale and Will Scarlock, Much and Little John, he blessed them as the best company that he was ever in. That gentle knight then spoke to Little John, 'Tomorrow I must go to St Mary's Abbey in York[17] and pay the abbot of that place £400. If I am not there by this night, my land will be lost for ever.'

Meanwhile in the hall of the Abbey of St Mary, the abbot spoke to his convent, 'Twelve months ago a knight came here and borrowed £400, pledging his lands as security. If he doesn't come today he will be disinherited.' 'It is still too early,' said the prior, 'the day is not yet over. If it were me I'd rather pay the £100 right away, but the knight is far beyond the sea fighting for England's right and suffers hunger and cold and many a sorry night.[18] It is a great pity to take his land. Abbot, you are too light of your conscience and do him much wrong.' The abbot replied, 'By God and St Richard of Chichester, you are always in my beard!'[19] At that moment the chief cellarer of the order, a big-headed monk, entered the room and said, 'The knight is either dead or hanged. By God that redeemed me, we shall have his £400 pounds a year income to spend in this place.'

The abbot and the high cellarer hurried on boldly because the high justice of England was in their pay. The justice and many others had taken the knight's debt in their hands and intended to do him wrong. The abbot and his accomplices judged him severely: 'Unless he comes today, he shall be dispossessed.' The justice added, 'I declare that the knight will not come.' But to their sorrow, the knight arrived at the abbey gate.

The noble knight then spoke to his retinue, 'Now put on your modest clothing that you brought over the sea.'[20] They put on their simple clothing and came to the abbey gate where the porter, standing ready, welcomed them all. 'Welcome, sir knight,' said the porter, 'my lord is at dinner, and so is many a noble man in your honour.' Looking at the knight's horse, the porter swore a great oath, 'By God that created me here is the best built horse that I've ever seen. Lead the horses into the stable so that they can be refreshed.' But the knight replied, 'By God that died on a tree, they shall not go within.'

In the abbot's hall, the lords were seated at dinner. The knight entered, knelt down, and greeted them all. 'Eat well, sir abbot, I have come as agreed upon.' The abbot responded at once, 'Have you brought me my money?' 'By God that created me, not one penny,' replied the knight. 'You are a wicked debtor,' said the abbot, as he turned to the justice and said, 'Sir justice, let's drink a toast to our victory!' The abbot then said, 'What are you doing here if you haven't brought my money?' 'To beg for an extension on my loan,' cried the knight. The justice blurted out, 'You have missed your payment and your land is lost.' 'Now good justice, be my friend and protect me from my enemies!', the knight begged. 'No,' said the justice, 'I have been retained by the abbot with both cloth and fee.' [21] Turning to the sheriff, the knight implored, 'Now, good sheriff, be my friend!' 'Nay, for God,' he replied. Finally turning to the abbot, the knight says, 'Now, good sir abbot, be my friend, and as an act of courtesy retain my lands in your hand until I have paid my debt to you! And I will be your true servant and serve you until I obtain the £400 of good money.' Swearing a great oath, the abbot replied, 'By God that died on a tree, get yourself land where you may but you get none from me.' 'By dear worthy God who created all this world,' said the knight, 'if I don't get my land again, someone is going to suffer for it. God who was born of a maiden grant us well to succeed! It is good to test a friend before a man has need.' The abbot looked on the knight with hatred and shamefully shouted at him, 'Get out, you false knight, hurry out of my hall!' 'By God who created us, abbot, you lie,' said the knight. 'I was never a false knight.' The noble knight then stood up and said to the abbot, 'You don't know good manners to allow a knight to kneel so long. I have been in jousts and tournaments and have been in as great danger as anyone I've ever seen.'

The high justice then asked the abbot, 'How much will you give so the knight will release his claim? Unless you do this you will never hold the land in peace.' The abbot replied, '£100.' 'Give him £200,' the justice said. 'No, by God,' said the knight, 'you won't get it that easy. Even if you gave a £1,000 more, you would be no nearer success – the abbot, justice and friar will never be my heirs.' The knight approached the round table and shook £400 out of a bag. 'Here, have your gold, sir abbot, that you lent me. If you had been courteous when I arrived you would have received a bonus.' The abbot sat still and ate no more of his splendid food. Lowering his head, he stared at the knight. 'Give me my gold again, sir justice, that I paid to you as a retainer,' said the abbot. 'By God who died on the Cross, no, not a penny,' replied the justice. 'Sir abbot and men of law,' said the knight, 'now that I have fulfilled my debt, I will have my land again in spite of anything you can say.' The knight went out the door without a care in the world, discarded his modest attire, put on his good clothing and went forth singing merrily.

When he arrived at his home in Verysdale,[22] his wife met him at the gate of his castle, and said, 'Welcome, my lord, are all your possessions lost?' 'Be merry, madam,' said the knight, 'and pray for Robin Hood that his soul go to heaven. He helped me out of trouble, and if it hadn't been for his kindness we would be beggars. The abbot and I reached an agreement, and he has been paid his money. The good yeoman lent it to me as I came along the road.'

The knight then dwelt pleasantly at home, to tell the truth, until he had collected the £400 with which to repay Robin Hood. He provided himself with one hundred bows with well-fitted strings and one hundred sheaves of good arrows with brightly burnished points. And every arrow was forty-five inches long, fletched with peacock feathers and nocked with white silver – they were a fine sight. He also purveyed one hundred archers, provided them and himself with gear and red and white liveries.[23] Bearing a light lance, he rode singing a song towards Barnsdale, while a servant carried his trunk.

When he reached Wentbridge, the knight stopped to watch a wrestling match.[24] All the best yeomen of the West Country were there. A splendid contest was going on, the winner receiving a white bull, a great horse with saddle and gold-burnished bridle, a pair of gloves, a red-gold ring and a cask of wine.[25] There was a yeoman, the best wrestler in the place, who was afraid he would be slain because he was a stranger in those parts. The knight took pity on the yeoman in the place where he stood. Because of his love of Robin Hood, he said that a yeoman should not be harmed. The knight and his one hundred men with their bent bows and sharp arrows pushed forward into the place in order to put that crowd to shame. Gathering together and making room, the crowd wanted to know what the knight had to say. He took the yeoman by the hand and declared him champion. Giving him five marks (£3 6s 8d) for the cask of wine lying on the ground, the knight ordered that it should be tapped and set running and invited all to drink. Thus this noble knight tarried until that sport was done. Meanwhile, Robin Hood, who was waiting for the knight in Barnsdale, went without food for three hours after noon.

Part 3

Attend and listen, gentlemen, all who be here now, about Little John, who was the knight's servant. You will hear some good mirth! Upon a merry day, the young men of Nottingham held a shooting match, and Little John fetched his bow at once and said that he would join them. He shot three rounds and always slit the wand sticking in the ground.[26] Standing by the targets, the proud Sheriff of Nottingham swore a great oath: 'By Him who died on the Cross, this man is the best archer that I've ever seen. Tell me now, strong young man, what is your name? In what country were you born, and where do you live?' Little John replied, 'Sir, indeed of my mother, I was born in Holdernes in east Yorkshire, and men call me Reynold Greenleaf when I'm at home.'[27] 'Tell me, Reynold Greenleaf,' said the sheriff, 'would you like to dwell with me? I'll give you twenty marks as your fee every year.' 'I already have a master', replied Little John, 'and he is a courteous knight. It would be best if you got his permission to retain me.'

After the sheriff obtained the knight's permission to employ Little John, he was retained for a period of twelve months, and at once he was given a good strong horse. Now is Little John the sheriff's man. May God grant us to succeed! But Little John's thought was always to pay him his just desert. 'So help me God,' he thought to himself, 'and by my true fidelity I shall be the worst servant to him that he ever had!'[28]

It happened on a Wednesday when the sheriff was gone hunting and Little John was left lying in his bed. Shortly after noon, Little John, who had not eaten yet, said to the keeper of the hall, 'Good sir steward, I ask you, give me my dinner. It is a long time for Greenleaf to be fasting, so I ask you, sir steward, give me my dinner.' The steward replied, 'You will not eat or drink until my lord comes back to town.' 'Upon my vow to God,' said Little John, 'I would rather crack your crown.' The butler was uncourteous where he stood on the floor. He walked to the butlery and shut fast the door. Little John gave him such a tap that nearly broke his back in two. Though he lived a hundred years, he would never walk the same again. Little John kicked the door open with his foot and there he took a large helping of both ale and wine. 'Since you will not dine,' said Little John, 'I'll give you something to drink. Even if you live one hundred years, you won't soon forget Little John.' Little John ate, and he drank as long as he wanted to. In his kitchen the sheriff had a cook, a stout and bold man. 'By God,' said the cook, 'to ask like this to dine, you are a cursed servant to dwell in anyone's house.' He then gave Little John three good blows. 'By God,' said Little John, 'I like these strokes! I think you are a bold and hearty man, and before I pass from this place I'm going to put you more to the test.' Little John drew a good sword, and the cook took another in hand. They gave no thought to fleeing but staunchly held their ground. For an hour they fiercely fought each other, but neither could hurt the other. 'By God,' exclaimed Little John, 'you are one of the best swordsmen I have ever seen. If you could wield a bow as well, I'd take you to the greenwood where Robin Hood will pay you a fee of twenty marks a year and two changes of clothing.'[29] 'Put up your sword', said the cook, 'and we'll be friends.'

The cook then fetched sweetbreads, good bread and wine for Little John, and they ate and drank. When they had drunk a draft or two, they promised each other that they would join Robin Hood that same evening. They quickly went to the sheriff's treasure room, broke the steel locks and took away the silver vessels, dishes and drinking cups, and they didn't even forget the spoons. They also took £300 and more, and they went straight to Robin Hood in the ancient greenwood. 'God save you and Christ watch over you, my dear master,' said Little John. 'Welcome to you and to that fair yeoman who is with you. Tell me, Little John, what news do you bring from Nottingham,' replied Robin. 'The proud sheriff greets you well and sends you by me his cook, his silver vessels and his £303,' bragged Little John. 'By God and the Trinity,' exclaimed Robin, 'it was never by the sheriff's good will that all these possessions came to me!'

Soon after Little John devised a crafty trick. Running five miles into the forest, all his wishes came true. Upon meeting the proud sheriff, who was hunting with hounds and horn, he knelt down out of courtesy before him and said, 'My dear master, God and Christ save and watch over you!' The sheriff asked, 'Reynold Greenleaf, where have you been?' 'I've been in the forest', answered Little John, ' and I've seen the fairest sight I've ever seen. Over there I saw a right fair hart, green in colour, with a herd of one hundred and forty deer altogether. Their antlers of more than sixty are so sharp, master, that I was afraid to shoot at them for fear they would slay me.'[30] 'By God,' said the sheriff, 'I would gladly see that sight.' 'Hasten you thither, dear master, and go with me,' said Little John. While the sheriff rode on horseback, Little John ran nimbly by his side, and when they came upon Robin Hood, John said, 'Lo, sir, here is the master hart.'

The proud sheriff, a sorry man was he, stood stone still and uttered, 'A plague on you, Reynold Greenleaf, because you have betrayed me!' 'By God,' said Little John, 'master, you are at fault for I was deprived of my dinner when I was at your home.' The sheriff quickly sat down to supper, but when he recognized his white silver he lost his appetite. 'Be of good cheer and for courtesy, sheriff; and for Little John's sake,' said Robin, 'I grant you your life'. When they had finished eating, the day was almost gone, and Robin ordered Little John to take off the sheriff's shoes and hose, as well as his tunic and furred short jacket. Robin gave him a green mantle to wrap himself in and commanded his sturdy young men under the greenwood tree to dress themselves in the same liveries so that the sheriff might see them. Because the proud sheriff lay on the ground all night in his britches and shirt, it was no wonder that his sides hurt. 'Be of good cheer and charity, sheriff,' said Robin, 'for this is our custom under the greenwood tree.' 'This is a crueller custom than any hermit or friar has to bear,' cried the sheriff. 'I would give all the gold in England not to stay here longer!' 'You shall remain here with me for twelve months', replied Robin, 'and I'll teach you, proud sheriff, how to be an outlaw.'[31] 'Before I stay here another night, Robin, I beg you to strike off my head and I will forgive you,' said the sheriff. 'For holy charity, let me go, and I'll be the best friend you ever had.' 'You shall swear an oath to me on my shining sword', replied Robin, 'that you will never plot me harm on land or water. And if you find any of my men at day or night, you will, upon your word, help them as far as you can.' When the sheriff swore his oath he started off for home. He was as full of the greenwood as ever a fruit was of its stone!

Part 4

The sheriff, who dwelt now in Nottingham, was glad that he was gone from the greenwood, and Robin and his merry men returned at once to the forest. 'Do we have dinner now?' asked Little John. 'No,' said Robin, 'I'm afraid Our Lady is angry with me because she hasn't sent my money.'[32] 'Have no doubt, master,' replied Little John, 'the sun has not yet set, and I safely swear that the knight is true and trustworthy.' Robin then commanded Little John, 'No man stay with me, but take your bow in your hand, walk up under the Saylis to Watling Street with Much and William Scarlock, and look for some unknown guest. Whether he be a messenger or minstrel, if he is poor he shall have some of my goods.' Little John started forth, a little angered and annoyed,[33] and girded himself with a good sword under his green mantle. The three yeomen went up to the Saylis, and looking both east and west they saw no man coming. But as they looked towards Barnsdale down the highway, they saw two Benedictine monks dressed in black, each on a good saddle horse. Little John then said, 'I bet my life these monks have brought our money. Be of good cheer and make ready your yew bows, and look that your hearts be sure and steadfast, your bow strings trusty and true. The monks have fifty-two men and seven strong packhorses. No bishop in this land rides so royally, I believe. Brothers, although we are only three, we must bring them to dinner lest we fail our master. Bend your bows and make that crowd stop. The life and death of the foremost monk are contained in my hand.' 'Stop! churl monk,' yelled Little John, 'don't go any farther. By dear worthy God, if you move your death is in my hand. Evil luck thrive on your head, right under your hatband, for you have made our master angry over fasting too long.' 'Who is your master?' asked the monk. 'Robin Hood,' answered Little John. 'He is a downright thief,' asserted the monk. 'I've heard nothing but bad about him.' 'You lie!' then said Little John, 'you shall regret what you said. Robin is a yeoman of the forest, who has commanded you to dine with him.' Much, who was ready with an arrow, aimed at the monk's chest, so that he dismounted. Of the fifty-two young yeomen, not one stayed save a little page and a groom who led the packhorses with Little John.

Whether he liked it or not, the monk was brought to the door of Robin's hut to speak with Robin Hood. When he saw the monk, Robin lowered his hood, but the monk was not as courteous because he left his hood in place. 'By God,' said Little John, 'he is a churl.' 'No matter,' replied Robin, 'he doesn't know how to be courteous. John, how many men had this monk?' 'Fifty-two when we met them, but most of them are gone,' answered John. 'Let's blow a horn', said Robin, 'so we may know our fellowship.' Immediately, seven score sturdy yeomen hurried to Robin's side, all of them dressed in striped scarlet mantles. They all came to Robin to know what he would say. The monk was made to wash and wipe his hands before sitting to dinner,[34] and Robin and Little John served him together. 'Eat with pleasure, monk,' said Robin. 'Thank you, sir,' the monk replied. 'When you are at home, where is your abbey? And who is your patron?' asked Robin. The monk answered, 'St Mary Abbey in York, though I am humble here.' 'What is your office?' Robin questioned. The monk replied, 'Sir, the chief steward.' 'So may I always prosper,' Robin added, 'you are most welcome. Fill our cups with the best wine, this monk shall drink to me.'

'All day long I have wondered why Our Lady has not sent me my money. I fear that she is angry with me,' Robin then said.[35] 'Have no doubt, master,' said Little John, 'you don't need to worry, I say, for the monk has brought it, I swear, because he is from the Virgin Mary's abbey.' Robin said, 'She was the guarantor of the money I lent the knight under the greenwood tree.' Turning to the monk, Robin said, 'And if you have brought that silver, I pray let me see it, and I shall help you in return if you have need of me.' With a miserable expression on his face, the monk swore a great oath and said, 'I have never heard of this matter before.' 'I swear to God, monk,' replied Robin, 'you are to blame because God and His Dame are righteous, and you cannot refuse because you said with your own tongue that you are Our Lady's servant and serve Her every day. And you are her messenger who will pay me my money. Therefore I thank you for coming today. Tell me the truth, what is in your coffers?' 'Sir,' answered the monk, 'so I may always prosper, twenty marks.' 'If there's no more than that', said Robin, 'I won't take a penny, and if you have need of more, sir, I'll lend it to you. But if I find more you will truly lose it all except for your travelling silver.[36] Little John, go forward and tell me the truth. If there's no more than twenty marks, I won't take a penny.'

Little John spread out the monk's mantle on the ground, as he had done before, and counted out more than £800 from his chest. Leaving the money on the ground, Little John ran to his master, and said, 'Sir, the monk is true enough, Our Lady has doubled your throw of the dice.' 'By God, monk,' said Robin, 'didn't I tell you that Our Lady is the truest woman that I ever found! By dear worthy God, searching throughout England I never found a better guarantor of my money. Let's fill our cups, drink a toast to the monk, and greet his gracious lady. And if she has need of Robin Hood, she will find a friend. And if she needs any more silver, you, monk, come again to me, and by this token she has sent to me she shall have three times as much.'

When Robin captured the monk, he was going to London to hold an important meeting in order to bring under foot the knight, Sir Richard at the Lee, who rode haughtily on his horse. Robin then asked, 'Monk, where are you going?' The monk replied, lying, 'Sir, I was going to our manors to deal with our crooked bailiffs, who have done much wrong.' 'Little John,' ordered Robin, 'come forward and listen to my tale. I don't know a better yeoman to search a monk's baggage.' 'Monk, tell us the truth,' asked Robin, 'how much money is that other horse carrying?' 'By Our Lady,' complained the monk, 'it is not courteous to ask a man to dinner and afterwards hold him!' 'It is our custom', said Robin, 'not to leave much behind.' Not wanting to stay any longer, the monk spurred his horse. Robin called after him, 'Before you ride away do you want another drink?' 'No, by God,' cried the monk, 'I regret that I came here for I could have dined more cheaply in Blyth or Doncaster!' 'Greet your abbot and prior for me', said Robin, 'and ask them to send me such a monk for dinner every day.'

Let's leave that monk in silence, and speak about the knight, Sir Richard, who came while it was still light on his appointed day to Robin Hood. He took himself straight to Barnsdale under the greenwood tree and found there Robin Hood and all his merry band. After the knight dismounted from his good horse, Robin courteously lowered his hood and knelt down. The knight exclaimed, 'God save you, Robin Hood and all this company.' And Robin replied, 'You are welcome, gentle knight, very welcome indeed.' Then Robin said to the knight so noble, 'What brings you to the greenwood? I pray, sir knight, tell me. Why have you been so long?' The knight replied, 'Because the abbot and the high justice would have had my land.' 'Tell me the truth,' asked Robin, 'do you have your land back again?'[37] 'Yes, by God,' replied the knight, 'and for that I thank God and you. But don't be offended that I have been so long for I came upon a wrestling match and there helped a poor yeoman who was being mistreated.' 'No, by God,' said Robin, 'Sir knight, I thank you for that. Any man who helps a good yeoman will be my friend.' Then the knight said, 'Here is the £400 that you lent me as well as twenty marks for your courtesy.'[38] 'No, by God,' replied Robin, 'you enjoy it forever because Our Lady, through her messenger the steward of St Mary's Abbey, has already sent me the money. And if I took the money twice, I would be ashamed. But truly, gentle knight, you are most welcome here.' When Robin told the knight his tale, he laughed and had good cheer, saying, 'By my word, your money is already here.' 'Use your money well, you generous knight', said Robin, 'and welcome to my trysting tree.'[39] But what are these bows and finely feathered arrows for?' asked Robin. 'By God,' then said the knight, 'they are a poor present for you.' 'Little John, come here,' said Robin, 'go to my money-box and bring me the £400 that the monk over-paid to me.' Robin said, 'Here, you gentle and true knight, have the £400. Go and buy yourself a horse with fine trappings and gild your spurs. And if you ever need any more money, come to Robin Hood, and, by my word, you shall never fail while I have any to give you. And use well the £400 that I lent you, and, if you will take my advice, don't dress so humbly.' Thus, good Robin helped the knight out of all his troubles. God, who sits in high heaven, grant us happiness!

Part 5

Now that the knight has taken his leave and gone on his way, Robin Hood and his merry men lived quietly for many days. Attend and listen, gentlemen, and hear what I am going to say about how the proud Sheriff of Nottingham announced a full fair contest. Upon a certain day all the best archers of the north should come together for a shooting, and he who shoots best of all will carry away the prize. Whoever shoots the farthest, fairest and lowest at a pair of fine butts[40] under the greenwood thicket will receive a right good arrow with a silver shaft and red-gold point and feathers. There is none like it in all of England. When Robin heard about the contest at his trysting tree, he said: 'You sturdy young men, prepare yourselves, I want to see that contest. Hurry, my merry young men, you will go with me, and I will test the sheriff's faithfulness to his oath.'

When they had readied their bows and finely feathered arrows, seven score sturdy young men stood by Robin's side. When they came to Nottingham, they found the target range fair and long. Many bold archers were shooting with strong bows. 'Only six of you will shoot with me,' said Robin, 'the others will protect my head. Stand by me with good bows ready in case I'm deceived by the sheriff.' Robin was the fourth outlaw to shoot his bow, and the proud sheriff was watching as he stood by the target. Robin shot three times and always split the wand sticking in the ground, and so did good Gilbert with the White Hand. Little John and Will Scarlock likewise were good archers, and Much and Reynold Greenleaf[41] were not much worse. When these good and fair archers all shot a bout, Robin Hood, in truth, was the best. The gold arrow was given to him as the best, and he courteously accepted the prize. As Robin was leaving for the greenwood, he heard the hue and cry and great horns sounding, and he said: 'Misery come to you! You will know evil for your treachery! You are truly evil! Woe to you, proud sheriff, pleasing your guest in this way! You promised me otherwise in yonder wild forest. If I had you in the greenwood at my trysting tree, you would leave me a better pledge than your word.'

Many an arrow were let loose there, many a tunic was rent, and many a side was hurt. The outlaws shot so fiercely that no man could drive them away, and the proud sheriff's men quickly fled. When Robin saw the ambush break out, he wished he was in the greenwood. Many an arrow was shot there among that company. Little John was so sorely hurt with an arrow in his knee that he couldn't run or ride. It was a great pity! To Robin then Little John said: 'Master, for the love of God who died on the Cross, and for the rewards of my service, if you ever loved me, don't let the proud sheriff find me alive. Take out your blood-stained sword, strike off my head, and give me deep and wide wounds.' 'No, I won't do that,' replied Robin, 'not for all the gold in England, though it lay in a pile.' 'God forbid', said Much, 'that you, Little John, should part from our company.' Much placed John on his back and carried him a mile, pausing only to take another shot. A little within the forest, they came upon a fair castle, double ditched and walled. And there dwelt that noble knight, Sir Richard at the Lee, to whom Robin had loaned the £400 under the greenwood tree. The knight took in Robin and all his band, and said: 'You are welcome, Robin Hood, and I thank you for your comfort, courtesy and kindness under the greenwood tree. I love no man in all this world as much as I do you. I will give you sanctuary from the proud Sheriff of Nottingham.'

The knight then gave orders to his men: 'Shut the gates and draw up the bridge, and let no one in. Arm yourselves and get ready. To the battlements!' 'I swear by St Quentin,[42] Robin,' said Sir Richard, 'I promise to maintain you and your men for forty days.' At once the tables were laid out and the clothes were quickly spread, and Robin and his merry men went to their meal.

Part 6

Attend and listen, gentlemen, and harken to your song. Hear how the proud Sheriff of Nottingham and his armed men raised the countryside militia in order to besiege the walls of the knight's castle.

The haughty sheriff then loudly proclaimed, 'You traitor knight, you are protecting the king's enemies against the law.'[43] 'Sir, I openly acknowledge the deeds I have done,' replied Sir Richard, 'but I swear upon my lands that I am a true knight. Go forth, sirs, on your way, and do no more to me until you discover our king's will and learn what he will say about this.'

Thus the sheriff had his answer, and it was no lie. He went to London to tell our king. There he told him about Sir Richard and also about Robin Hood and his bold archers, who were so noble and good. 'Dear Lord,' said the sheriff to the king, 'Sir Richard has admitted that he has maintained the strong outlaws.' 'Be warned,' said the sheriff, 'he intends to be lord of the north and reckons you worth nothing.' 'I will come to Nottingham', said the king, 'within this fortnight, and I will capture Robin Hood and that knight. Do as I bid, go home now and organize the militia of good archers from the entire countryside.' The sheriff took his leave of the king and went on his way.

Upon a certain day, Robin Hood returned to the greenwood. When Little John was healed of the wound in his knee, he went straight to Robin Hood under the greenwood tree. Because Robin was free to roam in the forest under the green leaves, the proud Sheriff of Nottingham was greatly vexed. Although the sheriff waited for Robin both by day and by night, he missed him and could not take his prey. He also stalked the noble knight, Sir Richard at the Lee, and one day, while the knight was hawking by the riverside, he was captured by heavily armed men and led bound hand and foot to Nottingham. Swearing a great oath, 'By Christ who died on the Cross,' the sheriff wished he'd captured Robin Hood instead.

When the knight's wife, a fair and noble lady, heard this, she mounted her saddle horse and rode to the greenwood. When she came into the forest under the greenwood tree, she found Robin Hood and his fair band there. 'God save you and your company,' said the lady, 'for the sake of our dear Virgin, I beg you to grant me a boon. Don't let my wedded lord be shamefully slain! Because of his love of you, he has been fast bound and taken to Nottingham.' Good Robin said at once to the noble lady, 'Who has taken your lord?' She then said, 'The proud Sheriff of Nottingham has taken him. In truth, he is not yet 3 miles from here.'

Robin jumped up as if he were mad, and said, 'Hurry you my merry men, and, by Christ who died on the Cross, if anyone refuse to serve he shall never live with me in the greenwood.' Immediately seven score archers with their bows scrambled over the hedges and ditches. 'I vow to God,' said Robin, 'if I find the sheriff and capture him, I will take revenge.'

And when they arrived in Nottingham, they walked through the streets and soon met up with the proud sheriff. 'Wait, you proud sheriff!' Robin said, 'wait, and speak to me. I want to hear what the king said. By dear worthy God, I haven't gone this fast on foot in the last seven years and, by God, it's not for your good!' All at once Robin shot an arrow from his bow and hit the proud sheriff so that he fell still on the ground. And before he could get up and stand on his feet, Robin struck off his head with his bright sword. 'Lie there, proud sheriff,' Robin said, 'badly may you end! No man could trust you while you were alive.' Robin's men drew out their sharp swords, attacked the sheriff's men, and chased them out without delay. Robin rushed to Sir Richard, cut his bonds in two, handed him a bow, and bade him stand and fight. 'Leave your horse behind', said Robin to the knight, 'and run with me through mire, moss and fen to the greenwood, until I've gotten the pardon of Edward, our handsome king.'[44]

Part 7

King Edward and his knights came to Nottingham in great force to capture Sir Richard and, if he might, Robin Hood. He asked the men of that country the whereabouts of the outlaw and the bold knight. When they told him what had happened, the king understood the situation, and he seized all the knight's lands. King Edward travelled through the whole of Lancashire until he came to Plompton Park,[45] where he found many of his deer missing. The king was used to seeing many herds there, but now he could scarcely find one deer with decent horns.[46] Enraged, the king swore by the Trinity, and said, 'I wish I had Robin Hood within my eyesight. And he who decapitates Sir Richard and brings his head to me shall have the knight's land. I will give it to him with my charter and seal it with my hand to have and to hold for ever more.'

Then spoke a fair old knight, who was true in his faith, 'O, my lord king, let me speak a word – there is no man in this country who can have the knight's lands while Robin Hood still rides with a bow in his hands. Robin won't lose his head, the "best ball in the hood",[47] by surrendering it to any man.' Our handsome King Edward lived in Nottingham half a year and more, but he didn't hear a word about Robin Hood or what part of the country he was in. Meantime, good Robin, travelling through hills and dales, continued to kill and enjoy the king's deer at will.

One day a proud forester, who was standing at the king's side, said, 'If you want to see good Robin, you must do what I say. Take five of your best knights, who are under your command, and walk down to yonder abbey and dress yourselves in monks' habits. I will be your guide and lead you, and before you reach Nottingham I wager my head that you will meet good Robin, if he is still alive, and see him with your own eyes.' After the king and the five knights were quickly clothed in monk's garments, they hastened thither. Our king, who was very tall, wore a broad hat on his head like an abbot. To tell you the truth, he also wore thick boots as he rode singing to the greenwood on the way to Nottingham. His 'convent of monks', all dressed in grey, his baggage horse, and his packhorses followed behind until they arrived in the greenwood about a mile in the forest. All of a sudden, they met good Robin and many bold archers standing in the middle of the road.[48] [See plate 20.]

Grabbing the reins of the king's horse, Robin said, 'Sir abbot, by your leave, you must stay here a little while. As yeomen of this forest, under these greenwood trees, we live on our king's deer for we have no other means. But you have churches, rents from your properties, and plenty of gold. For the sake of charity, give us some of your earnings.' Then soon spoke Edward, our handsome king, 'I have brought with me no more than £40 to the greenwood. For the last fortnight I've been staying with the king in Nottingham, and I've spent a great deal of money on the great lords there. And all I have left is £40, not a penny more, but if I had £100 I'd promise it to you.' Robin took the £40 and divided it into two parts – half he gave to his merry men and bade them to be merry. The other half Robin returned to the king, and courteously said, 'Sir, you can have this for your expenses. We shall meet another day.'[49] 'Thank you,' replied the king, 'but King Edward greets you and sends you his seal, bidding you to come to Nottingham to share both food and meat with him.' The king then took out his broad targe[50] and showed it to Robin, who knowing his courtesy, knelt down at once. Robin exclaimed, 'I love no man in all the world as much as I do my king. My lord's seal is most welcome here and, monk, so is your news. For the love of my king, sir abbot, you will dine with me today under my trysting tree.'

Robin led our handsome king by the hand to the place where many deer had been slain and quickly prepared. Robin blew loudly on a large horn, and seven score sturdy young men came running in a row and knelt before him. Swearing by St Augustine, the king said to himself, 'Here is an amazing sight! By God's sacrifice, his men are more obedient than mine.' Their dinner was quickly prepared and they went to eat. Both Robin and Little John served our king with all their skill. Before our king was set fat venison, good white bread, good red wine and also fine brown ale.

Robin said, 'Abbot, for charity, make good cheer and bless you for this news. You shall see what kind of life we lead, before you go away, so you can tell the king when you meet him.' Whereupon they jumped up and prepared their bows. Our king was so frightened because he thought he would be killed. As targets they set up two sticks fifty paces apart, but the king thought that they were too distant. And on both targets they placed a rose garland.[51] Robin said, 'Anyone who misses the rose garland shall forfeit his gear, no matter how fine, and give it to his master. As I drink ale or wine, I will spare no man, who will also receive a blow on his head.' It soon fell to Robin to strike them sorely. Twice Robin himself shot a round and he always split the stick, and so did Gilbert Whitehand.[52] But when Little John and good Scarlock missed the garland, Robin struck them sorely. Taking his final shot, Robin missed the target by more than three fingers' width.

Then spoke good Gilbert, 'Master, you have lost your gear. Stand and take your punishment.' Robin replied, 'If it may not be otherwise, sir abbot, I deliver my arrow to you. I pray you, sir, serve me the blow.' 'Robin, by your permission,' the abbot said, 'my religious order does not permit me to strike a good yeoman for fear I will hurt him.' 'Strike on boldly,' ordered Robin, 'I give you full permission.' With that word, the king, folding up his sleeve, gave Robin such a blow that he fell to the ground. 'By God!' said Robin, 'you are a stalwart friar! Your arms are so strong I warrant you can also shoot well.'

When the king came close to Robin, he gazed intently at our handsome king, as did Sir Richard at the Lee, and they both knelt down. When the wild outlaws saw them kneel, they did the same. 'My lord, the King of England,' exclaimed Robin, 'now I recognize you!'[53] 'Thanks, Robin,' said the king, 'for your goodness and your grace at your trysting tree for my men and me.' 'Yes, and may God save me,' cried Robin, 'I beg your mercy, my lord the king, for me and my men.' 'Yes, for the sake of God,' then said our king, 'I agree to it if you and your band will leave the greenwood and come home, sir, to my court and there dwell with me.' 'I vow to God', said Robin, 'that it shall be so. I'll come to your court to serve you, and I'll bring my seven score and three men with me. But if I don't like serving you, I'll return to the greenwood to shoot at the brown deer, as I'm used to doing.'

Part 8

'Do you have any green cloth', asked the king, 'that you'll sell to me now?' 'Yes, by God,' said Robin, '33 yards.' 'Robin,' said our king, 'I pray you now will sell me some of that cloth for me and my company.' 'Yes, by God,' answered Robin, 'or else I were a fool. You will clothe me, I believe, for Christmas.'[54] Casting off his monk's habit, the king put on the green garment, and, indeed, all the knights were soon wearing the hoods. When they were all dressed in Lincoln green,[55] they cast away their grey habits. To everyone there the king said, 'Now we shall go to Nottingham.'

Dressed as outlaws, they went toward Nottingham town shooting as they went. As our king and Robin rode together along the way,[56] they played the shooting game 'pluck buffet', and the king, who missed many targets, received many knocks from Robin Hood that day. Good Robin wasn't sparing in his payment of buffets! 'So help me God,' said the king, 'your game is not hard to learn. Though I practised shooting for a year, I couldn't beat you.' [See plate 21.]

As they rode into Nottingham, all the people stood and stared, and saw nothing but green mantles that covered the field. They said to each other, 'I fear our king has been slain. Robin Hood has come into town and he has left no one alive.' Both yeomen and boys began to flee, and old women, who could hardly walk, hopped away on their crutches. The king laughed out loud and gave orders to his people. When they saw our handsome king, they were very pleased indeed. They ate, drank and had a merry time singing high notes.

Then our handsome king spoke to Sir Richard at the Lee and gave him back his land. Robin thanked King Edward and knelt down. Robin lived in the king's court for fifteen months, and during that time he spent £100 in addition to his men's payments. Every where he went, Robin paid out even more for knights and squires in order to maintain his renown. By the end of the year, all those he had retained had gone except for Little John and good Will Scarlock. One day Robin saw men shooting their bows and arrows, and said, 'Alas, my wealth is gone!'[57] Sometime ago I was a good archer, hardy and strong, and was reckoned the best archer in merry England. Alas, if I live any longer with the king, my sorrow will slay me!' Robin went forth to the king, and said, 'My lord the King of England, grant me my request. I built a fair chapel in Barnsdale, dedicated to Mary Magdalene,[58] and I want to go there for seven days. I will neither eat or drink nor sleep a wink. As a pilgrim, I have been called to go there barefoot and dressed in sackcloth.' 'If it must be so,' answered the king, 'it cannot be otherwise. I give you leave for seven days, but no longer.' 'Thank you, lord,' then said Robin, settling himself on his knee.

Robin took his leave courteously and then he went to the greenwood. When he arrived in the forest on a merry morning, he heard the delicate notes of the birds merrily singing. 'It was long ago when I was last here,' said Robin, 'it pleases me to shoot at the brown deer.' Robin killed a large hart, and then blew his horn. Recognizing the sound, all the outlaws of the forest gathered together, and seven score sturdy young men hastened to Robin's side. Lowering their hoods, they knelt before him. 'Welcome our master', they said, 'under this greenwood tree.'

Robin lived in the greenwood for twenty-two years. For fear of King Edward, he didn't return to court. Yet he was tricked by a wicked woman, the prioress of

Kirkley Abbey,[59] who was related to him. Because of her love of a knight, Sir Roger of Donkesly, who was her favourite, may they suffer evil! Together they plotted how they might kill Robin Hood. Then spoke good Robin, 'Tomorrow I must go to Kirkley Abbey to have my blood let.' Sir Roger of Doncaster[60] lay with the prioress, and they betrayed good Robin Hood through their foul play.

Christ, who died on the Cross, have mercy on his soul because he was a good outlaw who did poor men much good!

ADAM BELL, CLIM OF THE CLOUGH AND WILLIAM OF CLOUDESLEY

Thomas Hahn

INTRODUCTION

As a lively, self-contained and substantive tale of outlawry, *Adam Bell, Clim of the Clough and William of Cloudesley* is the only work that rivals stories of Robin Hood in popularity and antiquity. No outlaw ballad, except the pivotal *A Gest of Robyn Hode*, was printed earlier than *Adam Bell*; the earliest fragments of the ballad survive from an edition of 1536, and the poem was then reprinted another half-dozen times or more within the next seventy-five years. *Adam Bell* is only one-third as long as *A Gest of Robyn Hode*, but it is twice the length of the earliest, unprinted Robin Hood ballads (*Robin Hood and the Monk, Robin Hood and the Potter*), and six times the length of the many seventeenth-century broadside ballads that celebrate the deeds of Robin Hood. Though the exploits of Adam, Clim and William never achieved inclusion in the 'garlands' (or cheap collections) that lionized Robin Hood into the nineteenth century, the outlaws were certainly well known to late medieval and early modern audiences: in 1432 a Wiltshire Parliament roll lists 'Adam Belle', 'Clim O'Cluw' and 'William Cloudesle' (alongside Robin Hood and other merry men) as local members, suggesting that the outlaws' notoriety had endowed their names with sufficient familiarity to be playful or defiant aliases in official contexts.[1]

The narrative was reprinted, presumably in its entirety, perhaps twice, in the 1540s, and again in 1557–8, 1582, 1586, 1594 and several more times in the first decade of the seventeenth century. Its remarkable popularity and commercial success inspired an anaemic sequel, added in 1586 and to most later editions; in this, William's oldest son (also here named William) grows up and, in the process of stealing off with his love Cisley, kills her former suitor and three rangers, and so becomes an outlaw.[2] 'Old William' pleads to the king for mercy; when this is denied, he and his old associates, Adam and Clim, join young William and Cisley and they resist the pursuit of fifty thousand of the king's men. When the king reverses policy and offers to take the outlaws into his service, Adam declares, 'Neare [never] had His Grace subjects more true, And sturdier than we'; the outlaws become courtiers, and the queen makes Cisley a lady, repeating to some degree the denouement of the original ballad. The colossal celebrity conferred on William and his comrades by the ballads must have touched every social stratum, and this pervasive familiarity was both acknowledged and ridiculed by self-consciously literary writers: in *Much Ado about Nothing* (1598–9), Shakespeare's Benedick vows that, should he fall in love, he will become a target, 'and he that hits me, let him be clapp'd on the shoulder, and call'd Adam' – an allusion to the unbelievable feats of archery performed by Adam and William in the ballad. In Ben Jonson's *The Alchemist* (1610), the trickster Face claims that his dupes are 'No cheating Clim-o'-the-Cloughs . . . that look as big as five-and-fifty and flush'. Both of these casual allusions draw upon the proverbial status of these outlaws among all audiences, even as they disdain the gross exaggerations typical of popular culture.

Though allusions to William, Adam and Clim would no doubt be lost on most modern audiences, the outlaws remained formidable rivals to Robin Hood and his band, in both oral and print culture, through to the end of the seventeenth century. Separate chapbooks of *Adam Bell*, usually running twenty to twenty-four pages, appeared in 1630, 1640, 1648, 1655, 1667, 1668 (discrete prints in London and Glasgow) and 1683. The mid-seventeenth century Percy folio manuscript, an antiquarian collection of 'ancient' ballads, copies both parts of *Adam Bell* alongside a sequence of Robin Hood texts and other popular narratives of adventure and violence. The fame of the three seems to have suffered eclipse in the eighteenth century, though the invented ballad, *Robin Hood's Birth, Breeding, Valour, and Marriage* (1716) casts Adam, Clim and William as an older generation of outlaws, contemporaries of Robin Hood's father.[3] The Scots man of letters, James Hogg, retold the ballad, as part of the general revival of ancient minstrelsy, in the earlier nineteenth century, and *Adam Bell* was reissued in the northern cities of Newcastle, Stirling and Glasgow (twice) in the course of the century. Pierce Egan, who had achieved a huge popular success in rewriting the Robin Hood stories, first in serial form and then as a self-contained novel for children (1838, 1840), produced a novelization of *Adam Bell* as well (serial, 1842; novel, 1851), though this seems to have had nothing like the impact of the earlier book. After another century of obscurity, several writers in the last decades have retold the story of *Adam Bell* (though focusing it explicitly on the exploits of William of Cloudesley): these include Jose Manuel Carbonell, *La Cenicienta* (Barcelona, Editorial Bruguera, 1963); Jennifer Westwood, *Tales and Legends* (New York, Coward, McCann & Geoghegan, 1971); and Roderick Hunt, *Myths and Legends*, Oxford Junior Readers, 5 (Oxford, OUP, 1981).

Though the outlaw heroes of *Adam Bell* may never recoup their former fame, the sources of their early appeal seem clear. Certainly by the sixteenth century, a conventional genre of outlaw narratives, set in a mythic medieval and national past, had emerged. Such writings chiefly centred on Robin Hood, and this mass of material (in songs, plays and other performances, and in published versions) seems to have exerted an irresistible influence over all kindred stories. *Adam Bell* accordingly opens in the merry greenwood, where men roam freely and enjoy untroubled relations with nature and with each other. William's decision to ignore his companions' warning, and to confront town life, civilization and the Law, predictably results in his downfall; his capture in turn sets up a stock but exciting rescue, entailing massive battles with officers of the law and government. Both of these episodes recall the central actions of one of the earliest outlaw ballads, *Robin Hood and the Monk*, in which Robin ventures into Nottingham unaccompanied, is captured after a bloody struggle, and is then ingeniously rescued by Little John and Much.[4] The final section of *Adam Bell* stages a variation on the archery contest that occurs regularly in Robin Hood ballads. The entire ballad thus interweaves a series of individual motifs that characteristically mark other outlaw narratives (especially *Robin Hood and the Monk*). These include the overthrow of brutal and corrupt local officials such as the sheriff and justice, the treachery of a much favoured minion (the old woman who skulks off to the authorities), the cold-blooded dispatch of arrogant lackeys such as the porter, the manipulation of the law and its instruments such as the king's seal, and the underlying fealty to and ultimate reconciliation with the king himself.

At the same time, *Adam Bell* introduces several distinctive and unexpected developments to the conventional outlaw story. The most striking of these is William's decision to leave the forest because he finds the exclusive fellowship of men inadequate; his longing to be back with his wife and children in Carlisle runs directly counter to the usual ethos of the greenwood, with its rejection of ordinary social and political responsibilities.[5] This fundamental commitment in *Adam Bell* to a 'mature masculinity' (an identity anchored in marriage, a sanctioned social position, ownership and inheritance, and intergenerational attachments) makes this ballad's conclusion seem fitting and consistent; in contrast, the love of adventure and evasion of conventional social ties that mark most outlaw tales make such 'socialized' endings, where they occur, seem purely magical resolutions. This narrative coherence (reinforced by the independent, self-contained character of the ballad's quatrains) endows *Adam Bell* with a less restless, episodic quality than most outlaw poems, both in its local effects and in its overall impact. Finally, the adaptation of the 'William Tell' episode – in which William of Cloudesley, under no compulsion from the king, insists on shooting an apple from the head of his trussed-up oldest son – transforms the traditional archery contest from a test of manly skill to an extravagant (even outrageous) personal and family melodrama. The king's threat to hang all three outlaws if William does not fulfill the precise conditions of his spoken oath is both conventional ballad leitmotif and a reaction to the potentially fatal consequences of William's reckless endangerment.

Adam Bell manifests, then, a thematic and narrative consistency unusual in outlaw tales, and it elaborates individual episodes through its use of local realism and explanatory detail (as in the false letter to dupe the porter). Nonetheless, the plot of *Adam Bell* remains utterly improbable. Ultimately, the appeal of the ballad depends upon a fantasy of invincible heroism, and upon the spectacular character of its action – in particular on its zest for martial encounter and unstinting, unrestrained violence. In the initial section, William (with the capable assistance of Fair Alice and her poleaxe) nearly succeeds in withstanding the whole town of Carlisle with his bow and then his sword; only when he is burnt out of his house, and has its charred fixtures thrown on top of him (as opposed to being bested in a fair fight or contest of skill), is he captured. In the second fitt (the shortest, at 188 lines and by far the most bloody), William and his associates kill more than three hundred of the king's agents and their supporters; they coolly execute the porter, they assassinate the sheriff and justice, and then fight their way through the streets of Carlisle, systematically mowing down all opposition. Because the ballad insists so fully on the audience's identification with the outlaws, these hundreds of deaths, rather than seeming an atrocity, become a platform for the display of the heroes' exploits. The violence of the third and longest fitt (291 lines) is, if not high tech, at least much more fine tuned: William puts on a shooting display (capped by his cold-blooded conscription of his child as the target support) that suggests his near preternatural skills place him in a class by himself as an archer.

Ballads like *Adam Bell* did not, of course, appeal to specialized audiences of skilled archers or violent sociopaths, but enjoyed a massive popularity with listeners and readers in all quarters. Many must have found pleasure in the 'tabloid realism' characteristic of these ballads, which insisted simultaneously upon the incredible character of the events they retold, and on the need to believe in their absolute actuality. Though the vividness of the episodes is often anchored in realism of detail, the excitement of these stories feeds upon the exaggerated, even hyper-realistic narrative style. In all these respects, early outlaw tales bear remarkable similarities to modern genres of pulp fiction, in particular to martial arts films and 'street fighter' arcade games. Both of these forms make use of fast-moving, episodic structures filled with spectacular masculine violence. The predominance of 'stars' who are at once fictional characters and real life people (Steven Seagal, Jean-Claude Van Damme, Jackie Chan) parallels the ambiguously 'historical' status of figures like Robin, William, Adam and Clim. Moreover, in both ballads and films, the hero's only role is to engage in a potentially limitless series of physical encounters that – in the name of truth, justice and freedom – highlight finely honed fighting techniques and justify any amount of mayhem. The relative triviality in such popular films of any complexity in motivation or character – as compared to the indispensability of unrelenting, spectacular displays of masculine potency – is even more apparent in modern arcade and computer games. Our awareness of these features in modern narratives and entertainments helps to locate the broad appeal of outlaw ballads in a recognizable cultural landscape, even if for *Adam Bell* that context is hundreds of years removed. Listeners, viewers and readers, from the Middle Ages to the twentieth century, have clearly savoured the spectacle of action pure and simple, and through their enormous appetite and huge pleasure, audiences have continuously sponsored such stories.

At the same time, *Adam Bell* possesses a number of distinctive ingredients that account for its fame and influence over several centuries. One of the most puzzling is William of Cloudesley's unprovoked desire to claim the role of respectable citizen, obtain pardon from the king, and become part not just of ordinary society – as exemplified by his wish to be with his wife and children – but ultimately of the official culture itself. In part, William's decision is no more than the necessary trigger for the action of the last fitt; it may also, however, contribute to William's role as 'noble' outlaw, since it rests upon his unquestioning trust of the king's law, and it allows the ballad to portray royal justice as ever the same throughout England's history. In ordering that the outlaws be hanged forthwith, the king values public order (and his own authority) over derring-do; the queen's contravention of the monarch's order, based upon her recognition of the outlaws' native manliness and decency, recurs as a motif in several Robin Hood ballads and in other stories as well. In the ensuing scene, the relatively powerless queen and outlaws seem to have gained the upper hand over their sovereign, who has pronounced a public pardon in ignorance of their latest crimes (in particular, the killing of three hundred people at Carlisle). What seems at first a low trick or a legal technicality (the rashly sworn oath, another common motif in outlaw tales), however, turns out to be a settlement the king relishes: William's display of manly bravado and skill convinces the monarch that the outlaws may be an even more potent force for keeping the peace than for breaking it. The conclusion of *Adam Bell*, in which outlaw careers end through co-option into the established structures of the law, finds many parallels in medieval and early modern judicial records.[6]

The ease with which William accepts his assimilation to officialdom is perhaps more plausible because the ballad presents him throughout as a family man. The capitulation of Adam and Clim, on the other hand, contrasts directly with the behaviour of outlaws in other tales; these 'wolves' heads' – non-entities before the law, who may be killed at will – are typically lone wolves who relish the freedom of the greenwood, and find it difficult or impossible to adjust to ordinary society or official roles. Though the transformation of the heroes in *Adam Bell* from sturdy, unvarnished yeomen of the countryside to newly coined 'Yeomen of the King' may figure some pattern of social mobility, it openly violates the fantasy of forest life that undergirds most narratives of this kind. Nonetheless, in its underlying ethos of a universal manhood that makes relations between king and yeomen outlaws possible, *Adam Bell* reproduces a staple element of other ballads. In its portrayal of resourceful, energetic common men who not only fend for themselves but become celebrities through their own main force, and of a monarchy that symbolizes timeless justice and reliable order, the narrative conjures a sense of the nation and its 'Englishness' that helped form the collective identity of audiences in the sixteenth century and beyond. The resort to specifics (on weapons or legal matters) and to local realism – in particular, the allusions to Inglewood Forest and Carlisle in the north, and the recourse to the king's court in the capital – sets the action in a 'medievalesque' framework that reinforces the continuity of English place and time even as it invents an improbably disconnected, legendary past. This deployment of 'faux history' to ground extravagant narratives remains a generic trait of romance novels and adventure stories early and late (Robin Hood, Hercules, Xena the Warrior Princess, Indiana Jones), but, at least for earlier audiences, it makes *Adam Bell* a story of national significance.

Finally, *Adam Bell*, as a tale of outlawry and adventure, is both typical and distinctive in centring its appeal on a fascination with weaponry, in particular the bow and arrow. Historians have pointed out that the bow (as opposed to the lance or the sword) is a non-aristocratic weapon, and that its featured role may signify the popular origins of a story. Nonetheless, the archery events depicted in poems like *Adam Bell* frequently require technical mastery and physical strength of the sort associated with modern athletic contests, and audiences – noble and common, medieval and modern – seem always to find excitement in such improbable feats and record-setting shots. William's performance in the several contests of the last fitt clearly gratifies this interest. Moreover, the lightness and portability of the weapon makes it the consummate amplification of the individual's power, at least before gunpowder; in using his bow, the hero is only once removed from the drama of direct bodily contact that is the essence of agonistic struggle, and he can do much greater (and more believable) damage than anyone might do with their hands alone. In outlaw tales like *Adam Bell*, the bow becomes a levelling device by which those outside officialdom can resist or overthrow tyrannical authority (as William does in the first fitt). Lastly, the bow also functions as an instrument of rampant violence and mass destruction, as the three heroes spectacularly prove in the middle section of the ballad. As crucial as William's unique shooting skills may be to the narrative, the capacity to defeat and destroy throngs of enemies seems even more integral to the fantasies of struggle, triumph and power that *Adam Bell* feeds.

In its own time, *Adam Bell* must first have circulated as popular song or recitation, and then as mass-produced entertainment. In making this momentous transition from oral to print culture, the ballad helped redefine what 'popular' literature might be, in terms of content, medium, audience, genre and so on. For many readers and listeners, the inexpensive chapbooks furnished a new outlet for cultural energies, an alternative to the cheap piety of religious pamphlets and sermons. Sir Thomas More's remark, that one should 'handle holie scripture in a more homely maner than a song of Robin Hood', exemplifies not only the disdain of the learned for popular culture, but the view that a 'song' or ballad like *Adam Bell* was essentially preliterate.[7] The survival of these outlaw narratives despite such 'official' hostility corroborates the depth and breadth of their appeal; after all, More himself must have been thoroughly familiar with these stories in order to reject them. While it is impossible for a poem like *Adam Bell* to impart to modern audiences the same allure and vitality that its early readers appreciated, the present translation attempts to convey at least some sense of these traditional forms and attractions, together with an understanding of the interests that produced and sustained them.

TRANSLATION OF *ADAM BELL, CLIM OF THE CLOUGH AND WILLIAM OF CLOUDESLEY*

Part I

It was merry in the green forest among the green leaves, where men walked in all directions with their bows and keen arrows, seeking to raise the deer out of their dens. Such sights as these which have often been seen by the yeomen of the north country are what I mean to talk about. One of these hunters was called Adam Bell, the second Clim of the Clough and the third William of Cloudesley, a fine archer indeed. Each of these three yeomen was outlawed for poaching deer, and one day they declared themselves sworn brothers and went to Inglewood Forest.[1]

Now attend and listen, gentlemen, who love to hear good stories. Two of the yeomen were single men, while the third had a wedded wife. William was the wedded man, and so his concerns were the greater. One day he said to his brothers that he would go to Carlisle[2] to speak with fair Alice his wife and with his three children. [See plate 22.]

'By my troth,' said Adam Bell, 'not by my counsel, for if you go to Carlisle, brother, and depart this wild wood, the law may get you, and your life would be at an end.' William replied, 'If I don't return by tomorrow at sunrise, brother, you can assume that I am captured or, if not, that I am slain.'

He took leave of his two brothers and is off to Carlisle. There he quickly knocked at his own window. 'Where are you, fair Alice my wife, and my three children? Quickly let in thy husband, William of Cloudesley.' 'Alas!' then said fair Alice, and she sighed with deep sorrow; 'For this half year and more this place has been besieged because of you.' 'Now that I am here', said Cloudesley, 'I would like to get inside. Now fetch us an abundance of meat and drink, and let us make good cheer.' She fetched him meat and drink aplenty, and pleased him, whom she loved as her life, with what she had.

Close by the hearth in that place lay an old woman, whom William in his charity had supported for more than seven years. Up she got, and stealthily walked out; evil may she fare therefore! For she had not set foot on the ground in the last seven years. She went to the hall of the Justice as fast as she could go. 'This night William of Cloudesley has come into this town.' The Justice was very pleased and so was the Sheriff also.[3] 'You shall not have come hither, dame, for nothing; you shall have your reward before you go.' They gave her a very nice gown, scarlet in colour, as I heard said. She took the gift and went home, and lay down again.

They raised the citizenry of merry Carlisle with all the haste they could, and they all came thronging to William's house. There they besieged the good yeoman on every side. William heard the loud noise of the people who were hurrying towards that place. Alice opened a shuttered window and looked all about. She was aware of both the Justice and the Sheriff, and the great crowd with them. 'Alas! treason,' cried Alice, 'may you forever suffer woe! Sweet William of Cloudesley, my husband,' she said, 'go into my chamber.'[4]

He took his sword and buckler, his bow and his three children and went into the strongest chamber where he thought he would be most secure. As a true lover, fair Alice followed him with a poleaxe in her hand. 'As long as I am able to stand, he shall be dead who comes through this door', she said. Cloudesley drew a good bow, which was made of trusty wood, and struck the Justice on the chest, but the arrow broke into three pieces. 'God's curse on the heart', said William, 'of whoever this day put your coat armour on. If it had been no better than mine, the arrow would have gone nearer the bone.'

'Yield thee, Cloudesley,' said the Justice, 'and throw thy bow and arrows from thee'. 'God's curse on his heart', said fair Alice, 'who so counsels my husband.' 'Set fire to the house,' said the sheriff, 'since it will no better be. And we will burn therein William, his wife and three children.' They set fire to the house in many places and the fire flew on high.[5]

'Alas!' then cried fair Alice, 'I see we shall die here.' William opened his back window that was in the upper chamber, and let his wife and his three children down on sheets. 'Have here my treasure,' said William, 'my wife and three children. For the love of Christ don't do them any harm, but all of you take your vengeance on me.'

William shot his bow wonderfully well until his arrows were all gone, and the fire had come so fully upon him that his bow string burned in two. The burning embers fell on him, good William of Cloudesley. He was then a woeful man, and said, 'To me this is a coward's death. I'd rather', said William, 'run among the throng with my sword than cruelly burn in front of my furious enemies.' He took his sword and buckler and ran among them all. Where the people were thickest he struck down many a man. He ran on them so fiercely there that no man might withstand his strokes. Then they threw windows and doors on top of him, and so captured that good yeoman. There they bound him both hand and foot, and cast him into a fortified dungeon.

'Now, Cloudesley,' said the chief Justice, 'thou shall be quickly hanged.' 'I shall make one vow,' said the Sheriff. 'I shall make for you a new pair of gallows, and all the gates of Carlisle shall be shut so that no man shall come in that way. Then neither Clim of the Clough, nor Adam Bell, shall help though they came with a thousand more – nor will all the devils in hell avail you.'

Early in the morning the Justice arose, went quickly to the gates, and quickly ordered every one of them to be tightly closed. Then he went to the market-place as fast as he could and set up a pair of new gallows beside the pillory. A little boy stood among them and asked what the gallow tree was for, and they said, 'To hang a good yeoman, called William of Cloudesley.' That little boy was the town swineherd, and kept there Alice's pigs. He had often seen Cloudesley in the woods, who gave him food. He went out of the town through a crevice in the wall, and quickly he went to the woods; there he met at once those sturdy young men. 'Alas!' then said the little boy, 'you tarry here all too long, for Cloudesley is captured and is condemned to death, and is set to be hanged.' 'Alas!' then said good Adam Bell, 'that ever we should see this day! He might have stayed safe with us here, as we often prayed him to do. He might have tarried in the green forest under the bright shadows, and kept him and us in peace, out of trouble and sorrow.'

Adam drew a right good bow; immediately a great hart he had slain. 'Take that, child,' he said, 'for thy dinner, and bring me my arrow again.' 'Now we go hence,' said these strong young men, 'tarry we no longer here. We shall ransom him, by God's grace, though we pay for it dearly.' To Carlisle went these good yeomen on a merry morning in May. Here is one fitt[6] of Cloudesley, and another is about to be said.

Part II

When they came to merry Carlisle on a fair morning, they found the gates shut against them on all sides. 'Alas!' then said good Adam Bell, 'that ever we were made! These gates are shut so wonderfully well that we may not come in.' Then spoke Clim of the Clough: 'We will get ourselves inside with a trick. Let's say we are messengers who have come straight from our king.' 'I have a letter that is well prepared,'[7] Adam said. 'Now let us act shrewdly; we will say we have the king's seal – I think the porter is no clerk.'[8]

With that, Adam beat on the gate with great and strong strokes. The porter heard such a great noise there that he rushed to the gate. 'Who is there now', said the porter, 'that makes all this knocking?' 'We are messengers', said Clim of the Clough, 'who have come directly from our king.'[9] 'We have a letter', said Adam Bell, 'that we must bring to the Justice. Let us in to deliver our message so we can return to our king.' 'No one comes in here,' said the porter, 'by Him who died on the Cross, until a false thief called William of Cloudesley is hanged.' Then spoke that good yeoman, Clim of the Clough, and swore by the gracious Virgin Mary: 'If we are made to stand any longer outside, you shall be hanged like a thief! Lo! Here we have the king's seal. What, fool, are you mad?' The porter thought that it had been as they said, and he quickly took off his hood. 'My lord's seal is welcome,' he said; 'for the sake of that, you shall come in.' He opened the gate at once – an evil opening for him!

'Now we are in,' said Adam Bell, 'for which we are very glad. But only Christ, who harrowed Hell, knows how we shall ever come out again.' 'Had we the keys,' said Clim of the Clough, 'we should do well enough then; we might get out easily when we saw the time and need.' They called the porter to take counsel with them, and wrung his neck in two, and cast him into a deep dungeon, and took the keys from him. 'Now am I the porter,' said Adam Bell. 'See, brother, we have the keys here, and I shall be the worst porter that merry Carlisle has had in one hundred years.[10] We will now draw our bows; into the town we will go, and deliver our dear brother, who lies in care and woe.'

Then they strung their good yew bows, making sure their strings were taut. At that point they dispersed themselves around the market-place of merry Carlisle. As they looked around, they saw there a pair of new gallows, and nearby was the Justice with the inquest of jurors, who had condemned Cloudesley to be hanged there. And Cloudesley himself lay waiting in a cart, tightly bound hand and foot, with a strong rope around his neck, all ready to be hanged. The Justice called a young boy over to him, who was to have Cloudesley's clothes, and told him to take the measure of that good yeoman, and thereupon to make his grave. 'I have seen as great a marvel', said Cloudesley, 'as between sunrise and now: he who makes this grave for me may himself lie therein.' 'You speak proudly,' said the Justice; 'I shall hang you with my own hand.' His two brothers heard that full well as they stood there silently.

Then Cloudesley cast his eyes around and saw his brothers standing there, in the corners of the market-place, their good bows ready in their hands, ready to chase the Justice. 'I see good comfort,' said Cloudesley; 'Even yet I hope to fare well. If I had my hands free, I would worry very little.' Then spoke good Adam Bell to Clim of the Clough: 'Brother, see you mark well the Justice; lo, yonder you may see him. And fiercely I will shoot at the Sheriff with a sharp arrow.' A better shot in merry Carlisle was not seen in the last seven years! They loosed their arrows both at once; of no man had they fear! The one shooter hit the Justice, the other the Sheriff, and both their sides began to bleed. All the townsmen scattered when the Justice fell to the ground, and the Sheriff fell near him; each one had his death wound. All the citizens fled at once – they dared hold their places no longer. The outlaws released Cloudseley at once where he was tied with ropes. William rushed up to a town officer, and wrenched his axe out of his hand; with it he struck down townsmen on every side, so that each one thought he had tarried too long. William said to his two brothers, 'Let us live or die together this day. If ever you have need as I now have had, you shall receive the same from me.' Because their bow strings were of such fine silk, they shot so well that day that they held the streets on every side; the battle raged for a long time. They fought together as true brothers, like hearty and bold men. They threw many a man to the ground and made many a heart cold.

But when all their arrows were gone, men pressed them very hard. Then they drew their swords at once, and cast their bows aside. They continued quickly on their victorious course, with swords and round bucklers. By the time it was midday, they had made many wounds. There were many horns sounding the alarm in Carlisle, and the bells were rung backwards; many women cried 'Alas!' and wrung their hands. The mayor of Carlisle then came forth with another large throng; these three yeomen feared him sorely; their lives stood in jeopardy. The mayor speedily came armed with a poleaxe in his hand. Many strong men were with him to withstand the outlaws there in that battleground. The mayor struck at Cloudesley with his axe; his shield split in two. Many a yeomen, suffering great hurt, cried out in woe, 'Alas, treason!' They ordered, 'Keep the gates shut fast, so these traitors cannot get out there.'[11] But all they did was for nothing: they were quickly mowed down, until the three outlaws, who fought so manfully, got outside in a rush. Adam Bell said, 'Here have your keys; I forsake my office as porter. If you take my advice, you will appoint a new porter.' He threw the keys at their heads, and wished bad luck to them, and to all that prevented any good yeomen to come and comfort his wife.

Thus, these good yeomen are gone to the woods, as light as leaves on a linden tree. They laugh and are merry in cheer because their enemies were far behind. When they came to Inglewood Forest under their trysting tree,[12] they found there good bows and plenty of arrows. 'So help me God,' said Adam Bell and worthy Clim of the Clough, 'I wish we were now in merry Carlisle, facing that huge host again!' They sat down and made good cheer, eating and drinking their fill. Here ends a fitt about these doughty yeomen, and another I shall tell you.

Part III

As they sat in Inglewood under their trysting tree, they thought they heard a woman weep, but they could not see her. Sorely sighed fair Alice there, and said, 'Alas that ever I see this day! For now is my dear husband slain, alas and alack! If I could speak with his dear brothers, with either of those two, to inform them about what happened to him, my heart would be out of pain.'[13] Cloudesley walked alongside and looked under the greenwood tree. He recognized his wife and children, full of woe in heart and mind. 'Welcome, wife,' then said William, 'to this trysting tree. I had thought yesterday, by sweet Saint John, that you would

never see me again.' 'Now good fortune is mine,' she said, 'for you are here. My
heart is out of woe.' 'Dame, be happy and glad,' William said, 'and thank my two
brothers.' 'To speak of such things', said Adam Bell, 'is truly of no consequence.[14]
The meat that we shall have for dinner is still running fast on its feet.' Then all
three of these noble archers went down into a clearing, and each of them slew a
fat hart, the best that they could see there. 'Here, Alice my wife, have the best,'
said William of Cloudesley, 'because you so boldly stood by me when I was nearly
slain.' Then they went to their supper with such meat as they had, and thanked
God for their fortune. They were merry and glad.

And when they had supped well, without any stinting, Cloudesley said, 'Let us
go to our king to get us a letter of peace.[15] Alice shall tarry in a nunnery near
here, and my two sons shall go with her, and shall stay there as well. My eldest
son shall go with me, for I have full confidence in him, and he shall bring you
word again about how we fared.'

Thus these rugged men went off to London, going as fast as they could until
they came to the king's palace, where they had to be. And when they came to the
king's court, to the very palace gate, they would ask permission of no man, but
boldly went in. They rushed headlong into the hall, fearful of no one. The porter
pursued and called after them, and began to chide them. This usher said, 'You
yeomen, what do you want? I pray you tell me; you are disrespecting our court
officials. Good sirs, where do you come from?' 'Sir, know for certain, we are
outlaws of the forest, and we've come here to our king to get a letter of peace.'

And when they came before our king, in accord with the law of the land, they
knelt down without delay and each held up his hand.[16] They said, 'Lord, we
beseech you here that you will grant us grace, for we have slain your fat fallow
deer in many places.'[17] 'Tell me at once', then said the king, 'what are your
names?' They said, 'Adam Bell, Clim of the Clough and William of Cloudesley.'
'Are you those thieves', then said our king, 'that men have spoken of to me?
I make a vow here to God, all three of you shall be hanged. You shall be dead
without reprieve, as I am king of this land.' He commanded all of his officers to
bind them fast.

They at once seized these good yeomen and arrested all three of them. 'By my
life,' said Adam Bell, 'I don't like this game.' They then said, 'But, good lord, we
beseech you now either to grant us grace, insofar as we have come to you freely,
or else let us depart from you with such weapons as we have, giving safe passage
till we are out of your place. And if we live another hundred years we will ask you
no further grace.'

'You speak proudly,' said the king; 'all three of you shall be hanged just the
same.' 'It would be a great pity,' said the queen, 'if there were no grace shown
here. My lord, when I first came into this land[18] to be your wedded wife, you
agreed you would at once grant me the first boon I asked. I have never asked
you one till now; therefore, good lord, grant it to me.' 'Now ask it, madam,' said

the king, 'and it shall be granted.' 'Then, good lord, I beseech you to grant me dominion over the yeomen.' 'Madam, you might easily have asked a boon that would have been worth more than those three. You might have asked for towers and towns, parks and forests plenty.' 'None are so pleasant to my liking,' she said, 'nor none so dear to me.' 'Madam, since it is your desire, your request shall be granted. But I'd rather given you three good market towns.'[19] The queen was a happy woman, and said, 'Lord, great thanks; I venture to pledge for them that they will be men true to you. But, good lord, speak some merry word, that they may feel some comfort.' 'I grant you grace,' then said our king;[20] 'Wash, fellows, and go to your meal.'

They had not sat at dinner long, to be sure, when messengers came from the north with letters for our king.[21] And when they came before the king, they knelt down upon their knees, and said, 'Lord, your officers from Carlisle in the north country greet you well.' 'How fares my justice and also my sheriff?' said the king. 'Sir, to tell the truth, they are slain and so are many more officers.' 'Who has slain them?' said the king; 'Tell me immediately!' 'Adam Bell, Clim of the Clough and William of Cloudesley.' 'Alas for pity!' then said our king, 'my heart is wondrously painful. I would have given a thousand pounds to have known of this before. For I have granted them a pardon, and that I regret. Had I known all this before, they would have been hanged all three.' The king opened the letter at once, and read it to himself; he discovered how these three outlaws had slain three hundred men and more: first the Justice and the Sheriff, and then the Mayor of the town of Carlisle. Of all the constables and sheriff's officers, not one was left alive. The outlaws had slain the bailiffs and beadles, the sergeants of the law and forty foresters of the region. They had transgressed the king's parks and slain his deer; of them all, they chose the best. Outlaws as menacing as these had never walked the ground anywhere. When the king had read this letter, he sighed sorely from his heart. At once he commanded, 'Take up the table, for I can eat no more.'

The king called his best archers to go to the shooting range with him. 'I will see these fellows shoot', he said, 'who have wrought this ruin in the north.' The king's bowmen prepared themselves at once, and the queen's archers as well, as did these three hardy yeomen, who decided to go with them. In order to test their hands, they shot two or three rounds, and these yeoman shot no shot that left the 'prick' standing.[22] Then spoke William of Cloudesley, 'By God who died for me, I consider him no archer who shoots at targets so wide.' 'At what sort of target then?' said our king; 'I pray you tell me.' 'At such a target, sire,' he said, 'as men use in my country.' William went into a field along with his two brothers, and there they set up two hazel sticks twenty score paces apart. 'I consider him an archer', said Cloudesley, 'who splits in two that wand yonder.' 'There is none such here,' said the king, 'nor anyone who can do that.' 'I shall try, sir,' said Cloudesley, 'before I do anything else.' Cloudesley cleft the wand in two with a flight arrow.[23]

'Truly thou are the best archer I've ever seen,' then said the king. 'And yet for your love,' said William, 'I will perform a greater feat. I have a son who is seven years old, and who is most beloved to me. I'll tie him to a stake – all will see who are here – and lay an apple upon his head; I will then go six score paces from him, and I myself, with a broad arrow will split the apple in two.'[24] 'By Him who died on the Cross,' said the king, 'now make haste; and unless you do as you have said, you shall be hanged. If you touch his head or his clothing, as any man here sees it, by all the saints there are in heaven, I shall hang all three of you.'[25] 'What I have promised I will never forsake,' said William. And there, right before the king, he drove a stake into the ground, and bound his eldest son there, telling him to stand still. He turned the child's face away from him so he would not flinch. He set an apple upon his head, and then strung his bow. Six score paces were measured out, and to that spot Cloudesley went. There he drew out a fine broad arrow; his bow was grand and long; he set that arrow in his bow, which was taut and strong. He entreated the people there to stand silent: 'He who shoots for such a wager must have a steady hand.' Many people prayed for Cloudesley, that his life might be saved, and when he got ready to shoot many an eye was weeping. Thus Cloudesley split the apple in two, which many a man witnessed. 'Our God forbid', said the king, 'that you should shoot at me! I hereby give you eighteen pence a day, if you will bear my bow. And I make you chief ranger over all the north country.'[26] 'And I give you twelve pence a day,' said the queen, 'by God and by my faith. Come fetch the payment when thou will, and no man shall say prevent you.' 'William, I make you a gentleman with clothing and with fee,' said the king.[27] 'And your two brothers I appoint yeomen of my chamber for they are so handsome to see. Because your son is of tender age, he shall assist in my wine cellar, and when he comes to manhood he shall be better advanced.' 'And William, bring me your wife,' said the queen, 'I long sorely to see her. She shall be my chief gentlewoman to govern my nursery.' The yeomen thanked them courteously, and said, 'We will go straight to Rome to be absolved of all the sins we have committed by the Pope's hand.' So these good yeomen went forth as fast as they could, and afterwards they came back and dwelt with the king, and all three died as good men. Thus ends the lives of these good yeomen; God send them eternal bliss. And may all those who shoot with hand-bows never miss heaven!

10

FROM *THE ACTS AND DEEDS OF SIR WILLIAM WALLACE*

Walter Scheps

INTRODUCTION

The Text and Translation

A single manuscript survives in the National Library of Scotland: MS Advocates 19.2.2. The colophon attributes the writing of the text to a John Ramsay and provides the date 1488. The first printed version dates from 1508, and it was followed by many subsequent editions. Within the last century *William Wallace* has been edited twice, first by James Moir for the Scottish Text Society in 1889, and, more recently, by Matthew P. McDiarmid for the Scottish Text Society in 1968–9. This translation is based upon McDiarmid's edition and adheres closely to the original in both sense and style.

Author and Date

Early editors, including James Moir, repeated the opinions of the Renaissance historian, John Mair, who identified the author of *William Wallace* with Blind Hary or Henry the Minstrel. Mair claimed that Hary, who was blind from birth, composed the poem in the vernacular, receiving food and clothing for his efforts. Mair also dated the composition of the poem in the time of his infancy (*meae infantiae tempore*), which James Moir supposed to be between 1450 and 1460 (pp. vii–viii). Because the year of Mair's birth is now known to be 1467, Matthew McDiarmid dates the poem to the years 1476–8 (p. xvi).

McDiarmid also shatters many of the misconceptions about the author and his work. Hary was born in about 1440 in or near Linlithgow of a family named Hary or Henry. His education enabled him to read French, Latin and Middle English (see sources below). He was not, as John Mair claimed, blind from birth, but lost his eyesight after completing *William Wallace*. He displays an intimate knowledge of military life and tactics, strongly suggesting that he served as a soldier early in his career. There is no truth to Hary's claim that he translated the story from a lost Latin book by John Blair. Instead, he wrote the work with the 'encouragement and connivance' of the contemporary Sir William Wallace, the descendant of the rebel, and Sir James Liddale. He may be the author of three additional works: *The Ballet of the Nine Nobles*, *Rauf Coilȝear* and *Golagros and Gawane* (McDiarmid, pp. lviii–lix).

Historical Context

Like Hereward, Eustache and Fouke fitz Waryn, William Wallace was a real person who led a short-lived but effective rebellion against 'Our old enemies . . . of Saxon's blood, That never yet to Scotland would do good'. Because a knowledge of the turbulent relations between England and Scotland in the late thirteenth century is vital to an appreciation of the poem, we include the following chronology:

1272–1307 Reign of Edward I 'Longshanks', son of Henry III (1216–72) and Eleanor of Provence (d. 1291). He is embroiled in a series of conflicts in Wales, Scotland and France
1267–77 Llywelyn, Prince of Wales, surrenders to Edward
1282–3 After Llywelyn dies in battle, his brother Dafydd is captured and executed in 1283, and Wales is annexed to England. To ensure the subjugation of the Welsh, Edward constructs a series of mighty strongholds in Wales and the Marches
1285 Alexander III of Scotland (reigned 1249–85) dies with no male issue
1290 Alexander III's granddaughter, Margaret, succeeds to the throne of Scotland, but she dies, and the direct line comes to an end. Of the thirteen claimants in the 'Great Cause', two Scottish barons were the main contenders: John Balliol and Robert Bruce
1292 John Balliol becomes king of Scotland and swears fealty to King Edward. The right to succeed was based on Balliol's claim that he was descended through the eldest daughter of King David I (1084–1153). Robert Bruce argued that he should succeed as the next surviving descendant of King David
1294 King Philip the Fair of France (1285–1314) tries to reduce the authority of Edward I in Gascony, one of the last English possessions in France. When war breaks out, Edward orders King John of Scotland to end all trade with France and to provide military service
1295 Fearing that King John will obey, the Scottish nobility divest him of his authority and negotiate a Franco-Scottish alliance requiring a Scottish invasion of England. Edward retaliates by seizing Scottish-owned properties in England
1296 Edward invades Scotland and captures Berwick upon Tweed as well as the principal castles. He strips Scotland of its national treasures, including the Black Rood of St Margaret and the Stone of Scone, on which every Scottish king had

been crowned. King John surrenders his kingship and Edward installs an occupation government

1297 The beginning of the short-lived outlawry and rebellion of William Wallace, who in May kills Hazelrig, the Sheriff of Lanark, in retaliation for murdering Marion Bradfute, his beloved. Wallace defeats the English at the Battle of Stirling Bridge on 11 September. He is subsequently knighted and elected Guardian of the Kingdom of Scotland

1298 Wallace is defeated by the English at the Battle of Falkirk in July and resigns his guardianship. He escapes to France in 1299

1305 Wallace is tried for treason and executed. The English chronicler, Matthew of Westminster, describes the execution: 'He was hung in a noose, and afterwards let down half-living; next his genitals were cut off and his bowels torn out and burned in a fire; then and not till then his head was cut off and his trunk cut into four pieces' (Gray, 152)

1306 Robert Bruce murders John Comyn, Earl of Badenoch, who was loyal to Edward, occupies the major castles, and is crowned king of Scotland in March

Structure

The 10,877-line poem, written in decasyllabic couplets, is divided by modern editors into twelve books of uneven length. The work employs a chronological time scheme to construct the life history of William Wallace, ranging from his 'tendyr age' when England invaded Scotland (1293–6), his outlawry in September 1296, his murder of the sheriff, Heselrig in May 1297, his victory at Stirling Bridge in August 1298, his invasion of England in 1298/9, his escape to France in 1299/1302, his defeat at the Battle of Falkirk in 1303, his second return to France in 1303/4, and his capture in Glasgow in 1306. Blind Hary's historical framework is, however, 'as unhistorical as its contents' (McDiarmid, p. lxxxi). As every Scottish schoolchild knows, the Battle of Stirling Bridge was fought in 1297, not 1298, and Wallace was executed in 1305, not 1306. Like Thomas Malory's *Le Morte D'Arthur*, the controlling image in the *Wallace* is the Wheel of Fortune. The work thus exemplifies the medieval notion of tragedy as defined by Chaucer in *The Prologue of the Monk's Tale*:

> Tragedie is to seyn a certeyn storie,
> As olde bookes maken us memorie,
> Of hym that stood in greet prosperitee,
> And is yfallen out of heigh degree
> Into myserie, and endeth wrecchedly. (VII, 1,973–77)

Genre and Sources

Pretending to be history, the work embraces 'a bewildering array of genres' (Goldstein, 250). To Walter Scheps's list of epic, romance, ballad and *débat*, Goldstein adds chronicle, saint's life and complaint. Sources adduced by McDiarmid include: Latin chronicles, such as Bower's version of Fordun's *Scotichronicon*; historical poems, such as John Barbour's *The Bruce* (*c.* 1375); histories, such as Froissart's *Chronicles of England, France and Spain* and Andrew of Wyntoun's *Original Chronicle*; didactic works, such as Boethius' *De Consolatione Philosophiae*; pseudo-travel literature such as *The Travels of Sir John Mandeville*; saints' legends; Chaucer's *Troilus and Criseyde* and *The Canterbury Tales*; and romances about Charlemagne, Arthur, and Alexander (pp. xxxvii–xxxviii).

The precise relationships between the *Wallace* and the other medieval outlaw tales has yet to be determined. McDiarmid identifies a number of episodes that appear to be based upon the popular 'gestes' of the day (p. lxvii), but he does not explore the parallels in any detail. That Blind Hary knew the 'Matter of the Greenwood' is indicated by his use of the Greenwood theme, the descriptions of archery, the disguises – especially the potter – and other narrative and verbal echoes.

Wallace and the Greenwood

As Maurice Keen observes, Blind Hary captured 'the spirit of the Greenwood extraordinarily well' (p. 73). After killing Selby's brutish son in Dundee (I, 227), the three English soldiers while fishing (I, 419) and the English braggart in Ayr (II, 43–4), Wallace seeks refuge in the forests of Scotland, asylums of freedom and security: 'He got his horse and headed for Laglane wood . . . thus he rode in safety into the wood. Many followed on horseback and on foot to take Wallace, but they were unsuccessful' (II, 66–70). The forest is also a place of plenty and, like Robin Hood or Adam Bell, the outlaws are not without venison: 'he slew a great hart with one shot, and his men made preparations for fresh venison' (IV, 284–5). Independent and free, the outlaws survive by their wits and martial prowess. In a passage strongly reminiscent of the most popular Robin Hood proverb, Wallace's skill with a bow is literally proverbial: 'He also bore a large and well-equipped bow as well as arrows that were long and sharp. There was no man who could draw Wallace's bow' (IV, 547–50). In a realistic touch not seen in the other tales, life in the Greenwood is also fraught with rigours and vicissitudes:

'Sometimes he had a great sufficiency within; now want, now has, now loss, now win, now happy, now sad, now blissful, now in torment. In haste, now hurt; now sorrowful, now healthy. Now faring well; now cold weather, now hot. Now moist, now drought, now changeable wind, now wet weather. So it went with him for Scotland's right in fierce and unrelenting strife for six years and seven months' (IV, 335–40).

Influence

From the time of its composition to the present, Hary's *Wallace* has been both popular and influential. William Hamilton of Gilbertfield's eighteenth-century modernization made the poem available to those who could not read Hary's lowland Scots and helped to spread Wallace's fame well beyond Scotland's borders. The poem has been taught in the Scottish schools, in both the original and modern English, and has served as the primary source of information about its hero as well as inspiration for poets like Robert Burns and Sir Walter Scott and for the recent film *Braveheart*.

Translator's Note

The translation is literal, often retaining the syntax of the Middle Scots. Because Hary's sentence structure is sometimes extremely loose, rendering his meaning somewhat obscure, I thought it advisable to adhere as closely to the original as possible.

TRANSLATION FROM *THE ACTS AND DEEDS OF SIR WILLIAM WALLACE*

Introduction (I, 1–20)

Our ancestors whom we should have read and held in mind, their noble worthy deeds we let fall into neglect through extreme sloth, and took ourselves always to other business. To honour enemies is our whole intent. It has been seen in times past our old enemies came of Saxon blood, enemies who never yet have done good to Scotland but always in force and with great power have enforced their will. How great kindness has been made known to them! It is well known on many diverse sides how they have wrought in their mighty pride to hold Scotland in subjection for evermore, but God above has made their might to weaken; yet we should think on our forebears. Of these parables now I say no more. We read of one right famous of renown, of worthy blood that rules in this region, and henceforth I will hold to my subject of William Wallace about whom you have been told.

Wallace slays young Selby and becomes an Outlaw (I, 144–276)

To Wallace again I will now go briefly. When he was but a youth, Scotland was lost and beset with our barbarous enemies. His father, Malcolm, fled into Lennox and took his eldest son with him. William's mother fled with him from Elrisle to the Gowrie district, and they lived in Kilspindie.[1] From there Malcolm sent them to his uncle who lived comfortably in Gowrie. An aged man, he received them gladly. They sent Wallace to school in Dundee until he was properly educated. In this manner did his youth pass. [See plate 23.]

Afterwards, when those of Saxon blood came into this realm, many did service of high vassalage, working the will of that false king, Edward.[2] They did many great wrongs in this region, destroying our lords and knocking their buildings down. They took both wives and widows as they wished, and it pleased them to slay nuns and maidens. In Scotland they played King Herod's part with many young children.[3] The bishoprics that were of greatest value they appropriated from their archbishops. Not for the Pope himself would they spare any churches but instead seized all by the violence of war. They assigned Glasgow to a diocese in Durham. It was a small benefice indeed that they would not pursue! They slew worthy clerics and hanged barons, and created much sorrow. It was well known that in the Barns of Ayr eighteen-score Scottish nobles were put to death.[4] But God above has sent us some remedy. The remembrance lies further in the tale. Now, I shall continue my narrative.

Even before he was a man of arms William Wallace thought it a great pity that Scotland had suffered such injuries. Reflection upon Scotland's wrongs made him melancholy because he was wise, worthy, strong and kind. At this time he still dwelt in Gowrie with his uncle. As he grew, his heart was sorrowful as he saw the numbers of the English constantly multiplying, but he kept his sadness to himself. The English had slain many of his kin. At this stage in his life he was seemly, strong and bold and but eighteen years of age. He bore weapons, either a good sword or a knife, for he frequently had occasion to use them in strife. When he found one enemy alone, that one did no grievance to Scots thereafter. He did not hesitate to cut his throat or stab him suddenly if he found him alone. Thus, many disappeared but none knew where or how, nor could anyone attribute these disappearances to Wallace. Both young and old he was of sober countenance, reticent, wise, courteous and gracious.

One day he was sent to Dundee. They knew little there of his fierce nature. The constable there was named Selby,[5] a brutal soldier, malicious and violent, who had done great harm to the Scots. Selby had a son who was almost twenty years of age and who was wont to go to town every day. He was an arrogant wretch who was usually accompanied by three or four others, all seeking to amuse themselves. Seeing Wallace, he approached him. A likely lad, big and well equipped, Wallace was dressed well in green.[6] Young Selby called to him, saying, 'You, Scot, wait. Why the Devil do you dress in so gay an outfit? It would be more appropriate for you to wear an Irish cloak with a Scottish knife in your belt and rough brogues on your rascally feet. Give me your knife. Why do you dress so fashionably?' He went towards Wallace to take his knife from him, but Wallace grasped him firmly by the collar and drew his knife; for all the men he had with him, young Selby had no hope of help but from himself. But Wallace stabbed him to death, and the squire's body fell to the ground. His men beset Wallace severely; the press was thick, and they harassed him closely. Wallace was terrified, but he was also agile and adept with the bloody knife in his hand. He spared none whom he found before him. He knew the house his uncle lived in and fled thither since he could gain nothing where he was. He saw the good woman then inside the courtyard and cried, 'Help, for the sake of Him who died on the Cross. The captain's son has fallen into strife with me.'

He went in at the door with this good wife who gave him a russet gown of her own which covered his clothes and a dirty kerchief for his head and neck. She affixed a woven white hat as the finishing touch, for they were not to tarry long at that inn. She gave him a spinning wheel and sat him down to spin.[7] The English sought Wallace in fear, not knowing at which gate he had entered. They searched for him carefully in that same house in which he had sought refuge, but he spun full cunningly – or as cunningly as his brief period of instruction would allow. They left him thus and went on their way with heavy hearts and sorrowful thoughts. They could get no more information about him then. The Englishmen, ready for hostilities, then ordered that all Scotsmen who were in that town be burned; yet this good wife hid Wallace until nightfall, comforted him, and cleverly let him out. She guided him quickly through a dark garden. In concealment, he went past the river, avoiding the gate with its watchmen.

His mother had been waiting in great despair. Thus, when she saw him she gave thanks to heaven's queen and said, 'Dear son, where have you been so long?' He told his mother of his unexpected adventure, whereupon she wept and often said, 'Alas, before you cease, you will surely be slain.' 'Mother,' he said, 'God is the ruler of us all. The people of England are insufferable, but part of their enmity at least I believe we should oppose.' His uncle knew full well that William had slain the squire and for fear his distress increased. As several days went by, this good man constantly fretted that Wallace should be taken for he knew that the English were extremely clever. When soon after they issued a great list of indictments for Scots and established a tribunal for the lawdays, Wallace would no longer remain there.

Wallace goes fishing (I, 368–433)

On the twenty-third day of April Wallace went to the River Irvine to fish as the spirit moved him. He took a child with him to carry his net, but before noon he was to be in great peril. He left his sword behind; so did he never again. It did him good although he suffered distress from the weight of having to carry it. Of that labour at this time he was not skilled. He was happy as he took fish abundantly. Before ten hours of the day had passed, there came riding near where Wallace was the Lord Percy who was then captain of Ayr. From thence he turned and made his way to Glasgow, but part of his retinue had seen Wallace's labour. Five of them clad suitably in green rode towards him. One immediately

said, 'Scot, we wish to have Martin's fish.'[8] Wallace meekly answered him, 'It
seems reasonable to me that you should have part of my catch. Game should
always be dealt out with a willing heart.' He ordered the child, 'Give them some
of our catch.' The Englishman said, 'We will not now have any of your dealing
out; you would give us too small a portion.' He got down from his horse and took
all from the child. Wallace then said to him, 'If you are noble men, leave us some
part, we pray, for charity. An aged knight serves Our Lady today. Good friend,
leave part, and do not take away all.' 'You shall have our permission to fish and
take more. All that you have here shall go with us. We serve a lord. These fish
shall go to him.' Wallace answered and said, 'Thou art in the wrong.' 'Whom are
you 'thou-ing', Scot? In faith you deserve a blow.'[9] He ran towards him and drew
a sword. William was sorry then that he had no weapons there except the netpole
which he bore in his hand. Wallace quickly hit him on the cheek with it with such
authority that he shook on his feet for a time. The sword flew from his hand a
good distance on the ground. Wallace was glad and immediately grasped it in his
hand and with the sword he gave him a crosswise stroke. Under his hat his neck
was drawn asunder.

By this time the remainder had alighted about Wallace. He had no help but
only God's grace. On either side of him they quickly rained blows on him; he
would have been in great peril had they lasted long. In great anger upon the head
he struck one; the piercing sword cut to the collarbone. Another he hit on the
arm so forcefully that both hand and sword lay on the ground. The other two
fled to their horses again. He stabbed the one who was last on the field of battle.
He slew three there; two fled with all their might after their lord, but he was out
of sight having taken to the moor before he and they had separated. They rode to
him before they would stop and cried, 'Wait, your men are martyred cruelly in
this false place. Five of our court here stopped at the river to bring fish, although
we were not successful. We have escaped, but three are slain.' The lord asked,
'How many were there?' 'We saw only one who has thwarted us all.' Then the
lord laughed and said, 'May foul things befall you, since one has put all of you to
confusion. Whoever means it most, may the Devil of hell drown him! In faith for
me this day he will not be sought.'

Wallace's adventures in Ayr (II, 19–72)

Wallace desired to see the town of Ayr. He took his servant with him and no
others. Wallace left his horse near the forest and then went on foot to the market
cross. At this time Lord Percy was in the castle of Ayr with many well-equipped
Englishmen. Ruling over all the town as they wished, they greatly oppressed
many Scots. Wallace boldly went among them; the hot blood of youth caused
him to have no fear. They had in that town a churl who could bear grievously
heavy burdens; often he would lift much more than any two others who could be

found, and also he had a sport that he participated in. 'He bore a bucket on a large pole that he would allow anyone to strike, as strongly as he could, on his broad back, only for the payment of three groats.'[10] When Wallace heard tell of that amusing game, he was pleased to be at that market and for a stroke he offered him three groats. The churl granted him permission; he was pleased with that proffer. Wallace was quite ready to pay the silver. Wallace took up the pole in his hand. Full sturdily he could stand before the churl. Wallace gave him a blow upon the back such that he split the backbone. The churl was dead. I speak of him no more.

The Englishmen then assembled against Wallace there, a great many of them on the field of warriors fighting fiercely, but he was undaunted and unafraid. He hit one upon the head with the pole and made the bone and brain fly in pieces. Another he struck on a steel helmet; the pole snapped and completely splintered. His pole was gone, but the Englishman was dead for his neck bone was broken in that place. Wallace drew a sword that helped him at need. He went through the thickest of the press and would have been quite glad to have found himself at his horse. Two Englishmen who were cruel and keen vexed him most. Wallace, being a man of great strength, counter-attacked, and at a stroke has slain the foremost. The other fled and dared not remain, but Wallace gave him a well-aimed stroke. In at the gushet [a piece of armour protecting the arm hole] he fiercely struck; the tempered sword cut through his rib. He slew five there before he left the town. He got his horse and headed for Laglane wood, kept his servant with him and would not let him remain. Thus he rode in safety into the wood. Many followed on horseback and on foot to take Wallace, but they were unsuccessful. The cover of trees saved him well, but he could not remain there at all.

Another game turns deadly for the English (III, 354–400)

Wallace took fifteen men with him and they went to the town [i.e., Ayr]. He saw an Englishman on the gate with a buckler in his hand playing at fencing. In fellowship Wallace went to stand near him. Lightly he asked, 'Why, Scot, do you dare to try yourself against me?' Wallace said, 'Yes, if you give me permission.' 'Smite on,' he said, 'I defy your action.' Wallace therewith gave him a blow on the crown. He made the sharp sword go through buckler, hand and skull as well to the shoulders. Whereupon he contemptuously returned to his own men again. The women cried, 'Our buckler player is slain!'

The man was dead. What more needs to be said? Many men of arms assembled about him there; seven score against sixteen were arrayed. But Wallace soon met well with the foremost. With anger and will he struck him on the head; through the bright helm he burst the brain asunder. Another he struck violently in the breast; his burnished blade sheared throughout the body. He made great room [i.e., he cut a wide swath]; his men were fighting steadfastly

and they made many a man full sore afraid, for they were powerful and well
versed in war. Quite boldly they bore down Englishmen. On their enemies they
made great martyrdom, so well could their hardy chieftain undertake the battle.
Those Englishmen who remained in his path never made further debate against
Scotland. Many soldiers had fallen underfoot; those of southern blood lay
stabbed to death in the street.

Reinforcements now came from the castle. Then Wallace feared and drew
aside; with good will he wished to avoid a defeat, for in war he was alert, strong
and wise. He quickly hewed harness and heads asunder; they passed by force out
of the thickest press. Wallace counter-attacked behind his men again. At the
rescue he slew many enemies. All the same he brought his men out of peril from
his enemies for all their power. They won through to their horses but more
remained there. For danger then to Laglane wood they rode. In that place they
left sixty-nine Englishmen who had been put to death.

Wallace's outlaw life and guerrilla war against the English
(IV, 267–342)

When the time seemed right to Wallace, the Scots issued forth into the night.
They went to the next wood with all their forces. The captain's wife, women
and three children went where they pleased, for Wallace let them be. He did
not wish to remain in that forest. They hurriedly went along the River Forth.
Because the moor was formidable, it was no advantage for them to ride.
Wallace was strong and light on his feet. They had few horses; thus they did not
rely on them. To save their lives they often sought many strongholds. Steven of
Ireland[11] was their guide that night to Kincardine; [12] then they rested in a
forest that was both long and wide and where the moor grew right to the side
of the water. After sunset Wallace walked about along the River Teith where he
saw many herds of wild beasts wandering in both woods and plain.
Immediately, he slew a great hart with one shot, and his men made
preparations for fresh venison. They had victuals, both bread and clear wine
with sufficient other provisions for their dinner. He gave his steel spear to
Kerly[13] for safekeeping and then they passed over the deep Teith water and
suddenly entered Strathern. Secretly they passed before the English could
detect them. Whenever they found any of Scotland's adversaries, their fatal
hour came without delay. Whoever they met who owed fealty to England they
slew immediately. They spared no one who was of English blood; such a one
immediately met his death regardless of how valiant he was. They saved neither
knight, squire nor knave, for this was the grace that Wallace gave to them. By
virtue of war, they slew all from that party that could wield bow or spear. Some
they slew through cunning, some through force, but Wallace thought they
destroyed not half enough.

They took silver and also gold that they found, and other good gear they casually took to hand. They cut throats and cast the bodies out of sight into caves, for they thought that best. At Blackfurd [in south-east Perthshire] as they prepared to pass, a squire came and with him four barons who were riding to Doune castle.[14] Thinking Wallace and his men Englishmen, he tarried among them to hear the news. Wallace quickly swung his sword and struck him upon the head with such great ire that he cut the neck asunder through bone and brain. The other four were soon taken and boldly stabbed to death before the Scots would stop. They took their horses and what of their gear they liked best, plundered them bare and then cast them into the brook. They did not tarry over this matter but passed forth on their way without delay. The warlike Scots, all of one mind, to the north over the River Ern made their way. In Methven wood[15] they took their lodging that night. In the morning, when it was daylight, Wallace arose and went into the forest where he saw many beasts dwelling, numerous animals both wild and tame walking. Then Wallace said, 'This country pleases me. Soldiers can make do with whatever food they have, but if they want meat they don't care about anything else.' Wallace paid no attention to an attractive diet, but meat and sleep were welcome as they came. Sometimes he had a great sufficiency within; now want, now has, now loss, now win, now happy, now sad, now blissful, now in torment. In haste, now hurt; now sorrowful, now healthy. Now faring well; now cold weather, now hot. Now moist, now drought, now changeable wind, now wet weather. So it went with him for Scotland's right in fierce and unrelenting strife for six years and seven months.[16] When he won peace and left Scotland for France, the Englishmen made a new conquest again.

Wallace's adventures in St Johnston [i.e., Perth] (IV, 346–90)

Wallace again went to his men and said, 'Here is a land of great abundance; may God be thanked for his high providence! Seven of you companions make yourselves ready immediately and go with me. I very much long to see St Johnston. Steven of Ireland, as God of heaven may save you, I make you master leader of the rest. Keep my men well, and let none out of your sight until I come again with all my might. Wait for me seven days in this strong forest. If I remain away so long, you can get food. You already have some, and God will send you more.' Then he turned and made his way to the town.

The mayor guarded the gate of that village; Wallace knew this well and sent him his messenger. The mayor was brought to him and saw a goodly man; with much respect he then greeted them. He asked him if they were all Scots. Wallace said, 'Yes, and it is time of peace [i.e., truce], we believe.' 'I grant', he said, 'that pleases us very much. True men of peace can always experience some friendship. What is your name? I pray you tell it to me.' 'Will Malcolmson,' he said, 'since you wish to know it.[17] My dwelling has been in Ettrick Forest.[18] I was born there among the bright trees. Now I desire to see this north land where I can find a better dwelling for myself.' The mayor said, 'Sir, I do not ask for any ill purpose, but many tidings are often brought to us of one Wallace who was born in the west. He holds our king's men in great distress, martyrs them – it is a great pity to see. Therefore we believe that he is out of the truce.' Wallace then said, 'I have heard tell of that man. However, I can tell you no news of him.' For him [the mayor] ordered a dwelling to be readied where none could come but he and his own men. His steward Kerle brought them in profusion enough good things that were in the town. Also Englishmen would invite him to drink, but he generally had nothing to do with them. In their presence he spent money reasonably, but he always paid for himself. He expended much goods on Scotsmen but nothing willingly upon those of English blood.

Wallace as archer in Shortwood Forest (IV, 525–82)

Harnessed on horseback in shining armour, they went forth together to seek Wallace. A thousand men well equipped for war, they rode toward the wood quite formidable in appearance, to Shortwood forest[19] and surrounded it all about with five armed groups of men who were stalwart and courageous. They made a fierce sixth to lie in wait where Wallace, full worthy in military matters, was. He [the English commander] took charge of the fortified position and ordered them to hold it on each side no matter who assailed it. Sir John Butler,[20] moved by sorrow in his intentions, went into the forest with two hundred men; in order to avenge his father's death, with his men at arms he quickly sought Wallace. They found a ravine with trees growing across the opening where they made a fortification and boldly waited. From one side they could issue forth to a plain and then return through the woods to their fortification. Wallace had twenty men who were noble archers against seven score of English bowmen. Four-score spearmen waited nearby to help them if the Scots sallied forth.

Wallace carried a bold and fierce shield. He also bore a large and well-equipped bow as well as arrows that were long and sharp. There was no man who could draw Wallace's bow.[21] Wallace was very strong and with his trusty gear boldly shot among those men of war. He drew a barbed-headed arrow up to the hook and slew the foremost son with one shot. English archers who were hardy and powerful shot with all their might among the Scots. Their awful shooting was fierce to abide; they wounded many of Wallace's men that time. Few of the Scots were reliable at archery. They were better – and were on an even footing – to remain on the field either with sword or spear.

Wallace perceived that his men took many casualties and ordered them to put on harnesses and not to remain in that place. He cast about for ways to keep them from death. He took great deeds upon himself; of the Southern men, he killed many of the archers from Lancashire who were in that place. A wounded archer lay in wait for Wallace at an opening where he frequently went. At him he drew a sure and painful shot under the chin through a collar of steel on the left side and hurt Wallace's neck somewhat. Wallace was astonished but not greatly aghast; he went out from his men who followed him quickly. In turning he shot the English archer in the neck so that the bone split asunder. Many more of them suffered the same fate; he shot fifteen that day with his own hand. By that time his arrows were used up and gone, but the English archers in truth wanted none [i.e., of Wallace's arrows]. Without these men the English were wary of renewing their attack; on each side the Scots pursued them.

Wallace is betrayed, but escapes (IV, 705–96)

Then Wallace said he would go to the town [St Johnston]. He arrayed himself well in a priest-like gown. In St Johnston he went disguised to this woman I spoke of earlier. She was very happy for his presence, and sorely afraid as to how he should safely leave. He stayed there from noon until almost night before he left. He told her when he would come again. Thus, on the third day she was extremely happy. Yet he was seen by enemies as he went. To Sir Gerald they told all his activities, and to Butler who wished to be avenged. Then they took that bright and shining woman and sternly accused her of sheltering an outlaw in this case. Many times she swore that she did not know Wallace. Then Butler said, 'We know well it was he, and unless you talk you shall die by burning. If you will help to bring that rebel down, we shall make you a lady of renown.' They gave her both gold and bright silver and said that she would be wedded to a knight, whomever she desired, in marriage as her reward. Thus they tempted her through speech and great rewards, so that she told them what time he would be there. Then they were glad, for they desired no more in all of Scotland than to have Wallace at their will; thus, they ordered her to fulfill this appointment. They got many men of arms ready hastily to keep the gates in order to catch sight of Wallace.

At the appointed time for the tryst, he entered the town, knowing nothing of all this false treason. He went immediately to her chamber without delay. She welcomed him and made things very pleasant for him. What they did I cannot readily say; I am quite imperfect in my knowledge of Venus's play. Hastily then he made himself ready to go. Then she embraced him and asked him if he grew weary. She asked him to remain that night with her. He immediately said, 'No, for the ill chance that may betide. My men are left in misrule for want of me. I may not sleep this night until I see home.' Then she wept and often said, 'Alas! Cursed be the time that I was conceived! Now I have lost the best man living. O feeble mind, to do so foul a misdeed. O cursed wit, fickle and variable, that has brought me to this mischievous chance! Alas,' she said, 'that I was wrought in the world! For I have brought all this pain upon myself! I have deserved to be burnt in a fire!'

When Wallace saw that she was nearly out of her wits, he took her in his arms very soberly and said, 'Dear heart, who has misdone anything, I?' 'No, I', she said, 'have falsely wrought this deception. I have sold [i.e., betrayed] you. Right now you will be slain.'[22] She told him her treason to the end as I have said; what need is there for more legend?[23] He asked her if she sorely regretted it. 'Woe, yes,' she said, 'and shall do evermore. I must fulfill my fickle fate in the world. I would burn on a hill in order to amend this misdeed.' He comforted her and told her not to fear. 'I will', he said, 'have some of your clothes.' He put on her gown and her coverchiefs also: 'God willing, I shall escape this false treason. I forgive you without more words.'

He kissed her, then took his leave to go. His burly sword, which often helped him in need, he hid under those clothes. He went by the quickest way to the south gate where he found enough armed men. His countenance disguised, he directed them to the chamber where he had been: 'Go quickly,' he said, 'Wallace is locked in.' From him they sought that place without noise or din. They came to that same house. Wallace then went out at the gate very fast, quite glad at heart when he was outside. He went very quickly with a fierce and strong pace. Two men saw him and said, 'We shall go see, for yonder woman seems indeed to be a stalwart "queen".' Those two followed him through the South Inch.[24] When Wallace saw that no more came with them, he turned back and slew the first. The other fled. Then Wallace with great strength struck him upon the head with his sword. He left them both dead, then went to the fortified place where his men were waiting. He reached his men who were very glad when they saw him. In haste he ordered them into a defensive formation, and immediately divested himself of the woman's clothing. Thus he escaped from that perilous situation.

Hazelrig and Marion Bradfute (V, 562–717)

Wallace often went into Lanark to amuse himself. When he went from Gilbank[25] to that town and found men who were from that false nation [i.e., England], they never did further grievance to Scotland. Some were stabbed, some had their throats cut asunder. Soon many were dead, but none knew who was responsible. Whomever he handled he let pass no further. There Hazelrig dwelt, that cursed knight of no value. He was sheriff of all the lands in that area, fierce, outrageous, pitiless in his deeds. Therefore, many had great dread of him. He thought it a marvel that someone dared to slay his people. He ordered a great number of men to go outside the town. When Wallace saw that they outnumbered him, he did nothing but greet them courteously. All four of his men bore themselves quietly. No Englishmen could see anything amiss in them, neither poor nor rich.

In Lanark there dwelt a noble woman, a mild maiden as my book [i.e., source] declares, eighteen years of age or a bit more. She was born to have some part of an inheritance, for her father was a man of honour and renown called Hugh Bradfute of Lamington, as many others were called in that country [i.e., his relatives]. They were noblemen of long standing. However, this good man and his wife were dead. The maiden then knew no other course of action but still lived on tribute in the town and had purchased King Edward's protection. She had servants with her and whatever friends she chose; thus, she lived without desire of ill [i.e., evil]. In this time of war she kept a quiet house, for Hazelrig had done her great harm, slain her brother who was eldest and the heir. She endured all and bore herself very humbly. She was amiable, well meaning, cautious and wise, courteous and sweet, filled with nobility of character, discreet of her tongue, proper in her bearing; of virtues she was worthy to be praised. She conducted herself humbly and thus purchased [i.e., obtained] a good name for herself. She kept herself from blame from all kinds of people. Truly righteous folk gave her great favour.

As she went to church one day, Wallace saw her as he looked about; the impression of love pierced him at the last so severely, through the beauty of that radiant girl, that he was able to remain in her presence only with the greatest unease. He knew her family and her blood quite well and how she was in honourable and good estate. At times he thought to love her above the rest, and at other times he thought about his betrayal and how his men were brought to confusion through his last love in St Johnston. Then he would think to leave and forget about Marion, but that thought would not remain long in his mind. He told Kerle of his new pleasant woe[26] and afterward asked him for his best, true counsel. 'Master,' he said, 'as far as I have knowledge, it may be extremely appropriate. Since you love so, take her in marriage. She is goodly, and she has heritage [i.e., is noble]. Suppose that you fell amiss in loving – God forbid it should be so with this!' 'I cannot thus yet expect to marry. I would first see a final end of war. I will no more go alone to my love. Give heed to me or fear that we suffer wrong. I would not try my skill to proffer love so soon. If I could leave off loving, in war I am pleased to live. What is this love? Nothing but foolishness. It can rob men of both their wits and their steadfastness.' Then he said thus, 'This will not readily be, love and war simultaneously to reign in me. It is quite true that if I stood in the bliss of love, where deeds were necessary I should prove the better, but well I know that where there is great anxiety in thought it hinders war in the wisest way it can be waged unless it is only to a deed. Then he who thinks to have success in love may do well if he has fortune and grace. But this stands completely in another case, a great kingdom overthrown by fierce foes. It is very hard to get amends from them and at the same time perform the observances which belong to love and its fickle chance. I have had an example; this I sorely regret. I vow to God it shall be so no more. I know the truth of this and her lineage. I did not know her [i.e., the woman in St Johnston]; therefore I lost a pledge.'

To Kerle he argued thus in this manner, but great desire remained in his mind to behold that lady lovely in appearance. For a time he left and did not come again into the town. He forced himself to concentrate on other things, proving to himself whether he could make that languor diminish. When Kerle saw that he suffered pain therefore, 'Dear sir,' he said, 'you live in idleness. Go see your love; then shall you get comfort.' At his counsel Wallace walked casually to the church where she made her residence. She knew him well, but as of eloquence she dared not make herself known in his presence. She was afraid the English would mark him, for Hazelrig had newly begun a matter and desired her in marriage to his son. Thus with her maiden [i.e., servant] she asked Wallace to dine with her, and privily brought him through a garden she had newly made so that Englishmen would not know of their meeting. Then he kissed this goodly woman with pleasure and afterward besought her very sincerely of her acquaintance. She answered him with wise, humble words: 'Were my acquaintance worthy to be prized, you should have it, as God saves me in happiness, but Englishmen make our power fail through their violence and their baronage which have well-nigh destroyed our lineage.'

When Wallace heard her complain thus piteously, he was greatly aggrieved in heart. Both ire and love sent him into a rage, but they did not lessen his courage. Of his matter he told, as I said earlier, to that goodly woman how love sorely constrained him. She answered him quite reasonably in return and said, 'I shall be ready to your service in completely honourable causes with all pleasure. And I trust that you would not, for your honour, try to do me dishonour, since I am a maiden and stand among many dangers from Englishmen to save my womanhood and have expended much to keep myself from their terror. With my good will I shall not be a lemman [lover] to any man born; therefore it seems to me that you should desire me only in goodliness. Perhaps you think I am too low to expect to be your righteous wife. In your service I would devote my entire life. Here I beseech you, for your honour in arms, that you charge me with no villainous harms, but rather defend me for the honour of your blood.' When Wallace well understood her true intent, in part it seemed to him her desire was reasonable; therefore, in conclusion he thanked her, and said, 'If through God's will it could be that our kingdom was free, I would wed you with all pleasure of heart; but at this time I may not take such a chance and for this reason, none other, I now crave. A man in war cannot have all pleasure.' Of their talk then I can tell you no more. Thus they concluded and then went to dinner. The sore grievance remained in his thought, loss of his men and the pleasant pain of love. At that time he took his leave to go and passed to Gilbank before it was night.

Wallace's adventures in Lanark (VI, 107–272)

Twelve hundred and ninety-seven years from the time that Christ, the rightful king of heaven,[27] was born, William Wallace happily goes into the town of

Lanark among his mortal foes. The Englishmen, who have always been false, with Hazelrig who was cruel and fierce and Robert Thorn a cruel, subtle knight, found the best means to oppose Wallace – by challenging him as by chance he came from the church that was outside the town while their forces were armed and ready. Sir John the Graham, hardy, wise and true,[28] came to Lanark in pursuit of Wallace out of concern for his welfare, as he had done many times previously. He had fifteen good men in a company and Wallace nine; there were no more companions.

In the morning they went to Mass, they and their men clad in goodly green. For the season such usage has long been the custom. When solemnly they had said their devotions, a man challenged them as they went through the town. He was the strongest man Hazelrig then knew, and he had a full quota of contemptuous words. He hailed them in a scornful manner: 'Dewgar [i.e., *Dieu garde*], good day, bone senyhour [i.e., *bon seigneur*] and good morning.' 'Whom do you scorn thus?' asked Wallace. 'Who taught you [i.e., who instructed you to speak thus].' 'Why, sir,' he said, 'haven't you newly come from over the sea? Pardon me then, for I thought you had been an ambassador assigned to bring a foreign queen here.' Wallace answered, 'Such pardon that we are accustomed to giving for such an offence, you shall not crave.' 'Since you are Scots, yet you shall be greeted: "Good day, dawch [drink; i.e., give me drink] Lord, bach lowch [i.e., furious champion], banyoch a de [i.e., God's blessing on you."'[29]

By this time more Englishmen had assembled near them, but Wallace at this time was loath to make a stir. One man made a gibe and pulled at Wallace's long sword. 'Hold your hand still,' he said, 'and speak your piece.' 'You make a great boast [i.e., display] with your long sword.' 'Of that, your judgment is worth little.' 'What cause do you have to wear that goodly green?' 'My main reason is to give you grief.' 'What should a Scot do with so fair a knife?' 'So said the priest who last bandied words with [i.e., seduced] your wife. That woman has long served him so well that in time his child will be worthy to be your heir.' 'It seems to me that you are putting me to scorn.' 'Your mother was seduced before you were born.'

By now the English forces had assembled there, two hundred men who were strong and brave. The Scots saw these forces coming; Sir Robert Thorn and Hazelrig were at hand, and the multitude there had weapons well burnished. The worthy Scots, who were cruel and fierce, among the English gave such blows then that blood burst forth from wide wounds. Wallace in battle was cruelly fighting. From an Englishman he struck off his right hand, and when that churl could fight no more with his left hand he held a buckler; then from the stump the blood spurted out rapidly and splattered into Wallace's face so that it obscured a good part of his sight. Sir John the Graham gave a stroke with his good sword to an English lord; that angry stroke drove him violently to death. The danger for the Scots was quite frightening, hard and strong. The battle endured for a miraculously long time.

The Englishmen gathered cruelly fast. At last the worthy Scots left at the gate. When they had slain and wounded many a man, to Wallace in the quickest way they knew they passed soon, defending themselves quite well. He and Sir John with strong, steel swords behind their men for a time defended the gate. The woman[30] then, who was full of despair, saw the peril with cruel noise and din and raised up the gate and let them enter in. From there, they were able to pass through to a fortified place. Fifty English at the gate were dead. This fair woman used all her craft and strength to delay the Englishmen with a trick while Wallace passed on into the forest. Then they immediately perceived Cartland Crags.[31]

When the English saw that Wallace had escaped, they turned back, took the woman and put her to death, I cannot tell you how. Of such a matter I will not now tarry. Where great dolour is yet unredeemed, renewing it [i.e., reopening discussion of it] is but increasing of pain. A true woman, who had served her long, left the town by the quickest way and told Wallace how all this deed was done. Immediately the painful woe sought his heart. Were it not for shame he would have sought the ground for the bitter woe that was bound in his breast. Sir John the Graham, wise, noble and generous, made great mourning so that it was a pity to see it, and all the others who were assembled there for pure sorrow wept with full woeful hearts. When Wallace saw that their courage was so small, he feigned courage in order to comfort all of them. 'Cease men,' he said, 'this is a fruitless pain. We cannot now choose life for her again.' He could barely bring out a word for grief. The woeful tears burst forth from his eyes. Sighing, he said, 'Never shall a man see me rest at ease until this deed, the guiltless slaughter of this happy and shining woman, has been avenged. This I swear to the Maker of Might, that from that nation I shall never forbear to slay young or old that is able to make war. I will not slay priests or women wrongfully unless they give me cause. Sir John,' he said, 'let all this mourning be and for her sake there shall ten thousand die. Where men must weep, their courage is the less; it slakes the anger at wrong that should be redressed.' Of their complaint as now I say no more.

Good Auchinleck of Gilbank, who lived there, when he heard of Wallace's vexation, he readied himself to go with ten men to Cartland wood.[32] He found Wallace during the night. In all haste they went to Lanark town; at that time the town watch took little heed of them. They divided their men and went through diverse gates. Sir John the Graham and his good company hurried to Sir Robert Thorn. Wallace and his men passed to Hazelrig where he was sleeping fast in a high [i.e., two-story] house. Wallace struck hard at the door with his foot so that he made both bar and brace lie on the floor. The sheriff cried, 'Who makes this great disturbance?' 'Wallace,' he said, 'whom you have sought all day. The woman's death, God willing, you shall dearly buy.' Hazelrig thought that this was no time to lie in bed; he would have been quite happy to have been out of that house. The night was dark, but Wallace had seen him and struck him sharply, as he came in great ire, upon the head so that flesh and bone burst. The glittering sword cut to his collarbone. Then he went out over the stair to be among his men. Good Auchinleck did not believe that Hazelrig was dead; thrice with a knife he stabbed him in that place.

The noise rose all about on the street; many of the remaining people were trampled underfoot. Young Hazelrig and mighty Wallace met; Wallace gave him a sure stroke so that he quickly fell off the stair dead. They slew many that night in Lanark town; some leaped off stairs and some were stabbed inside their houses. They were afraid with a hideous noise and din. Sir John the Graham set on fire the house in which Robert Thorn was burned up both flesh and bones. They slew twelve score who were born in England. In the morning they let women and priests pass their way, happily bore goods and swore that they would come no more again.

When Scots heard these fine tidings for the first time, out of all parts of Scotland they flocked to Wallace and replenished the town which was their heritage. Thus Wallace strove against that great baronage. So he began with strength and a stalwart hand to achieve again some room for independent Scots in Scotland. The worthy Scots who gathered to him there chose him for their chief, chieftain and leader.

Edward's offer to Wallace and Wallace's reply (VI, 341–427)

By this time the awful host of Edward had reached Biggar with sixty thousand men arrayed for war and cruel to see.[33] They planted their field with tents and pavilions where their clarions blew many mighty calls. They provided that place with good victuals and wine, their provender being transported in carts. The awful king ordered that two heralds be brought to him. He commanded them in all the haste they could make to order Wallace to come to him without condition and place himself in his power : 'Because we know he is a noble man, if he comes in my grace I shall save him. I will take responsibility for his life, and after this if he can make service to me he shall have wages which will suffice him well. That rascal is proud because he has done oppression to my people as chance favoured him. Against me however he cannot long endure. If he turns down this offer, I here swear that he shall be hanged high.'

A young squire who was brother to Fitzhugh thought he would disguise himself as a herald so that he could see this Wallace who took so high a part for himself.[34] He was born sister's son to King Edward. He put on a coat of arms and rode discreetly and without delay with the heralds to Tinto hill, where Wallace waited with his men in a defensive position. They found a likely host but with few men. They sought after Wallace and would not wait: 'If you are he who rules here, we have brought credentials from our worthy king.' Then Wallace ordered three knights called to him, and read the writ in the presence of them all. To them he said, 'You shall not have to ask for an answer. Written or oral, which would you rather have?' 'In writing,' they said, 'it is the most appropriate.' Then Wallace began to write [or, dictate] in haste. 'Thou, robber king, order me to come and put myself in your grace.[35] If I refuse, you say you will hang me. I vow to God that if ever I can take you, *you* shall be hanged to give an example to kings of thievery as long as I might live. You offer your wage to me. I defy you, your power and all who help you here from your false nation. God willing, you shall be put out of this region or die therein, even though you have sworn the contrary. You shall see us before nine o'clock tomorrow morning to give battle in spite of all your kin, for falsely you seek to invade our realm.'

This writ he gave to the heralds, but he was to give them a greater reward there. Jop, who had been with the English previously, knew well the squire young Fitzhugh and told Wallace for he was ever loyal to him. Then Wallace commanded that the heralds be taken; he made the serious accusation himself: 'Squire,' he said, 'since you have feigned arms, on you shall fall the first part of these punishments in order to give an example to all of your false nation.' He ordered them to set him down upon the hill and strike off his head before they proceeded further. To the herald he said without delay, 'Because you are false to arms and perjured through your jaws your tongue shall be cut out.' When that was done, then to the third said he, 'To judge arms you shall never readily see.' He ordered a smith with his pincers right there to put out his eyes, then gave them permission to leave: 'To your false king your fellow shall lead you; with my answer bundle his nephew's head. Thus sorely I dread your king and all his boasts.'

His dumb fellow led him to their host. When King Edward saw his two heralds thus, in pure anger he well nigh went mad for ire so that he did not know in what manner to avenge himself. For sorrow he could barely speak a word. A long while he stood writhing in rage. Aloud he said, 'This is a cruel outrage; the Scots will pay full dearly for this deed. So contemptuous a deed was never wrought in this world. I shall not go from this region until such time that I see that rascal hang.' Thus I leave him to dwell with his sorrow.

Wallace and the Potter (VI, 429–96)

Wallace then went right away from his men. He called to him Sir John Tinto the knight[36] and let him know that he himself would go to reconnoitre the English host and bade him tell no more whatever they asked until he should come again. Wallace disguised himself[37] and hurried over the plain. As he passed between Culter and Biggar[38] he noticed a workman who had pitchers to sell coming fast driving a mare. 'Good friend,' he said, 'in truth will you tell me where you are going with this merchandise.' 'To anyone, sir, who is willing to buy; it is my craft and I would sell them gladly.' 'I will buy them, so God save me from pain. Tell me your price and I will take them all.' 'Only half a mark, for such is the price I have paid.' 'Twenty shillings', Wallace said, 'you shall have; I will have more, pitchers and all the rest. Quickly take off your gown and hose and make an exchange for I shall give you mine, and your old hood for it is threadbare.' The man thought well that he had been scorned there. 'Do it, don't tarry, I'm telling you the truth.' The man took off his poor grey clothes and Wallace his and paid silver into his hand. 'Pass on,' he said, 'you are a proud merchant'. The gown and hose were caked with clay, the hood fastened with a hook; he prepared to go. He took the whip, then told the mare to go. Over a small hill the uppermost pot fell and broke on the ground. The man laughed at his misfortune: 'Unless you're careful, you will ruin your merchandise.' The sun by then had passed out of sight; day had gone and night had come.

Among the English Wallace passed very carefully. On each side he cast his eyes to see where the lords lay and where they had made their encampments as well as the king's pavilion with its heraldic leopards. Spying quickly where his advantage should be, he could well look and wink with one eye. Some scorned him, some called him a squint-eyed churl there; they were aggrieved for their herald's mishap. Some asked him how much he sold the best of his pitchers for. 'For forty pence,' he said, 'while they last.' Some broke a pot, some poked at his eye; Wallace fled and privately let them be. To his own host again he quickly passed. His men by then had taken Tinto the knight. Sir John the Graham ordered him bound securely for he knew well that he was last with Wallace. Some wanted to burn him, some hang him with a rope; they swore that he had deceived their lord. By this time Wallace had entered among them. To him [Tinto] he went and would not tarry long. He released him from his new bonds and said he was trusty, both wise and true.

They went immediately to supper without delay. He told them what marketing he had made and how he had spied full well on the English. Sir John the Graham was somewhat displeased and said to him, 'It was not chieftainlike through wilfulness to pass in such peril.' Wallace answered, 'Before we free Scotland, both you and I must be in more peril as well as many others who are full worthy. Now perhaps we do something a bit amiss. I would like us to have a bit of sleep and then look to see how we can gladden yonder men.'

Wallace's instructions to his men before battle (VI, 515–26)

Wallace immediately called his chieftains to him. He gave them these orders, whatever might happen. 'Take no heed of gear or of pillage, for they [i.e., the enemy] will flee like mad folk in a rage. Defeat first the men and you may have the goods afterwards. Give no heed to the cravings of covetousness. Through covetousness one loses both goods and life. I command you to forbear such temptation in our strife. See to it that you save no lord, captain or knight. Work this day for honour and for the right of our elders. God bless us so that in our voyage [i.e., endeavour] we can put these false folk out of our realm.'[39]

Wallace has a vision[40] (VII, 71–152)

In that slumber it seemed to him that he saw coming toward him quickly an aged man who immediately took him by the hand. 'I am', he said, 'charged to come to you.' He gave him a sword of strong, burnished steel. 'Good son,' he said, 'you shall well enjoy the use of this sword.' It seemed to him that the pommel was of topaz with both the hilt and handgrip glittering like glass. 'Dear son,' he said, 'we tarry here too long. You shall go where great wrong has been done.' Then he led him to a mountain on high. It seemed to him that he could see the entire world. He [the old man] left him there, and afterwards went from him. Wallace thought about what all this meant. He had a great desire to see more of him [the old man]. At this point he saw a cruel fire beginning which violently burned throughout the breadth of the land, throughout Scotland from Ross to Solway sand.

Then immediately there descended to him a queen surrounded by light and shining brightly. In her presence there appeared such great light that she put the fire out of his sight. She gave him a wand of red and green and with a sapphire blessed his face and eyes. 'Welcome,' she said, 'I choose you as my love. You are granted by the great God above the power to help people who suffer grievous wrongs. I may not now tarry with you long; you shall return to your own use [i.e., world] again. Your dearest kin are here in great pain; you can redeem all this region by right. Your last reward in earth shall be but small. Do not stop therefore from taking redress for this offence, for as your reward you shall have lasting bliss.' From her right hand she gave him a book. Humbly she immediately took her leave; she ascended on to a cloud and out of his sight. Wallace broke open the book with all his might. In three parts the book was well written. The first part was written in large brass letters, the second gold, the third shining silver. Wallace marvelled at what this writing might mean. He quickly busied himself to read the book; his spirit again passed to his waking mind. He rose up and suddenly went forth, found this clerk [i.e., John Blair, who is mentioned shortly before Wallace's vision] and told him his experience in this vision, as I have said before, completely through. What do we need with more words?

'Dear son,' he said, 'my wit is unable to interpret such a vision for fear I may say amiss. Yet I shall judge your vision though my cunning is small. God grant that there be no charge made against me after my words fall. It was St Andrew who gave you that sword in your hand; of saints he is the patron of Scotland. That mountain, where he took you on high, is knowledge of wrong that you can right. The fire represents cruel tidings which will be told in many different places before you depart this life. I cannot certainly determine what queen that lady should be, whether Fortune or Our Lady who is so generous. By the brightness that she brought, it is likely that she is the mother of Him who created all this world.[41] The part-coloured wand, I believe, assigns rule and cruel judgment. The red colour, for one who readily understands, betokens great battle and blood, the green, courage,[42] that now surrounds you. You shall continue in painful war for a very long time. The sapphire stone with which she blessed you is lasting grace which God wills to befall you.[43] The three-fold book is but this broken land which you may redeem by the worthiness of your hand. The brass letters betoken only this, the great oppression of war and great offence which you shall bring to right again; but for that you must suffer great pain. The gold betokens honour and worthiness, victory in arms which you shall have by God's grace. The silver shows a clean life and heaven's bliss. For your reward you shall not miss that joy. Therefore, dread not, be out of all despair. Further in this matter I can now do no more.'

Having invaded England, Wallace is visited by the English Queen (VIII, 1,215–469)

And as they walked about the green fields, they saw out of the south where the queen came riding solemnly toward the Scottish host. And fifty ladies valued for their discretion and judged to be renowned were in her company. Some were widows and some were religious [i.e., nuns]. She also travelled with seven aged priests. To such folk Wallace never did violence unless they made a great offence to him. Thus they approached the Scots. At the pavilion where they saw the lion [i.e., the heraldic symbol of Scotland], they alighted to the ground and fell on their knees; praying for peace, they cried with piteous countenances. Earl Malcolm said, 'Our chieftain is not here.' He bid the queen rise and said it was not right for a queen to kneel before any lower person. Up by the hand the good earl has taken her and across the field to Wallace have they gone.

When she saw him she would have knelt down, but Wallace immediately caught this queen with crown in arms and kissed her without more words.[44] Such had he never done to an English person before! 'Madam,' he said, 'you are very welcome. How does it please you to see our muster?' 'Very well,' she said, 'we have need of friendship. God grant that you will meet our needs with success. We must suffer although we like it ill, but trust well that it is against our will.' 'You shall remain. I must go with this lord. We shall not tarry long from your presence.'

He and the earl went to their pavilion to consider this deed further with good advice. Wallace immediately called them to a council. 'Lords,' he said, 'you know what is afoot. I have no pleasure in their coming, and henceforth we must work with foresight. Women may be a cause of shame in war among fools who cannot withstand them. I do not yet say this about the queen. I believe that she intends only good, but one should take to heart seriously examples from olden times. At Roncesvalles the treason was plainly made by women whom Ganelon brought with him and by Turkish wine; they could not forbear indulging themselves with them. Their long time at war made them succumb to their fleshly will, an occurrence which brought Charles the Great to grievous loss and harm. Through that foul deed the flower of France without redemption was brought to confusion.[45] Therefore command your men in a thrifty manner that they not behave in such a way upon pain of death. None may speak with them but wise men of great renown who are lords and who are sworn to this council.' Their orders they carried out as wisely as they could. This order was effected throughout the entire host.

Wallace and the earl both went to the queen, fairly received her and brought her to a tent made ready for dinner as well equipped as they were able and staffed with many a likely man. The queen had planned for good provisions to come with her. She took a sample of everything they had brought. Wallace saw this and said, 'We have no fear. I cannot believe that ladies would do such a deed, poison men, even to win all England.' The queen answered, 'If there is poison in anything which is brought here with me, you shall see sorrow first upon me.' Soon after eating, a marshal called the lords to go to a council. Ladies appeared in their presence with the queen. Wallace asked what her coming might mean. 'It is for peace', she said, 'that we have you sought. This burning war has brought many to woe. May you grant us peace for the sake of Him who died on the Cross.' Wallace answered, 'Madam, that may not be. England has done such great harms to us that we cannot pass over them and leave them thus.' 'Yes,' said the queen, 'since we are Christian folk for God's sake we desire no more, we ought to have peace.' 'Madam, that I deny. I shall show you the perfect reason, for you seek no peace except for your own advantage. When your false king had gripped all of Scotland, for nothing which he found before him would he permit the proper blood to rule in our land but stole their rents and then put them to death. Ransom of gold can make no remedy for us; his cruel, false war shall be seen on himself.' The queen then soberly answered him, 'Of these wrongs it is quite fair that there be amends made.' 'Madam,' he said, 'we ask no more of him than that he await us in battle, and as God is the judge, He knows who is the more righteous.' 'Such amends', she said, 'do not seem good to me. Peace would now be best if it could be obtained. If you would grant peace and take a truce with us, we should make prayers throughout all England; for you and they are likely to be lost in the war.' Then Wallace said, 'Where such a thing comes through boasting, of necessity a prayer to us, wherever it is made, helps little or not at all.' Carefully she said, 'Thus wise men have taught us, that after war peace is the final end. Wherefore you should cease of your great malice. The end of war is charity and peace. There is peace in heaven with bliss and everlastingness. We shall beseech the Pope of his high grace to order peace since we can do no more.' 'Madam,' he said, 'before your solicitation should arrive there, we think to have recompense from England.' 'What determined you thus,' she said, 'may God save you, if you do not like to remain in violent war?'

'Madam,' he said, 'I shall tell you the truth. After the time of Alexander's reign[46] our land stood desolate for three years without a king but kept itself well at peace and in good condition. Because two claimed the throne[47] there happened a great debate in earnest, but they could not come to any accord. They asked your king to be their arbiter. Slyly he passed through the fortified places of Scotland. Afterwards he took the kingdom in his own hand. Against our rightful law he made a king who should hold the region through [Edward's] permission. The entire baronage was against this arrangement, for as of yet Scotland had never been in thrall. Great Julius Caesar who got tribute through fear nevertheless got small winnings from Scotland. Then your false king under pretence and without more delay through an agreement he made with Bruce who is our heir rode throughout all Scotland with a great power and undid the king he had earlier made. To Bruce then afterward he kept no covenant. He said he would not go and conquer land from other men, and thus the case befell. Then throughout Scotland he ruled himself and slew our elders; it was a great pity to see this. In prison for a long time they tortured me before I was cast out from there and taken for dead. Thanks be to God, He sent me some remedy. I exerted all my strength to be avenged. Since then I have done many of their kin to death. The passion of youth made me desire a wife. That I sorely regretted and shall do all my life. A traitor knight, one Hazelrig, without mercy made her die only to spite me. Then I prevailed forth in cruel war and pain; after a time we had redeemed again part of our land. Then your cursed king desired a truce from us, a truce which Scotland soon regretted. During that peace they set up a subtle justice-ayr. They hanged there to death eighteen-score of nobles who were prudent and worthy of renown, of coat-armour the eldest [i.e., most senior] in that region. We plan to avenge their deed with all our might; the woman also who was so dolefully killed – that deed will never go out of my mind until God takes me from this wide world! Thus I can have no pity on the English. I think never more to spare your men in war.'

The tears burst forth from his eyes – it was a great pain to behold them – when he had told his tale. The queen wept for pity of Wallace. 'Alas,' she said, 'may misfortune befall this wretched case! In a cursed time was that Hazelrig born. Through his deed many are lost. He who slew such a guiltless one should have pain. Since then England has bought it dear enough, though she had been a queen or a princess.' 'Madam,' he said, 'as God gives me good grace, in her time she was as dear to me as a princess or queen, whatever her state was.' 'Wallace,' she said, 'we will cease this talk; the cure for this situation is good prayer and peace.' 'I grant', he said, 'that from me there will be no more; this is nothing but increasing our care.' The queen well found that language did not avail her. She believed that with gold he might be overthrown [i.e., convinced]. She ordered three thousand pounds of the finest red gold to be brought to Wallace in that place. 'Madam,' he said, 'we crave no such tribute. We would have another cure

from England before we return again from this region, some part of your false
blood which has slain our elders. For all the gold and riches you possess you get
no peace unless we have our desire from your king.' When she saw well that gold
might gain no relief for her, she thought to test him somewhat in sport. 'Wallace,'
she said, 'you have been called my love. I have boldly subjected myself to you
trusting therefore to slake your rancour. It seems to me you should do something
for my sake.' Very wisely he made answer to the queen. 'Madam,' he said, 'if the
truth were seen that you loved me, I would owe you love in return. These words
are nothing but vanity; such love as that is nothing praiseworthy, to suffer censure
and afterwards get no pleasure. In speech of love you English are subtle. You may
mock us when you see no more advantage.' 'In London', she said, 'I suffered
blame for you. Also our council will laugh when we come home. Thus may they
say: "Women are fierce in thought, to seek friendship and then get absolutely
nothing."' 'Madam,' he said, 'we know how you have been sent. You believe we
have but little to spend. Because you are rich and clever, first with your gold you
would blind us, since Scots are so gullible. Then pleasing words from you and
from fair ladies, as one who with a small pipe – for it will call most appealingly –
should drive birds into a snare. Madam, as yet you may not tempt us all. A great
part of our goods is left among our kin. Also in England we find enough goods to
obtain.'

She was abashed to make an answer to him. 'Dear sir,' she said, 'since this is
your will, war or peace, whatever you like best, let your high intelligence and
good counsel consider.' 'Madam,' he said, 'now you shall understand the reason
that I will make no treaty. I can bind no truce with you ladies, for hereafter your
false king, when he saw his time arrive, would find a way to break it at his will
and plainly say that he himself had never granted it. Then we would have none
but ladies to reproach. By God who is above, that shall not be! I will begin no
war upon women; in faith there is no honour to win from you. Upon himself he
shall take the whole burden of peace or war, whatever we happen to do.' The
queen granted his answer to be sufficient; so did the remainder who were present
in that place. They held his decision to be greatly advantageous and firm enough
to show to their council. The queen was sorry that her travail had not helped.
She took the gold that she had brought with her and gave it generously to the
host, to every man who wished to have any. She dealt gold out abundantly to
minstrels and heralds beseeching them to be her friends. When Wallace saw the
generosity of the queen, he said seriously, 'The truth has well been seen; women
may tempt the wisest who have ever been born. Your great generosity shall never
be fruitless. We assure you that our host will not move until you can send a
message to your king. If it be so that he and we accord, then for your sake things
shall be better. Also, your heralds shall safely come and go. For your generosity
we shall trouble you no more.' Many times she thanked him for his decision as
did all the ladies in a goodly fashion. They drank gladly in that place, the queen

and good Wallace as well as their lords and ladies. Without longer delay she took her leave. Five miles that night they rode to a nunnery. Upon the morrow they passed to London.

Wallace meets the Red Reiver (IX, 182–391)

[Having received an invitation from King Philip, Wallace, with fifty men, embarked for France.] Thus from Scotland with full sail they made their way forth, sailing throughout the first day and night. In the morning when the sun rose brightly, the ship's master went to the top castle. South-east he saw something that troubled his mind, sixteen sails arrayed all in a row, coloured red and drawing towards him. The glittering sun shone brightly upon them, and the sea all about was illuminated with the light. This man's spirit was sorely distracted. Down he went and said very sorrowfully, 'Alas, the day that I was born! Without help our lives are lost. In a cursed time I took on this responsibility. The best chieftain and rescuer of Scotland I have over recklessly taken upon me with weak forces to bring him through the sea. It would not matter if God wished me to be tormented as long as Wallace could escape with honour.'

When Wallace saw and heard this man's complaint, he went to him in good will to comfort him. 'Master,' he said, 'what has moved you thus?' 'Nothing for myself,' this man said piteously, 'but of a thing I venture to say that if all the ships of broad Britain were here [i.e., on our side] we should lose some; appointed Fortune has sworn it. The best war-man in the sea of those living today is before us, the king of the sea.' Wallace immediately asked, 'Do you know who he is?' 'In his fashion they call him the Red Reiver. It is an evil time in which I have seen him! I would make no mourning for my own life, but there is no man born whom that tyrant will take captive. He saves none for gold or other goods, but slays and drowns all fiercely in the sea. He gets no grace though he is king or knight; these sixteen years great wrong has he done. The power he controls is so strong that none may escape who come in his control. If we wish to board him there is no recourse but to begin. The worst ship in his fleet can sail us down into a dreadful death.'

Then Wallace said, 'Since you know no remedy, tell me his armourial bearing and how I shall know him, what is his military practice, and then go lodge yourself below.' The shipman says, 'Right well you may know him through plain tokens, full clearly by his means [of identifying himself, i.e., his coat of arms]. His coat armour is seen in many places always ready for battle and always ringed with red. He himself is in the first ship that pursues you so fast; he will not be afraid. He will hail you when he comes near you. Without delay then can you strike astern. He himself will enter first full boldly. These are the signs that you will know him by: a bar of blue within his shining shield, a green band describing the field. The red betokens blood and hardiness, the green courage increasing his intent; the blue he bears because he is a Christian man'.[48] Wallace answered soberly again, 'Though he is Christian, this is no goodly deed. Go below deck. May Saint Andrew grant us success.'

He made both the ship's master and the helmsman go into the hold. Without further delay he got his fifty men arrayed in their armour. Forty-eight on the leeward side lay low. He then called William Crawford to him and said, 'You have some maritime knowledge. Your custom has been to be often in the town of Ayr. I pray you take this instruction from me. See that you stand firmly by this mast. When they bid us to strike [sail as a sign of surrender], be ready to act. When I warn you, draw the sail again. Kneland, cousin, come take the helm in hand; I shall stand here on the bulwark near you. May God guide our ship! For now I say no more.'

The fight began with a full warlike show. The Red Reiver himself was aloft with a drawn sword and ordered his helmsman to lay them alongside Wallace's ship. He loudly cried, 'Strike your sails, dogs! You shall die!' Crawford let the sail drop a little way. The captain immediately leaped in and would not hold back. Wallace in haste grasped him by the throat, threw him on the upper deck where he stood while from his nose and mouth blood rushed out. Without delay he drew a forged knife. The warships were close together. The great ship had not yet grappled them fast with hooks. Crawford drew sail, slipped by and got past them. The Reiver cried with a piteous and clear voice for grace of his life. 'For Him who redeemed you with His life, mercy,' he said; 'for Him who died on the Cross, give me an opportunity to repent. I have spilled much blood. For my trespass I would make some atonement. Many guiltless people I have put to death.' Wallace knew well that even if the Red Reiver was killed there was no way he could escape from the others, but he could perhaps make some rescue of his life. A better purpose he soon took, and also he had pity on him for his life was ill led.

In Latin tongue[49] he spoke to him thus: 'I never yet took a man captive who was enemy to me. For God's sake I grant you your life.' He immediately took both knife and sword from him. By the hand he has taken him prisoner and on his sword keenly made him swear that from that day forth he should never do him harm. 'Command your men,' said Wallace, 'to honour our peace.' Their shot from guns was not easy to stop. The discharge of missiles was frightening on either side. The Red Reiver commanded them to halt and held out a glove in token of the truce. His men saw it and well recognized that sign; they ceased their shooting when they saw the signal. He called his largest ship to him: 'Let be your war; these are friends in accord with us. I trust to God that our worst days are over.' He asked Wallace to do whatever was his will. Without delay he said thus to him, 'To Rochelle I wish you to order them to sail. For I do not know what the English may intend.' He commanded them without more words: 'Turn sail and wind for fair Rochelle, for there, God willing, it is our purpose to be. Search about thoroughly for English skulkers in the sea.' They carried out his command with all the haste they could muster.

Wallace desired to talk more with this man. He asked soberly, 'In what land were you born?' 'In France,' said he, 'and my ancestors before me as well, and there we had some part of heritage [i.e., inherited lands]. Yet fierce Fortune has brought me to this enraged state.' Wallace asked, 'How did you come to this life?' 'In truth,' he said, 'through a sudden strife. It so happened to me in the king's presence to do great offence over recklessly; a noble man of great fame and renown through my deed was put to confusion, dead of a sword stroke. What is the use of more words? Though I repented sorely what had happened, nothing helped. Through friends at the court I escaped from that place and never since have been able to get the king's grace. For my sake [i.e., because of my act] they killed many of my kin, and when I saw that the situation could be no better unless I left the land – it behooved me to do this – one day I went to Bordeaux. One night I got on an English ship that was readied for the sea. Around me there assembled miscreants and others of like mind. In a short time we had multiplied so much that there were few who could stand against our power. In tyranny thus we have ruled for a long time. These sixteen years I have been on the sea and done great harm; therefore woe is me. I saved no one for gold or for ransom but slew and drowned them in the sea. I showed favour to folk of sundry lands, but no Frenchmen ever found friendship with me. As far as I could reign they got no grace. Thus on the sea I was called a king. Now I see well that my fortune has gone, vanquished by one; that makes me repent sorely! Who would have said this same day at morning that I should so easily be borne down by one man! My men would have greeted such a statement with great scorn. I believed myself a match for any man, but I have found very plainly that the opposite is true. Here I give up robbery for evermore. In such misrule I will never again bear arms, unless it is in honest use to defend myself. Now that I have told you the better part of my bliss and pain, for God's sake show me some kindness. My heart will break unless I know who you are, you who have so outrageously overcome me. For I know well that there is none living who could have taken me prisoner except Wallace who has redeemed Scotland, and who is called the best who wears a sword in this day and age.[50] In his war it is a great honour to labour. And now in the world I believe he has no equal.'

Thereat Wallace smiled and said, 'Friend, may you be well. Scotland has need of many such as he. What is your name, tell me, so may you have salvation?' 'In truth,' he said, 'Thomas of Longville.' 'Enjoy it well. Thus our strife ends. Work to please God in the amendment of your life. I shall be your faithful friend, and also I shall soon tell you my name. You should make no complaint about the chances of war, for as fate will work your fortune you must accept it. I am that man whom you praise so highly, and it has been but a short time since I came to sea. Born in Scotland my right name is Wallace.' He fell on his knees and thanked God for his grace: 'I dare to boast that my hand has been yielded to the best man who wears a sword. In truth,' he said, 'this makes me happier than if you gave me sixty-score florins.' Wallace answered, 'Since you are here through chance, my purpose is to travel in France; and since I am charged to see the king, as my reward I shall ask for your peace.' 'I would eagerly have peace from my rightful king, and no longer reign in that realm [i.e., the sea] but take my leave from there and come home again. I intend to remain in your service.' 'Service,' he said, 'Thomas, that may not be, but I desire good friendship from you.' He ordered the wine drawn, and each man made merry.[51]

X 1221-1246

A description of Wallace ~~(X, 1,221–46)~~

Wallace's stature, of breadth and of height, was judged thus with proper discretion by those who saw him both undressed in armour and dressed in armour. He was nine quarters of an ell in length [i.e., 7 feet tall]; a third part of that length was he broad in the shoulders, very seemly, strong and pleasing to see. His great limbs afforded him a vigorous and sound pace, his limbs were hard, his arms long and round; his hands were made like the leaves of a palm tree, of manly appearance with large and clear nails. His face was proportioned long and fair; he was sober in speech and able in courage. He had a broad and high chest with a great and sturdy neck; his lips were round, his nose was square and well shaped. He had curling brown hair on his brow with lighter coloured eye brows, clear sharp eyes like bright diamonds. Under the chin on the left side was seen a scar received through injury. His colour was sanguine. He had wounds in many diverse places, but his face was fair and well kept. He kept no riches for himself, but gave away what he won like King Alexander.[52] In peacetime he was as meek as a maid, but when war approached he was a veritable Hector. He gave great credence to Scottish men, but known enemies could not deceive him.[53] [See plate 24.]

On his second trip to France Wallace encounters treachery – and a lion (XII, 195–291)

The king had ordered a fierce lion to be brought within an enclosure because of the great harm that it did; thus caged in iron, the lion was powerless. In madness he exceeded all other beasts, but he was handsome and quite fierce in deeds. In that strong enclosure the king ordered men to feed him and to keep him away from people and other beasts. In the court dwelt two squires of great importance who were cousins to the two champions whom Wallace had slain earlier.[54] In perverse deceit they made a bond [i.e., swore an oath] to use their power to effect Wallace's confusion by any means, through fraud or subtlety. Afterwards, they did not care if they died as long as they could bring him to death or shame.

Thus, one day they went to the king: 'This man,' they said, 'whom you make so wealthy, sees nothing here that he cannot bring to confusion with his great prowess. Now he desires to fight your lion, and bids us ask you that for this strong battle you give him leave to go into that cage.' Soberly again to them the king answered, 'It seems grievous to me that he desires such a thing, but for neither grief nor great pleasure will I deny Wallace what he desires from France.' Then they went forth and soon met with Wallace. They told him a feigned tale of this case. 'Wallace,' they said, 'the king desires that you engage in battle which will be cruel to see and that you fight his lion.' Wallace answered in hasty conclusion and said, 'I shall do the king's will and do whatever is in my power to fulfill it.' Then he made his way to the king without delay. When Wallace approached, a lord of the court unwisely and without forethought asked, 'Wallace, do you dare to go and fight our lion?' And he said, 'Yes, if the king will allow me, or yourself if you think yourself better.' What will you hear more? This thing was agreed, that Wallace should pass through the barrier to the lion. The king ordered his men to bring him good harness, but he said, 'No may God shield me from such a case. I would take armour if I fought with a man, but for a dog that knows nothing about arms I will have nothing but what I now have with me.'[55]

He wound a large cloak about his hand and took his great sword; he took nothing else with him. Boldly he entered the enclosure. Great chains which were attached to the gate with a machine [i.e., a pulley] were pulled as soon as Wallace was therein. The mad lion bounded rampant towards where Wallace stood for the lion desired blood. With his crude paws he reached for the cloak. With his good sword of burnished steel Wallace then gave him a stroke across the back; it cut the body completely in two.

He then went in great ire to the king and said loudly, 'Was this all your desire, to waste a Scot so lightly in vain? Are there any more dogs that you would yet have slain? Go bring them forth since I must kill dogs in order to do your bidding while I dwell with you. It would profit me well to make ready to leave for Scotland, for men there have greater deeds upon hand than to strive with a dog in battle! From you in France forever I take my leave.' The king perceived that Wallace was aggrieved because he had so earnestly asked permission to leave; knowing the reputation and great nobility of Wallace which sprang forth in that time in many places, he was reluctant to allow him to undertake so base a deed as leaving in this manner. Humbly he said, 'You should not displease yourself. This [the fight with the lion] you desired. It never occurred to me, and by the faith I owe the crown of France I would never have charged you with such a danger, except that men of value requested it for you.' Wallace answered, 'I make a vow to God I never wished to be in such a battle. There is no reputation to be won from a dog.' The king conceived how this falsehood was wrought. The squires were both brought into his presence and could not deny what had happened when they came before him earlier. They recited their sin without delay; the king commanded that they be put to death, smote off their heads with no remedy.[56]

Lo, the champions for baseless envy Wallace brought to sudden death. The squires also, from the time their falseness was learned, envy brought them both to a sudden end. Lords, behold, envy the wily dragon[57] burns his region in cruel fire; for he who is bound in envy is nothing, since it brings him hastily to some mischief. Forsake envy, and you shall succeed the better.[58]

With the Scots short of food and a price on his head, Wallace foils his pursuers and feeds his men (XII, 548–655)

They rested that day in Methven Wood. When night came they went without resting to Barnan Wood[59] where they found the squire, good Ruane. He had long lived there as an outlaw on game when he could get no other provisions. They did not tarry but went to Athol[60] where food was scant. Then Wallace had great fear; they passed on to Lorn but found little in the way of food there. That country was made bare of both wild and tame beasts. In fortified places there was no food at all. The worthy Scots then made a piteous moan. Sir John Scot said that he would rather die with a good name and leave his heirs free than to remain bound in subjection. When Wallace saw these good men of renown stricken with hunger so that they might almost live no more, know that he sighed very sorely for them. 'Good men,' he said, 'I am the cause of this. As you desire I shall amend this misfortune, or leave you free to acquire some provisions.'

He readied himself to go from them alone and asked them to wait until he came again. Over a hill he passed to a plain. Out of their sight in a forest-side he sat down to wait under an oak. He leaned his sword and bow against a tree. In anguished grief and prostrate he turned this way and that. His piteous mind was so fixed on his men that he thought little about himself. 'O wretch,' he said, 'who could never be content with the great might that the great God lent you, but your fierce mind, willful and variable, could not remain stable with great lordship and willful wit to make Scotland free. God does not like what I have taken upon me. Those who were born far more noble than I are forlorn with hunger through my desire [i.e., actions]. I ask God to restore them again. I am the cause. I should have the pain.' While considering thus and arguing with himself, at last he fell asleep.

Three days before five men had followed him; they were determined to take him or to lose their lives.[61] The Earl of York had offered them such a great reward that they thought to put Wallace down by stealth. Three of them were men born of England and two were Scots of those who undertook this deed; and some said their [i.e., the Scots] third brother afterward betrayed Kildrummy castle, for which great sorrow was raised. They had a child with them who helped to bear food in the wilderness among the great mountains. They had all seen the departure of Wallace from his good men and where he now waited. In the thick woods in hiding they kept low until they perceived that he had fallen asleep, and then these five approached near to Wallace. They asked each other what was best to do. A man said thus: 'It would be a deed of great reputation if we could quickly lead him to St Johnston. Lo, how he lies. We can arrange our grips to our best advantage. He will get no help from his weapons. We shall bind him against his will and lead him thus to the backside of yonder hill so that his men shall know nothing about what has befallen him.' The other four assented to his counsel, and then these five made their way to Wallace and thought to bind him in that place through force.

What! These five thought to hold Wallace down? He was the manliest man and the strongest physically of anyone living, and also stood in such a righteous position, we trust well that God had his deeds in sight. They gripped him. Then he burst out of sleep. 'What does this mean?' he said quite suddenly. He turned about and thrust his arms up; in a knightly manner he struck blows upon those traitors. He grasped the strongest man in his arms and smashed him in his armour against a tree. He got a sword soon after he rose. Like a champion he goes among the four remaining men. Each man he killed with one blow. When two were dead the others would not stop but prepared themselves to flee; but by then there was no hope, for none living could pass from him on foot. He followed them quickly and soon brought them to death. Then he soberly sought after the child. 'What did you do here?' The child, with a pale face, fell on his knees and asked for Wallace's grace. 'I was with them and knew nothing of their plans. As a servant, as they ordered me, I did.' 'What do you bear here?' 'Only food,' the child said. 'Pack it up and come away with me. Food in this time is far better than gold.' Wallace and he went forth over the ground.

Who saved Wallace from his bold enemies? Who but the great God who has the world under His rule; He was his help in many cruel battles. With glad cheer thus he went to his men. There was roasted flesh as well as bread and cheese to succour those who were at the point of losing their lives to starvation. Then he distributed it to four men and a fifth who before had fasted for three days; then he took his share. He had fasted as long as they. Where have you ever heard in such a press, in hunger so, sleeping and weaponless, of anyone who recovered so well as Wallace did in this case, recovering completely before he vanquished his five enemies? You men of wit, decide this question. Without comment I will tell my tale further.

Wallace's execution (XII, 1,305–448)

On Wednesday the false English brought Wallace forth to martyr him as they had earlier devised.[62] Indeed it is true that Wallace was a martyr, just like Oswald, Edmund, Edward and Thomas.[63] A great host of men in arms led good Wallace, who looked about him with a bold spirit. He asked for a priest for God who died on the Cross. King Edward then commanded his clergy and said, 'I charge, upon pain of loss of life, that none be so bold to shrive yon tyrant; he has reigned long in defiance of my highness.' Immediately a blessed bishop who was present in that place – at that time he was the rightful lord of Canterbury – against the king made this righteous reply and said, 'Myself shall hear his confession, if I have the power, despite your authority. And if through force you will stop me from this thing, I vow to God, who is my rightful king, that all England I shall here interdict and make it known that you are a heretic. This sacrament of the church I shall give to him; so take your choice to execute him or let him live. It would be worth more in respect of your crown to keep such a one alive in your power than all the land and goods he has robbed you of. But covetousness has always driven you from honour. You have reigned in life through wrongful deeds, the consequences of which shall be seen in you or in your seed.'[64]

The king ordered that the bishop be seized, but wise lords counselled to let him go. All Englishmen said the bishop's desire was right. To Wallace he then went in their sight and soberly heard his confession until death. Humbly his spirit he there commended to God, humbly served him with heartfelt devotion upon his knees, and said his prayer. The bishop took his leave and rode to West monastery. The executioners then bore Wallace without delay to a place for his martyrdom for to his death he could make no further delay. From the first night he was captured in Scotland they kept him in the same bonds; he had nothing that would do him any good. Englishmen served him fleshly food. His worldly life desired the sustenance though it gave him no pleasure. Those thirty days they dared not lessen his bonds while he was bound to a bench of oak with iron chains that were both strong and sharp.

They set a clerk to hear what he would say. 'You Scot,' he said, 'who have done great wrongs, see that your fatal hour fast approaches. You should bear in mind your misdeeds so that clerks, when they read their psalms for Christian souls in their prayers, may include you in their number, for now you see that of necessity you must die.' Then Wallace said, 'For all your severe speech you have no authority – suppose that I did amiss – ; yonder blessed bishop has promised that I shall have bliss, and believe well that God shall permit it. Your feeble words shall not smite my conscience. I have comfort from the way that I should go; the most pain I feel at remaining here overlong.' Then the clerk said, 'Our king often sent for thee. You might have had all Scotland at your will to hold from him had you ceased your strife, and you could have reigned as a lord all your life.' Then Wallace said, 'You speak of mighty things. Had I lasted and gotten my rightful king, from the time that worthy Bruce had received his crown I thought to have made England subject to him so completely that it should have been at his will, as it pleased him, to save your king or kill him.' 'Well,' said this clerk, 'then you do not repent; of wickedness you have a fierce thought. There is no one in the world who has slain so many. Therefore it seems to me that you should be killed, by the grace of our king and then of his barons.' Then Wallace smiled a little at his language. 'I grant', he said, 'that I slew some Englishmen in my quarrel, it seemed to me not half enough. I began hostilities only to win back our own. To God and man the right of it is well known. Your vain words do naught but delay me; I command you, for God's sake, let me be.' A sheriff immediately made this clerk pass from him. Just as they dared, they granted what Wallace would ask.

Wallace always carried a psalter with him; from his childhood he would never be separated from it. It was better, he believed, to make haste in journeying. They stripped him of his clothing. He asked this favour of Lord Clifford that knight to let him have his psalter in his sight. He got a priest to hold it open before him while they did all that they would to him. Many English said that Wallace felt no pain. Good devotion so was his beginning, continued therewith, and fair was his ending; while speech and spirit at once went to lasting bliss, we believe, for evermore.

I will not tell how he was divided into five parts and ordained thus to pass. But thus his spirit in all likelihood was in bliss. Of Wallace's life whoever has further knowledge may display it forth with wit and eloquence, for I to this point have done my diligent best.[65] [See plate 25.]

Conclusion (XII, 1,449–64)

Go noble book, filled with good matter although you are barren of eloquence. Go, worthy book filled with true deeds, although in language you have great need of help. When good poets flourished well in Scotland, it was a great harm that you found none of them. Yet there are some who can praise you well; now bide your time and be a reminder of the events you describe. I beseech you, of your benevolence, whoever will not praise, do not find fault with my eloquence; it is well known I am an unlearned man, and here have spoken as well as I can. My mind knows no lofty terms.[66] Now beseech God, who is the giver of grace, who made hell and earth and set the heavens above, that He grant us some part of His everlasting love.

NOTES

GENERAL INTRODUCTION

1 Maurice Keen, *The Outlaws of Medieval Legend*, revised edn (Routledge & Kegan Paul, 1987).

2 The debate about the social class of the audience of the Robin Hood legend was initially waged in the journal *Past and Present* from 1958 to 1961. The articles have been conveniently reprinted in R.H. Hilton (ed.), *Peasants, Knights and Heretics* (Cambridge University Press, 1976), pp. 221–72. In brief, R.H. Hilton and Maurice Keen argued that the Robin Hood poems reflected peasant unrest over rents, services and social status that culminated in the Peasants' Revolt of 1381. J.C. Holt and T.H. Aston counter-argued that the poems, to use Holt's words, 'have nothing at all to do with the rift between landlord and peasant' (p. 243), but instead they are 'the literature of the county landowners, of knights and gentry' (p. 244). Holt concluded that the ballads were disseminated in the halls of the gentry's country households 'where the entertainment was aimed not only at the master but also at the members and the staff' (p. 249). Keen's views were subsequently published in his first edition of *The Outlaws of Medieval Legend* in 1961, while Holt's thesis was elaborated in his 1982 edition of *Robin Hood*. However, in the revised edition of 1977, Keen recanted his original position, throwing his support behind Holt. In spite of Keen's modification of his original views, the change only affects two of the fourteen chapters and, as a result, much of his analysis of the outlaw tales themselves is still valid. For a discussion of the audience of the Robin Hood ballads, in which I differ with both Keen and Holt, see the introduction to *A Gest of Robyn Hode*.

3 Eric Hobsbawm, *Bandits* (New York, Delacorte Press, 1969).

4 Ingrid Benecke, *Der gute Outlaw: Studien zu einem literarischen Typus im 13. Und 14 Jahrhundert* (Tübingen, Max Niemeyer, 1973).

5 Harry Rothwell (ed.), *English Historical Documents 1189–1327* (Oxford University Press, 1975), pp. 316–24.

6 Paul E. Sigmund, *Natural Law in Political Thought* (Cambridge, Massachusetts, Winthrop Publishers, 1971), pp. vii–viii.

7 A.P. D'Entreves (ed.), *Aquinas: Selected Political Writings* (Oxford, Basil Blackwell, 1948), p. 179.

8 Dino Bigongiari (ed.), *The Political Ideas of St Thomas Aquinas* (New York, Hafner, 1966), p. 195.

9 Edward Powell, 'Law and Justice', p. 32 in Rosemary Horrox (ed.), *Fifteenth-Century Attitudes: Perceptions of Society in Late Medieval England* (Cambridge University Press, 1994; repr. 1996).

10 Paul Radin, *The Trickster: A Study in American Indian Mythology* (Routledge and Kegan Paul, 1956), p. ix. See also William J. Hynes and William G. Doty (eds), *Mythical Trickster Figures: Contours, Contexts, and Criticisms* (Tuscaloosa, University of Alabama Press, 1993).

11 Mikhail Bakhtin, *Rabelais and His World* (Bloomington, Indiana University Press, 1984), p. 4.

1. THE OUTLAWRY OF EARL GODWIN FROM THE *VITA ÆDWARDI REGIS*

Introduction

1 See Andrew G. Watson, *The Library of Sir Simonds d'Ewes* (British Museum, 1966).

2 Bloch argues for a composition of about 1200 to allow for the development of the cult of King Edward, but Barlow follows Southern and Henningham in placing the composition at the time of the Norman Conquest (xli–xliv).

3 The twelfth-century chronicler William of Malmesbury gives this discussion of the competing representations of Godwin in his *History of the Kings of England*:

The English of our times vilify [Robert of Jumièges], together with the rest [of the Normans], as being the impeacher of Godwin and his sons, as the sower of discord, as the purchaser of the archbishopric; they say, too, that Godwin and his sons were men of liberal mind, the steadfast promoters and defenders of the government of Edward, and that it was not to be wondered at if they were indignant when they saw men of yesterday, and strangers, preferred to themselves; still, that they never uttered even a harsh word against the king whom they had formerly exalted to the throne. On the opposite hand, the Normans thus defend themselves: they allege that both Godwin and his sons acted with the greatest want of respect, as well as fidelity, to the king and his party, aiming at equal sovereignty with him, often ridiculing his simplicity, often hurling the shafts of their wit against him; that the Normans could not endure this, but endeavoured to weaken their power as much as possible (tr. John Stevenson, *The Church Historians of England*, III.i [London, 1854], p. 186).

4 See Heinrich Brunner, *Grundzüge der Deutschen Rechtgeschichte* (Leipzig, Duncker and Humblut, 1908), II, pp. 18ff.; Frederick Pollock and F.W Maitland, *The History of English Law, Before the Time of Edward I* (2nd edn, Cambridge University Press, 1969), II, p. 580; and Julius Goebel, *Felony and Misdemeanor: A Study in the History of Criminal Law* (Philadelphia, University of Pennsylvania Press, 1976), p. 15.

5 The Laws of Edward and Guthrum declare, regarding tax resisters: 'If he strikes a man to death, then he is an outlaw, and to be pursued with outcry by everyone who desires justice' (Felix Liebermann, *Die Gesetze der Angelsächsen* [Halle, Niemeyer, 1903–16], Edward and Guthrum 6.6). The mid-tenth-century laws of Edgar declare that 'at the fourth occasion he loses all that he owns and is an outlaw, unless the king allows him (to remain in) the land' (Liebermann, I Edgar 3.1). Translations of Anglo-Saxon and Latin are mine unless otherwise indicated.

6 Æthelstan's fifth set of laws orders that 'whoever aids (outlaws) or any of their men or sends any man to them, he is guilty himself' (Liebermann, Æthelstan 5. prologue).

7 The *Anglo-Saxon Chronicle* records that within four years of assuming the throne Cnut had outlawed four potentially threatening men: Eadwig Ætheling, Eadwig 'king of the peasants', Æthelweard and Thorkell the Tall. Although accounts are confusing, almost all are reported dead shortly thereafter. For the two Eadwigs, see the Worcester (D) and Peterborough (E) versions of the *Anglo-Saxon Chronicle* for the year 1017. The same texts report Æthelweard's banishment in 1020 and

Thorkell's outlawry in 1021. The Abingdon C Chronicle reports that the latter was reconciled with the king in 1023.

8 Eustace and his retinue entered Dover and demanded lodging. When they were refused by a resident of the town, a mêlée broke out and perhaps forty people were killed on both sides. Eustace immediately rode to the king and complained about the treatment and Edward responded by ordering Godwin to punish the men of Dover. When the earl refused, he was ordered to Gloucester to explain his lack of action. Both versions of the *Chronicle* imply that Eustace was more at fault in the exchange, Peterborough (E) by noting that Eustace and his men put on their armour before entering the town and Worcester (D) by calling their behaviour 'foolish'.

9 Gregory the Great, *Moralia in Job*, ed. M. Adrianen, Corpus Christianorum Series Latina 143B (Turnholt, Brepols, 1985), 27.10.

10 'Quid enim per Saul, nisi mali rectores; quid per David, nisi boni subditi designatur?' Gregory the Great, *Cura Pastoralis* III.4 (*Patrologia Latina* 77, pp. 54–6), tr. Henry Davis, *Ancient Christian Writers* 11 (Westminster, Maryland, The Newman Press, 1950).

11 'apud semetipsos dijudicent, ut tamen divino timore constricti ferre sub eis jugum reverentiae non recusent', *Cura Pastoralis* III.3.

12 'David ferire metuit, quia piae subditorum mentes ab omni se peste obtectrationis abstinentes praepositorum vitam nullo linguae gladio percutiunt, etiam cum de imperfectione reprehendunt', *Cura Pastoralis* III.3.

13 Compare his speech in the *Vita* to that in the excerpt from Walter Map's *De Nugis Curialium* or to his worm-tongued response to Jarl Ulfr's request for help in *Knýtlinga saga*: 'I don't think you Danes can expect much help from we English'.

Translation

1 Harthacnut died on 8 June 1042 and Edward was crowned on Easter Day 1043 (3 April). John of Worcester reports that he was able to claim the crown largely through the support of Earl Godwin and Lyfing, Bishop of Worcester (*The Chronicle of Florence of Worcester*, tr. Joseph Stevenson [1853; Felinfach, Llanerch, 1996], p. 278). William of Malmesbury credits Godwin's eloquence with convincing the leaders of England to accept Edward as king, but he also questions the earl's motivation (*History of the Kings of England*, tr. Joseph Stevenson [London, 1854], pp. 184–5).

2 Ælfweard died 25 July 1044. The appointment of Robert to the Bishopric of London was one of several preferments offered by Edward to Norman churchmen. In 1049 he gave Dorcester to Ulfr, a Norman priest, and when Robert moved to Canterbury in 1051, he was replaced in London by another Norman priest, William. See Frank Stenton, *Anglo-Saxon England*, 3rd edn (Oxford University Press, 1971), pp. 462–3.

3 I Corinthians 15:33: 'Do not be deceived: Bad companions corrupt good morals'.

4 Eadsig died 29 October 1050. Ælric of Canterbury is unknown outside of this account. The *Anglo-Saxon Chronicle* and subsequent chronicles make no mention of the dispute over the succession at Canterbury, though William of Malmesbury reports that Eadsig had named Siward, Abbot of Abingdon, as his successor 'lest any improper person should aspire to so great an eminence, either by solicitation or by purchase' (*History of the Kings of England*, 185).

5 Robert was installed 27 June 1051.

6 Stories of Godwin's acquisition of church property and lack of respect for ecclesiastical authority persisted long after his death, as the story from Walter Map recounted in the introduction indicates. Map also tells a tale of how Godwin set his son Swegn to seduce the prioress at Berkeley by Severn and as many nuns as possible so that he could take over the property on charges of corruption. Similarly, William of Malmesbury claims, regarding evils attributed to Edward's reign, 'the ruin of the monasteries and the iniquity of the judges, are said to have taken place without [Edward's] knowledge, through the insolence of Godwin and his sons, who used to laugh at the easiness of the king' (*History of the Kings of England*, 184).

7 Upon the death of Cnut on 12 November 1035 support in the kingdom was split between two potential successors. Harthacnut, the son of Cnut and Emma, was the choice of the queen, Godwin and the lords of Wessex, but he opted to consolidate his power in Denmark rather than immediately claim his rights in England. The northern lords supported Harold Harefoot, the son of Cnut and Ælfgifu of Northampton. A compromise was worked out by which Harold ruled as regent and Emma and Godwin represented Harthacnut's interests, but when Harthacnut remained in Denmark, Harold became, de facto, king until his death in 1040.

8 The story of Alfred's death is the subject of poems in the Abingdon B and Worcester (D) versions of the *Anglo-Saxon Chronicle*. The former blames Godwin directly for the attack, while the latter is vague about the identity of the perpetrators. The episode was commonly repeated by Norman historians who were anxious to discredit his entire family after Harold Godwinson claimed the throne in 1066 in opposition to William the Conqueror. The earl was further vilified in the lives of Edward the Confessor composed in the twelfth century. One reader of *La Vie du Eduoard* in Cambridge University Library MS Ee.3.59 apparently became so incensed with the earl's actions that he or she has poked out his eyes in two of the illustrations on folio 11v.

9 The council convened at Gloucester on 8 September 1051.

10 The accounts in the *Anglo-Saxon Chronicle* indicate that the northern lords were summoned in support of the king and against Godwin and his sons, but the wiser among them saw that a civil war was not in the best interests of the kingdom.

11 Stigand, Bishop of Winchester, was appointed archbishop of Canterbury to replace Robert of Jumièges in 1052. Robert, however, complained to Rome and Stigand was excommunicated by the reform-minded popes of the period. See Stenton, *Anglo-Saxon England*, pp. 465–6, 624, 659–60.

12 Baldwin V, Marquis of Flanders 1035–67.

13 The legality of the pursuit is questionable. If Godwin and his sons were outlawed because they failed to appear in court, then pursuit was imperative according to Anglo-Saxon law. On the other hand, if Godwin appeared and was exiled, then he had five days of grace to abjure the realm. The Worcester Chronicle (D) states that Godwin was outlawed for failing to appear, while the Peterborough Chronicle (E) records that he was given five days to leave. The *Vita* is vague on the point but appears to cite the pursuit as another offence of Robert.

14 See Daniel 11.

15 Joseph; see Genesis 39.

16 22 June 1052.

17 14 September 1052. The singing may be designed by the writer to recall the songs sung by the women of Israel in praise of David's victories; see I Samuel 18:6–7.

18 I Samuel 16:14–23.

19 I Samuel 18:25–7.

20 I Samuel 24:1–15; see Introduction, p. 3.

21 I Samuel 26:1–11; see Introduction, p. 3.

2. THE DEEDS OF HEREWARD

Introduction

1 The sobriquet 'le Wake' (i.e. the watchful one), albeit highly appropriate to a successful guerrilla leader, is first recorded in a fourteenth-century Peterborough manuscript – the so-called 'Chronicle of Abbot John' (*Chronicon Angliæ Petriburgense*, ed. J.A. Giles, [London, 1845], p. 55). Its present-day currency is due to the title of Kingsley's novel (see note 3).

2 For what we know of the historical Hereward see: John Hayward, 'Hereward the Outlaw', *Journal of Medieval History* 14 (1988), 293–304, and Cyril Hart, *The Danelaw* (London, 1992), pp. 625–48.

3 First issued in serial form as 'Hereward, the last of the English' in *Good Words*, Jan.–Dec. 1865, illustrated by Paul Gray, then published in book form with a modified title and new illustrations by H.C. Selous, the following year to coincide with the anniversary of the Norman Conquest.

4 Susan Reynolds, 'Eadric Silvaticus and the English resistance', *Bulletin of the Institute of Historical Research* 54 (1981), 102–5.

5 *The Anglo-Saxon Chronicle*, ed. Michael Swanton (London, 1996), p. 208.

6 Gaimar suggests that he was in charge of an English contingent fighting on behalf of William in Maine, and was subsequently killed by a bunch of jealous Norman knights (*L'Estoire des Engleis*, ed. A. Bell [Oxford, 1960], pp. 178–80).

7 *Liber Eliensis*, ed. E.O. Blake, Royal Historical Society, Camden Third Series 92 (London, 1962), p.188.

8 Cf. chapt. 2; a late medieval chronicle attributed to a twelfth-century abbot of Crowland (the pseudo-Ingulf): *Rerum Anglicarum Scriptorum Veterum*, ed. William Fulman (Oxford, 1684), I, pp. 1–132 (pp. 67–8).

9 *Beowulf*, ed. Michael Swanton, revised edn (Manchester, 1997), pp. 74–7, note pp. 193–4.

10 *Objective, Burma!*, Raoul Walsh (Warner Brothers, 1945).

11 *Anglo-Saxon Chronicle*, ed. Swanton, pp. 205–7.

12 Gaimar declared that if there had been only four such men in England, the Conquest could never have taken place (*L'Estoire des Engleis*, ed. Bell, pp. 180–1). Charles Macfarlane's novel *The Camp of Refuge* (London, 1844), pictures Hereward playing a dramatic role by the side of his king at Stamford Bridge and Hastings.

13 See generally Joost de Lange, 'The relation and development of english and Icelandic outlaw traditions' (dissertation, Utrecht, 1935), pp. 4–32; James Dunbar Pickering, 'The Legend of Hereward the Saxon: An investigation of De Gestis Herwardi Saxonis, its historical basis, its debt to saga and early romance, its place in English literary history' (dissertation, Columbia University, 1964).

Translation

1 The person to whom the Prefatory Letter is addressed, and who had apparently commissioned the work, was perhaps Hervey, first bishop of Ely, 1108–31, an incomer who we know was interested in the history of the place.

2 Bourne was a small manor on the western edge of the Fens. There is no evidence for Hereward or his family ever having been in possession of Bourne, although his documented estates lay round about (see map, plate 4). At the time of the Conquest Bourne was held by Earl Morcar (see note 52).

3 Now Bury St Edmunds, this was an ancient Anglo-Saxon monastery in nearby Suffolk, significant as the shrine of St Edmund, a ninth-century king of East Anglia martyred by the vikings (see note 76).

4 Mutilation of troublesome opponents was common practice; William treated Hereward's captured followers severely: 'Some he imprisoned, others he let go free, having cut off their hands or put out their eyes' (Florence of Worcester, *Chronicon ex Chronicis*, ed. B. Thorpe [London, 1848–9], II, p. 9).

5 Association with famous names would enhance the hero's status; of course, if he was actually related to one or other notable family, it would account for the prominence he is given in the record of resistance. We know nothing of a Leofric of Bourne, though a parcel of land there was held by one Leofwine and occasional confusion between the two names is not unknown at this date. Ralph the Staller ('stallers' held an office similar to that of latter-day marshal) was a Breton friend of Edward the Confessor from whom he held estates bordering the Fens in Norfolk; he acquiesced in the Conquest and was made Earl of Norfolk and Suffolk. 'Duke' Oslac was presumably Oslac ealdorman of Northumbria 963–75, who had Fenland origins; he was exiled for unknown reasons in 975, but was spoken about in celebratory terms: 'the famous earl . . . bold-hearted hero . . . wise and eloquent' (*Anglo-Saxon Chronicle*, ed. M. Swanton [London, 1996], pp. 120–1).

6 Great generosity remained a heroic virtue among the English. Contrast English and French versions of the early medieval tale of Sir Launfal: in the former his over-generous spirit (though partly responsible for his self-exile from Arthur's court) is duly celebrated, whereas in the latter his 'spendthrift' nature is not approved.

7 Edward 'the Confessor', 1043–66.

8 *Exulis*. The term 'outlaw' was a relatively recent introduction by Scandinavian settlers (Old Norse *útlagi*); prior to this the nearest English expression was merely 'fugitive' *(fliema)*.

9 Gilbert de Ghent, the son of Baldwin V of Flanders and thus nephew of the Conqueror's wife, Matilda. A major landowner, he held several manors close to Bourne.

10 *ultra Northumberland*. Scotland would provide an exciting scenario; here Malcolm and Macbeth were contending for the Scottish crown, and there were spectacular cross-border invasions by the English (*Anglo-Saxon Chronicle*, ed. Swanton, p. 185). But in view of the events there (see note 12) it might be the Viking islands west or north are envisaged.

11 Easter, Whitsun and Christmas were the traditional seasons at which great lords held ceremonial receptions (cf. *Anglo-Saxon Chronicle*, ed. Swanton, p. 219).

12 The story of the half-human bear which engendered the king of Norway is found in the Old Norse *Hrólfs saga kraka*, ed. D. Slay (Copenhagen, 1960), pp. 54–61.

13 *in choris canebant*.

14 We know nothing of Alef; possibly the name is a version of Old Norse Olaf or Anlaf. Rough Scab (*Ulcus Ferreus*) might possibly, though less probably, mean Cruel Avenger; either way the intention is apparent.

15 The link between Cornwall and Ireland was a natural one at this date: the Atlantic seaways permitting ready access to all the western coasts of Britain; it provides the background to the Tristan and Iscult story.

16 Sihtric 'Silkenbeard' ruled a significant Scandinavian kingdom centred on Dublin (989–1042). The events alluded to here are brought forward to allow Hereward to take part.

17 The Duke of Munster (south-west Ireland) is modelled on the Irish high king Brian Boru. The subsequent battle in which Hereward is made to play a prominent part bears a close resemblance to the historical Battle of Clontarf, 1014, as retailed by contemporary Scandinavian and Irish story-tellers (*Brennu-Njáls Saga*, ed. E.O. Sveinsson, Íslenzk Fornrit XII [Reykjavík, 1954], pp. 449–53; *The War of the Gædhil with the Gaill*, ed. J.H. Todd, Rolls Series 48 [London, 1897], pp. 184–211). The battle was fought on Good Friday 1014 between the Irish and the viking Dubliners assisted by viking allies from England and Scotland; Brian was too old to take part in the battle, and stayed praying in his tent, but was sought out and slain by a party of Norsemen. Here Hereward himself is said to have killed him, though Brian's name is not mentioned.

18 Singing in trio (*tripliciter*) might refer either to the close harmony said to be characteristic of the Anglo-Danish inhabitants of England (Giraldus Cambrensis, *Opera*, ed. J.S. Brewer et al., Rolls Series 21 [London, 1861–91], VI, pp. 189–90), or a troubadour dialogue form in which a subject is proposed and different viewpoints expressed in alternate stanzas, or in refrain.

19 The route that took Hereward to Orkney might seem a heroic circum-navigation of Britain but was not unusual, and had the advantage of going via the western Isles of Scotland where he could anticipate a friendly reception from Scandinavian settlers; the Earl of Orkney had been an ally of Sihtric at the Battle of Clontarf (see note 17). Shipwreck would not be unexpected by the audience, in view of the notoriously tumultuous nature of the ocean there.

20 Flanders, that part of the continent of Europe closest to England, witnessed a constant flow of cross-Channel traffic, and provided a natural refuge for English exiles, including Earl Godwin and his family.

21 St Bertin was an abbey close to Saint-Omer (see note 26).

22 Manasar the Old was Count of Saint-Pol in the Pas-de-Calais, owing allegiance to the Count of Flanders.

23 Harold was a common enough name; it may be no coincidence that just a little earlier Harold Godwinson found himself in a similar plight: detained at the court of Duke William of Normandy and engaging in similar military exploits (graphically portrayed in the Bayeux Tapestry, D.M. Wilson (ed.), *The Bayeux Tapestry* [London, 1985], pp. 197–8, pls 6–26).

24 Baldwin V, Count of Flanders 1035–67, whose daughter had married Duke William of Normandy ('the Conqueror').

25 Guines lies in the Pas-de-Calais.

26 Saint-Omer lay on the Aa, upriver from what was then a broad estuary and natural point of entry to Flanders; those who found refuge there included Earl Tostig (see note 52) ousted in 1065, and Harold Godwinson's mother Gytha after the Battle of Hastings.

27 St Valery, at the mouth of the Somme, was where Harold Godwinson was detained by a vassal of William of Normandy, and from where William's invasion fleet set sail in 1066.

28 *Pictavem*, possibly an error; Poitiers seems a long way to have gone but would be well known as a venue for such tournaments.

29 Zeeland is a region of large islands lying off the northern coast of Flanders.

30 Robert was Baldwin's younger son and eventual heir, 1071–93; his Zeeland campaign probably took place in 1067.

31 The tactic of feigned retreat and sudden counter-attack was a common one; the same is reported of the Normans at Hastings.

32 The Flemish 'great horse' was a superior breed of medieval warhorse native to the Low Countries.

33 Forty-nine seems a curiously specific number; perhaps, as in Biblical usage, 7×7 is simply indicative of 'many'.

34 Brand was the last English abbot of Peterborough (1066–9). Local annals emphasize that he was 'rather a good man'; after an internal election he sought confirmation of his appointment not from William but Edgar Ætheling whom he expected to become king (*Anglo-Saxon Chronicle*, ed. Swanton, p. 199). A fourteenth-century Peterborough chronicle calls him Hereward's uncle (loc. cit. in Introduction, note 1).

35 The Feast of Saints Peter and Paul was celebrated on 29 June; the word 'nativity' refers to their martyrdom and thus birth into new life.

36 The English tradition of clerical investiture was eventually abolished by the Council at Westminster in 1102.

37 Ely was admirably suited for defence, cut off by swamps and a network of hidden waterways, routes through which were known only to local people. (See map, plate 4).

38 William ('the Conqueror'), Duke of Normandy, had ousted the last English king, Harold Godwinson, at the Battle of Hastings in 1066, to become William I. See Introduction, 'Historical Background', p. 12–13.

39 William de Warenne was a close friend of William: a Norman baron who had fought at Hastings, and before his death in 1088 amassed one of the largest personal estates in England; here he is called 'old' to distinguish him from his like-named son who died in 1138. Frederick, was in fact not brother but brother-in-law of William; he held large estates in Norfolk.

40 Now Baldwin VI, Count of Flanders, 1067–70.

41 Pynkenni lay on the Somme near Amiens; members of this family subsequently held land in Northamptonshire.

42 Brabant was an important province to the east of Flanders.

43 Hugo and his brother, here called Breton are later said to be Norman; such confusion was not uncommon in England. Few of Hereward's companions can be identified with any certainty in external records.

44 This Guthlac perhaps refers to the renowned leader of a local war-band who eventually became a hermit in the Fens in the early eighth century (*Anglo-Saxon Prose*, ed. M. Swanton, 2nd edn [London, 1993], pp. 88–113); a major cult-figure in the region, he had founded Crowland Abbey, where Hereward was reputed to lie buried (see note 87).

45 The forest of Brunneswold seems to have lain not close to Bourne, but on high land two dozen miles away, stretching over west Cambridgeshire into east Northamptonshire.

46 Wroxham Bridge crossed the River Bure in Norfolk.

47 For the 'Earl of Warwick', and confusion between Tostig and Morcar, see note 52 below.

48 At Lincoln the ancient Roman walls and gateway towers were still standing, and kept in repair.

49 For Earl Edwin see note 52.

50 Thurstan, a local man from Witchford, had been appointed Abbot of Ely by Harold Godwinson in 1066, and was thus unsympathetic to the Conqueror's cause. Eventually, when threatened with sequestration of the abbey's outside estates, he would 'adopt a more prudent plan', i.e., secretly surrender; many a present-day institutional executive will speak in similar terms. The *Liber Eliensis* (p. 189) claims the surrender was due to famine.

51 Bardney on the River Witham below Lincoln, and the site of an ancient Anglo-Saxon abbey, ruined by the Danes but still venerated and restored by Gilbert de Ghent (see note 9). For minor locations see map, plate 4.

52 Edwin and Morcar were sons of Earl Ælfgar of Mercia, and thus grandsons of Lady Godiva. Edwin succeeded his father as Earl of Mercia, while Morcar became Earl of Northumbria (not Warwick). They joined the Conqueror's court, but in 1071 'ran off and travelled variously in woods and open country, until Edwin was killed by his own men, and Morcar turned by ship to Ely' (*Anglo-Saxon Chronicle*, ed. Swanton, pp. 206–8). Tostig Godwinson had been Earl of Northumbria until displaced by Morcar in 1065. By now he was already dead, slain in 1066 fighting on behalf of invading Danes (and against Edwin and Morcar) at Stamford Bridge. Or Tostig may possibly be a confused reference to one of his nephews who bore the same name.

53 *Alrehede* (for *Alreheðe*), 'Landing-place by the Alders', the narrowest of any crossing and providing the most obvious route to Ely (see map, plate 4).

54 Ordgar is a common enough name at this time but is probably to be identified with that Ordgar who had held Fenland estates and the office of sheriff before the Conquest. Thurcytel 'the Lad' was presumably the son of Thurcytel of Harringworth, a large landowner in the neighbourhood, whose estates had come into the hands of Frederick, brother-in-law of William de Warenne.

55 The Isle of Ely (*æl-ge*, 'eel-district') formed a tract of fertile land some 12 by 10 miles, capable of supporting 600 households according to Bede, *Ecclesiastical History*, IV, 19.

56 *apud foveam de Reche*. Reach lies on the water at one end of a massive prehistoric linear defensive earthwork (the Devil's Dyke); it formed a natural point at which to control any transfer between land and water transport.

57 Sheriff Osbeorht is undocumented, but there was a mint official of the name at this time.

58 No external evidence for this Thurstan exists; the list of known priors begins only in about 1109.

59 The Danes had entered the Humber and were promoting general insurrection in the north of England, although the *Gesta* makes no mention of their mission to Ely. It would be more than a year before William could leave to sort out the threat of trouble in Normandy.

60 Ivo de Taillebois came from a Norman baronial family, and was now sheriff and owner of large estates in the neighbouring district of swampy Holland (see note 71), and reputedly hostile to the monks of Crowland (see note 80). No doubt the French name was sufficient for the audience to suspect evil intent.

61 The leader's use of disguise in order personally to enter the enemy camp is a familiar motif. During the twelfth century similar stories were being told of Alexander disguised as a beggar visiting, and misleading, the king of India, and of King Alfred spying on his viking enemies in the guise of a minstrel (*Three Old English Prose Texts*, ed. S. Rypins, EETS OS 161 [London, 1924], pp. 26–8; William of Malmesbury, *Gesta Regum*, ed. W. Stubbs, Rolls Series 90 [London, 1887–9], I, p. 126). The disguise used by Hereward of a door-to-door pot-salesman is subsequently told of Eustache the Monk, Robin Hood and William Wallace.

62 *Brandune*; Brandon on the Little Ouse was a convenient location from which to direct water-borne operations – and in any case belonged to the monks of Ely! Possibly, though less likely, this may refer to Brampton, a royal manor in west Cambridgeshire, convenient for hunting in Brunneswold.

63 This potter's cry is possibly the translation of a rhythmic vernacular advertising jingle, cf. H. Paul, *Grundriss der Germanischen Philologie*, 2nd edn (Strassburg, 1901–9), II, p. 1088.

64 The castle visualized seems to be of the contemporary earth-bank and stockade, motte-and-bailey kind graphically depicted in *The Bayeux Tapestry*, ed. Wilson, pp. 213–15, pls 21–3, 49–50), but there is no evidence for such a fort ever having been built at either Brandon or Brampton.

65 Scandinavian witches typically uttered such hostile incantations raised on a scaffold (Old Norse *seiðhjallr*); for an example specifically intended to influence the outcome of a battle see *Hrólfs saga kraka*, ed. Slay, p. 119.

66 This act also is characteristic of witches in the Scandinavian tradition, the intention apparently being to 'overlook' the enemy upside down through the legs, and thus reverse the situation appertaining (cf. *Vatnsdæla Saga*, ed. E.O. Sveinsson, Íslenzk Fornrit VIII [Reykjavík, 1939], pp. 69–70); it does not work!

67 Peat (dead sedge and moss) constitutes a notoriously treacherous land surface: impossibly soggy when wet but a combustible crust when dry.

68 Ralph Guader, son of Ralph the Staller (see note 5), fought on William's side at Hastings, and succeeded his father as Earl of Norfolk and Suffolk. The notorious wedding plot to oust William actually took place four years later in 1075 (*Anglo-Saxon Chronicle*, ed. Swanton, pp. 210–12), but is here put back. Having the earls (unhistorically) join Ralph allows our hero to stand alone as the sole focus of resistance. The inclusion of ballad fragments in the *Anglo-Saxon Chronicle* suggests that the wedding plot itself was a subject for contemporary story-tellers.

69 Witchford is about 2 miles from Ely; to say it was merely a 'furlong' (*unius stadii*, 200 yards) is an understandably dramatic exaggeration since, with the enemy now in control of the narrow neck of the Isle, further resistance was impossible.

70 There is only a single reference to (the king's) forest in Northamptonshire in Domesday Book, but it must have been significant.

71 The county of Holland, a low-lying region bordering the Wash, was only later incorporated into Lincolnshire. Here Ivo de Taillebois was sheriff and held many estates.

72 This trick of reversed horseshoes is repeated in the stories of Eustache the Monk and Fouke fitz Waryn. It is remotely reminiscent of the classical brigand Cacus dragging oxen into a cave backwards to avoid detection (Livy, I, 7).

73 On the death of Abbot Brand (see note 34), the Conqueror replaced him with the tyrannical Norman abbot of Malmesbury, Turold, declaring that 'since Turold behaved more like a soldier than

a monk, he would provide him with somebody to fight', – i.e., Hereward (William of Malmesbury, *De Gestis Pontificum*, ed. N.E.S.A. Hamilton, Rolls Series 52 [London, 1870], p. 420).

74 The sequence of historical events is changed for dramatic purposes; Hereward's actual looting of Peterborough, resented and resisted by the monks, had taken place some time prior to the arrival of Turold (*Anglo-Saxon Chronicle*, ed. Swanton, pp. 205–7). Here the incident is delayed and excused by having the ransomed Turold renege on his agreement with our hero.

75 The figure, not surprisingly, is that of the patron saint of Peterborough, St Peter, who was said to hold the key to heaven (Matthew 16:19).

76 The guidance of a benevolent wolf is familiar from the local cult of St Edmund (cf. *Anglo-Saxon Prose*, ed. Swanton, p. 161); see note 3.

77 Such bioluminescence is a mysterious but natural phenomenon characteristic of marsh land.

78 This incident anticipates later fabliau; and, being set in the context of a guild dinner (cf. *Anglo-Saxon Prose*, ed. Swanton, pp. 33–4), was no doubt additionally humorous in that such pompous and exclusive bourgeois goings-on should be disturbed.

79 The name Dolfin may refer to the semi-independent ruler of what is now Cumbria, although at this stage he was still alive, being expelled by William in 1092 (*Anglo-Saxon Chronicle*, ed. Swanton, p. 227).

80 Crowland was an ancient Fenland abbey founded by St Guthlac (see note 44).

81 The Conqueror had given a man of this name both Bourne and Hereward's known estates round about (see map, plate 4).

82 Robert de Horepole was presumably warden of Bedford castle, built or rebuilt shortly after the Conquest.

83 Robert Malet was heir to a Norman barony, and now a substantial landowner and sheriff in eastern England, holding 281 manors in nearby Suffolk alone. He took a prominent part in suppressing the rebellion of Ralph Guader (see note 68); here he was no doubt concerned to avenge the death of his father who had apparently died fighting in the Fens.

84 Leofric the Deacon was the compiler of the original manuscript on which our author drew and was perhaps the source of this account!

85 Rockingham Castle, Northamptonshire, recently built by William the Conqueror.

86 There is no evidence that Hereward regained Bourne or any of his actual former estates; but a man called Hereward held lands in Warwickshire at the time of William's death – and had held these before the Conquest. The surname Hereward survived in Ely through the thirteenth century (thus Robert Hereward, bailiff and seneschal of the Bishop of Ely *c.* 1296).

87 The pseudo-Ingulf says that Hereward was finally buried as he had wished with Turfrida at Crowland (loc. cit. in Introduction, note 8).

3. *EUSTACHE THE MONK*

Translation

1 Saint Samer is the Benedictine abbey founded by St Wulmer in the seventh century and located about 8 miles from Boulogne.

2 Black Monks or Benedictines, founded in about 530 by St Benedict.

3 The city of Toledo in Spain had the reputation of being the locale of a school for magicians and sorcerers. Basin de Gênes and Maugis d'Aigremont (see vv. 280–302) were reputed to have done their apprenticeship there.

4 There is an interesting word play on the rhyme:

Il n'ot jusqu'a Saint Jake
Qui tans seüst de dyodake

The word '*dyodake*' means 'zodiac' but there are possible allusions to the Devil in the root prefix 'dio' or to the god Dio-nysos/Bacchus.

5 For an explanation of the various kinds of divination and incantation, see Burgess, *Two Medieval Outlaws*, p. 79, n. 2.

6 The exact location of Montferrand is uncertain. It might be Montferrand (Aude) or Clermont Ferrand (Puy de Dôme), both of which are more or less on the pilgrimage route to Compostella.

7 For a discussion of coinage, see Burgess, *Two Medieval Outlaws*, p. 79, n. 3.

8 A very common form of profanity, swearing by the body parts of Jesus Christ: 'by the bowels, the brains, the teeth'. The name Jesus Christ itself was not spoken in order to avoid blasphemy.

9 Basin de Gênes and Maugis d'Aigrement were well-known sorcerers. They appear as important characters in several *chanson de geste*.

10 The swords and their bearers are: Joyeuse (Charlemagne), Courte (Ogier le Danois), Hauteclaire (Oliver) and Durendal (Roland); see Burgess, *Two Medieval Outlaws*, p. 79, n. 6.

11 In criminal cases trial by combat was usually fought in person by the accuser and accused, and they fought to the death. Burgess (*Two Medieval Outlaws*, p. 11) suggests that the two parties chose champions because of age (Hainfrois) and religious vocation (Eustache).

12 The death of Manesier requires comment. Conlon notes in his edition of the romance (p. 103, n. 371) that this is one of the rare occasions, if not the unique example, where the innocent party loses in a trial by combat. In the Middle Ages the judgement of God was considered infallible in determining a just cause.

13 By refusing to appear when summoned by the count, Eustache is outlawed.

14 Interjections by the narrator protesting the truth of what he is presenting ('*Che fu la fine verités*'/'And that's the honest truth'!) are to be taken with a grain of salt. Yet apart from the normal exaggerations in the folklore elements, which are to be expected in the romance genre, our author gives a remarkably accurate account of the historical events reported. He appears, for example, to have detailed familiarity with the *vavasseurs* (vassals of a vassal) of the Boulonnais region (see line 533, *et passim*). Almost without exception, the characters of the romance are historical personages.

15 Once a Benedictine or Black Monk, Eustache now disguises himself as a Cistercian or White Monk.

16 St Honoré or Honoratus of Amiens, d. *c.* 500, patron saint of bakers and confectioners. His feastday is on 16 May and the rue Saint-Honoré in Paris is named after him. Burgess identifies him as the English saint and archbishop of Canterbury (d. 653), but why would the Count of Boulogne swear by an English saint?

17 St Remi or Remigius, d. 530?, Bishop of Reims and apostle of the Franks. His feastday is on 1 October.

18 Enticing the enemy into the forest is one of the outlaws' favourite tricks.

19 By emphasizing that Eustache pays for the hay, the story-teller makes a point of the fact that, although an outlaw, he does not rob the poor.

20 The outlaw game of 'truth or consequences' is also seen in *Fouke fitz Waryn* and *A Gest of Robyn Hode*.

21 As Burgess explains (*Two Medieval Outlaws*, p. 80, n. 11), by returning one of the ten stolen horses, Eustache is paying a tithe (or one-tenth of his income) to the count.

22 St Omer, a seventh-century monk who founded a monastery in the Flemish city named for him.

23 The potter disguise is also seen in *Hereward* and *William Wallace*, as well as in the early 'ryme', *Robin Hood and the Potter*.

24 By hiding in a tree and imitating the song of the nightingale, Eustache is adopting a most unusual disguise, unparalleled in the other tales.

25 This bawdy scene with its blunt language and strong sexual content is reminiscent of the Old French fabliau.

26 To swear an oath on the Virgin Mary's bowels is blasphemous, to say the least.

27 The outlaws' enemies are often clerics.

28 Philip Augustus II, King of France (1180–1223), and Louis VIII, King of France (1223–6).

29 Reversing the horseshoes to confuse the pursuing enemy is also employed by Hereward and Fouke fitz Waryn.

30 The strong opposition of the vassals to their lord, the Count of Boulogne, regarding the fate of Eustache borders on outright rebellion. The narrative at this point appears to emphasize justice of the Monk's cause. The reprimand of Renaud de Dammartin by Walet de Coupelle (v. 1,696) may in fact represent the commentary on Renaud by his contemporaries.

31 The second instance of the game of 'truth or consequences', and this time the victim lies.

32 Eustache impersonates a knight of the military-religious Order of the Hospital of Saint John of Jerusalem or the Hospitallers, founded in about 1070.

33 King John appropriately swears by an English saint; St Edmund is the ninth-century king of East Anglia martyred by the vikings.

34 Burgess (*Two Medieval Outlaws*, p. 81, n. 17) dismisses the two readings of Francisque Michel (Godehire equals Anglo-Saxon 'good lord' and Vincenesel equals St Vincent and help) in favour of 'God is here' and 'Winchelsea'. For Eustache's connection with Winchelsea in East Sussex, see Burgess, *Two Medieval Outlaws*, pp. 19, 32–4, 38–9.

35 St Winape equals Winnocus, *c.* 717, monk of Wormhoudt, near Dunkirk. His feastday is on 6 November.

36 Verse 2, 112 reads '*Si fist a lui tenser. I. flue*'. Burgess translates the word '*flue*' as a 'floodtide'. Berger and Petit, translators of the romance into modern French, render the line: 'Eustache provoked a tidal wave in order to protect himself' (p. 187). If that is an accurate interpretation, we would thus have Eustache near the end of his career again demonstrating his magical powers. In that sense the narrative appears to come full circle with Eustache, the Devil's magician, just prior to his violent death, performing marvels similar to those described at the very outset of the narrative.

37 The name Mauferas equals *mal* plus *feras* ('You will do evil').

38 For identifications of these *chansons de geste*, see Burgess, *Two Medieval Outlaws*, p. 81, n. 24.

39 Conlon (p. 18) notes that the *Nef de Boulogne* may have been a prototype of warships of the fifteenth and sixteenth centuries. It was an impressively big ship built in the shape of a castle.

40 Eustache is one of two outlaws in this volume who was executed; the other is William Wallace.

4. *THE OUTLAW'S SONG OF TRAILBASTON*

Introduction

1 For the poem's date and the institution of the Trailbaston Statutes, see Aspin, *Anglo-Norman Political Songs*, pp. 67–8. For the poem's scribe, his manuscripts and the date of his copying *Trailbaston*, see Ker, *Facsimile of BM MS Harley 2253*; Hathaway et al, *Fouke le Fitz Waryn*; and articles by Revard (1979, 1981, 1982a, 1982b, 1985).

2 Wright/Coss (*Political Songs of England*, pp. 383–5) reproduces the original Statutes of Trailbaston and (p. 273ff.) part of the royalist *Chronique de Piers Langtoft*, which approves the new *Trailbaston* courts. See also John Taylor, *English Historical Literature in the Fourteenth Century* (Oxford, 1987).

3 Vivid details are given by J.R. Maddicott (1975, 1978, 1986). The actual cases of 1305–6 in Hereford, heard before the Trailbaston judges named in the poem (Spigurnel et al.), can be studied in London, PRO JUST 1/306. Presumably one of these cases was that of the protagonist of *The Outlaw's Song of Trailbaston*: they include cases on the rolls for Delivery of Gaol, Fines and Redemptions, Indictments and *Querelas*.

4 Ker, *Facsimile of MS Harley 2253*; Hathaway et al, *Fouke le Fitz Waryn;* Revard, 1979, 1981, 1982a,b, 1985, 1997.

5 The charter, identified by the present writer in July 1988 as in the hand of the scribe of Harley MS 2253, is now Shropshire Record Office 5075/42. It is a quitclaim in form of letters patent dated from Richard's Castle on 8 March 1347, recording the release by John Talbot, lord of Richard's Castle, to Philip de Chenne of Ludlow, of all his rights in a *platea* of enclosed ground in Ludford Field.

6 A Thomas de Billebury, probably related to the chamberlain William de Billebury, was chaplain of the Virgin Mary in the parish Church of St Bartholomew in Richard's Castle from about 1316. The forty-one legal documents in the hand of the scribe of Harley MS *2253* show a pattern of names, dates and places that seem to point to their scribe's serving as parish clerk in the vicinity of Richard's Castle.

7 'G.E.C.', *The Complete Peerage* 9, 256–66, 'Mortimer of Richard's Castle', and 12, 606–32, 'Talbot of Credenhill' and 'Talbot of Richard's Castle'. For the marriage of Hugh and Maud, see John C. Parsons, *The Court and Household of Eleanor of Castile in 1290* (Toronto, 1977), pp. 16, 126–7 and notes 51, 194.

8 'Mortimer of Richard's Castle' (*Complete Peerage* 9,256–66); and see 'Billebury' in indices to the Calendars of Patent, Fine and Close Rolls for the years 1304–16. William of Billebury, after receiving his pardon for the events of 1304–5, continued to live in the lordship of Richard's Castle – at least, documents show a man of that name was active to 1341, when he was a juror on the *Inquisitione post mortem* of Joan, elder daughter and coheiress of Maud Mortimer of Richard's Castle.

9 Ker, *Facsimile of BM MS Harley 2253*, pp. xx–xxiii. Belregard is named among the manors of Trim handed over to Roger Mortimer, second Earl of March, by his grandmother Joan in 1354.

10 Revard, 1982b.

11 Edward II and Edward III had feed retainers called *histriones*: professional reciters/dramatic performers.

12 In medieval times the Man in the Moon was identified as Cain: see R.J. Menner, 'The Man in the Moon and Hedging', *Journal of English and Germanic Philology* 48.1 (1949), 1–14, and Carleton Brown, *English Lyrics of the XIIIth Century* (Oxford, Clarendon Press, 1932), pp. 160–1, 234–5.

13 See G.L. Harriss, *King, Parliament and Public Finance in Medieval England to 1369*, for an account of the crisis of 1339–41.

14 Anthony Verduyn, 'The Politics of Law and Order During the Early Years of Edward III', *English Historical Review* 108 (1993), pp. 842–67; see especially p. 866.

15 John Bellamy's account of the Coterel gang (*English Historical Review* 79, 1964), and E.L.G. Stones's account of the Folvilles (*Transactions of the Royal Historical Society*, 5th Series, 7 (1957), pp. 117–36), show how interwoven the criminal, the military and the royal administrative operations of ruthless men could be.

Translation

1 The poet calls this '*le bois de Belregard*' (l. 9) or '*vert bois de Belregard*' (l. 54). Literally, '*Belregard*' means 'Beautiful View', and commentators have followed Aspin (*Anglo-Norman Political Songs*, 1953, p. 77) by assuming it is, as she puts it, 'a fancy name, no doubt, chosen to support the alleged attractions of a life under the greenwood tree'. As pointed out above, however (Introduction, note 9), an Irish manor called Belregard did exist in the lordship of Trim, and would have been known to retainers of the noble families in the Ludlow area including servitors of the Mortimers of Wigmore, Mortimers of Richard's Castle, and county magnates including the Ludlows of Stokesay and Cheneys of Cheney Longville, one of whose retainers may have been the composer of the *Song of Trailbaston*. Since the scribe of the poem used fragments of an account-roll for a large household made during a visit (before 1314) to Trim and its manors, it is quite plausible that the poem's composer, once outlawed by Trailbaston judges during a sessions in Hereford or Ludlow, fled to Ireland and waited on the manor of Belregard for the royal pardon which eventually came.

2 Line 27 in French reads, '*Mes ore ne me sai je point cheuisaunce fere*'; Aspin translates, 'but now I do not know how to make a living'. In Chaucer's *Shipman's Tale* a French merchant obtains a loan to buy goods he can then sell for a profit, and '*chevisaunce*' is the term for this loan. So I have translated '*cheuisaunce fere*' as 'raise the funds'. Perhaps it should be 'float a loan'.

3 The outlaw's threat of violence is just the kind of behaviour the Trailbaston judges were sent to investigate and punish: see, for instance, Bellamy (1964) and Stones (1957). What we hear in the poem (see note 8 below) is in fact this outlaw's unintended self-indictment: he does here precisely what he was accused of doing, threatens judges so they will pardon an outlaw. He also implies that before his indictment he hung out with a gang of archers in the woods (stanza 22), associated with clerics and may himself have been one (stanza 15), and had considerable knowledge of the law, a hint that he might himself have been a 'chaplain' or parson with sufficient legal training to preside in, say, a manor court, to 'hear a reeve's reckoning' as Langland's Parson Sloth does – the same Parson Sloth

who also knows 'rymes of Robyn Hode' better than his Breviary. His self-portrait could be that of a literate manorial official, the sort of man who raked in his lord's taxes while extorting all he could from those under his jurisdiction: someone rather like the Devil disguised as Bailiff Itinerant in Chaucer's *Friar's Tale*.

4 A member of the clergy who was brought before secular justices could plead that as a cleric he must be tried in an ecclesiastical court. The outlaw here appeals to the kind of legally trained clergyman (sometimes, perhaps, a baronial chaplain) who might ride along with a gang, descend on a manor to loot its tenants, drive off its livestock and perhaps poach its game: accusations against such chaplains and parsons in the early fourteenth century, when this poem was composed and being circulated, are common in the *Calendar of Patent Rolls* for the period.

5 French '*Uncore attendroy grace*' refers to royal pardon as by the king's grace. On the Trailbaston Rolls for this period, many men found guilty and sentenced to hang, or outlawed under sentence of death, were actually granted reprieve and allowed to go as soldiers to kill abroad rather than at home. An 'X' would be put beside their names – a 'king's X', literally, with a note that their crimes were being pardoned because of good service to the king.

6 These lines clearly refer to gangs of expert bowmen with shady reputations who were actually living in the woods. It seems that the tales of Robin Hood had a basis in historical reality.

7 'Conspiracy' was indeed exactly the crime of which many of those who were brought before the Trailbaston judges were accused. It referred to the fact that members of a local power élite would conspire to 'fix' the outcomes of legal cases, and to bully, beat or bribe the jurors and judges into letting the conspirators have their way 'legally', often to extort money or obtain lands illegally.

8 Does the outlaw give himself away here as actually having killed someone, pleading in effect that he never meant to do it, that it was manslaughter or self-defence? The French lines read: '*Unqe ne fu homicide, certes a moun voler,/ Ne mal robberes pur gent damager*', hinting that whatever the outlaw did, it was either inadvertent ('The guy just up and died after I bashed him!'), or legal purveying or dues collecting, not armed robbery. It sounds rather like what the manor-lord's bailiff might say: 'I was merely collecting what they owed, and had to get rough before they'd pay up!' Elsewhere in the manuscript the scribe has copied a Middle English poem whose speaker is a manorial tenant who is protesting bitterly against such brutal and extortionate gathering of money and foodstuffs by the baronial and royal bailiffs: see Maddicott (1986) and Turville-Petre (1996) for discussions of this and other such protests.

5. *FOUKE FITZ WARYN*

Introduction

1 E.J. Hathaway, et al., pp. xlvii–li.

2 Hathaway, xxxviii, xliv.

3 Hathaway, p. xli.

4 Hathaway, p. xxi.

5 Hathaway, p. x.

6 Eric Hobsbawm, *Bandits* (New York, Delacorte Press, 1969), p. 35.

7 Ingrid Benecke, *Der gute Outlaw* (Tübingen, Max Niemeyer, 1973), p. 157.

8 Harry Rothwell (ed.), *English Historical Documents 1189–1327* (New York, Oxford University Press, 1975), p. 317.

9 Hathaway, p. xv.

10 A.P. D'Entreves (ed.), *Aquinas: Selected Political Writings* (Oxford, Basil Blackwell, 1948), p. xxx.

11. John Stevens, *Medieval Romance: Themes and Approaches* (New York, W.W. Norton and Company, 1974), pp. 97–8.

12 John Block Friedman, *The Monstrous Races in Medieval Art and Thought* (Cambridge, Massachusetts, Harvard University Press, 1981), pp. 5–8.

13 Friedman, p. 15.

Translation

1 The springtime opening is a commonplace in many medieval romances.

2 It is tempting to identify the patron of the work as one of the descendants of the hero Fouke III – a prime candidate would be Fouke VII, who succeeded Fouke VI in 1336. Given the numerous historical errors and omissions, however, it is unlikely, as Sidney Painter warns us, that the author had access to the Whittington documents. Carter Revard (in a personal communication) concludes that 'the prose redaction may well have been made for a household connected with the Fitz Warins in some fashion, but that household seems unlikely to have been at Whittington, or even a household anywhere whose clerks could inspect the Fitz Warin archival documents'. See also note 36.

3 William the Conqueror (Duke William II of Normandy, King William I of England) was born in 1027 or 1028, and he was the bastard son of Robert I, Duke of Normandy, and Herleve, the daughter of the tanner Fulbert. See David C. Douglas, *William the Conqueror: The Norman Impact upon England* (Berkeley and Los Angeles, University of California Press, 1964).

4 Harold II, King of England, 5 January to 14 October 1066.

5 As Hathaway et al. (*Fouke le fitz Waryn*, note p. 63), Owain was active around 1120 during the reign of King Henry II, and not at the time of the Norman Conquest. The author has confused him with Gruffydd ap Llewelyn, who raided the Normans along the Welsh border from 1055 to 1063. See also Burgess, *Two Medieval Outlaws*, p. 184.

6 Chester (Cheshire), the old Roman walled city, stands on the River Dee, near the Welsh border. Mount Gilbert, located south of Wellington, is one of the highest hills in Shropshire.

7 William made only one visit to Wales in 1081 (Hathaway et al., *Fouke le fitz Waryn*, p. 63).

8 William bestowed Shrewsbury and the surrounding county to his kinsmen, Roger de Montgomery, creating him Earl of Shrewsbury, Chichester and Arundel.

9 Hathaway identifies the abbey as Holy Cross Abbey in Shrewsbury (p. 133).

10 Located 20 miles south-east of Shrewsbury, the borough and market town received its name from a bridge over the River Severn. The castle was built or enlarged by Montgomery's son, Robert de Bellême.

11 The castle and town of Dynan have been identified as the borough, market town and parish of Ludlow, located 29 miles (south by east) from Shrewsbury. Given its proximity to Wales, the castle was maintained for the defence of the Welsh March.

12 Pembroke is the county town of Pembrokeshire, Wales.

13 William II Rufus, King of England, 1089–1100.

14 Hathaway et al., *Fouke le fitz Waryn*, mistakenly assert that the application of the name Dynan to Ludlow is a fabrication. As Carter Revard points out, legal documents in the hand of the scribe of *Fouke le fitz Waryn* (now in the Shropshire Record Office in Shrewsbury) show that in the thirteenth and fourteenth centuries the area of Ludlow adjacent to its castle was called Dynan.

15 Castell Bran, or the Old Border, is identified by Hathaway et al. (*Fouke le fitz Waryn*, p. 66) with the fortification of Castell Dinas Bran, near Llangollen.

16 This passage is drawn from Book I, Chapter 16 of Geoffrey of Monmouth's *Historia Regnum Britanniae* (*c.* 1136), in which the Welsh author recounts the legendary origins of Britain.

17 King Bran has been identified both with Bran, son of Dyfnwal Moelmud, in Geoffrey of Monmouth (Book II, 17 and Book III, 1) and with the myth of Bran the Blessed, the Celtic sea deity, in the second branch of the *Mabinogi*. See Hathaway et al., *Fouke le fitz Waryn*, p. 66, and Burgess, *Two Medieval Outlaws*, p. 185.

18 As Hathaway et al. note (*Fouke le fitz Waryn*, p. x), the battle between Payn Peverel and the giant Geomagog was probably inspired by the wrestling match between Coryneus and Geomagog in Geoffrey of Monmouth (Book I, 16).

19 The verse prophecy preserves part of the lost thirteenth-century romance. The Wolf is Fouke fitz Waryn III, who will drive away the Wild Boar (Morys of Powys) from Blaunche Launde (Whittington). The Leopard is an allusion to King John. See Hathaway et al., *Fouke le fitz Waryn*, p. 68, and Burgess, *Two Medieval Outlaws*, p. 185. The wolf is a fitting epithet for Fouke III because 'wolf's head' was a common synonym for an outlaw. See also note 91.

20 In order to pacify the Welsh March, William I settled Norman knights in various strategic strongholds: the Fitz Alans at Oswestry, Waryn de Metz at Alberbury and the Peverels at Whittington. As Hathaway et al. (*Fouke le fitz Waryn*, p. x), these land grants were actually made half a century later in the reign of Henry II.

21 The unnamed knight is Waryn de Metz.

22 William I died on 9 September 1087, and he was succeeded by his middle son, William II Rufus, who was killed in a hunting accident in New Forest in 1100. He was succeeded by his younger brother Henry I, who ruled from 1100 to 1135. The eldest brother, Duke Robert, who was passed over in the line of succession, invaded England from Normandy and was captured and imprisoned for the rest of his life.

23 Hathaway et al. (*Fouke le fitz Waryn*, p. 69) identify William Peverel with the Peverels of Dover and Bourn in Cambridgeshire. See also Burgess, *Two Medieval Outlaws*, p. 186, n. 9.

24 All of the places named are located in north-west Shropshire (Salop).

25 Whittington (Shropshire) is located 3 miles (east-south-east) from Oswestry.

26 Ellesmere (Shropshire) is located 16 miles (north-north-west) from Shrewsbury.

27 The River Ceirog is a tributary of the River Dee.

28 William II Peverel actually had four sisters (Hathaway et al., *Fouke le fitz Waryn*, p. 70).

29 Yervard has been identified with the Welsh prince, Iorwerth Goch or 'Red Edward', brother of Madog ap Meredith (Hathaway et al., *Fouke le fitz Waryn*, pp. 72, 81; see also Burgess, *Two Medieval Outlaws*, p. 186).

30 Guy has been identified as Guy fitz Candelou (Hathaway et al., *Fouke le fitz Waryn*, p. 73).

31 Joce de Dynan, Lord of Ludlow, was a royal vassal of King Henry II.

32 Walter de Lacy died in 1241, so he could not have taken part in the feud. The author means Gilbert de Lacy (Hathaway et al., *Fouke le fitz Waryn*, p. 73).

33 Champ Geneste (Bromfield, Shropshire) is 3 miles (north-west by west) from Ludlow.

34 8 August. In *A Gest of Robyn Hode*, Robin begs leave of King Edward to return to his chapel, dedicated to Mary Magdalene, in Barnsdale.

35 The Anglo-Norman of the original reads *jour d'amour*, which, as Hathaway et al. note (*Fouke le fitz Waryn*, note p. 77), is a mistranslation of Middle English *love-day*, a day for settling disputes by arbitration.

36 There is a blank space in the manuscript left for the name of the bishop, but it was never filled in. Hathaway et al. (*Fouke le fitz Waryn*, p. 77) list four bishops of Hereford between the Conquest and the death of Fouke II in 1197. This omission supports the claim by Sidney Painter and Carter Revard that the author of the prose redaction did not have access to the Whittington documents. See also note 2.

37 Identified by Hathaway et al. (*Fouke le fitz Waryn*, p. 77) as the seaport, Hartland, Devonshire.

38 See note 29.

39 As Hathaway et al. note (*Fouke le fitz Waryn*, p. 83), it is likely that Fouke was knighted by King Henry at this point in the story because he is referred to as Sir Fouke hereafter.

40 According to Hathaway et al. (*Fouke le fitz Waryn*, p. 83), the office of constable was actually held by Fouke VI at the time the manuscript was written.

41 Alveston (Gloucestershire) is located 3 miles (south by east) from Thornbury.

42 The dispossession of Whittington is one of the main causes of Fouke III's rebellion and outlawry in the second half of the romance.

43 Hathaway et al. (*Fouke le fitz Waryn*, p. 83) note that the presence of Fouke III in the court of Henry II is a 'flight of fancy'.

44 Although there is no evidence that Baldwin and the Fitz Waryns were related by blood, his name does appear on a royal pardon, dated November 1203 (Hathaway et al., *Fouke le fitz Waryn*, p. 85).

45 The granting of Whittington to Morys is one of the direct causes of Fouke III's outlawry.

46 Alberbury (Shropshire) is 8 miles west of Shrewsbury. Some remains survive of the castle and abbey built by Fouke fitz Waryn.

47 Audulph de Bracy is described elsewhere as Fouke's outlawed cousin, who accompanied him in exile to Brittany (Hathaway et al., *Fouke le fitz Waryn*, p. 86).

48 Emmeline de Higford, aunt of Fouke III, was the granddaughter of Waryn de Metz, not his daughter (Hathaway et al., *Fouke le fitz Waryn*, p. 86).

49 Babbins Wood is located near Whittington (Hathaway et al., *Fouke le fitz Waryn*, p. 128).

50 Braydon Forest is located in Wiltshire, near Fouke's holdings at Ashdown and Lambourn (Hathaway et al., *Fouke le fitz Waryn*, p. 87).

51 The game of truth or consequences occurs in two other outlaw tales: *Eustache the Monk* and *A Gest of Robyn Hode*.

52 For another cloth-measuring scene, see part one of *A Gest of Robyn Hode* in which Little John measures out the cloth for Sir Richard with his bow stave.

53 A William Malveysyn is listed among those who were pardoned in 1203 (Hathaway et al., *Fouke le fitz Waryn*, p. 88).

54 The scene in which the outlaws confront the porter at a locked gate occurs also in *Gamelyn* and *Adam Bell*.

55 Disguise as a monk occurs in three other outlaw tales: *The Deeds of Hereward, Eustache the Monk* and *The Acts and Deeds of William Wallace*.

56 Hubert Walter was archbishop of Canterbury from 1193 to 1205.

57 As Hathaway et al. note (*Fouke le fitz Waryn*, p. 89), Hubert Walter's brother Theobald was never surnamed *le Botiler*, but his son William adopted the name in 1221.

58 Assuming the name of a notorious outlaw, real or imaginary, appears to have been common practice. Accused of causing a riot and threatening violence at a fair in Willenhall in 1498, Roger Marshall of Wednesbury used the alias Robyn Hood (J.C. Holt, *Robin Hood* [1989], pp. 148–9).

59 The trick of reversing horseshoes to confuse the pursuers occurs also in *The Deeds of Hereward* and *Eustache the Monk*, but, interestingly, not in Robin Hood's story.

60 John de Rampaigne, in taking service with the enemy, closely resembles Little John in *A Gest of Robyn Hode* when he enters the service of the Sheriff of Nottingham disguised as Reynold Greenleaf.

61 The mocking of a disguised outlaw also appears in *The Deeds of Hereward* (chapt 23) and in *William Wallace*.

62 Porkington is Brogyntyn in Shropshire.

63 According to Hathaway et al. (*Fouke le fitz Waryn*, p. 90), 'Morys was dead before August 1, 1200, hence before the date (May 1201) usually assigned to Fouke's outlawry'.

64 Sir Lewys is Llewelyn the Great, Prince of Gwynedd, 1199–1240. His wife, Joan, was the daughter of King John, not Henry II. The marriage actually took place in 1204, long after the events related here (Hathaway et al., *Fouke le fitz Waryn*, p. 84, and Burgess, *Two Medieval Outlaws*, p. 187, n. 18).

65 The premature granting of a royal pardon is also seen in *Adam Bell*, when the king pardons the three outlaws only to discover that they had murdered the justice, sheriff and mayor of Carlisle.

66 According to Hathaway et al. (*Fouke le fitz Waryn*, p. 92), 'John was not at Shrewsbury until January 1209, long after his pardon of Fouke.'

67 Ford of Gymele equals Ffordd Gam Elen (Hathaway et al., *Fouke le fitz Waryn*, p. 93).

68 The remains of the castle are on the summit of a steep rock. Audley is located 5 miles north-west of Newcastle under Lyme in Staffordshire.

69 Sir Thomas Corbet (d. 1273) was the eldest son of Robert Corbet, Baron of Caus.

70 While attending a wedding feast in Ireland, Hereward (chapt 5) displays considerable musical skill as a harpist.

71 Pembridge is the Marcher castle on the River Monnow, 5 miles north of Monmouth (Hathaway et al. (*Fouke le fitz Waryn*, p. 94).

72 Hathaway et al. (*Fouke le fitz Waryn*, p. 94) identify the Maiden's Well as a tributary of the River Dee, located west of Llangollen.

73 A common Welsh place name was 'stone by the stream' (Hathaway et al., *Fouke le fitz Waryn*, p. 128).

74 Philip II Augustus, King of France, 1165–1223.

75 St Denis was the third-century bishop of Paris, martyr and patron saint of France.

76 This section begins three 'fairy tale' episodes: Fouke rescues seven damsels from the clutches of an old hag and her seven sons; Fouke sails round seven islands and encounters many marvels, including a serpent; and Fouke rescues a damsel by killing a dragon.

77 St Clement was the second-century bishop of Rome and martyr. He was drowned when his persecutors tied an anchor to his neck and threw him in the sea.

78 William I occasionally resided in Windsor (Berkshire), laid out its extensive parks, and enlarged the boundaries of the adjoining forest for his hunting pleasure. King John lived in Windsor Castle during his conflict with the barons.

79 The scene in which Fouke disguises himself as a collier or charcoal burner bears comparison with a similar episode in *Eustache the Monk*. Both King John and the Count of Boulogne are hunting in a forest; both Fouke and Eustache exchange clothing with a collier; and both greet their adversaries in disguise. While Fouke entices the king deeper into the forest with the promise of a long-antlered stag, Eustache sends the count to the real collier who is wearing his clothing. Eustache then trades the collier's clothing with a potter, further confusing the count.

80 This scene closely resembles the episode in *A Gest of Robyn Hode* when Little John, disguised as Reynold Greenleaf, entices the Sheriff of Nottingham into the forest with the promise of a fair hart and 140 deer. When the sheriff foolishly follows Little John, he is confronted by Robin Hood, the master hart, and his seven score men.

81 The parallels with *A Gest of Robyn Hode* continue when King John, like the Sheriff of Nottingham, first swears an oath not to harm Fouke and then breaks his promise.

82 Ralph de Blundeville, third Earl of Chester (1172–1232), was one of the barons who opposed King John during the Barons' Wars of 1215–16. He is listed as one of the 'venerable fathers' of *Magna Carta* (1216). Caught between Fouke, who is described as his cousin, and King John, he plays the role of conciliator by protesting Sir James of Normandy's charge that Fouke is a traitor and by urging Fouke to seek the king's peace. After his pardon, Fouke accompanies the earl to Ireland where, as the earl's champion, he defeats a giant.

83 In a strikingly close scene in *A Gest of Robyn Hode*, when Little John is wounded by an arrow, he begs Robin to cut off his head, and Robin, like Fouke, refuses.

84 Island of Beteloye. Another fairy tale episode begins.

85 John de Rampaigne's disguise as a Greek merchant allows him to infiltrate King John's court in London, to ascertain the whereabouts of Fouke's brother William, and to rescue him. Taking service with the enemy in disguise is a common theme in outlaw tales. In *A Gest of Robyn Hode*, Little John, disguised as the archer Reynold Greenleaf, takes service with the sheriff and later robs him.

86 Once stretching from the Wiltshire border to the coast, New Forest was created by William the Conqueror.

87 No explanation is given for the sudden royal pardon, but King John, according to Naomi D. Hurnard, 'granted a considerable number of pardons', some of which manifested 'the *voluntas regis* untrammelled by counsel or administrative formalities'. (*The King's Pardon for Homicide before AD 1307* [Oxford, Clarendon Press, 1969; rpr. 1997], pp. 35, 215.) The most likely explanation is that King John granted the pardon in exchange for military service, and Fouke's service in Ireland with the Earl of Chester seems to bear this out.

88 Another fairy tale episode.

89 Outlaws, as a condition of their royal pardon, were often required to 'expiate the slaying by some kind of religious penance rather than secular punishment' (Naomi D. Hurnard, pp. 35–6). The penance could take the form of entering a monastery, going on a crusade or pilgrimage, or, in Fouke's

case, founding a priory or church. At the end of *A Gest of Robyn Hode*, Robin begs leave of King Edward to visit the chapel he built in Barnsdale. See also note 46.

90 Visions or divine signs are common in outlaw tales. In *The Deeds of Hereward*, after Hereward plunders the abbey at Peterborough, he has a vision of an old man who warns him to return the possessions of the church. In *A Gest of Robyn Hode* Robin interprets the repayment of his loan by a monk of St Mary's Abbey as a miracle of the Virgin. William Wallace has a vision of an old man, who hands him a sword and takes him up to a mountain top where he sees a fire engulf Scotland.

91 This is the second of two verse prophecies derived from the lost thirteenth-century romance. The prophecy relates that the earlier prophecy has been fulfilled – the Wolf (Fouke III) has successfully driven the Leopard (King John) from his ancestral home. Both prophecies were either inspired by or derived from the *Libellus Merlini* (c. 1135), which Geoffrey of Monmouth incorporated into Book VII of the *Historia Regnum Britanniae*. See also note 19.

6. *THE TALE OF GAMELYN*

Introduction

1 Knight and Ohlgren, *Robin Hood and Other Outlaw Tales*, pp. 184–226.

2 F. Lindner, 'The Tale of Gamelyn,' *Englische Studien* 2 (1879), 94–114, 321–43, see pp. 112–13.

3 W.W. Skeat, *The Tale of Gamelyn* (Oxford, Clarendon Press, 1884), see p. vii.

4 Maurice Keen, *The Outlaws of Medieval Legend*, see p. 78; J.C. Holt, *Robin Hood*, see p. 71.

5 C.W. Dunn, 'Romances Derived from English Legend', in *Manual of Writings in Middle English, 1050–1500*, Fasc. 1, *Romances*, ed. J.B. Severs (1967), pp. 17–37, see p. 32.

6 R. Kaeuper, 'An Historian's Reading of *The Tale of Gamelyn*', *Medium Ævum* 52 (1983), 51–62; John Scattergood, '*The Tale of Gamelyn*: The Noble Robber as Provincial Hero', in *Readings in Medieval English Romance*, ed. Carol M. Meale (Cambridge, Brewer, 1994), pp. 159–94.

Translation

1 The original reads 'Lithes and listneth and harkeneth aright'. It is a triple imperative asking the audience to quiet down and listen to the story that follows.

2 In the manuscript the name is spelled 'Bonndes', but it is probably to be read as 'Boundes', meaning 'of the boundary' or 'of the territory'.

3 Since Sir John acquired most of his property during his lifetime, he held it in *purchas* or fee simple. As a result, he was entitled to divide it equally among his three sons, although this was against the standard practice of primogeniture.

4 Making an oath or asseveration to God, the Virgin or a saint is a common feature of these poems. Martin of Tours (d. 397) was a Roman calvary officer who divided his cloak with a beggar, had a vision of Christ and was converted to Christianity.

5 His inheritance of land from his father seems to contradict his prior claim, see note 3. A plough-measure is the amount of land that could be ploughed by eight oxen.

6 Sir John acquired part of his land in exchange for his military service.

7 To handle one's beard is a sign of male adolescence.

8 Donald Sands (ed.), *Middle English Verse Romances* (p.160), translates the line: 'dare to be the one to beat me'.

9 A pestle is a large club-shaped tool used for pounding food.

10 The poet is using euphemism or rhetorical understatement: to play is to fight.

11 A buckler is a small round shield worn or carried on the arm.

12 Probably St Richard of Chichester (Richard de Wych, 1197–1253). Perhaps an ironic parallel to Gamelyn, who, like the saint, worked on a farm as a youth.

13 Donald Sands (ed.), *Middle English Verse Romances* (p. 161), notes that 'with his mouth' means 'with deception', i.e., not with his heart.

14 A franklin ranked next below the knight and esquire. Chaucer's Frankeleyn is a prosperous landowner and country gentleman, an early type of the English country squire.

15 The idiom means something like 'as I live and breathe!'.

16 The idiom means something like 'if my eyes don't deceive me'.

17 It was customary to wash one's hands before and after eating.

18 Parodying religious language: Gamelyn is threatening to beat the clerics who have been invited to the banquet.

19 More parody of religious language. Gamelyn is beating the clerics with a wooden stave.

20 The idiom describes, perhaps, a bad hangover.

21 A proverbial expression: the nest is Sir John's manor house, the eggs are the escaped outlaws.

22 The outlaw is a metaphorical wolf, a beast to be hunted down and killed by the community. To grow the wolf's head (*genere caput lupinum*) was a legal synonym for outlawry.

23 An idiom meaning that Sir John was not able to bribe the jury this time.

7. THE SAGA OF ÁN BOW-BENDER

Introduction

1 Unless in quotations all Icelandic words and names will be given according to modern Icelandic practice. All translations from Icelandic and other languages are mine.

2 Carl Christian Rafn (ed.), *Fornaldar sögur Nordrlanda, eptir gömlum handritum* (3 vols, Copenhagen, 1829–30), vol. 2, pp. 323–62.

3 Guðni Jónsson (ed.), *Fornaldar sögur Norðurlanda* (4 vols, [Akureyri], 1954), vol. 2, pp. 365–403.

4 Ólafur Halldórsson (ed.), *Áns rímur bogsveigis* (Íslenzkar miðaldarímur 2, Stofnun Árna Magnússonar á Íslandi, Rit 4, Reykjavík, 1973), p. 74.

5 For a list see Torfi H. Tulinius, *La 'Matière du Nord': Sagas légendaires et fiction dans la littérature Islandaise en prose du XIIIe siècle* (voix germaniques, Paris, 1995), pp. 17–18. Tulinius argues that the surviving *fornaldar sögur* tell us more about the concerns of their thirteenth and fourteenth century composers and audiences in Iceland than they do about pre-ninth-century Scandinavia (pp. 161–8).

6 On the sources of *Áns saga* and its literary background, see Shaun F.D. Hughes, 'The Literary Antecedents of Áns saga bogsveigis', *Mediæval Scandinavia* 9 (1976), 198–235.

7 For the argument that these sagas constitute a 'tradition' and not a genre see Elizabeth Ashman Rowe, '"Fabulæ í þeim bestu sögum": Studies in the Genre of the Medieval Icelandic Mytho-heroic Saga' (unpublished dissertation, Cornell University, 1989), pp. 102–8.

8 Henry Goddard Leach, 'Outlaws', *American-Scandinavian Review* 4 (Nov.–Dec., 1916), p. 354.

9 Henry Goddard Leach, *Angevin Britain and Scandinavia* (Harvard Studies in Comparative Literature 6, Cambridge, 1921; repr. Milwood, New York, 1975), pp. 335–55.

10 Leach, *Angevin Britain and Scandinavia*, p. 342.

11 Leach, *Angevin Britain and Scandinavia*, p. 351.

12 The medieval English outlaw tradition has been thoroughly studied by Richard Howard Baum, 'The Medieval Outlaw: A Study in Protest' (unpublished dissertation, University of Utah, 1972), Ingrid Benecke, *Der gute Outlaw* and Maurice Keen, *The Outlaws of Medieval England*. Brief overviews in English of Icelandic outlaw traditions are Gabriel Turville-Petre, 'Outlawry', *Sjötíu ritgerðir helgaðar Jakobi Benediktssyni 20 júlí 1977*, eds Einar G. Pétursson and Jónas Kristjánsson (2 vols, Stofnun Árna Magnússonar á Íslandi, Rit 12, Reykjavík, 1977), vol. 2, pp. 769–78 and Frederic Amory, 'The Medieval Icelandic Outlaw: Life-Style, Saga, and Legend', *From Sagas to Society: Comparative Approaches to Early Iceland*, ed. Gísli Pálsson (Enfield Lock, 1992), pp. 189–203.

13 On the Ano Sagittarius episode in the *Gesta Danorum*, see Hughes, 'Literary Antecedents', pp. 202–7, 227–8. Ano is an aristocratic retainer and in Saxo there is no sign of the man happier as a farmer than a warrior, and who is in fact opposed to all royal authority.

14 Joost de Lange, *The Relation and Development of English and Icelandic Outlaw Traditions* (Nederlandsche Bijdragen op het Gebied van germaansche Philologie en Linguistiek 6, Haarlem, 1935), pp. 122–3.

15 De Lange, *Relation and Development*, pp. 130–1.

16 Jan Spoelstra, *De Vogelvrijen in de Ijslandse Letterkunde* (Nederlandsche Bijdragen op het Gebied van germaansche Philologie en Linguistiek 10, Haarlem, 1938), pp. 83–93.

17 Benecke, *Der gute Outlaw*, p. 6.

18 Benecke, *Der gute Outlaw*, pp. 132, 147–8.

19 Hughes, 'Literary Antecedents', p. 221.

20 After Iceland's loss of independence to Norway in 1262, for each of the four quarters of the country a *sýslumaður* ('sheriff' or 'bailiff') was appointed by the king. The office comes into existence too late to affect the medieval narratives, but it does play a role in the post-medieval Icelandic outlaw tradition. In the early centuries of foreign rule in Iceland, the king's representative was the *hirðstjóri* or governor. In 1361 the *hirðstjóri*, Smiður Andrésson, travelled to the north of Iceland, declared some of the most important farmers in the region outlaws, and indicated his intention to execute them. Smiður and his men were attacked by people of the district one evening when lodging at a farmstead and killed. An episode such as this may have given rise to the writing of the saga of Án bogsveigir in the form that we now have it.

21 Torfi Tulinius, *La 'Matière du Nord'*, pp. 58, 226–30.

22 Gísli Sigurðsson, 'Methodologies for the Study of the Oral in Medieval Iceland', in Hildegard L.C. Tristram (ed.), *Medieval Insular Literature between the Oral and the Written II: Continuity of Transmission* (ScriptOralia 97, Tübingen, 1997), p. 184.

23 The first to make a connection between the *rímur* and the *Gest* was Sir William A. Craigie, *Sýnisbók íslenzkra rímna frá upphafi rímnakveðskapar til loka nítjándu aldar* (Anthology of Icelandic *rímur* from

the beginning of the composition of *rímur* until the end of the nineteenth century) (3 vols, London and Reykjavík, 1952), vol. 1, pp. xvi, 285 (English translation). David Colbert, *The Birth of the Ballad: The Scandinavian Medieval Genre* (Skrifter udgivna av Svenskt Visarkiv 10, Stockholm, 1989), pp. 61–2, does not consider the *Gest* a ballad but a genre analogous to the *rímur*.

24 Dobson and Taylor, *Rymes of Robin Hood*, p. 8.

25 Knight and Ohlgren, *Robin Hood and Other Outlaw Tales*, pp. 7–8, 82–4. See also Stephen Knight, *Robin Hood: A Complete Study of the English Outlaw*, p. 74.

26 [R.] Barrie Dobson and John Taylor, '"Rymes of Robyn Hood": The Early Ballads and the Gest', in Kevin Carpenter, *Robin Hood: Die vielen Gesichter des edlen Räubers / The Many Faces of that Celebrated English Outlaw* (Oldenburg, 1995), p. 39.

27 David C. Fowler, *A Literary History of the Popular Ballad* (Durham, 1968), pp. 79–80; Knight, *Robin Hood*, p. 48; Knight and Ohlgren, *Robin Hood and Other Outlaw Tales*, p. 82.

28 Knight, *Robin Hood*, p. 71.

29 Knight, *Robin Hood*, pp. 80–1; James C. Holt, 'Robin Hood: The Origins of the Legend', in Carpenter, *Robin Hood*, p. 34; Dobson and Taylor, '"Rymes of Robyn Hood"', pp. 40–4; Dobson and Taylor, *Rymes of Robin Hood*, pp. xxxiv–xxxvi, 10–11; Knight and Ohlgren, *Robin Hood and Other Outlaw Tales*, pp. 81–2.

30 On the Icelandic ballads see Vésteinn Ólason, *The Traditional Ballads of Iceland: Historical Studies* (Stofnun Árna Magnússonar á Íslandi, Rit 22, Reykjavík, 1982).

31 Stanzas 12, 108, 119, 128, 152, 178, 205, 249, 265, 269, 299, 317, 340, 369, 383, 392, 396 in Dobson and Taylor, *Rymes of Robin Hood*.

32 Knight, *Robin Hood*, p. 72.

Translation

1 *Áns saga* was first translated into Latin by Þormóður Torfason (Torfæus) in his *Historia rerum Norvegicarum* (4 vols, Copenhagen, 1711), vol. 1, pp. 323–37, based on a slightly different recension of the saga than that printed by Rafn. Erik Julius Björner reprinted Torfæus's Latin version in his *Nordiska Kämper Dater* (Stockholm, 1735), separate foliation and pagination, thirty-five pages, accompanied by a Swedish translation and an Icelandic prose text. From time to time the Swedish translation adds details from other unidentified sources (Shaun F.D. Hughes, 'Áns rímur bogsveigis: Two Nineteenth Century Icelandic Metrical Romances' [unpublished dissertation, University of Washington, 1972], pp. 68, 76, 79–80). The Icelandic text in Björner's edition is a prose rendering of a lost version of *Áns rímur* but one which ultimately derives from the version of the poem found in the youngest of the three vellum manuscripts.

An earlier version of the present translation appeared in Hughes, 'Áns rímur bogsveigis', pp. 32–80, 219–22. Elizabeth Ashman Rowe translated the saga as Appendix B to '"Fabulæ í þeim bestu sögum"', pp. 206–32, and Willard Larsen privately published his translation as *The Saga of Aun the Bow-bender* in 1995.

2 The region (*fylki*) over which Ólafur and Ingjaldur ruled is Naumdælafylki, the region of Naumudalur, on the west coast of Norway, in modern Nord-Trøndelag.

3 The district of Firðir is in the central west coast of Norway in modern Nordfjord in Sogn og Fjørdane.

4 In *Egils saga-Grímssonar*, Arnviður, earl of Vermaland (Värmland in Sweden), has among his retainers two brothers called Úlfur, both of whom Egill kills when they try to ambush him in the Forest of Eiðaskógur.

5 In *Ketils saga hængs*, Ketill receives his appellative or nickname by killing an outlaw called Hængur. But the name is derived from hór (pot hook), and a jack salmon is called 'hængur' because of the shape of its lower jaw (Anthony Faulkes (ed.), *Two Icelandic Stories. Hreiðars þáttr. Órms þáttr* [Viking Society for Northern Research, Text Series 4, London, n.d.], p. 94).

6 Hamar is in the southern part of modern Hedmark on the east shore of Lake Mjøsa.

7 Pronounced 'own' as in 'town'.

8 In *Grettis saga Ásmundarsonar*, and *Orms þáttur Stórólfssonar*, Grettir and Ormur are both problem children like Án, although not 'male Cinderellas'. This is in contrast to the youthful sloth of Ketill 'the Jack-Salmon'. Ketill will later kill the loutish giant Surtur who will taunt him with being a *kolbítur* (cinder-eater). The common motif of the unpromising hero who is first lazy (Inger M. Boberg, *Motif-Index of Early Icelandic Literature* [Bibliotheca Arnamagnæana 27, Copenhagen, 1966], Motif L 114.1), and a hearthdweller or 'male Cinderella', i.e. a kolbítur (Boberg, *Motif-Index*, Motif L131), is frequently encountered in all genres of saga writing (see the list of occurrences in Boberg, *Motif-Index*, p. 189).

9 This episode is also found in *Ketils saga hængs*. Helga Reuschel, *Untersuchungen über Stoff und Stil der Fornaldarsaga* (Bausteine zur Volkskunde und Religions-wissenschaft 7, Bühl-Baden, 1933) p. 108, claims that this detail has been taken from *Áns saga* and inserted into *Ketils saga* in order to strengthen the relationship between the two sagas. But it might just as easily be the other way around.

10 The narrative detail of a young hero who has strained relations with his father, but is much beloved by his mother is also attributed to Grettir Ásmundarson.

11 Án's name is the basis for a series of puns in the text which have not been literally translated.

12 Reuschel, *Untersuchungen*, p. 58, points out that this phrase seems to have been taken from *Egils saga Skalla-Grímssonar*, chapter 57, where Egill is made an outlaw throughout all of Norway. As a *fylkiskonungur* (regional king), Ingjaldur does not have the authority to declare anyone an outlaw outside his own district.

13 A *kenning* (metaphor) for woman.

14 This is an allusion to Drífa, one of the meanings of whose name is 'snowfall'. Snowfall in calm weather ('logn') is called 'logndrífa' and in the verse the second element of this word is omitted, but the meaning of the line is parallel to line four, something like: 'From where are you coming, Drífa?'

15 The footpad ('stigamaður') is not exactly an outlaw, but someone who has taken himself to the margins of society. In *Hallfreðar saga Vandræðaskálds*, Hallfreður Óttarson kills the *stigamaður*, Önundur, in an encounter which is likely to have been the model for the description of the altercation between Án and Garan. In *Vatnsdæla saga*, Þorsteinn the son of Ketill 'oaf' and grandson of Án, kills the *stigamaður* Jökull Ingimundarson.

16 The 'hired killer' ('flugumaður') in thirteenth-century Iceland was an 'assassin-outlaw', someone who had been outlawed but who then sought out the protection of a powerful chieftain in return for carrying out assassination raids against the chieftain's enemies (Amory, 'Medieval Icelandic Outlaw', pp. 200–2).

17 The region of Upplönd comprises modern Oppland and Hedmark.

18 Two more puns which have only been approximately translated.

8. *A GEST OF ROBYN HODE*

Introduction

1 The standard source for the Robin Hood ballads is still volume three of Francis Child's *The English and Scottish Popular Ballads* (New York, The Folklore Press, 1957; repr., New York, Dover, 1965). For newly edited versions of twenty-four of the ballads, see Knight and Ohlgren (eds), *Robin Hood and Other Outlaw Tales*.

2 For more detailed treatments of these printed texts, see Child III, 39; Dobson and Taylor, *Rymes of Robin Hood*, pp. 71–4.

3 D.C. Fowler, *A Literary History of the Popular Ballad* (Durham, Duke University Press, 1968), p. 18. See also above, pp. 191–3.

4 The argument for a fifteenth-century copy text rests on the presence of some textual deficiencies and misprints in the extant printed versions; for a discussion, see Child, *The English and Scottish Popular Ballads*, p. 40.

5 See Thomas H. Ohlgren, 'Edwardus redivivus in *A Gest of Robyn Hode*', *Journal of English and Germanic Philology*, forthcoming.

6 It is not possible to ascertain the manipulation of the copy text by the sixteenth-century compositor, but we can assume that the compositor exercised some freedom in changing spelling and word order as well as in adding or omitting material.

7 Rodney H. Hilton, 'The Origins of Robin Hood', pp. 221–35 in *Peasants, Knights and Heretics: Studies in Medieval English Social History* (Cambridge University Press, 1976). Maurice Keen, in *The Outlaws of Medieval Legend*, initially agreed with Hilton on the audience of the Robin Hood poems, but he recanted his argument in the introduction (pp. xiii–xxi) to the revised paperback edition published by Routledge in 1987.

8 J.C. Holt, *Robin Hood*, pp. 109–58.

9 Dobson and Taylor, *Rymes of Robyn Hood*, p. 35.

10 A.R. Myers (ed.), *English Historical Documents 1327–1485* (New York, Oxford University Press, 1969), p. 929.

11 Mildred Campbell, *The English Yeoman in the Tudor and Early Stuart Age* (New York, Augustus M. Kelley, 1968), p. 39.

12 All citations to Chaucer are from *The Riverside Chaucer*, ed. Larry D. Benson (Boston, Houghton Mifflin), 1987.

13 See Sylvia L. Thrupp, *The Merchant Class of Medieval London 1300–1500* (Chicago, University of Chicago Press, 1948), pp. 76–80.

14 Martin Seliger, *Ideology and Politics* (London, 1976), p. 11.

15 Simon Schama, *Landscape and Memory* (New York, Vintage Books, 1996), p. 140.

16 Michael Nerlich, *Ideology of Adventure: Studies in Modern Consciousness 1100–1750*, tr. Ruth Crowley, (2 vols, Minneapolis, University of Minnesota Press, 1987), vol. 1, pp. 60–9.

17 For a representative sample of guild charters and ordinances, see William Herbert, *The History of the Twelve Great Livery Companies of London* (2 vols, London, published by the author, 1836–7; repr., New York, Augustus M. Kelley, 1968). See the notes for specific examples.

Translation

1 The status terms 'gentlemen' and 'yeomen' were used interchangeably in the early fifteenth century. 'Yeomen' denotes a broad social rank below knights and squires, including a small landowning farmer, an attendant, servant or lesser official in a royal or noble household, and even a tradesman, artificer, merchant and citizen (Middle English *yoman*, perhaps contraction of *yongman*).

2 Although the term 'outlaw' was generally applied to anyone who had committed a serious crime, such as robbery or murder, it had a more restricted legal meaning as well – those felons who refused to appear in court once summoned. The word is English in origin (Old English *utlaga*, from Old Norse *útlagi*).

3 Barnsdale has been identified as a tract of land in the West Riding of Yorkshire. As J.C. Holt notes, however, there was no forest or chase and he speculates that the three major locations of the legend – Barnsdale, Sherwood Forest and Nottingham – are all confused. The *Gest* clearly links Barnsdale with named places in the West Riding of Yorkshire. It does not mention Sherwood Forest in Nottinghamshire, but does set part of the story in Nottingham. See also note 9.

4 By refusing to eat until some unusual event occurs, Robin Hood is imitating the behaviour of royalty. In *Sir Gawain and the Green Knight*, for instance, King Arthur will not eat until he has been told of some adventurous thing, an unusual tale or some major marvel.

5 Reaching its height in Western Europe in the eleventh and twelfth centuries, the Marian cult is one of the major features of Roman Catholicism. Robin's devotion to the Virgin underlies one of the major episodes in the poem – the loan of £400 to Sir Richard at the Lee and its 'miraculous' repayment by a monk of St Mary's Abbey.

6 Robin Hood displays the chivalric ideal of protecting women, an obligation previously the preserve of knighthood: 'Wolde he never do compani harme/ That any woman was in'. In Sir Thomas Malory's *Le Morte D'Arthur* (Book III, Chapter XV), King Arthur decrees 'to do ladies, damosels, and gentlewomen succour, upon pain of death'.

7 In the early ballads Robin's outlaw activities are directed primarily at corrupt civil and ecclesiastical officials at the shire level. While some of his crimes, such as deer poaching, are capital offences, he is a loyal subject of the king.

8 The 'Saylis' and 'Watling Street' (actually Ermine Street) are located in Barnsdale, in the West Riding of Yorkshire.

9 The knight is later identified as Sir Richard at the Lee. He comes from 'Verysdale', which is probably the hamlet of Lee in Wyresdale in Lancashire.

10 Blyth and Doncaster are located on the main road south of the Barnsdale region.

11 Hand washing before a meal was a custom of civilized behaviour, reflecting yet again the influence of courtly romances on the *Gest*.

12 Robin bases his decision to rob his victims on how truthful they are. When victims are stopped on the road and waylaid into the forest, they are asked to answer truthfully how much money they are carrying. If they tell the truth – as does Sir Richard – they are allowed to keep their money, but if they lie – as the high cellarer of St Mary's Abbey later does – then they are robbed. This game of truth or consequences is also seen in *Eustache the Monk* and in *Fouke fitz Waryn*.

13 In a Parliamentary writ, dated 1278, Edward I ordered all sheriffs in England 'to distrain [compel] without delay all those of your bailiwick who have lands worth twenty pounds a year, or one whole knight's fee worth twenty pounds a year, and hold of us in chief and ought to be knights but

are not, to receive from us before Christmas or on that feast the arms of a knight' (Rothwell, *English Historical Documents* III, 413).

14 Because his son killed a knight and his squire in a joust, Sir Richard was forced to borrow £400 from the Abbot of St Mary's in York in order to obtain a pardon for his son.

15 When Robin asks for a guarantor for the loan of £400, the knight replies that he has none other than 'our dere Lady', who, because of his devotion to the Virgin, Robin readily accepts. The loan to Sir Richard and its miraculous repayment is one of the central episodes in the poem.

16 As the poem makes clear, the original colour of the outlaws' liveries is scarlet, not green. Robin is playing the role of a merchant when he orders Little John to measure out 3 yards of cloth for Sir Richard's new livery. Little John proceeds to measure the cloth with his bow stave, which is some 67 inches in length instead of the standard measure of a yard. Concerned about this display of excess and temper, Much the Miller's son accuses Little John of being a Devil's draper. There are other references to mercantile activities in the poem, which may suggest that the intended audience consisted of members of the urban gilds, such as the Drapers' Company and the Merchant Taylors.

17 York is located about 30 miles north of Barnsdale.

18 The Prior of St Mary's Abbey apparently has privileged information concerning the whereabouts of Sir Richard when he says he will be unable to repay the loan on time because he is 'ferre beyonde the see'. Previous scholars have assumed that he has been on a crusade or pilgrimage, but the mention of 'symple weeds' need not indicate a religious journey. Indeed, as I have argued elsewhere, the evidence suggests that Sir Richard was on a military campaign in France at the beginning of the Hundred Years War.

19 Probably St Richard of Chichester (Richard de Wych, 1197–1253).

20 Another reference to Sir Richard's recent return from abroad.

21 The predatory abbot has hired or retained the justice, or professional lawyer, to help him bankrupt the knight. The phrase *cloth and fee* refers to the payment of money and clothing for legal services.

22 Verysdale. See note 9.

23 Sir Richard's ability to raise and equip one hundred archers suggests that he served as a recruiting agent or purveyor for the crown, which was a lucrative business in times of war. This would explain how he was able to raise the £400 in order to repay the loan to Robin Hood.

24 As the poem suggests, wrestling was considered a yeoman sport. Chaucer's Miller 'at wrastlynge he wolde have alwey the ram'.

25 The usual prize for a wrestling match was a ram: in this contest, however, the victor wins a bull, a saddled horse, a pair of gloves, a gold ring and a cask of wine.

26 The frequent wars in Scotland and France in the fourteenth century necessitated that the populace practise archery on a regular basis. As a result, archery competitions were held on holidays and feast days throughout the country by royal order of Edward III. The sheriff is using the shooting match to identify the local talent and to recruit the best archers for eventual military service. Shooting at 'wands' or sticks stuck in the ground was the hardest challenge for any archer in the ballads; Little John split the stick each time.

27 When Little John wins the archery contest, the sheriff offers to retain his services for an annual fee. Since he has already been retained by Sir Richard, he is not permitted to change masters until

the sheriff receives the knight's permission. Because Little John has been outlawed, he uses the alias Reynold Greenleaf. In part 5 the poet treats Reynold as a separate character, perhaps forgetting that he previously used it as Little John's alias. See note 41.

28 When Little John says that he will be the worst servant the sheriff has ever seen, he is playing the role of the 'bad servant', a role he also plays when he recklessly miss measures the cloth at the end of part 1.

29 By offering the cook an annual fee and two changes of livery, Little John is retaining the services of the cook.

30 The green hart, with his herd of seven score deer, is an ironic reference to Robin Hood, the *mayster-herte* and his men. Their sharp antlers, of course, are their arrows.

31 The sheriff has become Robin's 'apprentice', which continues the mercantile theme.

32 Because the knight stopped to help the yeoman at the wrestling match, he is late for his appointment with Robin Hood, and Robin is impatiently waiting to be repaid the money he loaned to the knight. Robin's impatience, bordering on obsession, is further evidence of the mercantile theme.

33 This is another example of the strife between Little John and Robin Hood. Whenever Robin gives John a direct order, such as counting out the £400 for Sir Richard or measuring the cloth, John loses his temper. Their discord may be explained by the fact that Robin is the 'master', while John is the 'fellow' or, to continue the mercantile theme, the 'apprentice'.

34 Another reference to the custom of hand washing, see note 11.

35 Again Robin is preoccupied with being repaid the money loaned to the knight.

36 This is another example of the game of truth or consequences, and this time the monk lies that he has only twenty marks.

37 Robin's questions seem to be pointless because he surely knows that the knight recovered his land from the abbot of St Mary's.

38 In addition to repaying the loan of £400, Sir Richard offers a gift of twenty marks 'for your courtesy'. Because it was illegal to charge interest, 'gifts' were a way to avoid the charge of usury.

39 The 'trysting' tree is a tree in the forest, such as the Major Oak in Sherwood, selected by the outlaws as their place of rendezvous. The term originally designated a hunting station.

40 Butts are mounds (usually artificial) marking the limits of a shooting range.

41 When the sheriff retained Little John after the archery contest, John adopts the alias of Reynold Greenleaf. Here, however, Reynold appears as a separate character and a member of the outlaw band. This inconsistency may be the result of the fifteenth-century author's attempt to compile materials from different sources. See also note 27.

42 Saint Quentin or Quintinus was a Roman who went to Gaul as a missionary with St Lucian of Beauvais. He was so successful in preaching that he was arrested, imprisoned and tortured by prefect Rictiovarus, and later beheaded at Veromanduorum, now Saint-Quentin, a town in northern France. It seems odd that Sir Richard swears an oath on a minor French martyr and saint. The only reasonable explanation is that while abroad he was stationed in or near the French town, which was in fact the site of the first encounter between King Edward III and King Philip VI in September 1339.

43 When Sir Richard offers sanctuary to Robin Hood, he is of course breaking the law by maintaining the outlaws. The crime of maintenance involves giving favour and support to felons.

44 Three Edwards reigned in succession from 1272 to 1377: Edward I, 1272–1307; Edward II, 1307–27; Edward III, 1327–77. For evidence that the king is Edward III, see the introduction.

45 Helen Phillips (1988, p. 8) confirms Child's identification (III, pp. 54–5) of Plompton Park as a royal hunting preserve in Inglewood Forest in Cumberland, which is also the setting of *Adam Bell*.

46 The *Gest* is largely silent about the harsh forest laws of the twelfth and thirteenth centuries that protected 'vert' and 'venison'. Trespasses on 'vert', mainly cutting wood for fuel, are not mentioned at all. Offences against 'venison' are however numerous, but King Edward, who goes to investigate the disappearance of his deer, ends up pardoning Robin Hood. See also Knight and Ohlgren, *Robin Hood and Other Outlaw Tales*, pp. 164–5.

47 The phrase, 'the best ball in the hood', refers to the head, and may reflect games in which the ball was originally a human head.

48 The episode of King Edward meeting Robin Hood in the forest represents the story-type known as the 'King and the Subject', in which a subject of lower rank meets the king, usually in disguise and unrecognized, and after talking, drinking and eating, the king finally reveals himself and the subject is rewarded or pardoned.

49 Another instance of the 'game' of truth or consequences. See note 12.

50 A 'targe' is the king's private or privy seal.

51 The rose garland is a wreath of flowers used as the target.

52 Gilbert Whitehand is mentioned for the first time at the beginning of part 5.

53 Who can forget the famous recognition scene in the 1938 film, *The Adventures of Robin Hood*, when Errol Flynn recognizes King Richard the Lion Heart (played by Ian Hunter)?

54 Robin again plays the role of cloth merchant, selling 33 yards of green cloth to the king.

55 The outlaws' liveries are now described as Lincoln green in colour, whereas they were scarlet in colour at the beginning of the poem. This inconsistency can be explained by the fact that the poem represents a compilation of pre-existing materials, now mainly lost.

56 The procession on horseback from Sherwood to Nottingham resembles the gild 'ridings' in which gild members, dressed in their liveries, welcomed and escorted visiting dignitaries, including the king, into London. While riding on horseback, Robin and King Edward play another shooting game, called 'pluck buffet', in which the person missing the designated target receives a 'pluck' or blow.

57 After living at court for fifteen months, Robin exhausts all of his financial resources through excessive generosity, which borders on prodigality. Consequently, all of Robin's retainers, whom he was maintaining, leave except for Little John and Will Scarlock. Robin's wasteful extravagance becomes the chief cause of his outlawry in the later tradition of Richard Grafton's *Chronicle at Large* (1569), Anthony Munday's *The Downfall of Robert, Earle of Huntington* (1598), and Martin Parker's *A True Tale of Robin Hood* (1632).

58 The choice of this name can hardly be an accident – Mary Magdalene is a type of the converted sinner. She is popularly associated with the repentant and reformed prostitute who washed Christ's feet in Luke 7:36–50 and with the woman who witnessed Christ's resurrection.

59 The location of the nunnery has been identified with Kirklee or Kirkley abbey, 4 miles north of Huddersfield, Yorkshire.

60 Sir Roger of Doncaster (the earlier 'Donkesly' is probably a scribal error) is also called Red Roger in the mid-seventeenth-century ballad, *The Death of Robin Hood*. Although its printed version is late in

date, it preserves an earlier ballad dating from the mid-fifteenth century. It offers some details not included in the cryptic six verses in the *Gest*: after Robin's cousin, the prioress, drains his blood with surgical knives, Robin weakly blows his horn three times, summoning Little John. Robin then attempts to climb out of the window, but is stabbed through the side by Red Roger. Mortally wounded, Robin kills Red Roger. Robin then instructs Little John to bury him where his last arrow hits the ground.

9. *ADAM BELL, CLIM OF THE CLOUGH AND WILLIAM OF CLOUDESLEY*

Introduction

1 For an account of the early appearances of the name 'Robin Hood', and their possible resonances, see Stephen Knight, *Robin Hood*, pp. 22–36.

2 Francis James Child (III, pp. 34–9) edits *The Second Part of Adam Bell* as an Appendix to *Adam Bell*. Child declares the *Second Part* 'a pure manufacture, with no root in tradition, and . . . an absurd extravaganza besides'. Despite its early date and broad familiarity, Child disdains the ballad's lack of 'authenticity'. It is not included in the now definitive collection of earlier outlaw materials, Knight and Ohlgren, *Robin Hood and Other Outlaw Tales*.

3 For an edition with commentary of *Robin Hood's Birth*, see Knight and Ohlgren, *Robin Hood and Other Outlaw Tales*, pp. 527–40.

4 For an edition with commentary of *Robin Hood and the Monk*, see Knight and Ohlgren, *Robin Hood and Other Outlaw Tales*, pp. 31–56. This is one of only two Robin Hood ballads to survive in manuscript. Its early date (1450 or after) and its close similarity to *Adam Bell* in plot, suggest that the fundamental pattern for the outlaw story became fully established in the late fifteenth and early sixteenth centuries.

5 In contrast, Robin Hood's desire to go to Nottingham in *Robin Hood and the Monk* stems from his devotion to the Virgin Mary, as well as from a falling out with Little John.

6 For particularized accounts of the activities of medieval outlaw gangs – including what seems imitation of legendary outlaw practice and recruitment to royal service – see J.G. Bellamy, 'The Coterel Gang: an Anatomy of a Band of Fourteenth-century Criminals', *English Historical Review* 79 (1964), pp. 698–717 and E.L.G. Stones, 'The Folvilles of Ashby-Folville, Leicestershire, and their Associates in Crime, 1326–1347', *Transactions of the Royal Historical Society*, 5th series, 77 (1957), 117–36.

7 For the comments of More, together with other early reactions to outlaw material, see the Appendix of historical allusions in Knight, *Robin Hood*.

Translation

1 The original reads 'Englysshe-wood', which most scholars identify as Inglewood Forest in Cumberland. According to Francis Child, it was 16 miles in length, stretching from Carlisle to Penrith (III, pp. 21–2). Inglewood Forest was also identified as one of the haunts of Robin Hood in Andrew of Wyntoun's *Orygynale Chronicle* (*c.* 1420). See Knight and Ohlgren, *Robin Hood and Other Outlaw Tales*, p. 24. Inglewood Forest is also the setting for a large group of Gawain romances; see *Sir Gawain: Eleven Romances and Tales*, ed. Thomas Hahn, Kalamazoo, Michigan, Medieval Institute Publications, 1995.

2 Carlisle is the principal town of Cumberland. It is located on the border between England and Scotland, 302 miles (north-north-west) from London, and owing to its location it was the site of many border sieges and battles. As *Adam Bell* makes clear, it is a walled city with three gates. The setting of both outlaw stories and popular Arthurian romances in Carlisle suggest the symbolic importance of this locale at the edge of England, since such narratives regularly entail the crossing of borders that separate not simply physical geography and national territories, but other categories central to these ballads, such as law and lawlessness, popular and élite, and oral and written. Carlisle in this way serves as the symbolic centre for many popular romances (see *Sir Gawain: Eleven Romances and Tales*, above).

3 The justice or *iusticia regis* was a royal agent who handled the pleas of the crown. The position was created to weaken the power of the Norman sheriff, who was often corrupt.

4 Alice's cry of 'treason' – whether directed at the old woman, or at the Justice and the Sheriff – points up the contradictions and complications that pervade outlaw narratives: from the strict perspective of the law, it would be treasonous not to report William's appearance, or to seek his arrest, yet the narrator invites the audience to identify with William, so that his pursuers appear to be the traitors.

5 This entire episode – the outlaw besieged in his home with his wife and then burnt out – resembles two of the most memorable events in the thirteenth-century Icelandic outlaw tale, *Njals saga*.

6 Like the *Gest of Robyn Hode*, the poem is divided into parts or 'fitts'. The word 'fitt' may be related to a weaver's term 'the thread with which weavers mark off a day's work' (*OED*).

7 Adam brings forth a writ – an inscribed parchment – that can pass as an official document prepared in the King's court. Such 'letters' (whether genuine, stolen or counterfeited) were frequently used to swindle or coerce ordinary citizens and minor officials in the later Middle Ages.

8 Presenting a document that seemed official – possessing a seal of some kind, and perhaps written in Latin – was often sufficient evidence to compel compliance from those not acquainted with the law; even if the porter could read English, the apparatus of the courts (or its look-alike) would be enough to intimidate him, Adam surmises. The contrast sets those who are cowed by the very symbols of the law against those who literally take the law into their own hands.

9 The consistent use of the first-person plural possessive, 'our king', underscores the outlaws' fundamental allegiance to the monarch and central authority, even as they attack and subvert the powers of local officials.

10 When Adam Bell promises to be the worst porter that Carlisle has ever seen, he is playing the role of the 'bad servant', a popular theme also seen in *A Gest of Robyn Hode* when Little John steals the sheriff's silver.

11 The ballad clearly suggests that hostility to the outlaws is not confined to the local officials (justice, sheriff, mayor), but is shared by the citizens of Carlisle, who energetically join in the attack on Adam and his associates. A fundamental feature of noble outlaw stories is the support for the outlaws by the local community, for without such support those outside the law could hardly survive, let alone become heroes (Hobsbawm, *Bandits* [New York, Delacorte Press, 1969]). The mutual enmity here between the criminals and the townspeople is therefore somewhat unusual.

12 The term 'trysting tree' originally designated a hunting station, but here means meeting place.

13 The action seems unclear here: Alice obviously has not witnessed the events in Carlisle, and she wishes either to find out from Adam and Clim what happened to William, or to inform them (erroneously) that William is dead. Within the plot, her ignorance becomes the pretext for the reunion of the family within the forest, away from the ordinary precincts of domesticity in the city.

14 Adam's point is that William need not even mention his gratitude; any sworn brother would do the same, as William himself had declared in the midst of the fight in Carlisle.

15 The King's court was the court of highest authority and final appeal; there are many instances of medieval criminals – those who had been outlawed by local or lower courts – obtaining the king's pardon for their misdeeds. Many of these were repeat felons, and the revoking of their outlaw status seems often to have been an effort to recruit their power of intimidation to the side of official justice. The ease and expediency endemic in such procedures made the distinction between outlaws and officials – the point in dispute here between William and the porter – difficult for medieval people to maintain.

16 The outlaws make the gesture of fealty – holding out their hands to be clasped in their lord's hands – traditionally associated with feudal subordination and service. Here, as throughout the story, they acknowledge the authority of the king as lord of the realm, even as they oppose (and overthrow and sometimes even kill) corrupt local officials and bureaucratic structures.

17 In taking deer in the forest, the outlaws have openly transgressed against the king's authority, since from the times of William the Conqueror uncultivated forest had been declared the king's own land. It is striking that the ballad presents this violation of the king's personal domain as more important than the killing of his officials.

18 Since every English monarch from Edward I to Henry VI married a foreign bride, it is not possible to identify the queen in the poem.

19 The king's explicit equation of the worth of the outlaws' lives and three 'market towns' underscores the usual conflict in such stories between life and property; the queen here intervenes to preserve life, whose value the king can think to measure only in terms of real estate and revenue.

20 The queen asks that the king render his favour to her and his pardon to the outlaws effective by speaking the words out loud; the fate of the outlaws remains in jeopardy until the king pronounces the words, and lets them 'feel comfort'. Once the king speaks his words and grants the outlaws pardon, he cannot take them back. This technicality becomes crucial as the episode develops, since the king must stay true to his word and let them go free even after he discovers they have killed hundreds of his officials and retainers. Manipulation of spoken oaths and legal rituals is a staple of outlaw stories, as, for example, in *Njals saga*.

21 The border country of the north – epitomized here by Inglewood Forest and Carlisle – was a source of trouble to English kings, and their territorial and national claims, from the time of William the Conqueror; William Wallace (*Braveheart*) is merely one in a string of Scots champions who challenged royal authority externally. The activities of Adam, Clim and William were manifestations of internal resistance to central governmental control in England.

22 In archery, the 'prick' is the mark aimed at in shooting, i.e., the bull's-eye.

23 William Cloudesley uses a 'bearyng arow' or flight arrow (long and thin) as opposed to a 'brode arow' or broad arrow, used in shorter range archery.

24 As Francis Child points out (III, pp. 16–21), the story of shooting an apple off the boy's head was related in seven versions in Germanic and Norse literature, including the early thirteenth-

century *Gesta Danorum* by Saxo Grammaticus and the mid-thirteenth-century Icelandic saga of *Dietrich of Bern*. There are variants in many other cultures. The best-known retelling is of course the story of the Swiss William Tell.

25 Improbable as William's unsolicited offer – to put his own child's life in danger – may seem, the king's reaction seems even more curious: rather than apprise William of possible charges of maiming or manslaughter, he informs William that he will hold him to his word on pain of his life. As in the earlier scene in court, the spoken word becomes the bond by which men live or die; the exchange of words between men (rather than the content, intentions or implications of the words) itself becomes the substance of heroic action.

26 The king's response to William's prowess – this man's too dangerously skillful to be anywhere outside royal service – and his immediate attempt to purchase William's talents seem at once typical narrative exaggerations and accurate reflections of history. Medieval kings often attempted to co-opt their most dangerous opposition in just this way, and they frequently commissioned them to 'keep the peace' in their own regions, as William and his cohorts are returned to the 'north country' here.

27 The change in rank from yeomanry to nobility required a change in clothing that was not merely symbolic (sumptuary laws prescribed what only knights could wear), and a 'fee' – an income-producing estate held of the king, which would provide the stable source of wealth needed by a gentleman.

10. FROM *THE ACTS AND DEEDS OF SIR WILLIAM WALLACE*

Translation

1 Kilspindie is 10 miles from Dundee.

2 i.e., Edward I (1239–1307) of England.

3 i.e., they killed them. The allusion is to Herod the Great (37–4 BC) and his massacre of the innocents, a popular subject in medieval art and literature. The Biblical account is in Matthew 2.

4 This incident, in which Scottish nobles are invited to a conference with the English and then slaughtered, is loosely based on Barbour's *Bruce*, Bk IV, ll. 95ff. but is essentially Hary's fabrication.

5 There is no surviving confirmation of Selby as constable of Dundee castle at this time.

6 Wallace's attire is perhaps prophetic, since green is traditionally associated with woodsmen generally (see e.g., Chaucer's Yeoman in the *General Prologue* to the *The Canterbury Tales*) and outlaws in particular, most notably Robin Hood.

7 Wallace will again disguise himself as a woman to escape from St Johnston (IV, 768ff., translated below, IV, 705–96).

8 The reference is obscure. McDiarmid notes the proverb, 'Everie man for himself quod Schir Marteine' (II, p. 144, n. 383), and suggests that the allusion may be to the kingfisher or 'martin'.

9 Wallace has changed his form of address from the formal 'ye' to the familiar 'thou'.

10 McDiarmid's translation, II, p. 145, n. 33–5.

11 See McDiarmid's translation, II, pp. 159–60, n.173.

12 The parish of Kincardine in south-east Perthshire.

13 One of Wallace's closest companions; see McDiarmid, II, pp. 61–2, n. 194.

14 Doune castle is 3 miles west of Dunblane.

15 Located 6 miles from Perth.

16 Wallace's rebellion actually lasted only two years.

17 i.e., William, son of Malcolm Wallace. The riddling response to the request for the hero's name is a folk motif that goes back at least as far as Homer's *Odyssey* in which Odysseus tells Polyphemous that his name is Noman.

18 As McDiarmid notes, Ettrick Forest 'was celebrated as the haunt of "reif and fellonie"' (II, p. 164, n. 369).

19 A forest in the parish of Cargill.

20 Sir John Butler, who held lands in Scotland, swore fealty to King Edward in 1296 and fought on his side at the Battle of Stirling in 1304 (McDiarmid, II, p. 164).

21 The unique attribute or object, from Arthur's Excalibur to Superman's X-ray vision, is common in heroic narrative. Wallace's bow may derive from the sources of the relatively late ballad, *Robin Hood's Progress to Nottingham* (Knight and Ohlgren, p. 507) and the account of Robin Hood's life in the Sloane MS 715 (see Child, *The English and Scottish Popular Ballads*, III, p. 175). Hary's reference is similar to one of the best-known Robin Hood proverbs, 'Many speak of Robin Hood that never bent his bow'. However, in contradistinction to the English proverb, Hary's statement is literal.

22 The use of 'sold' here refers not only to the material rewards she's been promised but recalls the betrayal of Jesus by Judas. In the Middle English ballad, *Judas* (Child, *The English and Scottish Popular Ballads*), for example, Christ says, 'Ic am iboust ant isold to day . . .' ('I am bought and sold today').

23 The term 'legend' means 'saint's life' and continues the motif begun with the use of 'sold' (see note 22 above). It is here being employed ironically for the woman and seriously for Wallace.

24 McDiarmid notes that the North and South Inches were two parks or meadows located immediately outside the town of Perth (II, p. 166, n. 787).

25 McDiarmid locates Gilbank 'three miles W. Lanark' (II, p. 174, n. 467).

26 The oxymoron here is typical of the effects of courtly love; cf. Chaucer's Pandarus who tells his niece, Criseyde, 'I have a joly wo, a lusty sorwe', *Troilus and Criseyde*, II, p. 1,099.

27 Hary consistently contrasts rightful (Christ, Philip of France) and unrightful kingship (Edward).

28 Wallace's loyal and steadfast companion who bears some resemblance to Robin Hood's Little John. See McDiarmid's discussion of the Grahams, II, pp. 173–4, n. 437–45.

29 The mocking greetings, first in French then in Scots Gaelic, are ostensibly occasioned by the smartness of Wallace's dress; cf. the incident with young Selby translated above (I, 144–276) and the comments below (l. 147).

30 The woman is Marion Bradfute, Wallace's beloved and betrothed; see the translation of V, 562–717.

31 McDiarmid locates Cartland Crags 'two miles N.W. Lanark' (II, p. 186, n. 190).

32 Hary had earlier indicated that Graham had fifteen men (l. 122) and Wallace nine (l. 123), making a total of thirty-five.

33 Biggar is 'twelve miles E.S.E Lanark' (McDiarmid, II, p.189, n. 343). As McDiarmid notes, the number of men is conventional and may be based on an account in Froissart.

34 McDiarmid notes that the 'Fitzhughs of Ravensworth castle, county Durham, fought at Bannockburn (Barbour), Homildon, and Otterburn' (II, p. 189, n. 363).

35 McDiarmid notes that this form of address is common in the Alexander romances (II, p. 190, n. 381).

36 See McDiarmid, II, p. 189, n. 336.

37 For Wallace's disguise and its connections, see note 7 above. Robin Hood, Hereward the Wake and Eustache the Monk all disguise themselves as potters.

38 See note 33 for the location of Biggar.

39 Wallace's words are similar to those found in Sir Gilbert Haye's *Buik of Alexander* (a translation of the French *Roman d'Alexandre*) and to Bruce's speech before the battle of Bannockburn (*Bruce*, XII, ll. 303ff.). See McDiarmid, II, p. 191, n. 516–26.

40 As McDiarmid notes, the first part of the vision owes something to Bower in the *Scotichronicon*, the second to the alliterative *Morte Arthure* (II, pp. 199–200, 71–152n).

41 The Virgin Mary's appearance to Wallace recalls Robin Hood's frequent devotions to her; see e.g., 'Robyn loved Oure dere Lady', *Gest*, l. 10.

42 Given the symbolic significance of the colour, we can better understand why Wallace, and of course Robin Hood are so frequently dressed in green as well as young Selby's disapproval of Wallace's garb (see above I, 144–276).

43 The colour blue is traditionally associated with the Virgin who often appears in medieval art wearing a blue cloak or gown. See, for example, Emma Pirani, *Gothic Illuminated Manuscripts*, trans. Margaret Crosland (London, Hamlyn, 1966), pp. 13, 50, 55 and 62.

44 Wallace's manner of greeting the queen is not unusual for the time.

45 Several of the Charlemagne romances describe the incident Wallace refers to; see McDiarmid, II, p. 230, n. 1,251–62.

46 Alexander III (1241–85); reigned 1249–85.

47 The two are John de Baliol, who swore fealty to Edward and was appointed king in 1292, and Robert Bruce whom Wallace supports. In July 1296, Baliol surrendered his kingdom to Antony Bek, Bishop of Durham, Edward's representative.

48 These colours are identical to those in Wallace's vision; compare the description of the Virgin Mary there (VII, 71–152).

49 Presumably Wallace knows no French and would have learned Latin in school, as the Red Reiver obviously has.

50 Praise of the outlaw by one who does not know he is addressing him is a common motif. See, for example, *Robin Hood and Guy of Gisborne* (Child, *The English and Scottish Popular Ballads*, p. 118), st. 25 *et seq.* and *Robin Hood and the Potter* (Child, *The English and Scottish Popular Ballads*, p. 121), st. 56. Obviously, this motif is connected to the disguise motif discussed above, note 7.

51 The parallels and contrasts between Wallace's situation and Longville's should be noted. Both are outlaws and both, as a consequence, have had many of their kin slain. Neither takes prisoners. Each is a kind of monarch in his own domain (Wallace is scornfully called 'King of Kyle', VIII, 21), Wallace in Scotland, Longville on the sea. But Longville's outlawry stems from his own actions, however unintentional, and he longs to be reconciled with his king, while Wallace is declared outlaw by a king whom he sees as an outlaw himself.

52 The reference here is almost certainly to Alexander the Great who with Charlemagne and King Arthur was one of the three great heroes of medieval romance. However, Hary may also be referring to King Alexander III of Scotland who had been mentioned earlier (I, 41, VIII, 1,327).

53 This physical description owes far more to descriptions of other literary heroes than to historical accuracy. Wallace's great height is traditional, but the other features are based on sources as diverse as the Charlemagne romances, Chaucer's *Knight's Tale* and Barbour's *Bruce*, as well as medieval treatises on physiognomy. McDiarmid's discussion is both full and illuminating; see II, pp. 254–7.

54 Hary had described the champions as being envious of Wallace (see XII, 147ff.), hence his moral disquisition on envy, one of the Seven Deadly Sins, at the end of this passage.

55 Wallace's scornful rejection of the king's offer of armour is reminiscent of Beowulf's refusal to arm himself against Grendel.

56 This remarkable incident may have actually occurred. McDiarmid cites the eighteenth-century antiquary, Sir Richard Hay of Drumboote, who in his *Notes on the Life of Sir William Wallace*, MS 33.4.18 in the National Library, Edinburgh, describes the incident as Hary does but with some additional details (II, pp. 269–70, n. 195–286).

57 The Devil is often portrayed as a dragon. McDiarmid compares Dunbar's 'Done is a battell on the dragon black' (II, p. 270, n. 287).

58 This address to lords to eschew envy is reminiscent of similar advice in Chaucer and Dunbar, both court poets, and may refer to some specific contemporary issue.

59 The Birnam Wood of *Macbeth* near Dunkeld (see McDiarmid, II, p. 246, n. 820).

60 North of Barnan Wood; see McDiarmid, II, pp. 132–3, n. 102.

61 McDiarmid notes a somewhat similar incident in *Bruce,* VII, ll. 400–87 (II, p. 271, n. 568–653).

62 After Wallace returns from France in 1305, he is captured in Glasgow on 8 July 1305.

63 Wallace is here compared to four famous English martyrs: St Oswald, King of Northumbria, d. 870; St Edmund, King of East Anglia, d. 870; St Edward, brother of King Ethelred, d. 979; and St Thomas Becket, Archbishop of Canterbury, d. 1170. See McDiarmid, II, p. 280.

64 King Edward orders his clergy not to give Wallace last rites, but the Archbishop of Canterbury threatens Edward with excommunication, and he relents.

65 See the Introduction for the details of Wallace's execution.

66 The modesty topos and envoy, or direct address to the book, are both common in fifteenth-century Scottish poetry, especially poetry influenced by Chaucer. See, e.g., *The Kingis Quair*, st. 197, Dunbar's *The Goldyn Targe*, ll. 271–9, et al.

SELECT BIBLIOGRAPHY

1. THE OUTLAWRY OF EARL GODWIN FROM THE
VITA ÆDWARDI REGIS

Manuscript

British Library, Harley MS 526, fols 38–57

Editions

Barlow, Frank. *The Life of King Edward*, Oxford University Press, 1962; repr. Thomas Nelson and Sons, 1984

Luard, Henry R. *Lives of Edward the Confessor*, Rolls Series 3, London, 1858

Related Primary Texts

Anglo-Saxon Chronicle, ed. Michael Swanton, Dent, 1996

Knýtlinga saga, tr. H. Palsson and Paul Edwards, Odense University Press, 1986

Walter Map. *De Nugis Curialium*, eds and trs M.R. James, Revd C.N.L. Brooke and R.A.B. Mynors, Oxford, Clarendon Press, 1983

Vita Haroldi Regis, tr. Michael Swanton, in *Three Lives of the Last Englishmen*, New York, Garland, 1984

Critical Commentary

Bloch, Marc. 'The Life of Edward the Confessor', *Analecta Bollandiana* 41 (1923), 17–44

Henningham, Eleanor K. 'The Genuiness of the *Vita Æduuardi Regis*', *Speculum* 21 (1946), 419–56

Jones, Timothy S. 'Redemptive Fictions: The Contexts of Outlawry in Medieval English Chronicle and Romance', dissertation, University of Illinois at Urbana-Champaign, 1994

Southern, R.W. 'The First Life of Edward the Confessor', *English Historical Review* 58 (1943), 385–400

2. *THE DEEDS OF HEREWARD*

Manuscript
Peterborough Cathedral Manuscript 1, fols 320–39

Text
The Latin text is available in T.D. Hardy and C.T. Martin (eds), *Lestorie des Engles solum la translacion Maistre Geffrei Gaimar*, Rolls Series 91, 2 vols, London, 1898–9, I, pp. 339–404

Commentary and Criticism
Hart, Cyril. 'Hereward "the Wake"', in *The Danelaw*, London and Rio Grande, The Hambledon Press, 1992, pp. 625–48

Hayward, John. 'Hereward the Outlaw', *Journal of Medieval History* 14 (1988), 293–304

Head, Victor. *Hereward*, Stroud, Alan Sutton, 1995

Lange, Joost de. 'The relation and development of English and Icelandic outlaw traditions', dissertation, Utrecht, 1935

Noack, Georg. 'Sagenhistorische Untersuchungen zu den Gesta Herwardi', inaugural dissertation, Universität Halle-Wittenberg, 1914

Pickering, James Dunbar. 'The Legend of Hereward the Saxon: An investigation of *De Gestis Herwardi Saxonis*, its historical basis, its debt to saga and early romance, its place in English literary history', dissertation, Columbia University, 1964

Schmidt, P.G. 'Biblisches und hagiographisches kolorit in den Gesta Herwardi', in K. Walsh and D. Wood (eds), *The Bible in the Medieval World: Essays in Memory of Beryl Smalley*, Oxford, 1985, pp. 85–95

Wilson, R.M. *The Lost Literature of Medieval England*, London, Methuen, 1952, revd 1970

Wright, C.E. *The Cultivation of Saga in Anglo-Saxon England*, Edinburgh and London, Oliver and Boyd, 1939

3. *EUSTACHE THE MONK*

Editions
Conlon, Denis Joseph, (ed.). *Li Romans de Witasse le Moine: Roman du treizième siècle. Édité d'après le manuscrit, Fonds Français 1553, de la Bibliothèque Nationale, Paris*, University of North Carolina Studies in Romance Languages and Literatures, Number 126, Chapel Hill, University of North Carolina Press, 1972

Translations

Berger, Roger, and Petit, Aimé. In *Contes à rire du Nord de la France*, Troesnes, Corps 9 Editions (Trésors littéraires médiévaux du Nord de la France), 1987, pp. 149–99

Burgess, Glyn S. *Two Medieval Outlaws: Eustace the Monk and Fouke Fitz Waryn*, Woodbridge, Suffolk, D.S. Brewer, 1997

Kelly, Thomas E. Excerpts from *Eustache the Monk* in Knight and Ohlgren, *Robin Hood and Other Outlaw Tales*, pp. 668–86

Historical Background

Painter, Sidney. *The Reign of King John*, Baltimore, Johns Hopkins Press, 1949

Turner, Ralph V. *King John*, Longman, 1994

Scholarship and Commentary

Burgess, Glyn S. *Two Medieval Outlaws* (see above), pp. 3–49, 79–87

Busby, Keith. 'The Diabolic Hero in Medieval French Narrative: *Trubert* and *Witasse le Moine*', pp. 415–26, in Evelyn Mullally and John Thompson (eds), *The Court and Cultural Diversity, selected papers from the Eighth Triennial Congress of the International Courtly Literature Society (The Queen's University of Belfast 26 July–1 August 1995)*, D.S. Brewer, Cambridge, 1997

Carpenter, David A. 'Eustace the Monk', in C.S. Nicholls (ed.), *Dictionary of National Biography, Missing Persons*, Oxford University Press, 1993, pp. 212–13

Keen, Maurice. 'The Romance of Eustace the Monk', in *The Outlaws of Medieval Legend*, pp. 53–63

4. THE OUTLAW'S SONG OF TRAILBASTON

Manuscript

The poem is extant in a single copy: British Library Harley MS 2253, fols 113v–114v, for which see N.R. Ker, *Facsimile of BM MS Harley 2253*, Oxford, Early English Text Society 255, 1964

Printed Editions

First printed by Francis Palgrave in 1818, the poem was re-edited with translation by Thomas Wright in *Political Songs of England from the Reign of John to that of Edward II*, Camden Society, 1839, pp. 231–6. Wright's notes (pp. 383–5) include the original Statutes of Trailbaston, and his Appendix (273ff.) has excerpts from the *Chronicle of Piers Langtoft* in Anglo-Norman. Langtoft's account links the Trailbaston Statutes of 1304–5 to the 1305 capture and execution of Sir William Wallace, the Scots 'rebel', dismissing Wallace as one of the felons whom the Trailbaston Justices were rightly seizing. A definitive modern edition with historical notes and prose translation is provided by Isabel S.T. Aspin, *Anglo-Norman Political Songs*, Anglo-Norman Text Society No. 11 (Oxford, Basil Blackwell, 1953). It is reprinted with translation and notes in R.B. Dobson and J. Taylor, *Rymes of Robyn Hood*, pp. 250–4

Historical and Literary Background

Bellamy, John. 'The Coterel Gang: an Anatomy of a Band of Fourteenth-century Criminals', *English Historical Review* 79 (1964)

——. *Robin Hood, an Historical Enquiry*, Bloomington, Indiana University Press, 1985

Brie, Friedrich W.D. (ed.). *The Brut*, Early English Text Society 131, 1906

Brown, Carleton. *English Lyrics of the XIIIth Century*, Oxford, Clarendon Press, 1932

Burgess, Glyn S. *Two Medieval Outlaws: Eustace the Monk and Fouke Fitz Waryn*, Woodbridge, Suffolk, D.S. Brewer, 1997

Coss, Peter. *Thomas Wright's Political Songs of England*, Cambridge University Press, 1996: reprint of Wright's 1839 Camden Society volume, with introduction by Coss, pp. xi–lxvi, cited as Wright/Coss

Gransden, Antonia. *Historical Writing in England, c. 550–c. 1367*, Ithaca, Cornell University Press, 1974

Haines, Roy Martin. *The Church and Politics in Fourteenth-Century England: The Career of Adam Orleton, c. 1275–1345*, Cambridge University Press, 1978

——. *Archbishop John Stratford*, Toronto, Pontifical Institute of Medieval Studies, 1986

Harriss, G.L. *King, Parliament, and Public Finance in Medieval England to 1369*, Oxford, Clarendon Press, 1975

Hathaway, E.J., Ricketts, P.T., Robson, C.A. and Wilshere, A.D. (eds). *Fouke le fitz Waryn*, Oxford, Anglo-Norman Text Society, 26–8, Oxford, Basil Blackwell, 1975, 26–8

Jeffrey, David L. and Levy, Brian J. *The Anglo-Norman Lyric*, Toronto, Pontifical Institute of Medieval Studies, 1990

Legge, M. Dominica. *Anglo-Norman Literature and its Background*, corr. edn, Oxford, Clarendon Press, 1971

Maddicott, J.R. *The English Peasantry and the Demands of the Crown 1294–1341*, Oxford, Past and Present Society Supplement 1 (1975)

——. *Law and Lordship: Royal Justices as Retainers in Thirteenth and Fourteenth Century England*, Oxford, Past and Present Society Supplement 4 (1978)

——. 'Poems of Social Protest in Early Fourteenth-Century England', in W.M. Ormrod (ed.), *England in the Fourteenth Century*, Woodbridge, 1986, 130–44

'Mortimer of Richard's Castle', in 'G.E.C.', *The Complete Peerage* 9 256–66

Putnam, Bertha. *The Place in Legal History of Sir William Shareshull*, Cambridge University Press, 1950

Revard, Carter. 'Richard Hurd and MS. Harley 2253', *Notes and Queries* 224 (1979), 199–202

——. 'Three more holographs in the hand of the scribe of MS Harley 2253 in Shrewsbury', *Notes and Queries* 226 (1981), 199–200

——. 'Scribe of MS Harley 2253', *Notes and Queries* 227, (1982), 62–3

——. 'Gilote et Johane: an interlude in BL MS. Harley 2253', *Studies in Philology* 79 (1982), 122–46

——. 'A New ME O-and-I Lyric and its Provenance', *Medium Ævum* 54.1 (1985), 33–46

Robbins, Rossell Hope, (ed.). *Historical Poems of the XIVth and XVth Centuries*, New York, Columbia University Press, 1959

Stones, E.L.G., 'The Folvilles of Ashby-Folville, Leicestershire, and their Associates in Crime, 1326–47', *Transactions of the Royal Historical Society*, 5th Serics, 7 (1957), 117–36

'Talbot of Credenhill' and 'Talbot of Richard's Castle' in 'G.E.C', *The Complete Peerage* 12: 606–32.

Taylor, John. *English Historical Literature in the Fourteenth Century*, Oxford, Clarendon Press, 1987

Turville-Petre, Thorlac. *England, The Nation*, Oxford, Clarendon Press, 1996

Verduyn, Anthony. 'The Politics of Law and Order During the Early Years of Edward III', *English Historical Review* 108 (1993), 842–67

5. *FOUKE FITZ WARYN*

Manuscript

British Library, Royal 12 C. XII, ff. 33–61.

Editions

Brandin, Louis. *Fouke fitz Warin: roman du XIVe siècle*, Classiques Français du Moyen Age, 63, Paris, Champion, 1932

Hathaway, E. J., Ricketts, P.T,. Robson, C.A., and Wilshere, A.D. (eds). *Fouke le fitz Waryn*, Anglo-Norman Text Society, 26–8, Oxford, Basil Blackwell, 1975

Stevenson Joseph, (ed. and tr.). *The Legend of Fulk fitz-Warin*, Rolls Series 66, London, 1857; reprinted Kraus Reprint, 1965

Wright, Thomas. *The History of Fulk Fitz Warine, an Outlawed Baron in the Reign of King John*, The Warton Club, 1855

Translations

Burgess, Glyn S. *Two Medieval Outlaws: Eustache the Monk and Fouke fitz Waryn*, Woodbridge, Suffolk, D.S. Brewer, 1997, pp. 132–83

Kelly, Thomas E. *Fouke le Fitz Waryn*, pp. 687–723 in Knight and Ohlgren, *Robin Hood and Other Outlaw Tales*
See also J. Stevenson and Thomas Wright above

Critical Commentary

Benecke, Ingrid. *Der gute Outlaw*, Tübingen, Niemeyer, 1973
Burgess, Glyn S. *Two Medieval Outlaws: Eustache the Monk and Fouke fitz Waryn*, pp. 91–131
Hathaway, E.J. et al., see above
Jones, Timothy. 'Geoffrey of Monmouth, *Fouke le Fitz Waryn*, and National Mythology', *Studies in Philology* 91 (1994), 233–49.
Kelly, Thomas E., see above
Legge, M. Dominica. *Anglo-Norman Literature and Its Background*, corr. edn, Oxford, Clarendon Press, 1971
Meisel, Janet. *Barons of the Welsh Frontier: The Corbet, Pantulf, and Fitz Warin Families, 1066–1272*, Lincoln, Nebraska, University of Nebraska Press, 1980
Painter, Sidney. *The Reign of King John*, Baltimore, Johns Hopkins Press, 1949
——. 'The Sources of Fouke fitz Warin', *Modern Language Notes* 50 (1935), 13–15

6. *THE TALE OF GAMELYN*

Manuscripts

Gamelyn is found in twenty-five of the manuscripts of *The Canterbury Tales*, in the *c* and *d* families. It has been edited three times from manuscript:

Skeat, W.W. (ed.). *The Tale of Gamelyn*, Oxford, Clarendon Press, 1884 (from Harley 7334). (This text also used in the Appendix to *The Works of Geoffrey Chaucer*, 7 vols, vol. VI, Oxford University Press, 1895.)
Daniel, Neil (ed.). *The Tale of Gamelyn: A New Edition*, Indiana University Ph.D., 1967. (From Corpus manuscript.)
Knight and Ohlgren, *Robin Hood and Other Outlaw Tales*, pp. 184–226
Another edition: Sands, Donald B. (ed.). *Middle English Verse Romances*, New York, Holt, 1966, pp. 154–81

Commentary and Criticism

Barron, W.R.J. *Medieval English Romances*, Longman, 1987
Bennett, J.A.W and Gray, D., *Middle English Literature*, Oxford, Clarendon, 1986
Duby, Georges. 'Youth in Medieval Society', in C. Postan (tr.). *The Chivalrous Society*, Arnold, 1977, pp. 112–22
Dunn, C.W. 'Romances Derived from English Legend', in J.B. Severs (ed.), *Manual of Writings in Middle English, 1050–1500*, Fasc. 1, *Romances*, 1967, pp. 17–37

Hibberd, Laura. *Medieval Romance in England*, New York, Oxford University Press, 1924

Kaeuper, R. 'An Historian's Reading of *The Tale of Gamelyn*', *Medium Ævum* 52 (1983), 51–62

Knight, Stephen. '"harkeneth aright": Reading *Gamelyn* for text not Context', in Rosalind Field (ed.), *Romance: Tradition and Transformation: Proceedings of the 1996 Conference on Romance in Medieval England*, Cambridge, D.S. Brewer, 1998

Knight, S. and Ohlgren, T. *Robin Hood and Other Outlaw Tales*, pp. 184–93

Lange, Joost de. *The Relation and Development of English and Icelandic Outlaw Traditions*, Haarlem, Willink, 1935

Lindner, F. 'The Tale of Gamelyn', *Englische Studien* 2 (1879), 94–114, 321–43

Mehl, Dieter. *The Middle English Romances of the Thirteenth and Fourteenth Centuries*, Routledge, 1968

Pearsall, D.A. 'The Development of Middle English Romance', *Medieval Studies*, 27 (1965), 91–116

Prideaux, W.F. 'Who Was Robin Hood ?', *Notes and Queries*, 7th Series, II (1886), 421–4

Ramsey, Lee C. *Chivalric Romances*, Bloomington, Indiana University Press, 1983

Scattergood, John. '*The Tale of Gamelyn*: The Noble Robber as Provincial Hero', in Carol M. Meale (ed.), *Readings in Medieval English Romance*, Cambridge, Brewer, 1994, pp. 159–94

Schmidt, A.V.C. and Jacobs, Nicolas. *Medieval English Romances*, 2 vols, Hodder and Stoughton, 1980

Shannon jr, Edgar F., 'Mediaeval Law in *The Tale of Gamelyn*', *Speculum* 28 (1951), 458–64

7. *THE SAGA OF ÁN BOW BENDER*

Amory, Frederic. 'The Medieval Icelandic Outlaw: Life-Style, Saga, and Legend', in Gísli Pálsson (ed.). *From Sagas to Society: Comparative Approaches to Early Iceland*, Enfield Lock, Hisarlik Press, 1992, pp. 189–203

Baum, Richard Howard. 'The Medieval Outlaw: A Study in Protest', unpublished dissertation, University of Utah, 1972

Benecke, Ingrid. *Der gute Outlaw: Studien zu einem literarischen Typus im 13. und 14. Jahrhundert*, Studien zur englischen Philologie, NF 17, Tübingen, Niemeyer, 1973

Boberg, Inger M. *Motif-Index of Early Icelandic Literature*, Bibliotheca Arnamagnæana 27, Copenhagen, Munksgaard, 1966

Carpenter, Kevin (ed.). *Robin Hood: Die vielen Gesichter des edlen Räubers / The Many Faces of that Celebrated English Outlaw*, Oldenburg, BIS, 1995

Colbert, David. *The Birth of the Ballad: The Scandinavian Medieval Genre*, Skrifter udgivna av Svenskt Visarkiv 10, Stockholm, Svenskt Visarkiv, 1989

Craigie, Sir William A. *Synisbók íslenzkra rímna frá upphafi rímnakveðskapar til loka nítjándu aldar* (Anthology of Icelandic *rímur* from the beginning of the composition of *rímur* until the end of the nineteenth century), 3 vols, London and Reykjavík, Nelson and Leiftur, 1952

Dobson, [R.] Barrie and Taylor, John. '"Rymes of Robyn Hood": The Early Ballads and the Gest', in Carpenter, *Robin Hood*, pp. 35–44

Faulkes, Anthony (ed.). *Two Icelandic Stories. Hreiðars þáttr. Orms þáttr*, Viking Society for Northern Research, Text Series 4, London, Viking Society for Northern Research, n.d.

Fowler, David C. *A Literary History of the Popular Ballad*, Durham, Duke University Press, 1968

Gísli Sigurðsson. 'Methodologies for the Study of the Oral in Medieval Iceland', in Hildegard L.C. Tristram (ed.), *Medieval Insular Literature between the Oral and the Written II: Continuity of Transmission*, ScriptOralia 97, Tübingen, Gunter Narr, 1997, pp. 177–92

Guðni Jónsson (ed.). *Fornaldar sögur Norðurlanda*, 4 vols, Akureyri, Íslendingasagnaútgáfan, 1954

Holt, James C. 'Robin Hood: The Origins of the Legend', in Carpenter, *Robin Hood*, pp. 27–34

Hughes, Shaun F.D. 'Áns rímur bogsveigis: Two Nineteenth Century Icelandic Metrical Romances', unpublished dissertation, University of Washington, 1972

———. 'The Literary Antecedents of Áns saga bogsveigis', *Mediæval Scandinavia* 9 (1976), 198–235

Lange, Joost de. *The Relation and Development of English and Icelandic Outlaw Traditions*, Nederlandsche Bijdragen op het Gebied van germaansche Philologie en Linguistiek 6, Haarlem, Tjeenk Willink, 1935

Larsen, Willard (tr.). *The Saga of Aun the Bow-bender*, Baltimore, Gateway Press, 1995

Leach, Henry Goddard. *Angevin Britain and Scandinavia*, Harvard Studies in Comparative Literature 6, Cambridge, Harvard University Press 1921; repr. Milwood, NY, Kraus, 1975

———. 'Outlaws', *American-Scandinavian Review* 4 (Nov. Dec., 1916), 360–54

Ólafur Halldórsson (ed.). *Áns rímur bogsveigis*, Íslenzkar miðaldarímur 2, Stofnun Árna Magnússonar á Íslandi, Rit 4, Reykjavík, Stofnun Árna Magnússonar á Íslandi, 1973

Rafn, Carl Christian (ed.). *Fornaldar sögur Nordrlanda, eptir gömlum handritum*, 3 vols, Copenhagen, Hartvig Popp, 1829–30

Reuschel, Helga. *Untersuchungen über Stoff und Stil der Fornaldarsaga*, Bausteine zur Volkskunde und Religionswissenschaft 7, Bühl-Baden, Konkordia, 1933

Rowe, Elizabeth Ashman. '"Fabulæ í þeim bestu sögum": Studies in the Genre of the Medieval Icelandic Mytho-heroic Saga', unpublished dissertation, Cornell University, 1989

Spoelstra, Jan. *De Vogelvrijen in de Ijslandse Letterkunde*, Nederlandsche Bijdragen op
    het Gebied van germaansche Philologie en Linguistiek 10, Haarlem, Tjeenk
    Willink, 1938
Tofæus (Þormóður Torfason). *Historia rerum Norvegicarum*, 4 vols, Copenhagen,
    Typographeus Joachimi Schmitgenii, 1711
Tulinius, Torfi H. *La 'Matière du Nord': Sagas légendaires et fiction dans la littérature
    Islandaise en prose du XIIIe siècle*, voix germaniques, Paris, Presses de l'Université
    de Paris-Sorbonne, 1995
Turville-Petre, Gabriel. 'Outlawry', in Einar G. Pétursson and Jónas Kristjánsson
    (eds) *Sjötíu ritgerðir helgaðar Jakobi Benediktssyni 20 júlí 1977*, 2 vols, Stofnun Árna
    Magnússonar á Íslandi, Rit 12, Reykjavík, Stofnun Árna Magnússonar á
    Íslandi, 1977, 2, 769–78
Vésteinn Ólason. *The Traditional Ballads of Iceland: Historical Studies*, Stofnun Árna
    Magnússonar á Íslandi, Rit 22, Reykjavík, Stofnun Árna Magnússonar á
    Íslandi, 1982

8. *A GEST OF ROBYN HODE*

Early Printed Texts

A Gest of Robyn Hode ('Lettersnijder' ed.), Antwerp, Jan van Doesborch, *c.* 1510–15
A Lytell Geste of Robyn Hode, London, Wynkyn de Worde, ?1506–10. Now in
    Cambridge University Library MS. Sel. 5. 18
Fragments of an early printed version, perhaps by Wynkyn de Worde, of the *Gest*,
    now in the Douce Collection, Bodleian Library, Oxford
A Mery Geste of Robyn Hoode, London, William Copland, *c.* 1560
A Merry Iest of Robin Hood, London, Edward White, late sixteenth century
Ritson, Joseph (ed.). *Robin Hood, A Collection of all the Ancient Poems, Songs, and
    Ballads Now extant Relative to the Celebrated English Outlaw*, 2 vols, Egerton and
    Johnson, 1795
Gutch, J.M. (ed.). *A Lytelle Gest of Robin Hood and other Auncient and Modern Ballads
    and Songs Relating to the Celebrated Yeoman*, 2 vols, Longman, 1847

Editions

Child, F.J. *The English and Scottish Popular Ballads*, pp. 56–78
Dobson and Taylor. *Rymes of Robin Hood*, pp. 79–112
Knight and Ohlgren. *Robin Hood and Other Outlaw Tales*, pp. 90–148

Commentary and Criticism

Bellamy, John. *Robin Hood: An Historical Enquiry*, Bloomington, Indiana University
    Press, 1985

Bessinger, jr, J.B. 'The *Gest of Robin Hood* Revisited', in L.D. Benson (ed.), *The Learned and the Lewed: Studies in Chaucer and Medieval Literature*, Cambridge, Harvard University Press, 1974, pp. 355–69

Child, Francis J. *The English and Scottish Popular Ballads*, pp. 39–56

Clawson, William H. *The Gest of Robin Hood*, Toronto, University of Toronto Library, 1909

Coss, Peter R. 'Aspects of Cultural Diffusion in Medieval England: The Early Romances, Local Society and Robin Hood', *Past and Present* 108 (1985), 35–79

Dobson and Taylor, *Rymes of Robin Hood*, especially pp. 71–9

Fowler, David C. *A Literary History of the Popular Ballad*, Durham, Duke University Press, 1968

Gray, Douglas. 'The Robin Hood Poems', *Poetica* 18 (1984), 1–39

Hilton, Rodney H. 'The Origins of Robin Hood', *Past and Present* 14 (1958), 30–44; reprinted in R.H. Hilton (ed.), *Peasants, Knights and Heretics*, Cambridge, University Press, 1976, pp. 221–35

Holt, J.C. 'The Origins and Audience of the Ballads of Robin Hood', *Past and Present* 18 (1960), 89–110; reprinted in Hilton, 1976, see above, pp. 236–57

Knight and Ohlgren, *Robin Hood and Other Outlaw Tales*, pp. 80–9

Maddicott, J.R. 'The Birth and Setting of the Ballads of Robin Hood', *English Historical Review* 93 (1979), 276–99

Ohlgren, Thomas H. 'Edwardus redivivus in *A Gest of Robyn Hode*', *Journal of English and Germanic Philology*, forthcoming

Phillips, Graham and Keatman, Martin. *Robin Hood: The Man Behind the Myth*, Michael O'Mara Books, 1995

Phillips, Helen. *The Awntyrs of Arthure at the Terne Wathelyne*, University of Lancaster English Department, 1988

Tardif, Richard. 'The "Mistery" of Robin Hood: A New Social Context for the Texts', in Stephen Knight and S.N. Mukherjee (eds), *Worlds and Words: Studies in the Social Role of Verbal Culture*, Sydney, Sydney Association for Studies in Society and Culture, 1983, pp. 130–45

9. *ADAM BELL, CLIM OF THE CLOUGH AND WILLIAM OF CLOUDESLEY*

Early Printed Texts

Two fragments, lines 452–506, 642–80, by John Byddell, printer, London, 1536, in Cambridge University Library

A fragment, lines 211–446, perhaps by printer Wynkyn de Worde

Adambel, Clym of the Clough, and William of Cloudesle, London, William Copeland, *c.* 1550–60. This is the earliest full version

Adam Bell, Clim of the Clough, and William of Cloudesle, London, James Roberts, *c.* 1605

Manuscript

Thomas Percy's folio manuscript, British Library, Add. MSS 27879

Editions

Child, F.J. *The English and Scottish Popular Ballads*, pp. 22–34
Dobson and Taylor. *Rymes of Robin Hood*, pp. 258–73
Knight and Ohlgren. *Robin Hood and Other Outlaw Tales*, pp. 241–67
Percy, Thomas (ed.). *Reliques of English Poetry*, 3 vols, London, J. Dodsley, 1765, I, 129–60
Ritson, Joseph (ed.). *Pieces of Ancient Popular Poetry*, London, C. Clark for T. and J. Egerton, 1791, pp. 1–30

Criticism

Child, F.J. *The English and Scottish Popular Ballads*, pp. 14–22
Dobson and Taylor. *Rymes of Robin Hood*, pp. 258–60
Fowler, David C. *A Literary History of the Popular Ballad*, Durham, Duke University Press, 1968, p. 71
Gray, Douglas. 'The Robin Hood Ballads', *Poetica* 18 (1984), 1–39
Knight and Ohlgren. *Robin Hood and Other Outlaw Tales*, pp. 235–40

10. FROM *THE ACTS AND DEEDS OF SIR WILLIAM WALLACE*

Manuscript

Edinburgh, National Library of Scotland, MS Adv. 19.2.2, dated 1488

Editions

Henry the Minstrel. *The actis and deidis of the illustre and vailzeand campioun Schir William Wallace, Knicht of Ellerslie*, ed. James Moir, The Scottish Text Society, Edinburgh and London, William Blackwood, 1889
Hary's Wallace (Vita Nobilissimi Defensoris Scoti Wilelmi Wallace Militis), ed. Matthew P. McDiarmid, 2 vols, The Scottish Text Society, Edinburgh and London, William Blackwood, 1968

Historical Context

Brown, P. Hume. *History of Scotland*, 3 vols, Cambridge University Press, 1902–9
Gray, D.J. *William Wallace: The King's Enemy*, New York, Barnes & Noble, 1991
Hallam, Elizabeth (ed.). *Four Gothic Kings*, New York, Weidenfeld and Nicolson, 1978
Morgan, Kenneth O. (ed.). *The Oxford Illustrated History of Britain*, Oxford and New

York, Oxford University Press, 1984

Rothwell, Harry (ed.). *English Historical Documents 1189–1327*, New York, Oxford University Press, 1975

Salzman, Louis F. *Edward I*, New York, Praeger, 1968

Criticism

Balaban, John. 'Blind Harry and The Wallace', *The Chaucer Review* 8 (1974), 241–51

Goldstein, R. James. *The Matter of Scotland: Historical Narrative in Medieval Scotland*, Lincoln, University of Nebraska Press, 1993

Lindsay, Maurice. *History of Scottish Literature*, Robert Hale, 1977

McDiarmid, Matthew P., see above, pp. lxxiv–cviii

Scheps, Walter. 'Barbour's Bruce and Harry's Wallace: The Question of Influence', *Tennessee Studies in Literature* 17 (1972), 19–24

——. 'Middle English Poetic Usage and Blind Harry's Wallace', *The Chaucer Review* 4 (1970), 291–302

——. 'Possible Sources for Two Instances of Historical Inaccuracy in Blind Harry's Wallace', *Notes and Queries* 16 (1969), 125–6

INDEX